COLLECTED POEMS

THE MACMILLAN COMPANY
NEW YORK · BOSTON · CHICAGO · DALLAS
ATLANTA · SAN FRANCISCO

MACMILLAN & CO., LIMITED
LONDON · BOMBAY · CALCUTTA
MELBOURNE

THE MACMILLAN CO. OF CANADA, LTD.
TORONTO

From a painting by Lilla Cabot Perry.

COLLECTED POEMS

BY

EDWIN ARLINGTON ROBINSON

New York
THE MACMILLAN COMPANY
1921

All rights reserved

PRINTED IN THE UNITED STATES OF AMERICA

COPYRIGHT, 1896, 1897, 1902, and 1915,
BY EDWIN ARLINGTON ROBINSON

COPYRIGHT, 1910,
BY CHARLES SCRIBNER'S SONS

COPYRIGHT, 1920,
BY THOMAS SELTZER

COPYRIGHT, 1916, 1917, 1920, and 1921,
BY THE MACMILLAN COMPANY
Set up and electrotyped. Published October, 1921.

The author begs to acknowledge his indebtedness to Messrs. Charles Scribner's Sons for permission to include in this collection the contents of the volumes entitled "The Children of the Night," and "The Town Down the River," to Mr. Thomas Seltzer for permission to include the poem entitled "Lancelot," and to the editors of *Scribner's Magazine, The Atlantic Monthly, The Yale Review, The North American Review, The Nation, The Dial, The New Republic, The Bookman, The Outlook, Collier's, Poetry, The Literary Review,* and other periodicals, for permission to reprint several poems.

CONTENTS

	PAGE
THE MAN AGAINST THE SKY (1916)	1
Flammonde	3
The Gift of God	6
The Clinging Vine	8
Cassandra	11
John Gorham	13
Stafford's Cabin	14
Hillcrest	15
Old King Cole	17
Ben Jonson Entertains a Man from Stratford	20
Eros Turannos	32
Old Trails	33
The Unforgiven	37
Theophilus	39
Veteran Sirens	40
Siege Perilous	41
Another Dark Lady	41
The Voice of Age	42
The Dark House	43
The Poor Relation	45
The Burning Book	47
Fragment	48
Lisette and Eileen	49
Llewellyn and the Tree	50
Bewick Finzer	55
Bokardo	56
The Man Against the Sky	60
THE CHILDREN OF THE NIGHT (1890-1897)	71
John Evereldown	73
Luke Havergal	74
Three Quatrains	75
An Old Story	76
Ballade by the Fire	76
Ballade of Broken Flutes	77

CONTENTS

	PAGE
Her Eyes	78
Two Men	80
Villanelle of Change	80
The House on the Hill	81
Richard Corey	82
Boston	83
Calvary	83
Dear Friends	83
The Story of the Ashes and the Flame	84
Amaryllis	84
Zola	85
The Pity of the Leaves	85
Aaron Stark	86
The Garden	86
Cliff Klingenhagen	87
Charles Carville's Eyes	87
The Dead Village	88
Two Sonnets	89
The Clerks	90
Fleming Helphenstine	90
Thomas Hood	91
Horace to Leuconoë	91
Reuben Bright	92
The Altar	92
The Tavern	93
Sonnet	93
George Crabbe	94
Credo	94
On the Night of a Friend's Wedding	95
Sonnet	95
Verlaine	96
Sonnet	96
Supremacy	97
The Chorus of Old Men in "Ægeus"	97
The Wilderness	99
Octaves	100
The Torrent	108
L'envoy	108
CAPTAIN CRAIG, ETC. (1902)	111
Captain Craig	113
Isaac and Archibald	169
The Return of Morgan and Fingal	181
Aunt Imogen	184
The Klondike	189

CONTENTS

	PAGE
The Growth of "Lorraine"	191
The Sage	192
Erasmus	193
The Woman and The Wife	194
The Book of Annandale	195
Sainte-Nitouche	211
As a World Would Have It	218
The Corridor	220
Cortège	221
Partnership	222
Twilight Song	223
Variations of Greek Themes	225
The Field of Glory	231

MERLIN (1917) . . . 233

Merlin . . . 235

THE TOWN DOWN THE RIVER (1910) . . . 315

The Master	317
The Town Down the River	319
An Island	323
Calverly's	330
Leffingwell	331
Clavering	333
Lingard and the Stars	334
Pasa Thalassa Thalassa	335
Momus	336
Uncle Ananias	337
The Whip	338
The White Lights	340
Exit	340
Leonora	341
The Wise Brothers	341
But for the Grace of God	342
For Arvia	344
The Sunken Crown	344
Doctor of Billiards	345
Shadrach O'Leary	345
How Annandale Went Out	346
Alma Mater	346
Miniver Cheevy	347
The Pilot	348
Vickery's Mountain	349
Bon Voyage	351
The Companion	353

CONTENTS

	PAGE
Atherton's Gambit	353
For a Dead Lady	355
Two Gardens in Linndale	355
The Revealer	359
LANCELOT (1920)	363
Lancelot	365
THE THREE TAVERNS (1920)	451
The Valley of the Shadow	453
The Wandering Jew	456
Neighbors	459
The Mill	460
The Dark Hills	461
The Three Taverns	461
Demos	471
The Flying Dutchman	472
Tact	473
On the Way	474
John Brown	486
The False Gods	491
Archibald's Example	492
London Bridge	493
Tasker Norcross	499
A Song at Shannon's	509
Souvenir	509
Discovery	510
Firelight	510
The New Tenants	511
Inferential	511
The Rat	512
Rahel to Varnhagen	513
Nimmo	520
Peace on Earth	523
Late Summer	525
An Evangelist's Wife	528
The Old King's New Jester	528
Lazarus	530
AVON'S HARVEST, ETC. (1921)	541
Avon's Harvest	543
Mr. Flood's Party	573
Ben Trovato	575
The Tree in Pamela's Garden	576

	PAGE
Vain Gratuities	576
Job the Rejected	577
Lost Anchors	577
Recalled	578
Modernities	578
Afterthoughts	579
Caput Mortuum	580
Monadnock Through the Trees	580
The Long Race	581
Many Are Called	581
Rembrandt to Rembrandt	582

THE MAN AGAINST THE SKY
(1916)

*To the Memory of
William Edward Butler*

COLLECTED POEMS

FLAMMONDE

The man Flammonde, from God knows where,
With firm address and foreign air,
With news of nations in his talk
And something royal in his walk,
With glint of iron in his eyes,
But never doubt, nor yet surprise,
Appeared, and stayed, and held his head
As one by kings accredited.

Erect, with his alert repose
About him, and about his clothes,
He pictured all tradition hears
Of what we owe to fifty years.
His cleansing heritage of taste
Paraded neither want nor waste;
And what he needed for his fee
To live, he borrowed graciously.

He never told us what he was,
Or what mischance, or other cause,
Had banished him from better days
To play the Prince of Castaways.
Meanwhile he played surpassing well

COLLECTED POEMS

A part, for most, unplayable;
In fine, one pauses, half afraid
To say for certain that he played.

For that, one may as well forego
Conviction as to yes or no;
Nor can I say just how intense
Would then have been the difference
To several, who, having striven
In vain to get what he was given,
Would see the stranger taken on
By friends not easy to be won.

Moreover, many a malcontent
He soothed and found munificent;
His courtesy beguiled and foiled
Suspicion that his years were soiled;
His mien distinguished any crowd,
His credit strengthened when he bowed;
And women, young and old, were fond
Of looking at the man Flammonde.

There was a woman in our town
On whom the fashion was to frown;
But while our talk renewed the tinge
Of a long-faded scarlet fringe,
The man Flammonde saw none of that,
And what he saw we wondered at—
That none of us, in her distress,
Could hide or find our littleness.

There was a boy that all agreed
Had shut within him the rare seed
Of learning. We could understand,

FLAMMONDE

But none of us could lift a hand.
The man Flammonde appraised the youth,
And told a few of us the truth;
And thereby, for a little gold,
A flowered future was unrolled.

There were two citizens who fought
For years and years, and over nought;
They made life awkward for their friends,
And shortened their own dividends.
The man Flammonde said what was wrong
Should be made right; nor was it long
Before they were again in line,
And had each other in to dine.

And these I mention are but four
Of many out of many more.
So much for them. But what of him—
So firm in every look and limb?
What small satanic sort of kink
Was in his brain? What broken link
Withheld him from the destinies
That came so near to being his?

What was he, when we came to sift
His meaning, and to note the drift
Of incommunicable ways
That make us ponder while we praise?
Why was it that his charm revealed
Somehow the surface of a shield?
What was it that we never caught?
What was he, and what was he not?

How much it was of him we met
We cannot ever know; nor yet

Shall all he gave us quite atone
For what was his, and his alone;
Nor need we now, since he knew best,
Nourish an ethical unrest:
Rarely at once will nature give
The power to be Flammonde and live.

We cannot know how much we learn
From those who never will return,
Until a flash of unforeseen
Remembrance falls on what has been.
We've each a darkening hill to climb;
And this is why, from time to time
In Tilbury Town, we look beyond
Horizons for the man Flammonde.

THE GIFT OF GOD

Blessed with a joy that only she
Of all alive shall ever know,
She wears a proud humility
For what it was that willed it so,—
That her degree should be so great
Among the favored of the Lord
That she may scarcely bear the weight
Of her bewildering reward.

As one apart, immune, alone,
Or featured for the shining ones,
And like to none that she has known
Of other women's other sons,—
The firm fruition of her need,
He shines anointed; and he blurs

THE GIFT OF GOD

Her vision, till it seems indeed
A sacrilege to call him hers.

She fears a little for so much
Of what is best, and hardly dares
To think of him as one to touch
With aches, indignities, and cares;
She sees him rather at the goal,
Still shining; and her dream foretells
The proper shining of a soul
Where nothing ordinary dwells.

Perchance a canvass of the town
Would find him far from flags and shouts,
And leave him only the renown
Of many smiles and many doubts;
Perchance the crude and common tongue
Would havoc strangely with his worth;
But she, with innocence unwrung,
Would read his name around the earth.

And others, knowing how this youth
Would shine, if love could make him great,
When caught and tortured for the truth
Would only writhe and hesitate;
While she, arranging for his days
What centuries could not fulfill,
Transmutes him with her faith and praise,
And has him shining where she will.

She crowns him with her gratefulness,
And says again that life is good;
And should the gift of God be less
In him than in her motherhood,
His fame, though vague, will not be small,

As upward through her dream he fares,
Half clouded with a crimson fall
Of roses thrown on marble stairs.

THE CLINGING VINE

"Be calm? And was I frantic?
  You'll have me laughing soon.
I'm calm as this Atlantic,
  And quiet as the moon;
I may have spoken faster
  Than once, in other days;
For I've no more a master,
  And now—'Be calm,' he says.

"Fear not, fear no commotion,—
  I'll be as rocks and sand;
The moon and stars and ocean
  Will envy my command;
No creature could be stiller
  In any kind of place
Than I . . . No, I'll not kill her;
  Her death is in her face.

"Be happy while she has it,
  For she'll not have it long;
A year, and then you'll pass it,
  Preparing a new song.
And I'm a fool for prating
  Of what a year may bring,
When more like her are waiting
  For more like you to sing.

"You mock me with denial,
  You mean to call me hard?

THE CLINGING VINE

You see no room for trial
    When all my doors are barred?
You say, and you'd say dying,
    That I dream what I know;
And sighing, and denying,
    You'd hold my hand and go.

"You scowl—and I don't wonder;
    I spoke too fast again;
But you'll forgive one blunder,
    For you are like most men:
You are,—or so you've told me,
    So many mortal times,
That heaven ought not to hold me
    Accountable for crimes.

"Be calm? Was I unpleasant?
    Then I'll be more discreet,
And grant you, for the present,
    The balm of my defeat:
What she, with all her striving,
    Could not have brought about,
You've done. Your own contriving
    Has put the last light out.

"If she were the whole story,
    If worse were not behind,
I'd creep with you to glory,
    Believing I was blind;
I'd creep, and go on seeming
    To be what I despise.
You laugh, and say I'm dreaming,
    And all your laughs are lies.

"Are women mad? A few are,
    And if it's true you say—

If most men are as you are—
　We'll all be mad some day.
Be calm—and let me finish;
　There's more for you to know.
I'll talk while you diminish,
　And listen while you grow.

"There was a man who married
　Because he couldn't see;
And all his days he carried
　The mark of his degree.
But you—you came clear-sighted,
　And found truth in my eyes;
And all my wrongs you've righted
　With lies, and lies, and lies.

"You've killed the last assurance
　That once would have me strive
To rouse an old endurance
　That is no more alive.
It makes two people chilly
　To say what we have said,
But you—you'll not be silly
　And wrangle for the dead.

"You don't? You never wrangle?
　Why scold then,—or complain?
More words will only mangle
　What you've already slain.
Your pride you can't surrender?
　My name—for that you fear?
Since when were men so tender,
　And honor so severe?

"No more—I'll never bear it.
　I'm going. I'm like ice.

CASSANDRA

My burden? You would share it?
   Forbid the sacrifice!
Forget so quaint a notion,
   And let no more be told;
For moon and stars and ocean
   And you and I are cold."

CASSANDRA

I HEARD one who said: "Verily,
   What word have I for children here?
Your Dollar is your only Word,
   The wrath of it your only fear.

"You build it altars tall enough
   To make you see, but you are blind;
You cannot leave it long enough
   To look before you or behind.

"When Reason beckons you to pause,
   You laugh and say that you know best;
But what it is you know, you keep
   As dark as ingots in a chest.

"You laugh and answer, 'We are young;
   O leave us now, and let us grow.'—
Not asking how much more of this
   Will Time endure or Fate bestow.

"Because a few complacent years
   Have made your peril of your pride,
Think you that you are to go on
   Forever pampered and untried?

"What lost eclipse of history,
  What bivouac of the marching stars,
Has given the sign for you to see
  Millenniums and last great wars?

"What unrecorded overthrow
  Of all the world has ever known,
Or ever been, has made itself
  So plain to you, and you alone?

"Your Dollar, Dove and Eagle make
  A Trinity that even you
Rate higher than you rate yourselves;
  It pays, it flatters, and it's new.

"And though your very flesh and blood
  Be what your Eagle eats and drinks,
You'll praise him for the best of birds,
  Not knowing what the Eagle thinks.

"The power is yours, but not the sight;
  You see not upon what you tread;
You have the ages for your guide,
  But not the wisdom to be led.

"Think you to tread forever down
  The merciless old verities?
And are you never to have eyes
  To see the world for what it is?

"Are you to pay for what you have
  With all you are?"—No other word
We caught, but with a laughing crowd
  Moved on. None heeded, and few heard.

JOHN GORHAM

JOHN GORHAM

"Tell me what you're doing over here, John Gorham,
Sighing hard and seeming to be sorry when you're not;
Make me laugh or let me go now, for long faces in the moonlight
Are a sign for me to say again a word that you forgot."—

"I'm over here to tell you what the moon already
May have said or maybe shouted ever since a year ago;
I'm over here to tell you what you are, Jane Wayland,
And to make you rather sorry, I should say, for being so."—

"Tell me what you're saying to me now, John Gorham,
Or you'll never see as much of me as ribbons any more;
I'll vanish in as many ways as I have toes and fingers,
And you'll not follow far for one where flocks have been before."—

"I'm sorry now you never saw the flocks, Jane Wayland,
But you're the one to make of them as many as you need.
And then about the vanishing. It's I who mean to vanish;
And when I'm here no longer you'll be done with me indeed."—

"That's a way to tell me what I am, John Gorham!
How am I to know myself until I make you smile?
Try to look as if the moon were making faces at you,
And a little more as if you meant to stay a little while."—

"You are what it is that over rose-blown gardens
Make a pretty flutter for a season in the sun;
You are what it is that with a mouse, Jane Wayland,
Catches him and lets him go and eats him up for fun."—

"Sure I never took you for a mouse, John Gorham;
All you say is easy, but so far from being true
That I wish you wouldn't ever be again the one to think so;
For it isn't cats and butterflies that I would be to you."—

"All your little animals are in one picture—
One I've had before me since a year ago to-night;
And the picture where they live will be of you, Jane Wayland,
Till you find a way to kill them or to keep them out of sight."—

"Won't you ever see me as I am, John Gorham,
Leaving out the foolishness and all I never meant?
Somewhere in me there's a woman, if you know the way to find her.
Will you like me any better if I prove it and repent?"—

"I doubt if I shall ever have the time, Jane Wayland;
And I dare say all this moonlight lying round us might as well
Fall for nothing on the shards of broken urns that are forgotten,
As on two that have no longer much of anything to tell."

STAFFORD'S CABIN

Once there was a cabin here, and once there was a man;
And something happened here before my memory began.
Time has made the two of them the fuel of one flame
And all we have of them is now a legend and a name.

All I have to say is what an old man said to me,
And that would seem to be as much as there will ever be.
"Fifty years ago it was we found it where it sat."—
And forty years ago it was old Archibald said that.

HILLCREST

"An apple tree that's yet alive saw something, I suppose,
Of what it was that happened there, and what no mortal knows.
Some one on the mountain heard far off a master shriek,
And then there was a light that showed the way for men to seek.

"We found it in the morning with an iron bar behind,
And there were chains around it; but no search could ever find,
Either in the ashes that were left, or anywhere,
A sign to tell of who or what had been with Stafford there.

"Stafford was a likely man with ideas of his own—
Though I could never like the kind that likes to live alone;
And when you met, you found his eyes were always on your shoes,
As if they did the talking when he asked you for the news.

"That's all, my son. Were I to talk for half a hundred years
I'd never clear away from there the cloud that never clears.
We buried what was left of it,—the bar, too, and the chains;
And only for the apple tree there's nothing that remains."

Forty years ago it was I heard the old man say,
"That's all, my son."—And here again I find the place to-day,
Deserted and told only by the tree that knows the most,
And overgrown with golden-rod as if there were no ghost.

HILLCREST

(To Mrs. Edward MacDowell)

No sound of any storm that shakes
Old island walls with older seas
Comes here where now September makes
An island in a sea of trees.

Between the sunlight and the shade
A man may learn till he forgets
The roaring of a world remade,
And all his ruins and regrets;

And if he still remembers here
Poor fights he may have won or lost,—
If he be ridden with the fear
Of what some other fight may cost,—

If, eager to confuse too soon,
What he has known with what may be,
He reads a planet out of tune
For cause of his jarred harmony,—

If here he venture to unroll
His index of adagios,
And he be given to console
Humanity with what he knows,—

He may by contemplation learn
A little more than what he knew,
And even see great oaks return
To acorns out of which they grew.

He may, if he but listen well,
Through twilight and the silence here,
Be told what there are none may tell
To vanity's impatient ear;

And he may never dare again
Say what awaits him, or be sure
What sunlit labyrinth of pain
He may not enter and endure.

OLD KING COLE

Who knows to-day from yesterday
May learn to count no thing too strange:
Love builds of what Time takes away,
Till Death itself is less than Change.

Who sees enough in his duress
May go as far as dreams have gone;
Who sees a little may do less
Than many who are blind have done;

Who sees unchastened here the soul
Triumphant has no other sight
Than has a child who sees the whole
World radiant with his own delight.

Far journeys and hard wandering
Await him in whose crude surmise
Peace, like a mask, hides everything
That is and has been from his eyes;

And all his wisdom is unfound,
Or like a web that error weaves
On airy looms that have a sound
No louder now than falling leaves.

OLD KING COLE

In Tilbury Town did Old King Cole
A wise old age anticipate,
Desiring, with his pipe and bowl,
No Khan's extravagant estate.
No crown annoyed his honest head,
No fiddlers three were called or needed;
For two disastrous heirs instead
Made music more than ever three did.

Bereft of her with whom his life
Was harmony without a flaw,
He took no other for a wife,
Nor sighed for any that he saw;
And if he doubted his two sons,
And heirs, Alexis and Evander,
He might have been as doubtful once
Of Robert Burns and Alexander.

Alexis, in his early youth,
Began to steal—from old and young.
Likewise Evander, and the truth
Was like a bad taste on his tongue.
Born thieves and liars, their affair
Seemed only to be tarred with evil—
The most insufferable pair
Of scamps that ever cheered the devil.

The world went on, their fame went on,
And they went on—from bad to worse;
Till, goaded hot with nothing done,
And each accoutred with a curse,
The friends of Old King Cole, by twos,
And fours, and sevens, and elevens,
Pronounced unalterable views
Of doings that were not of heaven's.

And having learned again whereby
Their baleful zeal had come about,
King Cole met many a wrathful eye
So kindly that its wrath went out—
Or partly out. Say what they would,
He seemed the more to court their candor;
But never told what kind of good
Was in Alexis and Evander.

OLD KING COLE

And Old King Cole, with many a puff
That haloed his urbanity,
Would smoke till he had smoked enough,
And listen most attentively.
He beamed as with an inward light
That had the Lord's assurance in it;
And once a man was there all night,
Expecting something every minute.

But whether from too little thought,
Or too much fealty to the bowl,
A dim reward was all he got
For sitting up with Old King Cole.
"Though mine," the father mused aloud,
"Are not the sons I would have chosen,
Shall I, less evilly endowed,
By their infirmity be frozen?

"They'll have a bad end, I'll agree,
But I was never born to groan;
For I can see what I can see,
And I'm accordingly alone.
With open heart and open door,
I love my friends, I like my neighbors;
But if I try to tell you more,
Your doubts will overmatch my labors.

"This pipe would never make me calm,
This bowl my grief would never drown.
For grief like mine there is no balm
In Gilead, or in Tilbury Town.
And if I see what I can see,
I know not any way to blind it;
Nor more if any way may be
For you to grope or fly to find it.

"There may be room for ruin yet,
And ashes for a wasted love;
Or, like One whom you may forget,
I may have meat you know not of.
And if I'd rather live than weep
Meanwhile, do you find that surprising?
Why, bless my soul, the man's asleep!
That's good. The sun will soon be rising."

BEN JONSON ENTERTAINS A MAN FROM STRATFORD

You are a friend then, as I make it out,
Of our man Shakespeare, who alone of us
Will put an ass's head in Fairyland
As he would add a shilling to more shillings,
All most harmonious,—and out of his
Miraculous inviolable increase
Fills Ilion, Rome, or any town you like
Of olden time with timeless Englishmen;
And I must wonder what you think of him—
All you down there where your small Avon flows
By Stratford, and where you're an Alderman.
Some, for a guess, would have him riding back
To be a farrier there, or say a dyer;
Or maybe one of your adept surveyors;
Or like enough the wizard of all tanners.
Not you—no fear of that; for I discern
In you a kindling of the flame that saves—
The nimble element, the true caloric;
I see it, and was told of it, moreover,
By our discriminate friend himself, no other.
Had you been one of the sad average,
As he would have it,—meaning, as I take it,

BEN JONSON ENTERTAINS A MAN FROM STRATFORD

The sinew and the solvent of our Island,
You'd not be buying beer for this Terpander's
Approved and estimated friend Ben Jonson;
He'd never foist it as a part of his
Contingent entertainment of a townsman
While he goes off rehearsing, as he must,
If he shall ever be the Duke of Stratford.
And my words are no shadow on your town—
Far from it; for one town's as like another
As all are unlike London. Oh, he knows it,—
And there's the Stratford in him; he denies it,
And there's the Shakespeare in him. So, God help him!
I tell him he needs Greek; but neither God
Nor Greek will help him. Nothing will help that man.
You see the fates have given him so much,
He must have all or perish,—or look out
Of London, where he sees too many lords.
They're part of half what ails him: I suppose
There's nothing fouler down among the demons
Than what it is he feels when he remembers
The dust and sweat and ointment of his calling
With his lords looking on and laughing at him.
King as he is, he can't be king *de facto,*
And that's as well, because he wouldn't like it;
He'd frame a lower rating of men then
Than he has now; and after that would come
An abdication or an apoplexy.
He can't be king, not even king of Stratford,—
Though half the world, if not the whole of it,
May crown him with a crown that fits no king
Save Lord Apollo's homesick emissary:
Not there on Avon, or on any stream
Where Naiads and their white arms are no more,
Shall he find home again. It's all too bad.
But there's a comfort, for he'll have that House—

The best you ever saw; and he'll be there
Anon, as you're an Alderman. Good God!
He makes me lie awake o'nights and laugh.

And you have known him from his origin,
You tell me; and a most uncommon urchin
He must have been to the few seeing ones—
A trifle terrifying, I dare say,
Discovering a world with his man's eyes,
Quite as another lad might see some finches,
If he looked hard and had an eye for nature.
But this one had his eyes and their foretelling,
And he had you to fare with, and what else?
He must have had a father and a mother—
In fact I've heard him say so—and a dog,
As a boy should, I venture; and the dog,
Most likely, was the only man who knew him.
A dog, for all I know, is what he needs
As much as anything right here to-day,
To counsel him about his disillusions,
Old aches, and parturitions of what's coming,—
A dog of orders, an emeritus,
To wag his tail at him when he comes home,
And then to put his paws up on his knees
And say, "For God's sake, what's it all about?"

I don't know whether he needs a dog or not—
Or what he needs. I tell him he needs Greek;
I'll talk of rules and Aristotle with him,
And if his tongue's at home he'll say to that,
"I have your word that Aristotle knows,
And you mine that I don't know Aristotle."
He's all at odds with all the unities,
And what's yet worse, it doesn't seem to matter;
He treads along through Time's old wilderness
As if the tramp of all the centuries

BEN JONSON ENTERTAINS A MAN FROM STRATFORD

Had left no roads—and there are none, for him;
He doesn't see them, even with those eyes,—
And that's a pity, or I say it is.
Accordingly we have him as we have him—
Going his way, the way that he goes best,
A pleasant animal with no great noise
Or nonsense anywhere to set him off—
Save only divers and inclement devils
Have made of late his heart their dwelling place.
A flame half ready to fly out sometimes
At some annoyance may be fanned up in him,
But soon it falls, and when it falls goes out;
He knows how little room there is in there
For crude and futile animosities,
And how much for the joy of being whole,
And how much for long sorrow and old pain.
On our side there are some who may be given
To grow old wondering what he thinks of us
And some above us, who are, in his eyes,
Above himself,—and that's quite right and English.
Yet here we smile, or disappoint the gods
Who made it so: the gods have always eyes
To see men scratch; and they see one down here
Who itches, manor-bitten to the bone,
Albeit he knows himself—yes, yes, he knows—
The lord of more than England and of more
Than all the seas of England in all time
Shall ever wash. D'ye wonder that I laugh?
He sees me, and he doesn't seem to care;
And why the devil should he? I can't tell you.

I'll meet him out alone of a bright Sunday,
Trim, rather spruce, and quite the gentleman.
"What ho, my lord!" say I. He doesn't hear me;
Wherefore I have to pause and look at him.
He's not enormous, but one looks at him.

A little on the round if you insist,
For now, God save the mark, he's growing old;
He's five and forty, and to hear him talk
These days you'd call him eighty; then you'd add
More years to that. He's old enough to be
The father of a world, and so he is.
"Ben, you're a scholar, what's the time of day?"
Says he; and there shines out of him again
An aged light that has no age or station—
The mystery that's his—a mischievous
Half-mad serenity that laughs at fame
For being won so easy, and at friends
Who laugh at him for what he wants the most,
And for his dukedom down in Warwickshire;—
By which you see we're all a little jealous. . . .
Poor Greene! I fear the color of his name
Was even as that of his ascending soul;
And he was one where there are many others,—
Some scrivening to the end against their fate,
Their puppets all in ink and all to die there;
And some with hands that once would shade an eye
That scanned Euripides and Æschylus
Will reach by this time for a pot-house mop
To slush their first and last of royalties.
Poor devils! and they all play to his hand;
For so it was in Athens and old Rome.
But that's not here or there; I've wandered off.
Greene does it, or I'm careful. Where's that boy?

Yes, he'll go back to Stratford. And we'll miss him?
Dear sir, there'll be no London here without him.
We'll all be riding, one of these fine days,
Down there to see him—and his wife won't like us;
And then we'll think of what he never said
Of women—which, if taken all in all

BEN JONSON ENTERTAINS A MAN FROM STRATFORD

With what he did say, would buy many horses.
Though nowadays he's not so much for women:
"So few of them," he says, "are worth the guessing."
But there's a worm at work when he says that,
And while he says it one feels in the air
A deal of circumambient hocus-pocus.
They've had him dancing till his toes were tender,
And he can feel 'em now, come chilly rains.
There's no long cry for going into it,
However, and we don't know much about it.
But you in Stratford, like most here in London,
Have more now in the *Sonnets* than you paid for;
He's put one there with all her poison on,
To make a singing fiction of a shadow
That's in his life a fact, and always will be.
But she's no care of ours, though Time, I fear,
Will have a more reverberant ado
About her than about another one
Who seems to have decoyed him, married him,
And sent him scuttling on his way to London,—
With much already learned, and more to learn,
And more to follow. Lord! how I see him now,
Pretending, maybe trying, to be like us.
Whatever he may have meant, we never had him;
He failed us, or escaped, or what you will,—
And there was that about him (God knows what,—
We'd flayed another had he tried it on us)
That made as many of us as had wits
More fond of all his easy distances
Than one another's noise and clap-your-shoulder.
But think you not, my friend, he'd never talk!
Talk? He was eldritch at it; and we listened—
Thereby acquiring much we knew before
About ourselves, and hitherto had held
Irrelevant, or not prime to the purpose.

And there were some, of course, and there be now,
Disordered and reduced amazedly
To resignation by the mystic seal
Of young finality the gods had laid
On everything that made him a young demon;
And one or two shot looks at him already
As he had been their executioner;
And once or twice he was, not knowing it,—
Or knowing, being sorry for poor clay
And saying nothing. . . . Yet, for all his engines,
You'll meet a thousand of an afternoon
Who strut and sun themselves and see around 'em
A world made out of more that has a reason
Than his, I swear, that he sees here to-day;
Though he may scarcely give a Fool an exit
But we mark how he sees in everything
A law that, given we flout it once too often,
Brings fire and iron down on our naked heads.
To me it looks as if the power that made him,
For fear of giving all things to one creature,
Left out the first,—faith, innocence, illusion,
Whatever 'tis that keeps us out o' Bedlam,—
And thereby, for his too consuming vision,
Empowered him out of nature; though to see him,
You'd never guess what's going on inside him.
He'll break out some day like a keg of ale
With too much independent frenzy in it;
And all for cellaring what he knows won't keep,
And what he'd best forget—but that he can't.
You'll have it, and have more than I'm foretelling;
And there'll be such a roaring at the Globe
As never stunned the bleeding gladiators.
He'll have to change the color of its hair
A bit, for now he calls it Cleopatra.
Black hair would never do for Cleopatra.

BEN JONSON ENTERTAINS A MAN FROM STRATFORD

But you and I are not yet two old women,
And you're a man of office. What he does
Is more to you than how it is he does it,—
And that's what the Lord God has never told him.
They work together, and the Devil helps 'em;
They do it of a morning, or if not,
They do it of a night; in which event
He's peevish of a morning. He seems old;
He's not the proper stomach or the sleep—
And they're two sovran agents to conserve him
Against the fiery art that has no mercy
But what's in that prodigious grand new House.
I gather something happening in his boyhood
Fulfilled him with a boy's determination
To make all Stratford 'ware of him. Well, well,
I hope at last he'll have his joy of it,
And all his pigs and sheep and bellowing beeves,
And frogs and owls and unicorns, moreover,
Be less than hell to his attendant ears.
Oh, past a doubt we'll all go down to see him.

He may be wise. With London two days off,
Down there some wind of heaven may yet revive him;
But there's no quickening breath from anywhere
Small make of him again the poised young faun
From Warwickshire, who'd made, it seems, already
A legend of himself before I came
To blink before the last of his first lightning.
Whatever there be, there'll be no more of that;
The coming on of his old monster Time
Has made him a still man; and he has dreams
Were fair to think on once, and all found hollow.
He knows how much of what men paint themselves
Would blister in the light of what they are;
He sees how much of what was great now shares

An eminence transformed and ordinary;
He knows too much of what the world has hushed
In others, to be loud now for himself;
He knows now at what height low enemies
May reach his heart, and high friends let him fall;
But what not even such as he may know
Bedevils him the worst: his lark may sing
At heaven's gate how he will, and for as long
As joy may listen, but *he* sees no gate,
Save one whereat the spent clay waits a little
Before the churchyard has it, and the worm.
Not long ago, late in an afternoon,
I came on him unseen down Lambeth way,
And on my life I was afear'd of him:
He gloomed and mumbled like a soul from Tophet,
His hands behind him and his head bent solemn.
"What is it now," said I,—"another woman?"
That made him sorry for me, and he smiled.
"No, Ben," he mused; "it's Nothing. It's all Nothing.
We come, we go; and when we're done, we're done;
Spiders and flies—we're mostly one or t'other—
We come, we go; and when we're done, we're done;"
"By God, you sing that song as if you knew it!"
Said I, by way of cheering him; "what ails ye?"
"I think I must have come down here to think,"
Says he to that, and pulls his little beard;
"Your fly will serve as well as anybody,
And what's his hour? He flies, and flies, and flies,
And in his fly's mind has a brave appearance;
And then your spider gets him in her net,
And eats him out, and hangs him up to dry.
That's Nature, the kind mother of us all.
And then your slattern housemaid swings her broom,
And where's your spider? And that's Nature, also.
It's Nature, and it's Nothing. It's all Nothing.

BEN JONSON ENTERTAINS A MAN FROM STRATFORD

It's all a world where bugs and emperors
Go singularly back to the same dust,
Each in his time; and the old, ordered stars
That sang together, Ben, will sing the same
Old stave to-morrow."

                              When he talks like that,
There's nothing for a human man to do
But lead him to some grateful nook like this
Where we be now, and there to make him drink.
He'll drink, for love of me, and then be sick;
A sad sign always in a man of parts,
And always very ominous. The great
Should be as large in liquor as in love,—
And our great friend is not so large in either:
One disaffects him, and the other fails him;
Whatso he drinks that has an antic in it,
He's wondering what's to pay in his insides;
And while his eyes are on the Cyprian
He's fribbling all the time with that damned House.
We laugh here at his thrift, but after all
It may be thrift that saves him from the devil;
God gave it, anyhow,—and we'll suppose
He knew the compound of his handiwork.
To-day the clouds are with him, but anon
He'll out of 'em enough to shake the tree
Of life itself and bring down fruit unheard-of,—
And, throwing in the bruised and whole together,
Prepare a wine to make us drunk with wonder;
And if he live, there'll be a sunset spell
Thrown over him as over a glassed lake
That yesterday was all a black wild water.

God send he live to give us, if no more,
What now's a-rampage in him, and exhibit,

With a decent half-allegiance to the ages
An earnest of at least a casual eye
Turned once on what he owes to Gutenberg,
And to the fealty of more centuries
Than are as yet a picture in our vision.
"There's time enough,—I'll do it when I'm old,
And we're immortal men," he says to that;
And then he says to me, "Ben, what's 'immortal'?
Think you by any force of ordination
It may be nothing of a sort more noisy
Than a small oblivion of component ashes
That of a dream-addicted world was once
A moving atomy much like your friend here?"
Nothing will help that man. To make him laugh,
I said then he was a mad mountebank,—
And by the Lord I nearer made him cry.
I could have eat an eft then, on my knees,
Tail, claws, and all of him; for I had stung
The king of men, who had no sting for me,
And I had hurt him in his memories;
And I say now, as I shall say again,
I love the man this side idolatry.

He'll do it when he's old, he says. I wonder.
He may not be so ancient as all that.
For such as he, the thing that is to do
Will do itself,—but there's a reckoning;
The sessions that are now too much his own,
The roiling inward of a stilled outside,
The churning out of all those blood-fed lines,
The nights of many schemes and little sleep,
The full brain hammered hot with too much thinking,
The vexed heart over-worn with too much aching,—
This weary jangling of conjoined affairs
Made out of elements that have no end,

BEN JONSON ENTERTAINS A MAN FROM STRATFORD

And all confused at once, I understand,
Is not what makes a man to live forever.
O no, not now! He'll not be going now:
There'll be time yet for God knows what explosions
Before he goes. He'll stay awhile. Just wait:
Just wait a year or two for Cleopatra,
For she's to be a balsam and a comfort;
And that's not all a jape of mine now, either.
For granted once the old way of Apollo
Sings in a man, he may then, if he's able,
Strike unafraid whatever strings he will
Upon the last and wildest of new lyres;
Nor out of his new magic, though it hymn
The shrieks of dungeoned hell, shall he create
A madness or a gloom to shut quite out
A cleaving daylight, and a last great calm
Triumphant over shipwreck and all storms.
He might have given Aristotle creeps,
But surely would have given him his *katharsis*.

He'll not be going yet. There's too much yet
Unsung within the man. But when he goes,
I'd stake ye coin o' the realm his only care
For a phantom world he sounded and found wanting
Will be a portion here, a portion there,
Of this or that thing or some other thing
That has a patent and intrinsical
Equivalence in those egregious shillings.
And yet he knows, God help him! Tell me, now,
If ever there was anything let loose
On earth by gods or devils heretofore
Like this mad, careful, proud, indifferent Shakespeare!
Where was it, if it ever was? By heaven,
'Twas never yet in Rhodes or Pergamon—
In Thebes or Nineveh, a thing like this!

No thing like this was ever out of England;
And that he knows. I wonder if he cares.
Perhaps he does. . . . O Lord, that House in Stratford!

EROS TURANNOS

SHE fears him, and will always ask
　What fated her to choose him;
She meets in his engaging mask
　All reasons to refuse him;
But what she meets and what she fears
Are less than are the downward years,
Drawn slowly to the foamless weirs
　Of age, were she to lose him.

Between a blurred sagacity
　That once had power to sound him,
And Love, that will not let him be
　The Judas that she found him,
Her pride assuages her almost,
As if it were alone the cost.—
He sees that he will not be lost,
　And waits and looks around him.

A sense of ocean and old trees
　Envelops and allures him;
Tradition, touching all he sees,
　Beguiles and reassures him;
And all her doubts of what he says
Are dimmed with what she knows of days—
Till even prejudice delays
　And fades, and she secures him.

The falling leaf inaugurates
　The reign of her confusion;

OLD TRAILS

The pounding wave reverberates
   The dirge of her illusion;
And home, where passion lived and died,
Becomes a place where she can hide,
While all the town and harbor side
   Vibrate with her seclusion.

We tell you, tapping on our brows,
   The story as it should be,—
As if the story of a house
   Were told, or ever could be;
We'll have no kindly veil between
Her visions and those we have seen,—
As if we guessed what hers have been,
   Or what they are or would be.

Meanwhile we do no harm; for they
   That with a god have striven,
Not hearing much of what we say,
   Take what the god has given;
Though like waves breaking it may be,
Or like a changed familiar tree,
Or like a stairway to the sea
   Where down the blind are driven.

OLD TRAILS

(Washington Square)

I MET him, as one meets a ghost or two,
Between the gray Arch and the old Hotel.
"King Solomon was right, there's nothing new,"
Said he. "Behold a ruin who meant well."

He led me down familiar steps again,
Appealingly, and set me in a chair.
"My dreams have all come true to other men,"
Said he; "God lives, however, and why care?

"An hour among the ghosts will do no harm."
He laughed, and something glad within me sank.
I may have eyed him with a faint alarm,
For now his laugh was lost in what he drank.

"They chill things here with ice from hell," he said;
"I might have known it." And he made a face
That showed again how much of him was dead,
And how much was alive and out of place,

And out of reach. He knew as well as I
That all the words of wise men who are skilled
In using them are not much to defy
What comes when memory meets the unfulfilled.

What evil and infirm perversity
Had been at work with him to bring him back?
Never among the ghosts, assuredly,
Would he originate a new attack;

Never among the ghosts, or anywhere,
Till what was dead of him was put away,
Would he attain to his offended share
Of honor among others of his day.

"You ponder like an owl," he said at last;
"You always did, and here you have a cause.
For I'm a confirmation of the past,
A vengeance, and a flowering of what was.

OLD TRAILS

"Sorry? Of course you are, though you compress,
With even your most impenetrable fears,
A placid and a proper consciousness
Of anxious angels over my arrears.

"I see them there against me in a book
As large as hope, in ink that shines by night
Surely I see; but now I'd rather look
At you, and you are not a pleasant sight.

"Forbear, forgive. Ten years are on my soul,
And on my conscience. I've an incubus:
My one distinction, and a parlous toll
To glory; but hope lives on clamorous.

"'Twas hope, though heaven I grant you knows of what—
The kind that blinks and rises when it falls,
Whether it sees a reason why or not—
That heard Broadway's hard-throated siren-calls;

"'Twas hope that brought me through December storms,
To shores again where I'll not have to be
A lonely man with only foreign worms
To cheer him in his last obscurity.

"But what it was that hurried me down here
To be among the ghosts, I leave to you.
My thanks are yours, no less, for one thing clear:
Though you are silent, what you say is true.

"There may have been the devil in my feet,
For down I blundered, like a fugitive,
To find the old room in Eleventh Street.
God save us!—I came here again to live."

We rose at that, and all the ghosts rose then,
And followed us unseen to his old room.
No longer a good place for living men
We found it, and we shivered in the gloom.

The goods he took away from there were few,
And soon we found ourselves outside once more,
Where now the lamps along the Avenue
Bloomed white for miles above an iron floor.

"Now lead me to the newest of hotels,"
He said, "and let your spleen be undeceived:
This ruin is not myself, but some one else;
I haven't failed; I've merely not achieved."

Whether he knew or not, he laughed and dined
With more of an immune regardlessness
Of pits before him and of sands behind
Than many a child at forty would confess;

And after, when the bells in *Boris* rang
Their tumult at the Metropolitan,
He rocked himself, and I believe he sang.
"God lives," he crooned aloud, "and I'm the man!"

He was. And even though the creature spoiled
All prophecies, I cherish his acclaim.
Three weeks he fattened; and five years he toiled
In Yonkers,—and then sauntered into fame.

And he may go now to what streets he will—
Eleventh, or the last, and little care;
But he would find the old room very still
Of evenings, and the ghosts would all be there.

THE UNFORGIVEN

I doubt if he goes after them; I doubt
If many of them ever come to him.
His memories are like lamps, and they go out;
Or if they burn, they flicker and are dim.

A light of other gleams he has to-day
And adulations of applauding hosts;
A famous danger, but a safer way
Than growing old alone among the ghosts.

But we may still be glad that we were wrong:
He fooled us, and we'd shrivel to deny it;
Though sometimes when old echoes ring too long,
I wish the bells in *Boris* would be quiet.

THE UNFORGIVEN

WHEN he, who is the unforgiven,
Beheld her first, he found her fair:
No promise ever dreamt in heaven
Could then have lured him anywhere
That would have been away from there;
And all his wits had lightly striven,
Foiled with her voice, and eyes, and hair.

There's nothing in the saints and sages
To meet the shafts her glances had,
Or such as hers have had for ages
To blind a man till he be glad,
And humble him till he be mad.
The story would have many pages,
And would be neither good nor bad.

And, having followed, you would find him
Where properly the play begins;

But look for no red light behind him—
No fumes of many-colored sins,
Fanned high by screaming violins.
God knows what good it was to blind him,
Or whether man or woman wins.

And by the same eternal token,
Who knows just how it will all end?—
This drama of hard words unspoken,
This fireside farce, without a friend
Or enemy to comprehend
What augurs when two lives are broken,
And fear finds nothing left to mend.

He stares in vain for what awaits him,
And sees in Love a coin to toss;
He smiles, and her cold hush berates him
Beneath his hard half of the cross;
They wonder why it ever was;
And she, the unforgiving, hates him
More for her lack than for her loss.

He feeds with pride his indecision,
And shrinks from what will not occur,
Bequeathing with infirm derision
His ashes to the days that were,
Before she made him prisoner;
And labors to retrieve the vision
That he must once have had of her.

He waits, and there awaits an ending,
And he knows neither what nor when;
But no magicians are attending
To make him see as he saw then,
And he will never find again

THEOPHILUS

The face that once had been the rending
Of all his purpose among men.

He blames her not, nor does he chide her,
And she has nothing new to say;
If he were Bluebeard he could hide her,
But that's not written in the play,
And there will be no change to-day;
Although, to the serene outsider,
There still would seem to be a way.

THEOPHILUS

By what serene malevolence of names
Had you the gift of yours, Theophilus?
Not even a smeared young Cyclops at his games
Would have you long,—and you are one of us.

Told of your deeds I shudder for your dream
And they, no doubt, are few and innocent.
Meanwhile, I marvel; for in you, it seems,
Heredity outshines environment.

What lingering bit of Belial, unforeseen,
Survives and amplifies itself in you?
What manner of devilry has ever been
That your obliquity may never do?

Humility befits a father's eyes,
But not a friend of us would have him weep.
Admiring everything that lives and dies,
Theophilus, we like you best asleep.

Sleep—sleep; and let us find another man
To lend another name less hazardous:
Caligula, maybe, or Caliban,
Or Cain,—but surely not Theophilus.

VETERAN SIRENS

The ghost of Ninon would be sorry now
To laugh at them, were she to see them here,
So brave and so alert for learning how
To fence with reason for another year.

Age offers a far comelier diadem
Than theirs; but anguish has no eye for grace,
When time's malicious mercy cautions them
To think a while of number and of space.

The burning hope, the worn expectancy,
The martyred humor, and the maimed allure,
Cry out for time to end his levity,
And age to soften its investiture;

But they, though others fade and are still fair,
Defy their fairness and are unsubdued;
Although they suffer, they may not forswear
The patient ardor of the unpursued.

Poor flesh, to fight the calendar so long;
Poor vanity, so quaint and yet so brave;
Poor folly, so deceived and yet so strong,
So far from Ninon and so near the grave.

ANOTHER DARK LADY

SIEGE PERILOUS

Long warned of many terrors more severe
To scorch him than hell's engines could awaken,
He scanned again, too far to be so near,
The fearful seat no man had ever taken.

So many other men with older eyes
Than his to see with older sight behind them
Had known so long their one way to be wise,—
Was any other thing to do than mind them?

So many a blasting parallel had seared
Confusion on his faith,—could he but wonder
If he were mad and right, or if he feared
God's fury told in shafted flame and thunder?

There fell one day upon his eyes a light
Ethereal, and he heard no more men speaking;
He saw their shaken heads, but no long sight
Was his but for the end that he went seeking.

The end he sought was not the end; the crown
He won shall unto many still be given.
Moreover, there was reason here to frown:
No fury thundered, no flame fell from heaven.

ANOTHER DARK LADY

Think not, because I wonder where you fled,
That I would lift a pin to see you there;
You may, for me, be prowling anywhere,
So long as you show not your little head:

No dark and evil story of the dead
Would leave you less pernicious or less fair—
Not even Lilith, with her famous hair;
And Lilith was the devil, I have read.

I cannot hate you, for I loved you then.
The woods were golden then. There was a road
Through beeches; and I said their smooth feet showed
Like yours. Truth must have heard me from afar,
For I shall never have to learn again
That yours are cloven as no beech's are.

THE VOICE OF AGE

She'd look upon us, if she could,
As hard as Rhadamanthus would;
Yet one may see,—who sees her face,
Her crown of silver and of lace,
Her mystical serene address
Of age alloyed with loveliness,—
That she would not annihilate
The frailest of things animate.

She has opinions of our ways,
And if we're not all mad, she says,—
If our ways are not wholly worse
Than others, for not being hers,—
There might somehow be found a few
Less insane things for us to do,
And we might have a little heed
Of what Belshazzar couldn't read.

She feels, with all our furniture,
Room yet for something more secure

THE DARK HOUSE

Than our self-kindled aureoles
To guide our poor forgotten souls;
But when we have explained that grace
Dwells now in doing for the race,
She nods—as if she were relieved;
Almost as if she were deceived.

She frowns at much of what she hears,
And shakes her head, and has her fears;
Though none may know, by any chance,
What rose-leaf ashes of romance
Are faintly stirred by later days
That would be well enough, she says,
If only people were more wise,
And grown-up children used their eyes.

THE DARK HOUSE

Where a faint light shines alone,
Dwells a Demon I have known.
Most of you had better say
"The Dark House," and go your way.
Do not wonder if I stay.

For I know the Demon's eyes,
And their lure that never dies.
Banish all your fond alarms,
For I know the foiling charms
Of her eyes and of her arms,

And I know that in one room
Burns a lamp as in a tomb;
And I see the shadow glide,
Back and forth, of one denied
Power to find himself outside.

There he is who is my friend,
Damned, he fancies, to the end—
Vanquished, ever since a door
Closed, he thought, for evermore
On the life that was before.

And the friend who knows him best
Sees him as he sees the rest
Who are striving to be wise
While a Demon's arms and eyes
Hold them as a web would flies.

All the words of all the world,
Aimed together and then hurled,
Would be stiller in his ears
Than a closing of still shears
On a thread made out of years.

But there lives another sound,
More compelling, more profound;
There's a music, so it seems,
That assuages and redeems,
More than reason, more than dreams.

There's a music yet unheard
By the creature of the word,
Though it matters little more
Than a wave-wash on a shore—
Till a Demon shuts a door.

So, if he be very still
With his Demon, and one will,
Murmurs of it may be blown
To my friend who is alone
In a room that I have known.

THE POOR RELATION

After that from everywhere
Singing life will find him there;
Then the door will open wide,
And my friend, again outside,
Will be living, having died.

THE POOR RELATION

No longer torn by what she knows
And sees within the eyes of others,
Her doubts are when the daylight goes,
Her fears are for the few she bothers.
She tells them it is wholly wrong
Of her to stay alive so long;
And when she smiles her forehead shows
A crinkle that had been her mother's.

Beneath her beauty, blanched with pain,
And wistful yet for being cheated,
A child would seem to ask again
A question many times repeated;
But no rebellion has betrayed
Her wonder at what she has paid
For memories that have no stain,
For triumph born to be defeated.

To those who come for what she was—
The few left who know where to find her—
She clings, for they are all she has;
And she may smile when they remind her,
As heretofore, of what they know
Of roses that are still to blow
By ways where not so much as grass
Remains of what she sees behind her.

They stay a while, and having done
What penance or the past requires,
They go, and leave her there alone
To count her chimneys and her spires.
Her lip shakes when they go away,
And yet she would not have them stay;
She knows as well as anyone
That Pity, having played, soon tires.

But one friend always reappears,
A good ghost, not to be forsaken;
Whereat she laughs and has no fears
Of what a ghost may reawaken,
But welcomes, while she wears and mends
The poor relation's odds and ends,
Her truant from a tomb of years—
Her power of youth so early taken.

Poor laugh, more slender than her song
It seems; and there are none to hear it
With even the stopped ears of the strong
For breaking heart or broken spirit.
The friends who clamored for her place,
And would have scratched her for her face,
Have lost her laughter for so long
That none would care enough to fear it.

None live who need fear anything
From her, whose losses are their pleasure;
The plover with a wounded wing
Stays not the flight that others measure;
So there she waits, and while she lives,
And death forgets, and faith forgives,
Her memories go foraging
For bits of childhood song they treasure.

THE BURNING BOOK

And like a giant harp that hums
On always, and is always blending
The coming of what never comes
With what has past and had an ending,
The City trembles, throbs, and pounds
Outside, and through a thousand sounds
The small intolerable drums
Of Time are like slow drops descending.

Bereft enough to shame a sage
And given little to long sighing,
With no illusion to assuage
The lonely changelessness of dying,—
Unsought, unthought-of, and unheard,
She sings and watches like a bird,
Safe in a comfortable cage
From which there will be no more flying.

THE BURNING BOOK

Or the Contented Metaphysician

To the lore of no manner of men
  Would his vision have yielded
When he found what will never again
  From his vision be shielded,—
Though he paid with as much of his life
  As a nun could have given,
And to-night would have been as a knife,
  Devil-drawn, devil-driven.

For to-night, with his flame-weary eyes
  On the work he is doing,
He considers the tinder that flies
  And the quick flame pursuing.

In the leaves that are crinkled and curled
    Are his ashes of glory,
And what once were an end of the world
    Is an end of a story.

But he smiles, for no more shall his days
    Be a toil and a calling
For a way to make others to gaze
    On God's face without falling.
He has come to the end of his words,
    And alone he rejoices
In the choiring that silence affords
    Of ineffable voices.

To a realm that his words may not reach
    He may lead none to find him;
An adept, and with nothing to teach,
    He leaves nothing behind him.
For the rest, he will have his release,
    And his embers, attended
By the large and unclamoring peace
    Of a dream that is ended.

FRAGMENT

FAINT white pillars that seem to fade
As you look from here are the first one sees
Of his house where it hides and dies in a shade
Of beeches and oaks and hickory trees.
Now many a man, given woods like these,
And a house like that, and the Briony gold,
Would have said, "There are still some gods to please,
And houses are built without hands, we're told."

LISETTE AND EILEEN

There are the pillars, and all gone gray.
Briony's hair went white. You may see
Where the garden was if you come this way.
That sun-dial scared him, he said to me;
"Sooner or later they strike," said he,
And he never got that from the books he read.
Others are flourishing, worse than he,
But he knew too much for the life he led.

And who knows all knows everything
That a patient ghost at last retrieves;
There's more to be known of his harvesting
When Time the thresher unbinds the sheaves;
And there's more to be heard than a wind that grieves
For Briony now in this ageless oak,
Driving the first of its withered leaves
Over the stones where the fountain broke.

LISETTE AND EILEEN

"WHEN he was here alive, Eileen,
    There was a word you might have said;
So never mind what I have been,
    Or anything,—for you are dead.

"And after this when I am there
    Where he is, you'll be dying still.
Your eyes are dead, and your black hair,—
    The rest of you be what it will.

"'Twas all to save him? Never mind,
    Eileen. You saved him. You are strong.
I'd hardly wonder if your kind
    Paid everything, for you live long.

"You last, I mean. That's what I mean.
I mean you last as long as lies.
You might have said that word, Eileen,—
And you might have your hair and eyes.

"And what you see might be Lisette,
Instead of this that has no name.
Your silence—I can feel it yet,
Alive and in me, like a flame.

"Where might I be with him to-day,
Could he have known before he heard?
But no—your silence had its way,
Without a weapon or a word.

"Because a word was never told,
I'm going as a worn toy goes.
And you are dead; and you'll be old;
And I forgive you, I suppose.

"I'll soon be changing as all do,
To something we have always been;
And you'll be old. . . . He liked you, too,
I might have killed you then, Eileen.

"I think he liked as much of you
As had a reason to be seen,—
As much as God made black and blue.
He liked your hair and eyes, Eileen."

LLEWELLYN AND THE TREE

Could he have made Priscilla share
  The paradise that he had planned,
Llewellyn would have loved his wife
  As well as any in the land.

LLEWELLYN AND THE TREE

Could he have made Priscilla cease
    To goad him for what God left out,
Llewellyn would have been as mild
    As any we have read about.

Could all have been as all was not,
    Llewellyn would have had no story;
He would have stayed a quiet man
    And gone his quiet way to glory.

But howsoever mild he was
    Priscilla was implacable;
And whatsoever timid hopes
    He built—she found them, and they fell.

And this went on, with intervals
    Of labored harmony between
Resounding discords, till at last
    Llewellyn turned—as will be seen.

Priscilla, warmer than her name,
    And shriller than the sound of saws,
Pursued Llewellyn once too far,
    Not knowing quite the man he was.

The more she said, the fiercer clung
    The stinging garment of his wrath;
And this was all before the day
    When Time tossed roses in his path.

Before the roses ever came
    Llewellyn had already risen.
The roses may have ruined him,
    They may have kept him out of prison.

And she who brought them, being Fate,
   Made roses do the work of spears,—
Though many made no more of her
   Than civet, coral, rouge, and years.

You ask us what Llewellyn saw,
   But why ask what may not be given?
To some will come a time when change
   Itself is beauty, if not heaven.

One afternoon Priscilla spoke,
   And her shrill history was done;
At any rate, she never spoke
   Like that again to anyone.

One gold October afternoon
   Great fury smote the silent air;
And then Llewellyn leapt and fled
   Like one with hornets in his hair.

Llewellyn left us, and he said
   Forever, leaving few to doubt him;
And so, through frost and clicking leaves,
   The Tilbury way went on without him.

And slowly, through the Tilbury mist,
   The stillness of October gold
Went out like beauty from a face.
   Priscilla watched it, and grew old.

He fled, still clutching in his flight
   The roses that had been his fall;
The Scarlet One, as you surmise,
   Fled with him, coral, rouge, and all.

LLEWELLYN AND THE TREE

Priscilla, waiting, saw the change
   Of twenty slow October moons;
And then she vanished, in her turn
   To be forgotten, like old tunes.

So they were gone—all three of them,
   I should have said, and said no more,
Had not a face once on Broadway
   Been one that I had seen before.

The face and hands and hair were old,
   But neither time nor penury
Could quench within Llewellyn's eyes
   The shine of his one victory.

The roses, faded and gone by,
   Left ruin where they once had reigned;
But on the wreck, as on old shells,
   The color of the rose remained.

His fictive merchandise I bought
   For him to keep and show again,
Then led him slowly from the crush
   Of his cold-shouldered fellow men.

"And so, Llewellyn," I began—
   "Not so," he said; "not so at all:
I've tried the world, and found it good,
   For more than twenty years this fall.

"And what the world has left of me
   Will go now in a little while."
And what the world had left of him
   Was partly an unholy guile.

"That I have paid for being calm
  Is what you see, if you have eyes;
For let a man be calm too long,
  He pays for much before he dies.

"Be calm when you are growing old
  And you have nothing else to do;
Pour not the wine of life too thin
  If water means the death of you.

"You say I might have learned at home
  The truth in season to be strong?
Not so; I took the wine of life
  Too thin, and I was calm too long.

"Like others who are strong too late,
  For me there was no going back;
For I had found another speed,
  And I was on the other track.

"God knows how far I might have gone
  Or what there might have been to see;
But my speed had a sudden end,
  And here you have the end of me."

The end or not, it may be now
  But little farther from the truth
To say those worn satiric eyes
  Had something of immortal youth.

He may among the millions here
  Be one; or he may, quite as well,
Be gone to find again the Tree
  Of Knowledge, out of which he fell.

BEWICK FINZER

He may be near us, dreaming yet
   Of unrepented rouge and coral;
Or in a grave without a name
   May be as far off as a moral.

BEWICK FINZER

Time was when his half million drew
   The breath of six per cent;
But soon the worm of what-was-not
   Fed hard on his content;
And something crumbled in his brain
   When his half million went.

Time passed, and filled along with his
   The place of many more;
Time came, and hardly one of us
   Had credence to restore,
From what appeared one day, the man
   Whom we had known before.

The broken voice, the withered neck,
   The coat worn out with care,
The cleanliness of indigence,
   The brilliance of despair,
The fond imponderable dreams
   Of affluence,—all were there.

Poor Finzer, with his dreams and schemes,
   Fares hard now in the race,
With heart and eye that have a task
   When he looks in the face
Of one who might so easily
   Have been in Finzer's place.

He comes unfailing for the loan
    We give and then forget;
He comes, and probably for years
    Will he be coming yet,—
Familiar as an old mistake,
    And futile as regret.

BOKARDO

Well, Bokardo, here we are;
    Make yourself at home.
Look around—you haven't far
    To look—and why be dumb?
Not the place that used to be,
Not so many things to see;
But there's room for you and me.
    And you—you've come.

Talk a little; or, if not,
    Show me with a sign
Why it was that you forgot
    What was yours and mine.
Friends, I gather, are small things
In an age when coins are kings;
Even at that, one hardly flings
    Friends before swine.

Rather strong? I knew as much,
    For it made you speak.
No offense to swine, as such,
    But why this hide-and-seek?
You have something on your side,
And you wish you might have died,
So you tell me. And you tried
    One night last week?

BOKARDO

You tried hard? And even then
   Found a time to pause?
When you try as hard again,
   You'll have another cause.
When you find yourself at odds
With all dreamers of all gods,
You may smite yourself with rods—
   But not the laws.

Though they seem to show a spite
   Rather devilish,
They move on as with a might
   Stronger than your wish.
Still, however strong they be,
They bide man's authority:
Xerxes, when he flogged the sea,
   May've scared a fish.

It's a comfort, if you like,
   To keep honor warm,
But as often as you strike
   The laws, you do no harm.
To the laws, I mean. To you—
That's another point of view,
One you may as well indue
   With some alarm.

Not the most heroic face
   To present, I grant;
Nor will you insure disgrace
   By fearing what you want.
Freedom has a world of sides,
And if reason once derides
Courage, then your courage hides
   A deal of cant.

Learn a little to forget
  Life was once a feast;
You aren't fit for dying yet,
  So don't be a beast.
Few men with a mind will say,
Thinking twice, that they can pay
Half their debts of yesterday,
  Or be released.

There's a debt now on your mind
  More than any gold?
And there's nothing you can find
  Out there in the cold?
Only—what's his name?—Remorse?
And Death riding on his horse?
Well, be glad there's nothing worse
  Than you have told.

Leave Remorse to warm his hands
  Outside in the rain.
As for Death, he understands,
  And he will come again.
Therefore, till your wits are clear,
Flourish and be quiet—here.
But a devil at each ear
  Will be a strain?

Past a doubt they will indeed,
  More than you have earned.
I say that because you need
  Ablution, being burned?
Well, if you must have it so,
Your last flight went rather low.
Better say you had to know
  What you have learned.

BOKARDO

And that's over. Here you are,
   Battered by the past.
Time will have his little scar,
   But the wound won't last.
Nor shall harrowing surprise
Find a world without its eyes
If a star fades when the skies
   Are overcast.

God knows there are lives enough,
   Crushed, and too far gone
Longer to make sermons of,
   And those we leave alone.
Others, if they will, may rend
The worn patience of a friend
Who, though smiling, sees the end,
   With nothing done.

But your fervor to be free
   Fled the faith it scorned;
Death demands a decency
   Of you, and you are warned.
But for all we give we get
Mostly blows? Don't be upset;
You, Bokardo, are not yet
   Consumed or mourned.

There'll be falling into view
   Much to rearrange;
And there'll be a time for you
   To marvel at the change.
They that have the least to fear
Question hardest what is here;
When long-hidden skies are clear,
   The stars look strange

THE MAN AGAINST THE SKY

Between me and the sunset, like a dome
Against the glory of a world on fire,
Now burned a sudden hill,
Bleak, round, and high, by flame-lit height made higher,
With nothing on it for the flame to kill
Save one who moved and was alone up there
To loom before the chaos and the glare
As if he were the last god going home
Unto his last desire.

Dark, marvelous, and inscrutable he moved on
Till down the fiery distance he was gone,
Like one of those eternal, remote things
That range across a man's imaginings
When a sure music fills him and he knows
What he may say thereafter to few men,—
The touch of ages having wrought
An echo and a glimpse of what he thought
A phantom or a legend until then;
For whether lighted over ways that save,
Or lured from all repose,
If he go on too far to find a grave,
Mostly alone he goes.

Even he, who stood where I had found him,
On high with fire all round him,
Who moved along the molten west,
And over the round hill's crest
That seemed half ready with him to go down,
Flame-bitten and flame-cleft,
As if there were to be no last thing left
Of a nameless unimaginable town,—

THE MAN AGAINST THE SKY

Even he who climbed and vanished may have taken
Down to the perils of a depth not known,
From death defended though by men forsaken,
The bread that every man must eat alone;
He may have walked while others hardly dared
Look on to see him stand where many fell;
And upward out of that, as out of hell,
He may have sung and striven
To mount where more of him shall yet be given,
Bereft of all retreat,
To sevenfold heat,—
As on a day when three in Dura shared
The furnace, and were spared
For glory by that king of Babylon
Who made himself so great that God, who heard,
Covered him with long feathers, like a bird.

Again, he may have gone down easily,
By comfortable altitudes, and found,
As always, underneath him solid ground
Whereon to be sufficient and to stand
Possessed already of the promised land,
Far stretched and fair to see:
A good sight, verily,
And one to make the eyes of her who bore him
Shine glad with hidden tears.
Why question of his ease of who before him,
In one place or another where they left
Their names as far behind them as their bones,
And yet by dint of slaughter toil and theft,
And shrewdly sharpened stones,
Carved hard the way for his ascendency
Through deserts of lost years?
Why trouble him now who sees and hears
No more than what his innocence requires,

And therefore to no other height aspires
Than one at which he neither quails nor tires?
He may do more by seeing what he sees
Than others eager for iniquities;
He may, by seeing all things for the best,
Incite futurity to do the rest.

Or with an even likelihood,
He may have met with atrabilious eyes
The fires of time on equal terms and passed
Indifferently down, until at last
His only kind of grandeur would have been,
Apparently, in being seen.
He may have had for evil or for good
No argument; he may have had no care
For what without himself went anywhere
To failure or to glory, and least of all
For such a stale, flamboyant miracle;
He may have been the prophet of an art
Immovable to old idolatries;
He may have been a player without a part,
Annoyed that even the sun should have the skies
For such a flaming way to advertise;
He may have been a painter sick at heart
With Nature's toiling for a new surprise;
He may have been a cynic, who now, for all
Of anything divine that his effete
Negation may have tasted,
Saw truth in his own image, rather small,
Forbore to fever the ephemeral,
Found any barren height a good retreat
From any swarming street,
And in the sun saw power superbly wasted;
And when the primitive old-fashioned stars
Came out again to shine on joys and wars

THE MAN AGAINST THE SKY

More primitive, and all arrayed for doom,
He may have proved a world a sorry thing
In his imagining,
And life a lighted highway to the tomb.

Or, mounting with infirm unsearching tread,
His hopes to chaos led,
He may have stumbled up there from the past,
And with an aching strangeness viewed the last
Abysmal conflagration of his dreams,—
A flame where nothing seems
To burn but flame itself, by nothing fed;
And while it all went out,
Not even the faint anodyne of doubt
May then have eased a painful going down
From pictured heights of power and lost renown,
Revealed at length to his outlived endeavor
Remote and unapproachable forever;
And at his heart there may have gnawed
Sick memories of a dead faith foiled and flawed
And long dishonored by the living death
Assigned alike by chance
To brutes and hierophants;
And anguish fallen on those he loved around him
May once have dealt the last blow to confound him,
And so have left him as death leaves a child,
Who sees it all too near;
And he who knows no young way to forget
May struggle to the tomb unreconciled.
Whatever suns may rise or set
There may be nothing kinder for him here
Than shafts and agonies;
And under these
He may cry out and stay on horribly;
Or, seeing in death too small a thing to fear,

He may go forward like a stoic Roman
Where pangs and terrors in his pathway lie,—
Or, seizing the swift logic of a woman,
Curse God and die.

Or maybe there, like many another one
Who might have stood aloft and looked ahead,
Black-drawn against wild red,
He may have built, unawed by fiery gules
That in him no commotion stirred,
A living reason out of molecules
Why molecules occurred,
And one for smiling when he might have sighed
Had he seen far enough,
And in the same inevitable stuff
Discovered an odd reason too for pride
In being what he must have been by laws
Infrangible and for no kind of cause.
Deterred by no confusion or surprise
He may have seen with his mechanic eyes
A world without a meaning, and had room,
Alone amid magnificence and doom,
To build himself an airy monument
That should, or fail him in his vague intent,
Outlast an accidental universe—
To call it nothing worse—
Or, by the burrowing guile
Of Time disintegrated and effaced,
Like once-remembered mighty trees go down
To ruin, of which by man may now be traced
No part sufficient even to be rotten,
And in the book of things that are forgotten
Is entered as a thing not quite worth while.
He may have been so great
That satraps would have shivered at his frown,

THE MAN AGAINST THE SKY

And all he prized alive may rule a state
No larger than a grave that holds a clown;
He may have been a master of his fate,
And of his atoms,—ready as another
In his emergence to exonerate
His father and his mother;
He may have been a captain of a host,
Self-eloquent and ripe for prodigies,
Doomed here to swell by dangerous degrees,
And then give up the ghost.
Nahum's great grasshoppers were such as these,
Sun-scattered and soon lost.

Whatever the dark road he may have taken,
This man who stood on high
And faced alone the sky,
Whatever drove or lured or guided him,—
A vision answering a faith unshaken,
An easy trust assumed of easy trials,
A sick negation born of weak denials,
A crazed abhorrence of an old condition,
A blind attendance on a brief ambition,—
Whatever stayed him or derided him,
His way was even as ours;
And we, with all our wounds and all our powers,
Must each await alone at his own height
Another darkness or another light;
And there, of our poor self dominion reft,
If inference and reason shun
Hell, Heaven, and Oblivion,
May thwarted will (perforce precarious,
But for our conservation better thus)
Have no misgiving left
Of doing yet what here we leave undone?
Or if unto the last of these we cleave,

65

Believing or protesting we believe
In such an idle and ephemeral
Florescence of the diabolical,—
If, robbed of two fond old enormities,
Our being had no onward auguries,
What then were this great love of ours to say
For launching other lives to voyage again
A little farther into time and pain,
A little faster in a futile chase
For a kingdom and a power and a Race
That would have still in sight
A manifest end of ashes and eternal night?
Is this the music of the toys we shake
So loud,—as if there might be no mistake
Somewhere in our indomitable will?
Are we no greater than the noise we make
Along one blind atomic pilgrimage
Whereon by crass chance billeted we go
Because our brains and bones and cartilage
Will have it so?
If this we say, then let us all be still
About our share in it, and live and die
More quietly thereby.

Where was he going, this man against the sky?
You know not, nor do I.
But this we know, if we know anything:
That we may laugh and fight and sing
And of our transience here make offering
To an orient Word that will not be erased,
Or, save in incommunicable gleams
Too permanent for dreams,
Be found or known.
No tonic and ambitious irritant
Of increase or of want

THE MAN AGAINST THE SKY

Has made an otherwise insensate waste
Of ages overthrown
A ruthless, veiled, implacable foretaste
Of other ages that are still to be
Depleted and rewarded variously
Because a few, by fate's economy,
Shall seem to move the world the way it goes;
No soft evangel of equality,
Safe-cradled in a communal repose
That huddles into death and may at last
Be covered well with equatorial snows—
And all for what, the devil only knows—
Will aggregate an inkling to confirm
The credit of a sage or of a worm,
Or tell us why one man in five
Should have a care to stay alive
While in his heart he feels no violence
Laid on his humor and intelligence
When infant Science makes a pleasant face
And waves again that hollow toy, the Race;
No planetary trap where souls are wrought
For nothing but the sake of being caught
And sent again to nothing will attune
Itself to any key of any reason
Why man should hunger through another season
To find out why 'twere better late than soon
To go away and let the sun and moon
And all the silly stars illuminate
A place for creeping things,
And those that root and trumpet and have wings,
And herd and ruminate,
Or dive and flash and poise in rivers and seas,
Or by their loyal tails in lofty trees
Hang screeching lewd victorious derision
Of man's immortal vision.

Shall we, because Eternity records
Too vast an answer for the time-born words
We spell, whereof so many are dead that once
In our capricious lexicons
Were so alive and final, hear no more
The Word itself, the living word
That none alive has ever heard
Or ever spelt,
And few have ever felt
Without the fears and old surrenderings
And terrors that began
When Death let fall a feather from his wings
And humbled the first man?
Because the weight of our humility,
Wherefrom we gain
A little wisdom and much pain,
Falls here too sore and there too tedious,
Are we in anguish or complacency,
Not looking far enough ahead
To see by what mad couriers we are led
Along the roads of the ridiculous,
To pity ourselves and laugh at faith
And while we curse life bear it?
And if we see the soul's dead end in death,
Are we to fear it?
What folly is here that has not yet a name
Unless we say outright that we are liars?
What have we seen beyond our sunset fires
That lights again the way by which we came?
Why pay we such a price, and one we give
So clamoringly, for each racked empty day
That leads one more last human hope away,
As quiet fiends would lead past our crazed eyes
Our children to an unseen sacrifice?
If after all that we have lived and thought,

THE MAN AGAINST THE SKY

All comes to Nought,—
If there be nothing after Now,
And we be nothing anyhow,
And we know that,—why live?
'Twere sure but weaklings' vain distress
To suffer dungeons where so many doors
Will open on the cold eternal shores
That look sheer down
To the dark tideless floods of Nothingness
Where all who know may drown.

THE CHILDREN OF THE NIGHT
(1890-1897)

*To the Memory of
My Father and Mother*

JOHN EVERELDOWN

"Where are you going to-night, to-night,—
  Where are you going, John Evereldown?
There's never the sign of a star in sight,
  Nor a lamp that's nearer than Tilbury Town.
Why do you stare as a dead man might?
Where are you pointing away from the light?
And where are you going to-night, to-night,—
  Where are you going, John Evereldown?"

"Right through the forest, where none can see,
  There's where I'm going, to Tilbury Town.
The men are asleep,—or awake, may be,—
  But the women are calling John Evereldown.
Ever and ever they call for me,
And while they call can a man be free?
So right through the forest, where none can see,
  There's where I'm going, to Tilbury Town."

"But why are you going so late, so late,—
  Why are you going, John Evereldown?
Though the road be smooth and the way be straight,
  There are two long leagues to Tilbury Town.
Come in by the fire, old man, and wait!
Why do you chatter out there by the gate?
And why are you going so late, so late,—
  Why are you going, John Evereldown?"

"I follow the women wherever they call,—
  That's why I'm going to Tilbury Town.
God knows if I pray to be done with it all,
  But God is no friend to John Evereldown.
So the clouds may come and the rain may fall,
The shadows may creep and the dead men crawl,—
But I follow the women wherever they call,
  And that's why I'm going to Tilbury Town."

LUKE HAVERGAL

Go to the western gate, Luke Havergal,
There where the vines cling crimson on the wall,
And in the twilight wait for what will come.
The leaves will whisper there of her, and some,
Like flying words, will strike you as they fall;
But go, and if you listen she will call.
Go to the western gate, Luke Havergal—
Luke Havergal.

No, there is not a dawn in eastern skies
To rift the fiery night that's in your eyes;
But there, where western glooms are gathering,
The dark will end the dark, if anything:
God slays Himself with every leaf that flies,
And hell is more than half of paradise.
No, there is not a dawn in eastern skies—
In eastern skies.

Out of a grave I come to tell you this,
Out of a grave I come to quench the kiss
That flames upon your forehead with a glow
That blinds you to the way that you must go.

THREE QUATRAINS

Yes, there is yet one way to where she is,
Bitter, but one that faith may never miss.
Out of a grave I come to tell you this—
To tell you this.

There is the western gate, Luke Havergal,
There are the crimson leaves upon the wall.
Go, for the winds are tearing them away,—
Nor think to riddle the dead words they say,
Nor any more to feel them as they fall;
But go, and if you trust her she will call.
There is the western gate, Luke Havergal—
Luke Havergal.

THREE QUATRAINS

I

As long as Fame's imperious music rings
    Will poets mock it with crowned words august;
And haggard men will clamber to be kings
    As long as Glory weighs itself in dust.

II

Drink to the splendor of the unfulfilled,
    Nor shudder for the revels that are done:
The wines that flushed Lucullus are all spilled,
    The strings that Nero fingered are all gone.

III

We cannot crown ourselves with everything,
    Nor can we coax the Fates for us to quarrel:

No matter what we are, or what we sing,
   Time finds a withered leaf in every laurel.

AN OLD STORY

Strange that I did not know him then,
   That friend of mine!
I did not even show him then
   One friendly sign;

But cursed him for the ways he had
   To make me see
My envy of the praise he had
   For praising me.

I would have rid the earth of him
   Once, in my pride. . . .
I never knew the worth of him
   Until he died.

BALLADE BY THE FIRE

Slowly I smoke and hug my knee,
   The while a witless masquerade
Of things that only children see
   Floats in a mist of light and shade:
   They pass, a flimsy cavalcade,
And with a weak, remindful glow,
   The falling embers break and fade,
As one by one the phantoms go.

BALLADE OF BROKEN FLUTES

Then, with a melancholy glee
    To think where once my fancy strayed,
I muse on what the years may be
    Whose coming tales are all unsaid,
    Till tongs and shovel, snugly laid
Within their shadowed niches, grow
    By grim degrees to pick and spade,
As one by one the phantoms go.

But then, what though the mystic Three
    Around me ply their merry trade?—
And Charon soon may carry me
    Across the gloomy Stygian glade?—
    Be up, my soul; nor be afraid
Of what some unborn year may show;
    But mind your human debts are paid,
As one by one the phantoms go.

ENVOY

Life is the game that must be played:
    This truth at least, good friends, we know;
So live and laugh, nor be dismayed
    As one by one the phantoms go.

BALLADE OF BROKEN FLUTES

(To A. T. Schumann)

In dreams I crossed a barren land,
    A land of ruin, far away;
Around me hung on every hand
    A deathful stillness of decay;
    And silent, as in bleak dismay

That song should thus forsaken be,
 On that forgotten ground there lay
The broken flutes of Arcady.

The forest that was all so grand
 When pipes and tabors had their sway
Stood leafless now, a ghostly band
 Of skeletons in cold array.
 A lonely surge of ancient spray
Told of an unforgetful sea,
 But iron blows had hushed for aye
The broken flutes of Arcady.

No more by summer breezes fanned,
 The place was desolate and gray;
But still my dream was to command
 New life into that shrunken clay.
 I tried it. And you scan to-day,
With uncommiserating glee,
 The songs of one who strove to play
The broken flutes of Arcady.

ENVOY

So, Rock, I join the common fray,
 To fight where Mammon may decree;
And leave, to crumble as they may,
 The broken flutes of Arcady.

HER EYES

Up from the street and the crowds that went,
 Morning and midnight, to and fro,
Still was the room where his days he spent,
 And the stars were bleak, and the nights were slow.

HER EYES

Year after year, with his dream shut fast,
   He suffered and strove till his eyes were dim,
For the love that his brushes had earned at last,
   And the whole world rang with the praise of him.

But he cloaked his triumph, and searched, instead,
   Till his cheeks were sere and his hairs were gray.
"There are women enough, God knows," he said . . .
   "There are stars enough—when the sun's away."

Then he went back to the same still room
   That had held his dream in the long ago,
When he buried his days in a nameless tomb,
   And the stars were bleak, and the nights were slow.

And a passionate humor seized him there—
   Seized him and held him until there grew
Like life on his canvas, glowing and fair,
   A perilous face—and an angel's too.

Angel and maiden, and all in one,—
   All but the eyes. They were there, but yet
They seemed somehow like a soul half done.
   What was the matter? Did God forget? . . .

But he wrought them at last with a skill so sure
   That her eyes were the eyes of a deathless woman,—
With a gleam of heaven to make them pure,
   And a glimmer of hell to make them human.

God never forgets.—And he worships her
   There in that same still room of his,
For his wife, and his constant arbiter
   Of the world that was and the world that is.

And he wonders yet what her love could be
To punish him after that strife so grim;
But the longer he lives with her eyes to see,
The plainer it all comes back to him.

TWO MEN

There be two men of all mankind
    That I should like to know about;
But search and question where I will,
    I cannot ever find them out.

Melchizedek, he praised the Lord,
    And gave some wine to Abraham;
But who can tell what else he did
    Must be more learned than I am.

Ucalegon, he lost his house
    When Agamemnon came to Troy;
But who can tell me who he was—
    I'll pray the gods to give him joy.

There be two men of all mankind
    That I'm forever thinking on:
They chase me everywhere I go,—
    Melchizedek, Ucalegon.

VILLANELLE OF CHANGE

Since Persia fell at Marathon,
    The yellow years have gathered fast:
Long centuries have come and gone.

THE HOUSE ON THE HILL

And yet (they say) the place will don
  A phantom fury of the past,
Since Persia fell at Marathon;

And as of old, when Helicon
  Trembled and swayed with rapture vast
(Long centuries have come and gone),

This ancient plain, when night comes on,
  Shakes to a ghostly battle-blast,
Since Persia fell at Marathon.

But into soundless Acheron
  The glory of Greek shame was cast:
Long centuries have come and gone,

The suns of Hellas have all shone,
  The first has fallen to the last:—
Since Persia fell at Marathon,
Long centuries have come and gone.

THE HOUSE ON THE HILL

They are all gone away,
  The House is shut and still,
There is nothing more to say.

Through broken walls and gray
  The winds blow bleak and shrill:
They are all gone away.

Nor is there one to-day
  To speak them good or ill:
There is nothing more to say.

Why is it then we stray
   Around the sunken sill?
They are all gone away,

And our poor fancy-play
   For them is wasted skill:
There is nothing more to say.

There is ruin and decay
   In the House on the Hill:
They are all gone away,
There is nothing more to say.

RICHARD CORY

Whenever Richard Cory went down town,
We people on the pavement looked at him:
He was a gentleman from sole to crown,
Clean favored, and imperially slim.

And he was always quietly arrayed,
And he was always human when he talked;
But still he fluttered pulses when he said,
"Good-morning," and he glittered when he walked.

And he was rich—yes, richer than a king—
And admirably schooled in every grace:
In fine, we thought that he was everything
To make us wish that we were in his place.

So on we worked, and waited for the light,
And went without the meat, and cursed the bread;
And Richard Cory, one calm summer night,
Went home and put a bullet through his head.

DEAR FRIENDS

BOSTON

My northern pines are good enough for me,
But there's a town my memory uprears—
A town that always like a friend appears,
And always in the sunrise by the sea.
And over it, somehow, there seems to be
A downward flash of something new and fierce,
That ever strives to clear, but never clears
The dimness of a charmed antiquity.

CALVARY

Friendless and faint, with martyred steps and slow,
Faint for the flesh, but for the spirit free,
Stung by the mob that came to see the show,
The Master toiled along to Calvary;
We gibed him, as he went, with houndish glee,
Till his dimned eyes for us did overflow;
We cursed his vengeless hands thrice wretchedly,—
And this was nineteen hundred years ago.

But after nineteen hundred years the shame
Still clings, and we have not made good the loss
That outraged faith has entered in his name.
Ah, when shall come love's courage to be strong!
Tell me, O Lord—tell me, O Lord, how long
Are we to keep Christ writhing on the cross!

DEAR FRIENDS

Dear friends, reproach me not for what I do,
Nor counsel me, nor pity me; nor say
That I am wearing half my life away
For bubble-work that only fools pursue.

And if my bubbles be too small for you,
Blow bigger then your own: the games we play
To fill the frittered minutes of a day,
Good glasses are to read the spirit through.

And whoso reads may get him some shrewd skill;
And some unprofitable scorn resign,
To praise the very thing that he deplores;
So, friends (dear friends), remember, if you will,
The shame I win for singing is all mine,
The gold I miss for dreaming is all yours.

THE STORY OF THE ASHES AND THE FLAME

No matter why, nor whence, nor when she came,
There was her place. No matter what men said,
No matter what she was; living or dead,
Faithful or not, he loved her all the same.
The story was as old as human shame,
But ever since that lonely night she fled,
With books to blind him, he had only read
The story of the ashes and the flame.

There she was always coming pretty soon
To fool him back, with penitent scared eyes
That had in them the laughter of the moon
For baffled lovers, and to make him think—
Before she gave him time enough to wink—
Her kisses were the keys to Paradise.

AMARYLLIS

Once, when I wandered in the woods alone,
An old man tottered up to me and said,
"Come, friend, and see the grave that I have made
For Amaryllis." There was in the tone

THE PITY OF THE LEAVES

Of his complaint such quaver and such moan
That I took pity on him and obeyed,
And long stood looking where his hands had laid
An ancient woman, shrunk to skin and bone.

Far out beyond the forest I could hear
The calling of loud progress, and the bold
Incessant scream of commerce ringing clear;
But though the trumpets of the world were glad,
It made me lonely and it made me sad
To think that Amaryllis had grown old.

ZOLA

BECAUSE he puts the compromising chart
Of hell before your eyes, you are afraid;
Because he counts the price that you have paid
For innocence, and counts it from the start,
You loathe him. But he sees the human heart
Of God meanwhile, and in His hand was weighed
Your squeamish and emasculate crusade
Against the grim dominion of his art.

Never until we conquer the uncouth
Connivings of our shamed indifference
(We call it Christian faith) are we to scan
The racked and shrieking hideousness of Truth
To find, in hate's polluted self-defence
Throbbing, the pulse, the divine heart of man.

THE PITY OF THE LEAVES

VENGEFUL across the cold November moors,
Loud with ancestral shame there came the bleak
Sad wind that shrieked, and answered with a shriek,
Reverberant through lonely corridors.

The old man heard it; and he heard, perforce,
Words out of lips that were no more to speak—
Words of the past that shook the old man's cheek
Like dead, remembered footsteps on old floors.

And then there were the leaves that plagued him so!
The brown, thin leaves that on the stones outside
Skipped with a freezing whisper. Now and then
They stopped, and stayed there—just to let him know
How dead they were; but if the old man cried,
They fluttered off like withered souls of men.

AARON STARK

Withal a meagre man was Aaron Stark,
Cursed and unkempt, shrewd, shrivelled, and morose.
A miser was he, with a miser's nose,
And eyes like little dollars in the dark.
His thin, pinched mouth was nothing but a mark;
And when he spoke there came like sullen blows
Through scattered fangs a few snarled words and close,
As if a cur were chary of its bark.

Glad for the murmur of his hard renown,
Year after year he shambled through the town,
A loveless exile moving with a staff;
And oftentimes there crept into his ears
A sound of alien pity, touched with tears,—
And then (and only then) did Aaron laugh.

THE GARDEN

There is a fenceless garden overgrown
With buds and blossoms and all sorts of leaves;
And once, among the roses and the sheaves,
The Gardener and I were there alone.

CHARLES CARVILLE'S EYES

He led me to the plot where I had thrown
The fennel of my days on wasted ground,
And in that riot of sad weeds I found
The fruitage of a life that was my own.

My life! Ah, yes, there was my life, indeed!
And there were all the lives of humankind;
And they were like a book that I could read,
Whose every leaf, miraculously signed,
Outrolled itself from Thought's eternal seed.
Love-rooted in God's garden of the mind.

CLIFF KLINGENHAGEN

CLIFF KLINGENHAGEN had me in to dine
With him one day; and after soup and meat,
And all the other things there were to eat,
Cliff took two glasses and filled one with wine
And one with wormwood. Then, without a sign
For me to choose at all, he took the draught
Of bitterness himself, and lightly quaffed
It off, and said the other one was mine.

And when I asked him what the deuce he meant
By doing that, he only looked at me
And smiled, and said it was a way of his.
And though I know the fellow, I have spent
Long time a-wondering when I shall be
As happy as Cliff Klingenhagen is.

CHARLES CARVILLE'S EYES

A MELANCHOLY face Charles Carville had,
But not so melancholy as it seemed,
When once you knew him, for his mouth redeemed
His insufficient eyes, forever sad:

In them there was no life-glimpse, good or bad,
Nor joy nor passion in them ever gleamed;
His mouth was all of him that ever beamed,
His eyes were sorry, but his mouth was glad.

He never was a fellow that said much,
And half of what he did say was not heard
By many of us: we were out of touch
With all his whims and all his theories
Till he was dead, so those blank eyes of his
Might speak them. Then we heard them, every word.

THE DEAD VILLAGE

Here there is death. But even here, they say,
Here where the dull sun shines this afternoon
As desolate as ever the dead moon
Did glimmer on dead Sardis, men were gay;
And there were little children here to play,
With small soft hands that once did keep in tune
The strings that stretch from heaven, till too soon
The change came, and the music passed away.

Now there is nothing but the ghosts of things,—
No life, no love, no children, and no men;
And over the forgotten place there clings
The strange and unrememberable light
That is in dreams. The music failed, and then
God frowned, and shut the village from His sight.

TWO SONNETS

I

Just as I wonder at the twofold screen
Of twisted innocence that you would plait
For eyes that uncourageously await
The coming of a kingdom that has been,
So do I wonder what God's love can mean
To you that all so strangely estimate
The purpose and the consequent estate
Of one short shuddering step to the Unseen.

No, I have not your backward faith to shrink
Lone-faring from the doorway of God's home
To find Him in the names of buried men;
Nor your ingenious recreance to think
We cherish, in the life that is to come,
The scattered features of dead friends again.

II

Never until our souls are strong enough
To plunge into the crater of the Scheme—
Triumphant in the flash there to redeem
Love's handsel and forevermore to slough,
Like cerements at a played-out masque, the rough
And reptile skins of us whereon we set
The stigma of scared years—are we to get
Where atoms and the ages are one stuff.

Nor ever shall we know the cursed waste
Of life in the beneficence divine
Of starlight and of sunlight and soul-shine
That we have squandered in sin's frail distress,
Till we have drunk, and trembled at the taste,
The mead of Thought's prophetic endlessness.

THE CLERKS

I DID not think that I should find them there
When I came back again; but there they stood,
As in the days they dreamed of when young blood
Was in their cheeks and women called them fair.
Be sure, they met me with an ancient air,—
And yes, there was a shop-worn brotherhood
About them; but the men were just as good,
And just as human as they ever were.

And you that ache so much to be sublime,
And you that feed yourselves with your descent,
What comes of all your visions and your fears?
Poets and kings are but the clerks of Time,
Tiering the same dull webs of discontent,
Clipping the same sad alnage of the years.

FLEMING HELPHENSTINE

AT first I thought there was a superfine
Persuasion in his face; but the free glow
That filled it when he stopped and cried, "Hollo!"
Shone joyously, and so I let it shine.
He said his name was Fleming Helphenstine,
But be that as it may;—I only know
He talked of this and that and So-and-So,
And laughed and chaffed like any friend of mine.

But soon, with a queer, quick frown, he looked at me,
And I looked hard at him; and there we gazed
In a strained way that made us cringe and wince:
Then, with a wordless clogged apology
That sounded half confused and half amazed,
He dodged,—and I have never seen him since.

HORACE TO LEUCONOË

THOMAS HOOD

THE man who cloaked his bitterness within
This winding-sheet of puns and pleasantries,
God never gave to look with common eyes
Upon a world of anguish and of sin:
His brother was the branded man of Lynn;
And there are woven with his jollities
The nameless and eternal tragedies
That render hope and hopelessness akin.

We laugh, and crown him; but anon we feel
A still chord sorrow-swept,—a weird unrest;
And thin dim shadows home to midnight steal,
As if the very ghost of mirth were dead—
As if the joys of time to dreams had fled,
Or sailed away with Ines to the West.

HORACE TO LEUCONOË

I PRAY you not, Leuconoë, to pore
With unpermitted eyes on what may be
Appointed by the gods for you and me,
Nor on Chaldean figures any more.
'T were infinitely better to implore
The present only:—whether Jove decree
More winters yet to come, or whether he
Make even this, whose hard, wave-eaten shore
Shatters the Tuscan seas to-day, the last—
Be wise withal, and rack your wine, nor fill
Your bosom with large hopes; for while I sing,
The envious close of time is narrowing;—
So seize the day, or ever it be past,
And let the morrow come for what it will.

REUBEN BRIGHT

Because he was a butcher and thereby
Did earn an honest living (and did right),
I would not have you think that Reuben Bright
Was any more a brute than you or I;
For when they told him that his wife must die,
He stared at them, and shook with grief and fright,
And cried like a great baby half that night,
And made the women cry to see him cry.

And after she was dead, and he had paid
The singers and the sexton and the rest,
He packed a lot of things that she had made
Most mournfully away in an old chest
Of hers, and put some chopped-up cedar boughs
In with them, and tore down to the slaughter-house.

THE ALTAR

Alone, remote, nor witting where I went,
I found an altar builded in a dream—
A fiery place, whereof there was a gleam
So swift, so searching, and so eloquent
Of upward promise, that love's murmur, blent
With sorrow's warning, gave but a supreme
Unending impulse to that human stream
Whose flood was all for the flame's fury bent.

Alas! I said,—the world is in the wrong.
But the same quenchless fever of unrest
That thrilled the foremost of that martyred throng
Thrilled me, and I awoke . . . and was the same
Bewildered insect plunging for the flame
That burns, and must burn somehow for the best.

SONNET

THE TAVERN

Whenever I go by there nowadays
And look at the rank weeds and the strange grass,
The torn blue curtains and the broken glass,
I seem to be afraid of the old place;
And something stiffens up and down my face,
For all the world as if I saw the ghost
Of old Ham Amory, the murdered host,
With his dead eyes turned on me all aglaze.

The Tavern has a story, but no man
Can tell us what it is. We only know
That once long after midnight, years ago,
A stranger galloped up from Tilbury Town,
Who brushed, and scared, and all but overran
That skirt-crazed reprobate, John Evereldown.

SONNET

Oh for a poet—for a beacon bright
To rift this changeless glimmer of dead gray;
To spirit back the Muses, long astray,
And flush Parnassus with a newer light;
To put these little sonnet-men to flight
Who fashion, in a shrewd mechanic way,
Songs without souls, that flicker for a day,
To vanish in irrevocable night.

What does it mean, this barren age of ours?
Here are the men, the women, and the flowers,
The seasons, and the sunset, as before.
What does it mean? Shall there not one arise
To wrench one banner from the western skies,
And mark it with his name forevermore?

GEORGE CRABBE

Give him the darkest inch your shelf allows,
Hide him in lonely garrets, if you will,—
But his hard, human pulse is throbbing still
With the sure strength that fearless truth endows.
In spite of all fine science disavows,
Of his plain excellence and stubborn skill
There yet remains what fashion cannot kill,
Though years have thinned the laurel from his brows.

Whether or not we read him, we can feel
From time to time the vigor of his name
Against us like a finger for the shame
And emptiness of what our souls reveal
In books that are as altars where we kneel
To consecrate the flicker, not the flame.

CREDO

I cannot find my way: there is no star
In all the shrouded heavens anywhere;
And there is not a whisper in the air
Of any living voice but one so far
That I can hear it only as a bar
Of lost, imperial music, played when fair
And angel fingers wove, and unaware,
Dead leaves to garlands where no roses are.

No, there is not a glimmer, nor a call,
For one that welcomes, welcomes when he fears,
The black and awful chaos of the night;
For through it all—above, beyond it all—
I know the far-sent message of the years,
I feel the coming glory of the Light.

SONNET

ON THE NIGHT OF A FRIEND'S WEDDING

If ever I am old, and all alone,
I shall have killed one grief, at any rate;
For then, thank God, I shall not have to wait
Much longer for the sheaves that I have sown.
The devil only knows what I have done,
But here I am, and here are six or eight
Good friends, who most ingenuously prate
About my songs to such and such a one.

But everything is all askew to-night,—
As if the time were come, or almost come,
For their untenanted mirage of me
To lose itself and crumble out of sight,
Like a tall ship that floats above the foam
A little while, and then breaks utterly.

SONNET

The master and the slave go hand in hand,
Though touch be lost. The poet is a slave,
And there be kings do sorrowfully crave
The joyance that a scullion may command.
But, ah, the sonnet-slave must understand
The mission of his bondage, or the grave
May clasp his bones, or ever he shall save
The perfect word that is the poet's wand.

The sonnet is a crown, whereof the rhymes
Are for Thought's purest gold the jewel-stones;
But shapes and echoes that are never done
Will haunt the workshop, as regret sometimes
Will bring with human yearning to sad thrones
The crash of battles that are never won.

VERLAINE

Why do you dig like long-clawed scavengers
To touch the covered corpse of him that fled
The uplands for the fens, and rioted
Like a sick satyr with doom's worshippers?
Come! let the grass grow there; and leave his verse
To tell the story of the life he led.
Let the man go: let the dead flesh be dead,
And let the worms be its biographers.

Song sloughs away the sin to find redress
In art's complete remembrance: nothing clings
For long but laurel to the stricken brow
That felt the Muse's finger; nothing less
Than hell's fulfilment of the end of things
Can blot the star that shines on Paris now.

SONNET

When we can all so excellently give
The measure of love's wisdom with a blow,—
Why can we not in turn receive it so,
And end this murmur for the life we live?
And when we do so frantically strive
To win strange faith, why do we shun to know
That in love's elemental over-glow
God's wholeness gleams with light superlative?

Oh, brother men, if you have eyes at all,
Look at a branch, a bird, a child, a rose,
Or anything God ever made that grows,—
Nor let the smallest vision of it slip,
Till you may read, as on Belshazzar's wall,
The glory of eternal partnership.

THE CHORUS OF OLD MEN IN "ÆGEUS"

SUPREMACY

There is a drear and lonely tract of hell
From all the common gloom removed afar:
A flat, sad land it is, where shadows are,
Whose lorn estate my verse may never tell.
I walked among them and I knew them well:
Men I had slandered on life's little star
For churls and sluggards; and I knew the scar
Upon their brows of woe ineffable.

But as I went majestic on my way,
Into the dark they vanished, one by one,
Till, with a shaft of God's eternal day,
The dream of all my glory was undone,—
And, with a fool's importunate dismay,
I heard the dead men singing in the sun.

THE CHORUS OF OLD MEN IN "ÆGEUS"

Ye gods that have a home beyond the world,
Ye that have eyes for all man's agony,
Ye that have seen this woe that we have seen,—
Look with a just regard,
And with an even grace,
Here on the shattered corpse of a shattered king,
Here on a suffering world where men grow old
And wander like sad shadows till, at last,
Out of the flare of life,
Out of the whirl of years,
Into the mist they go,
Into the mist of death.

O shades of you that loved him long before
The cruel threads of that black sail were spun,
May loyal arms and ancient welcomings
Receive him once again
Who now no longer moves
Here in this flickering dance of changing days,
Where a battle is lost and won for a withered wreath,
And the black master Death is over all
To chill with his approach,
To level with his touch,
The reigning strength of youth,
The fluttered heart of age.

Woe for the fateful day when Delphi's word was lost—
Woe for the loveless prince of Æthra's line!
Woe for a father's tears and the curse of a king's release—
Woe for the wings of pride and the shafts of doom!
And thou, the saddest wind
That ever blew from Crete,
Sing the fell tidings back to that thrice unhappy ship!—
Sing to the western flame,
Sing to the dying foam.
A dirge for the sundered years and a dirge for the years to be!

Better his end had been as the end of a cloudless day,
Bright, by the word of Zeus, with a golden star,
Wrought of a golden fame, and flung to the central sky,
To gleam on a stormless tomb for evermore:—
Whether or not there fell
To the touch of an alien hand
The sheen of his purple robe and the shine of his diadem,
Better his end had been
To die as an old man dies,—
But the fates are ever the fates, and a crown is ever a crown.

THE WILDERNESS

Come away! come away! there's a frost along the marshes,
And a frozen wind that skims the shoal where it shakes the dead black water;
There's a moan across the lowland and a wailing through the woodland
Of a dirge that sings to send us back to the arms of those that love us.
There is nothing left but ashes now where the crimson chills of autumn
Put off the summer's languor with a touch that made us glad
For the glory that is gone from us, with a flight we cannot follow,
To the slopes of other valleys and the sounds of other shores.

Come away! come away! you can hear them calling, calling,
Calling us to come to them, and roam no more.
Over there beyond the ridges and the land that lies between us,
There's an old song calling us to come!

Come away! come away!—for the scenes we leave behind us
Are barren for the lights of home and a flame that's young forever;
And the lonely trees around us creak the warning of the night-wind,
That love and all the dreams of love are away beyond the mountains.
The songs that call for us to-night, they have called for men before us,
And the winds that blow the message, they have blown ten thousand years;
But this will end our wander-time, for we know the joy that waits us
In the strangeness of home-coming, and a woman's waiting eyes.

Come away! come away! there is nothing now to cheer us—
Nothing now to comfort us, but love's road home:—
Over there beyond the darkness there's a window gleams to greet us,
And a warm hearth waits for us within.

Come away! come away!—or the roving-fiend will hold us,
And make us all to dwell with him to the end of human faring:
There are no men yet may leave him when his hands are clutched upon them,
There are none will own his enmity, there are none will call him brother.
So we'll be up and on the way, and the less we boast the better
For the freedom that God gave us and the dread we do not know:—
The frost that skips the willow-leaf will again be back to blight it,
And the doom we cannot fly from is the doom we do not see.

Come away! come away! there are dead men all around us—
Frozen men that mock us with a wild, hard laugh
That shrieks and sinks and whimpers in the shrill November rushes,
And the long fall wind on the lake.

OCTAVES

I

We thrill too strangely at the master's touch;
We shrink too sadly from the larger self
Which for its own completeness agitates
And undetermines us; we do not feel—
We dare not feel it yet—the splendid shame
Of uncreated failure; we forget,

OCTAVES

The while we groan, that God's accomplishment
Is always and unfailingly at hand.

II

TUMULTUOUSLY void of a clean scheme
Whereon to build, whereof to formulate,
The legion life that riots in mankind
Goes ever plunging upward, up and down,
Most like some crazy regiment at arms,
Undisciplined of aught but Ignorance,
And ever led resourcelessly along
To brainless carnage by drunk trumpeters.

III

To me the groaning of world-worshippers
Rings like a lonely music played in hell
By one with art enough to cleave the walls
Of heaven with his cadence, but without
The wisdom or the will to comprehend
The strangeness of his own perversity,
And all without the courage to deny
The profit and the pride of his defeat.

IV

WHILE we are drilled in error, we are lost
Alike to truth and usefulness. We think
We are great warriors now, and we can brag
Like Titans; but the world is growing young,
And we, the fools of time, are growing with it:—
We do not fight to-day, we only die;
We are too proud of death, and too ashamed
Of God, to know enough to be alive.

V

There is one battle-field whereon we fall
Triumphant and unconquered; but, alas!
We are too fleshly fearful of ourselves
To fight there till our days are whirled and blurred
By sorrow, and the ministering wheels
Of anguish take us eastward, where the clouds
Of human gloom are lost against the gleam
That shines on Thought's impenetrable mail.

VI

When we shall hear no more the cradle-songs
Of ages—when the timeless hymns of Love
Defeat them and outsound them—we shall know
The rapture of that large release which all
Right science comprehends; and we shall read,
With unoppressed and unoffended eyes,
That record of All-Soul whereon God writes
In everlasting runes the truth of Him.

VII

The guerdon of new childhood is repose:—
Once he has read the primer of right thought,
A man may claim between two smithy strokes
Beatitude enough to realize
God's parallel completeness in the vague
And incommensurable excellence
That equitably uncreates itself
And makes a whirlwind of the Universe.

VIII

There is no loneliness:—no matter where
We go, nor whence we come, nor what good friends

OCTAVES

Forsake us in the seeming, we are all
At one with a complete companionship;
And though forlornly joyless be the ways
We travel, the compensate spirit-gleams
Of Wisdom shaft the darkness here and there,
Like scattered lamps in unfrequented streets.

IX

WHEN one that you and I had all but sworn
To be the purest thing God ever made
Bewilders us until at last it seems
An angel has come back restigmatized,—
Faith wavers, and we wonder what there is
On earth to make us faithful any more,
But never are quite wise enough to know
The wisdom that is in that wonderment.

X

WHERE does a dead man go?—The dead man dies;
But the free life that would no longer feed
On fagots of outburned and shattered flesh
Wakes to a thrilled invisible advance,
Unchained (or fettered else) of memory;
And when the dead man goes it seems to me
'T were better for us all to do away
With weeping, and be glad that he is gone.

XI

STILL through the dusk of dead, blank-legended,
And unremunerative years we search
To get where life begins, and still we groan
Because we do not find the living spark

Where no spark ever was; and thus we die,
Still searching, like poor old astronomers
Who totter off to bed and go to sleep,
To dream of untriangulated stars.

XII

WITH conscious eyes not yet sincere enough
To pierce the glimmered cloud that fluctuates
Between me and the glorifying light
That screens itself with knowledge, I discern
The searching rays of wisdom that reach through
The mist of shame's infirm credulity,
And infinitely wonder if hard words
Like mine have any message for the dead.

XIII

I GRANT you friendship is a royal thing,
But none shall ever know that royalty
For what it is till he has realized
His best friend in himself. 'T is then, perforce,
That man's unfettered faith indemnifies
Of its own conscious freedom the old shame,
And love's revealed infinitude supplants
Of its own wealth and wisdom the old scorn.

XIV

THOUGH the sick beast infect us, we are fraught
Forever with indissoluble Truth,
Wherein redress reveals itself divine,
Transitional, transcendent. Grief and loss,
Disease and desolation, are the dreams
Of wasted excellence; and every dream

OCTAVES

Has in it something of an ageless fact
That flouts deformity and laughs at years.

XV

We lack the courage to be where we are:—
We love too much to travel on old roads,
To triumph on old fields; we love too much
To consecrate the magic of dead things,
And yieldingly to linger by long walls
Of ruin, where the ruinous moonlight
That sheds a lying glory on old stones
Befriends us with a wizard's enmity.

XVI

Something as one with eyes that look below
The battle-smoke to glimpse the foeman's charge,
We through the dust of downward years may scan
The onslaught that awaits this idiot world
Where blood pays blood for nothing, and where life
Pays life to madness, till at last the ports
Of gilded helplessness be battered through
By the still crash of salvatory steel.

XVII

To you that sit with Sorrow like chained slaves,
And wonder if the night will ever come,
I would say this: The night will never come,
And sorrow is not always. But my words
Are not enough; your eyes are not enough;
The soul itself must insulate the Real,
Or ever you do cherish in this life—
In this life or in any life—repose.

XVIII

Like a white wall whereon forever breaks
Unsatisfied the tumult of green seas,
Man's unconjectured godliness rebukes
With its imperial silence the lost waves
Of insufficient grief. This mortal surge
That beats against us now is nothing else
Than plangent ignorance. Truth neither shakes
Nor wavers; but the world shakes, and we shriek.

XIX

Nor jewelled phrase nor mere mellifluous rhyme
Reverberates aright, or ever shall,
One cadence of that infinite plain-song
Which is itself all music. Stronger notes
Than any that have ever touched the world
Must ring to tell it—ring like hammer-blows,
Right-echoed of a chime primordial,
On anvils, in the gleaming of God's forge.

XX

The prophet of dead words defeats himself:
Whoever would acknowledge and include
The foregleam and the glory of the real,
Must work with something else than pen and ink
And painful preparation: he must work
With unseen implements that have no names,
And he must win withal, to do that work,
Good fortitude, clean wisdom, and strong skill.

XXI

To curse the chilled insistence of the dawn
Because the free gleam lingers; to defraud

TWO QUATRAINS

The constant opportunity that lives
Unchallenged in all sorrow; to forget
For this large prodigality of gold
That larger generosity of thought,—
These are the fleshly clogs of human greed,
The fundamental blunders of mankind.

XXII

FOREBODINGS are the fiends of Recreance;
The master of the moment, the clean seer
Of ages, too securely scans what is,
Ever to be appalled at what is not;
He sees beyond the groaning borough lines
Of Hell, God's highways gleaming, and he knows
That Love's complete communion is the end
Of anguish to the liberated man.

XXIII

HERE by the windy docks I stand alone,
But yet companioned. There the vessel goes,
And there my friend goes with it; but the wake
That melts and ebbs between that friend and me
Love's earnest is of Life's all-purposeful
And all-triumphant sailing, when the ships
Of Wisdom loose their fretful chains and swing
Forever from the crumbled wharves of Time.

TWO QUATRAINS

I

As eons of incalculable strife
Are in the vision of one moment caught,
So are the common, concrete things of life
Divinely shadowed on the walls of Thought.

COLLECTED POEMS

II

We shriek to live, but no man ever lives
Till he has rid the ghost of human breath;
We dream to die, but no man ever dies
Till he has quit the road that runs to death.

THE TORRENT

I found a torrent falling in a glen
Where the sun's light shone silvered and leaf-split;
The boom, the foam, and the mad flash of it
All made a magic symphony; but when
I thought upon the coming of hard men
To cut those patriarchal trees away,
And turn to gold the silver of that spray,
I shuddered. Yet a gladness now and then
Did wake me to myself till I was glad
In earnest, and was welcoming the time
For screaming saws to sound above the chime
Of idle waters, and for me to know
The jealous visionings that I had had
Were steps to the great place where trees and torrents go.

L'ENVOI

Now in a thought, now in a shadowed word,
Now in a voice that thrills eternity,
Ever there comes an onward phrase to me
Of some transcendent music I have heard;
No piteous thing by soft hands dulcimered,
No trumpet crash of blood-sick victory,
But a glad strain of some vast harmony
That no brief mortal touch has ever stirred.

L'ENVOI

There is no music in the world like this,
No character wherewith to set it down,
No kind of instrument to make it sing.
No kind of instrument? Ah, yes, there is;
And after time and place are overthrown,
God's touch will keep its one chord quivering.

CAPTAIN CRAIG, ETC.
(1902)

*To the Memory of
John Hays Gardiner*

CAPTAIN CRAIG

I

I DOUBT if ten men in all Tilbury Town
Had ever shaken hands with Captain Craig,
Or called him by his name, or looked at him
So curiously, or so concernedly,
As they had looked at ashes; but a few—
Say five or six of us—had found somehow
The spark in him, and we had fanned it there,
Choked under, like a jest in Holy Writ,
By Tilbury prudence. He had lived his life
And in his way had shared, with all mankind,
Inveterate leave to fashion of himself,
By some resplendent metamorphosis,
Whatever he was not. And after time,
When it had come sufficiently to pass
That he was going patch-clad through the streets,
Weak, dizzy, chilled, and half starved, he had laid
Some nerveless fingers on a prudent sleeve,
And told the sleeve, in furtive confidence,
Just how it was: "My name is Captain Craig,"
He said, "and I must eat." The sleeve moved on,
And after it moved others—one or two;
For Captain Craig, before the day was done,
Got back to the scant refuge of his bed
And shivered into it without a curse—
Without a murmur even. He was cold,

And old, and hungry; but the worst of it
Was a forlorn familiar consciousness
That he had failed again. There was a time
When he had fancied, if worst came to worst,
And he could do no more, that he might ask
Of whom he would. But once had been enough,
And soon there would be nothing more to ask.
He was himself, and he had lost the speed
He started with, and he was left behind.
There was no mystery, no tragedy;
And if they found him lying on his back
Stone dead there some sharp morning, as they might,—
Well, once upon a time there was a man—
Es war einmal ein König, if it pleased him.
And he was right: there were no men to blame:
There was just a false note in the Tilbury tune—
A note that able-bodied men might sound
Hosannas on while Captain Craig lay quiet.
They might have made him sing by feeding him
Till he should march again, but probably
Such yielding would have jeopardized the rhythm;
They found it more melodious to shout
Right on, with unmolested adoration,
To keep the tune as it had always been,
To trust in God, and let the Captain starve.

He must have understood that afterwards—
When we had laid some fuel to the spark
Of him, and oxidized it—for he laughed
Out loud and long at us to feel it burn,
And then, for gratitude, made game of us:
"You are the resurrection and the life,"
He said, "and I the hymn the Brahmin sings;
O Fuscus! and we'll go no more a-roving."

CAPTAIN CRAIG

We were not quite accoutred for a blast
Of any lettered nonchalance like that,
And some of us—the five or six of us
Who found him out—were singularly struck.
But soon there came assurance of his lips,
Like phrases out of some sweet instrument
Man's hand had never fitted, that he felt
"No penitential shame for what had come,
No virtuous regret for what had been,—
But rather a joy to find it in his life
To be an outcast usher of the soul
For such as had good courage of the Sun
To pattern Love." The Captain had one chair;
And on the bottom of it, like a king,
For longer time than I dare chronicle,
Sat with an ancient ease and eulogized
His opportunity. My friends got out,
Like brokers out of Arcady; but I—
May be for fascination of the thing,
Or may be for the larger humor of it—
Stayed listening, unwearied and unstung.
When they were gone the Captain's tuneful ooze
Of rhetoric took on a change; he smiled
At me and then continued, earnestly:
"Your friends have had enough of it; but you,
For a motive hardly vindicated yet
By prudence or by conscience, have remained;
And that is very good, for I have things
To tell you: things that are not words alone—
Which are the ghosts of things—but something firmer.
"First, would I have you know, for every gift
Or sacrifice, there are—or there may be—
Two kinds of gratitude: the sudden kind
We feel for what we take, the larger kind
We feel for what we give. Once we have learned

As much as this, we know the truth has been
Told over to the world a thousand times;—
But we have had no ears to listen yet
For more than fragments of it: we have heard
A murmur now and then, an echo here
And there, and we have made great music of it;
And we have made innumerable books
To please the Unknown God. Time throws away
Dead thousands of them, but the God that knows
No death denies not one: the books all count,
The songs all count; and yet God's music has
No modes, his language has no adjectives."

"You may be right, you may be wrong," said I;
"But what has this that you are saying now—
This nineteenth-century Nirvana-talk—
To do with you and me?" The Captain raised
His hand and held it westward, where a patched
And unwashed attic-window filtered in
What barren light could reach us, and then said,
With a suave, complacent resonance: "There shines
The sun. Behold it. We go round and round,
And wisdom comes to us with every whirl
We count throughout the circuit. We may say
The child is born, the boy becomes a man,
The man does this and that, and the man goes,—
But having said it we have not said much,
Not very much. Do I fancy, or you think,
That it will be the end of anything
When I am gone? There was a soldier once
Who fought one fight and in that fight fell dead.
Sad friends went after, and they brought him home
And had a brass band at his funeral,
As you should have at mine; and after that
A few remembered him. But he was dead,

CAPTAIN CRAIG

They said, and they should have their friend no more.—
However, there was once a starveling child—
A ragged-vested little incubus,
Born to be cuffed and frighted out of all
Capacity for childhood's happiness—
Who started out one day, quite suddenly,
To drown himself. He ran away from home,
Across the clover-fields and through the woods,
And waited on a rock above a stream,
Just like a kingfisher. He might have dived,
Or jumped, or he might not; but anyhow,
There came along a man who looked at him
With such an unexpected friendliness,
And talked with him in such a common way,
That life grew marvelously different:
What he had lately known for sullen trunks
And branches, and a world of tedious leaves,
Was all transmuted; a faint forest wind
That once had made the loneliest of all
Sad sounds on earth, made now the rarest music;
And water that had called him once to death
Now seemed a flowing glory. And that man,
Born to go down a soldier, did this thing.
Not much to do? Not very much, I grant you:
Good occupation for a sonneteer,
Or for a clown, or for a clergyman,
But small work for a soldier. By the way,
When you are weary sometimes of your own
Utility, I wonder if you find
Occasional great comfort pondering
What power a man has in him to put forth?
'Of all the many marvelous things that are,
Nothing is there more marvelous than man,'
Said Sophocles; and he lived long ago;
'And earth, unending ancient of the gods

He furrows; and the ploughs go back and forth,
Turning the broken mould, year after year.' . . .

"I turned a little furrow of my own
Once on a time, and everybody laughed—
As I laughed afterwards; and I doubt not
The First Intelligence, which we have drawn
In our competitive humility
As if it went forever on two legs,
Had some diversion of it: I believe
God's humor is the music of the spheres—
But even as we draft omnipotence
Itself to our own image, we pervert
The courage of an infinite ideal
To finite resignation. You have made
The cement of your churches out of tears
And ashes, and the fabric will not stand:
The shifted walls that you have coaxed and shored
So long with unavailing compromise
Will crumble down to dust and blow away,
And younger dust will follow after them;
Though not the faintest or the farthest whirled
First atom of the least that ever flew
Shall be by man defrauded of the touch
God thrilled it with to make a dream for man
When Science was unborn. And after time,
When we have earned our spiritual ears,
And art's commiseration of the truth
No longer glorifies the singing beast,
Or venerates the clinquant charlatan,—
Then shall at last come ringing through the sun,
Through time, through flesh, a music that is true.
For wisdom is that music, and all joy
That wisdom:—you may counterfeit, you think,
The burden of it in a thousand ways;

CAPTAIN CRAIG

But as the bitterness that loads your tears
Makes Dead Sea swimming easy, so the gloom,
The penance, and the woeful pride you keep,
Make bitterness your buoyance of the world.
And at the fairest and the frenziedest
Alike of your God-fearing festivals,
You so compound the truth to pamper fear
That in the doubtful surfeit of your faith
You clamor for the food that shadows eat.
You call it rapture or deliverance,—
Passion or exaltation, or what most
The moment needs, but your faint-heartedness
Lives in it yet: you quiver and you clutch
For something larger, something unfulfilled,
Some wiser kind of joy that you shall have
Never, until you learn to laugh with God."
And with a calm Socratic patronage,
At once half sombre and half humorous,
The Captain reverently twirled his thumbs
And fixed his eyes on something far away;
Then, with a gradual gaze, conclusive, shrewd,
And at the moment unendurable
For sheer beneficence, he looked at me.

"But the brass band?" I said, not quite at ease
With altruism yet.—He made a sort
Of reminiscent little inward noise,
Midway between a chuckle and a laugh,
And that was all his answer: not a word
Of explanation or suggestion came
From those tight-smiling lips. And when I left,
I wondered, as I trod the creaking snow
And had the world-wide air to breathe again,—
Though I had seen the tremor of his mouth
And honored the endurance of his hand—

Whether or not, securely closeted
Up there in the stived haven of his den,
The man sat laughing at me; and I felt
My teeth grind hard together with a quaint
Revulsion—as I recognize it now—
Not only for my Captain, but as well
For every smug-faced failure on God's earth;
Albeit I could swear, at the same time,
That there were tears in the old fellow's eyes.
I question if in tremors or in tears
There be more guidance to man's worthiness
Than—well, say in his prayers. But oftentimes
It humors us to think that we possess
By some divine adjustment of our own
Particular shrewd cells, or something else,
What others, for untutored sympathy,
Go spirit-fishing more than half their lives
To catch—like cheerful sinners to catch faith;
And I have not a doubt but I assumed
Some egotistic attribute like this
When, cautiously, next morning I reduced
The fretful qualms of my novitiate,
For most part, to an undigested pride.
Only, I live convinced that I regret
This enterprise no more than I regret
My life; and I am glad that I was born.

That evening, at "The Chrysalis," I found
The faces of my comrades all suffused
With what I chose then to denominate
Superfluous good feeling. In return,
They loaded me with titles of odd form
And unexemplified significance,
Like "Bellows-mender to Prince Æolus,"

CAPTAIN CRAIG

"Pipe-filler to the Hoboscholiast,"
"Bread-fruit for the Non-Doing," with one more
That I remember, and a dozen more
That I forget. I may have been disturbed,
I do not say that I was not annoyed,
But something of the same serenity
That fortified me later made me feel
For their skin-pricking arrows not so much
Of pain as of a vigorous defect
In this world's archery. I might have tried,
With a flat facetiousness, to demonstrate
What they had only snapped at and thereby
Made out of my best evidence no more
Than comfortable food for their conceit;
But patient wisdom frowned on argument,
With a side nod for silence, and I smoked
A series of incurable dry pipes
While Morgan fiddled, with obnoxious care,
Things that I wished he wouldn't. Killigrew,
Drowsed with a fond abstraction, like an ass,
Lay blinking at me while he grinned and made
Remarks. The learned Plunket made remarks.

It may have been for smoke that I cursed cats
That night, but I have rather to believe
As I lay turning, twisting, listening,
And wondering, between great sleepless yawns,
What possible satisfaction those dead leaves
Could find in sending shadows to my room
And swinging them like black rags on a line,
That I, with a forlorn clear-headedness
Was ekeing out probation. I had sinned
In fearing to believe what I believed,
And I was paying for it.—Whimsical,
You think,—factitious; but "there is no luck,

No fate, no fortune for us, but the old
Unswerving and inviolable price
Gets paid: God sells himself eternally,
But never gives a crust," my friend had said;
And while I watched those leaves, and heard those cats,
And with half mad minuteness analyzed
The Captain's attitude and then my own,
I felt at length as one who throws himself
Down restless on a couch when clouds are dark,
And shuts his eyes to find, when he wakes up
And opens them again, what seems at first
An unfamiliar sunlight in his room
And in his life—as if the child in him
Had laughed and let him see; and then I knew
Some prowling superfluity of child
In me had found the child in Captain Craig
And let the sunlight reach him. While I slept,
My thought reshaped itself to friendly dreams,
And in the morning it was with me still.

Through March and shifting April to the time
When winter first becomes a memory
My friend the Captain—to my other friend's
Incredulous regret that such as he
Should ever get the talons of his talk
So fixed in my unfledged credulity—
Kept up the peroration of his life,
Not yielding at a threshold, nor, I think,
Too often on the stairs. He made me laugh
Sometimes, and then again he made me weep
Almost; for I had insufficiency
Enough in me to make me know the truth
Within the jest, and I could feel it there
As well as if it were the folded note
I felt between my fingers. I had said

CAPTAIN CRAIG

Before that I should have to go away
And leave him for the season; and his eyes
Had shone with well-becoming interest
At that intelligence. There was no mist
In them that I remember; but I marked
An unmistakable self-questioning
And a reticence of unassumed regret.
The two together made anxiety—
Not selfishness, I ventured. I should see
No more of him for six or seven months,
And I was there to tell him as I might
What humorous provision we had made
For keeping him locked up in Tilbury Town.
That finished—with a few more commonplace
Prosaics on the certified event
Of my return to find him young again—
I left him neither vexed, I thought, with us,
Nor over much at odds with destiny.
At any rate, save always for a look
That I had seen too often to mistake
Or to forget, he gave no other sign.

That train began to move; and as it moved,
I felt a comfortable sudden change
All over and inside. Partly it seemed
As if the strings of me had all at once
Gone down a tone or two; and even though
It made me scowl to think so trivial
A touch had owned the strength to tighten them,
It made me laugh to think that I was free.
But free from what—when I began to turn
The question round—was more than I could say:
I was no longer vexed with Killigrew,
Nor more was I possessed with Captain Craig;
But I was eased of some restraint, I thought,

Not qualified by those amenities,
And I should have to search the matter down;
For I was young, and I was very keen.
So I began to smoke a bad cigar
That Plunket, in his love, had given me
The night before; and as I smoked I watched
The flying mirrors for a mile or so,
Till to the changing glimpse, now sharp, now faint,
They gave me of the woodland over west,
A gleam of long-forgotten strenuous years
Came back, when we were Red Men on the trail,
With Morgan for the big chief Wocky-Bocky;
And yawning out of that I set myself
To face again the loud monotonous ride
That lay before me like a vista drawn
Of bag-racks to the fabled end of things.

II

YET that ride had an end, as all rides have;
And the days coming after took the road
That all days take,—though never one of them
Went by but I got some good thought of it
For Captain Craig. Not that I pitied him,
Or nursed a mordant hunger for his presence;
But what I thought (what Killigrew still thinks)
An irremediable cheerfulness
Was in him and about the name of him,
And I fancy that it may be most of all
For cheer in them that I have saved his letters.
I like to think of him, and how he looked—
Or should have looked—in his renewed estate,
Composing them. They may be dreariness
Unspeakable to you that never saw
The Captain; but to five or six of us

CAPTAIN CRAIG

Who knew him they are not so bad as that.
It may be we have smiled not always where
The text itself would seem to indicate
Responsive titillation on our part,—
Yet having smiled at all we have done well,
Knowing that we have touched the ghost of him.
He tells me that he thinks of nothing now
That he would rather do than be himself,
Wisely alive. So let us heed this man:—

"The world that has been old is young again,
The touch that faltered clings; and this is May.
So think of your decrepit pensioner
As one who cherishes the living light,
Forgetful of dead shadows. He may gloat,
And he may not have power in his arms
To make the young world move; but he has eyes
And ears, and he can read the sun. Therefore
Think first of him as one who vegetates
In tune with all the children who laugh best
And longest through the sunshine, though far off
Their laughter, and unheard; for 't is the child,
O friend, that with his laugh redeems the man.
Time steals the infant, but the child he leaves;
And we, we fighters over of old wars—
We men, we shearers of the Golden Fleece—
Were brutes without him,—brutes to tear the scars
Of one another's wounds and weep in them,
And then cry out on God that he should flaunt
For life such anguish and flesh-wretchedness.
But let the brute go roaring his own way:
We do not need him, and he loves us not.

"I cannot think of anything to-day
That I would rather do than be myself,

Primevally alive, and have the sun
Shine into me; for on a day like this,
When chaff-parts of a man's adversities
Are blown by quick spring breezes out of him—
When even a flicker of wind that wakes no more
Than a tuft of grass, or a few young yellow leaves,
Comes like the falling of a prophet's breath
On altar-flames rekindled of crushed embers,—
Then do I feel, now do I feel, within me
No dreariness, no grief, no discontent,
No twinge of human envy. But I beg
That you forego credentials of the past
For these illuminations of the present,
Or better still, to give the shadow justice,
You let me tell you something: I have yearned
In many another season for these days,
And having them with God's own pageantry
To make me glad for them,—yes, I have cursed
The sunlight and the breezes and the leaves
To think of men on stretchers or on beds,
Or on foul floors, things without shapes or names,
Made human with paralysis and rags;
Or some poor devil on a battle-field,
Left undiscovered and without the strength
To drag a maggot from his clotted mouth;
Or women working where a man would fall—
Flat-breasted miracles of cheerfulness
Made neuter by the work that no man counts
Until it waits undone; children thrown out
To feed their veins and souls on offal . . . Yes,
I have had half a mind to blow my brains out
Sometimes; and I have gone from door to door,
Ragged myself, trying to do something—
Crazy, I hope.—But what has this to do
With Spring? Because one half of humankind

CAPTAIN CRAIG

Lives here in hell, shall not the other half
Do any more than just for conscience' sake
Be miserable? Is this the way for us
To lead these creatures up to find the light,—
Or to be drawn down surely to the dark
Again? Which is it? What does the child say?

"But let us not make riot for the child
Untaught, nor let us hold that we may read
The sun but through the shadows; nor, again,
Be we forgetful ever that we keep
The shadows on their side. For evidence,
I might go back a little to the days
When I had hounds and credit, and grave friends
To borrow my books and set wet glasses on them,
And other friends of all sorts, grave and gay,
Of whom one woman and one man stand out
From all the rest, this morning. The man said
One day, as we were riding, 'Now, you see,
There goes a woman cursed with happiness:
Beauty and wealth, health, horses,—everything
That she could ask, or we could ask, is hers,
Except an inward eye for the dim fact
Of what this dark world is. The cleverness
God gave her—or the devil—cautions her
That she must keep the china cup of life
Filled somehow, and she fills it—runs it over—
Claps her white hands while some one does the sopping
With fingers made, she thinks, for just that purpose,
Giggles and eats and reads and goes to church,
Makes pretty little penitential prayers,
And has an eighteen-carat crucifix
Wrapped up in chamois-skin. She gives enough,
You say; but what is giving like hers worth?

What is a gift without the soul to guide it?
"Poor dears, and they have cancers?—Oh!" she says;
And away she works at that new altar-cloth
For the Reverend Hieronymus Mackintosh—
Third person, Jerry. "Jerry," she says, "can say
Such lovely things, and make life seem so sweet!"
Jerry can drink, also.—And there she goes,
Like a whirlwind through an orchard in the springtime—
Throwing herself away as if she thought
The world and the whole planetary circus
Were a flourish of apple-blossoms. Look at her!
And here is this infernal world of ours—
And hers, if only she might find it out—
Starving and shrieking, sickening, suppurating,
Whirling to God knows where . . . But look at her!'

"And after that it came about somehow,
Almost as if the Fates were killing time,
That she, the spendthrift of a thousand joys,
Rode in her turn with me, and in her turn
Made observations: 'Now there goes a man,'
She said, 'who feeds his very soul on poison:
No matter what he does, or where he looks,
He finds unhappiness; or, if he fails
To find it, he creates it, and then hugs it:
Pygmalion again for all the world—
Pygmalion gone wrong. You know I think
If when that precious animal was young,
His mother, or some watchful aunt of his,
Had spanked him with *Pendennis* and *Don Juan,*
And given him the *Lady of the Lake,*
Or *Cord and Creese,* or almost anything,
There might have been a tonic for him? Listen:
When he was possibly nineteen years old

CAPTAIN CRAIG

He came to me and said, "I understand
You are in love"—yes, that is what he said,—
"But never mind, it won't last very long;
It never does; we all get over it.
We have this clinging nature, for you see
The Great Bear shook himself once on a time
And the world is one of many that let go."
And yet the creature lives, and there you see him·
And he would have this life no fairer thing
Than a certain time for numerous marionettes
To do the Dance of Death. Give him a rose,
And he will tell you it is very sweet,
But only for a day. Most wonderful!
Show him a child, or anything that laughs,
And he begins at once to crunch his wormwood
And then runs on with his "realities."
What does he know about realities,
Who sees the truth of things almost as well
As Nero saw the Northern Lights? Good gracious!
Can't you do something with him? Call him something—
Call him a type, and that will make him cry:
One of those not at all unusual,
Prophetic, would-be-Delphic manger-snappers
That always get replaced when they are gone;
Or one of those impenetrable men,
Who seem to carry branded on their foreheads,
"We are abstruse, but not quite so abstruse
As possibly the good Lord may have wished;"
One of those men who never quite confess
That Washington was great;—the kind of man
That everybody knows and always will,—
Shrewd, critical, facetious, insincere,
And for the most part harmless, I'm afraid.
But even then, you might be doing well
To tell him something.'—And I said I would.

"So in one afternoon you see we have
The child in absence—or, to say the least,
In ominous defect,—and in excéss
Commensurate, likewise. Now the question is,
Not which was right and which was wrong, for each,
By virtue of one-sidedness, was both;
But rather—to my mind, as heretofore—
Is it better to be blinded by the lights,
Or by the shadows? By the lights, you say?
The shadows are all devils, and the lights
Gleam guiding and eternal? Very good;
But while you say so do not quite forget
That sunshine has a devil of its own,
And one that we, for the great craft of him,
But vaguely recognize. The marvel is
That this persuasive and especial devil,
By grace of his extreme transparency,
Precludes all common vision of him; yet
There is one way to glimpse him and a way,
As I believe, to test him,—granted once
That we have ousted prejudice, which means
That we have made magnanimous advance
Through self-acquaintance. Not an easy thing
For some of us; impossible, may be,
For most of us: the woman and the man
I cited, for example, would have wrought
The most intractable conglomerate
Of everything, if they had set themselves
To analyze themselves and not each other;
If only for the sake of self-respect,
They would have come to no place but the same
Wherefrom they started; one would have lived awhile
In paradise without defending it,
And one in hell without enjoying it;
And each had been dissuaded neither more

CAPTAIN CRAIG

Nor less thereafter. There are such on earth
As might have been composed primarily
For mortal warning: he was one of them,
And she—the devil makes us hesitate.
'T is easy to read words writ well with ink
That makes a good black mark on smooth white paper;
But words are done sometimes with other ink
Whereof the smooth white paper gives no sign
Till science brings it out; and here we come
To knowledge, and the way to test a devil.

"To most of us, you say, and you say well,
This demon of the sunlight is a stranger;
But if you break the sunlight of yourself,
Project it, and observe the quaint shades of it,
I have a shrewd suspicion you may find
That even as a name lives unrevealed
In ink that waits an agent, so it is
The devil—or this devil—hides himself
To all the diagnoses we have made
Save one. The quest of him is hard enough—
As hard as truth; but once we seem to know
That his compound obsequiousness prevails
Unferreted within us, we may find
That sympathy, which aureoles itself
To superfluity from you and me,
May stand against the soul for five or six
Persistent and indubitable streaks
Of irritating brilliance, out of which
A man may read, if he have knowledge in him,
Proportionate attest of ignorance,
Hypocrisy, good-heartedness, conceit,
Indifference,—by which a man may learn
That even courage may not make him glad
For laughter when that laughter is itself

The tribute of recriminating groans.
Nor are the shapes of obsolescent creeds
Much longer to flit near enough to make
Men glad for living in a world like this;
For wisdom, courage, knowledge, and the faith
Which has the soul and is the soul of reason—
These are the world's achievers. And the child—
The child that is the saviour of all ages,
The prophet and the poet, the crown-bearer,
Must yet with Love's unhonored fortitude,
Survive to cherish and attain for us
The candor and the generosity,
By leave of which we smile if we bring back
The first revealing flash that wakened us
When wisdom like a shaft of dungeon-light
Came searching down to find us.

                              "Halfway back
I made a mild allusion to the Fates,
Not knowing then that ever I should have
Dream-visions of them, painted on the air,—
Clotho, Lachesis, Atropos. Faint-hued
They seem, but with a faintness never fading,
Unblurred by gloom, unshattered by the sun,
Still with eternal color, colorless,
They move and they remain. The while I write
These very words I see them,—Atropos,
Lachesis, Clotho; and the last is laughing.
When Clotho laughs, Atropos rattles her shears;
But Clotho keeps on laughing just the same.
Some time when I have dreamed that Atropos
Has laughed, I'll tell you how the colors change—
The colors that are changeless, colorless."

CAPTAIN CRAIG

I fear I may have answered Captain Craig's
Epistle Number One with what he chose,
Good-humoredly but anxiously, to take
For something that was not all reverence;
From Number Two it would have seemed almost
As if the flanges of the old man's faith
Had slipped the treacherous rails of my allegiance,
Leaving him by the roadside, humorously
Upset, with nothing more convivial
To do than be facetious and austere:—

"If you decry *Don César de Bazan*,
There is an imperfection in your vitals.
Flamboyant and old-fashioned? Overdone?
Romantico-robustious?—Dear young man,
There are fifteen thousand ways to be one-sided,
And I have indicated two of them
Already. Now you bait me with a third—
As if it were a spider with nine legs;
But what it is that you would have me do,
What fatherly wrath you most anticipate,
I lack the needed impulse to discern;
Though I who shape no songs of any sort,
I who have made no music, thrilled no canvas,—
I who have added nothing to the world
The world would reckon save long-squandered wit—
Might with half-pardonable reverence
Beguile my faith, maybe, to the forlorn
Extent of some sequestered murmuring
Anent the vanities. No doubt I should,
If mine were the one life that I have lived;
But with a few good glimpses I have had
Of heaven through the little holes in hell,
I can half understand what price it is
The poet pays, at one time and another,

For those indemnifying interludes
That are to be the kernel in what lives
To shrine him when the new-born men come singing.

"So do I comprehend what I have read
From even the squeezed items of account
Which I have to my credit in that book
Whereof the leaves are ages and the text
Eternity. What do I care to-day
For pages that have nothing? I have lived,
And I have died, and I have lived again;
And I am very comfortable. Yes,
Though I look back through barren years enough
To make me seem—as I transmute myself
In downward retrospect from what I am—
As unproductive and as unconvinced
Of living bread and the soul's eternal draught
As a frog on a Passover-cake in a streamless desert,—
Still do I trust the light that I have earned,
And having earned, received. You shake your head,
But do not say that you will shake it off.

"Meanwhile I have the flowers and the grass,
My brothers here the trees, and all July
To make me joyous. Why do you shake your head?
Why do you laugh?—because you are so young?
Do you think if you laugh hard enough the truth
Will go to sleep? Do you think of any couch
Made soft enough to put the truth to sleep?
Do you think there are no proper comedies
But yours that have the fashion? For example,
Do you think that I forget, or shall forget,
One friendless, fat, fantastic nondescript
Who knew the ways of laughter on low roads,—
A vagabond, a drunkard, and a sponge,

CAPTAIN CRAIG

But always a free creature with a soul?
I bring him back, though not without misgivings,
And caution you to damn him sparingly.

"Count Pretzel von Würzburger, the Obscene
(The beggar may have had another name,
But no man to my knowledge ever knew it)
Was a poet and a skeptic and a critic,
And in his own mad manner a musician:
He found an old piano in a bar-room,
And it was his career—three nights a week,
From ten o'clock till twelve—to make it rattle;
And then, when I was just far down enough
To sit and watch him with his long straight hair,
And pity him, and think he looked like Liszt,
I might have glorified a musical
Steam-engine, or a xylophone. The Count
Played half of everything and 'improvised'
The rest: he told me once that he was born
With a genius in him that 'prohibited
Complete fidelity,' and that his art
'Confessed vagaries,' therefore. But I made
Kind reckoning of his vagaries then:
I had the whole great pathos of the man
To purify me, and all sorts of music
To give me spiritual nourishment
And cerebral athletics; for the Count
Played indiscriminately—with an *f,*
And with incurable presto—cradle-songs
And carnivals, spring-songs and funeral marches,
The Marseillaise and Schubert's Serenade—
And always in a way to make me think
Procrustes had the germ of music in him.
And when this interesting reprobate
Began to talk—then there were more vagaries:

He made a reeking fetich of all filth,
Apparently; but there was yet revealed
About him, through his words and on his flesh,
That ostracizing nimbus of a soul's
Abject, apologetic purity—
That phosphorescence of sincerity—
Which indicates the curse and the salvation
Of a life wherein starved art may never perish.

"One evening I remember clearliest
Of all that I passed with him. Having wrought,
With his nerve-ploughing ingenuity,
The *Träumerei* into a Titan's nightmare,
The man sat down across the table from me
And all at once was ominously decent.
' "The more we measure what is ours to use," '
He said then, wiping his froth-plastered mouth
With the inside of his hand, ' "the less we groan
For what the gods refuse." I've had that sleeved
A decade for you. Now but one more stein,
And I shall be prevailed upon to read
The only sonnet I have ever made;
And after that, if you propitiate
Gambrinus, I shall play you that Andante
As the world has never heard it played before.'
So saying, he produced a piece of paper,
Unfolded it, and read, 'SONNET UNIQUE
DE PRETZEL VON WURZBURGER, DIT L'OBSCÉNE:—

" 'Carmichael had a kind of joke-disease,
And he had queer things fastened on his wall.
There are three green china frogs that I recall
More potently than anything, for these
Three frogs have demonstrated, by degrees,
What curse was on the man to make him fall:

CAPTAIN CRAIG

*"They are not ordinary frogs at all,
They are the Frogs of Aristophanes."*

" 'God! how he laughed whenever he said that;
And how we caught from one another's eyes
The flash of what a tongue could never tell!
We always laughed at him, no matter what
The joke was worth. But when a man's brain dies,
We are not always glad . . . Poor Carmichael!'

" 'I am a sowbug and a necrophile,'
Said Pretzel, 'and the gods are growing old;
The stars are singing *Golden hair to gray,
Green leaf to yellow leaf,*—or chlorophyl
To xanthophyl, to be more scientific,—
So speed me one more stein. You may believe
That I'm a mendicant, but I am not:
For though it look to you that I go begging,
The truth is I go giving—giving all
My strength and all my personality,
My wisdom and experience—all myself,
To make it final—for your preservation;
Though I be not the one thing or the other,
Though I strike between the sunset and the dawn,
Though I be cliff-rubbed wreckage on the shoals
Of Circumstance,—doubt not that I comprise,
Far more than my appearance. Here he comes;
Now drink to good old Pretzel! Drink down Pretzel!
Quousque tandem, Pretzel, and O Lord,
How long! But let regret go hang: the good
Die first, and of the poor did many cease
To be. Beethoven after Wordsworth. *Prosit!*
There were geniuses among the trilobites,
And I suspect that I was one of them.'

"How much of him was earnest and how much
Fantastic, I know not; nor do I need
Profounder knowledge to exonerate
The squalor or the folly of a man
Than consciousness—though even the crude laugh
Of indigent Priapus follow it—
That I get good of him. And if you like him,
Then some time in the future, past a doubt,
You'll have him in a book, make metres of him,—
To the great delight of Mr. Killigrew,
And the grief of all your kinsmen. Christian shame
And self-confuted Orientalism
For the more sagacious of them; vulture-tracks
Of my Promethean bile for the rest of them;
And that will be a joke. There's nothing quite
So funny as a joke that's lost on earth
And laughed at by the gods. Your devil knows it.

"I come to like your Mr. Killigrew,
And I rejoice that you speak well of him.
The sprouts of human blossoming are in him,
And useful eyes—if he will open them;
But one thing ails the man. He smiles too much.
He comes to see me once or twice a week,
And I must tell him that he smiles too much.
If I were Socrates, it would be simple."

Epistle Number Three was longer coming.
I waited for it, even worried for it—
Though Killigrew, and of his own free will,
Had written reassuring little scraps
From time to time, and I had valued them
The more for being his. "The Sage," he said,

CAPTAIN CRAIG

"From all that I can see, is doing well—
I should say very well. Three meals a day,
Siestas, and innumerable pipes—
Not to the tune of water on the stones,
But rather to the tune of his own Ego,
Which seems to be about the same as God.
But I was always weak in metaphysics,
And pray therefore that you be lenient.
I'm going to be married in December,
And I have made a poem that will scan—
So Plunket says. You said the other wouldn't:

> *"Augustus Plunket, Ph.D.,*
>   *And oh, the Bishop's daughter;*
> *A very learned man was he*
>   *And in twelve weeks he got her;*
>
> *And oh, she was as fair to see*
> *As pippins on the pippin tree . . .*
> *Tu, tui, tibi, te,—chubs in the mill water.*

"Connotative, succinct, and erudite;
Three dots to boot. Now goodman Killigrew
May wind an epic one of these glad years,
And after that who knoweth but the Lord—
The Lord of Hosts who is the King of Glory?"

Still, when the Captain's own words were before me,
I seemed to read from them, or into them,
The protest of a mortuary joy
Not all substantiating Killigrew's
Off-hand assurance. The man's face came back
The while I read them, and that look again,
Which I had seen so often, came back with it.

COLLECTED POEMS

I do not know that I can say just why,
But I felt the feathery touch of something wrong:—

"Since last I wrote—and I fear weeks have gone
Too far for me to leave my gratitude
Unuttered for its own acknowledgment—
I have won, without the magic of Amphion
Without the songs of Orpheus or Apollo,
The frank regard—and with it, if you like,
The fledged respect—of three quick-footed friends.
('Nothing is there more marvelous than man,'
Said Sophocles; and I say after him:
'He traps and captures, all-inventive one,
The light birds and the creatures of the wold,
And in his nets the fishes of the sea.')
Once they were pictures, painted on the air,
Faint with eternal color, colorless,—
But now they are not pictures, they are fowls.

"At first they stood aloof and cocked their small,
Smooth, prudent heads at me and made as if,
With a cryptic idiotic melancholy,
To look authoritative and sagacious;
But when I tossed a piece of apple to them,
They scattered back with a discord of short squawks
And then came forward with a craftiness
That made me think of Eden. Atropos
Came first, and having grabbed the morsel up,
Ran flapping far away and out of sight,
With Clotho and Lachesis hard after her;
But finally the three fared all alike,
And next day I persuaded them with corn.
In a week they came and had it from my fingers
And looked up at me while I pinched their bills
And made them sneeze. Count Pretzel's Carmichael

CAPTAIN CRAIG

Had said they were not ordinary birds
At all,—and they are not: they are the Fates,
Foredoomed of their own insufficiency
To be assimilated.—Do not think,
Because in my contented isolation
It suits me at this time to be jocose,
That I am nailing reason to the cross,
Or that I set the bauble and the bells
Above the crucible; for I do nought,
Say nought, but with an ancient levity
That is the forbear of all earnestness.

"The cross, I said.—I had a dream last night:
A dream not like to any other dream
That I remember. I was all alone,
Sitting as I do now beneath a tree,
But looking not, as I am looking now,
Against the sunlight. There was neither sun
Nor moon, nor do I think of any stars;
Yet there was light, and there were cedar trees,
And there were sycamores. I lay at rest,
Or should have seemed at rest, within a trough
Between two giant roots. A weariness
Was on me, and I would have gone to sleep,
But I had not the courage. If I slept,
I feared that I should never wake again;
And if I did not sleep I should go mad,
And with my own dull tools, which I had used
With wretched skill so long, hack out my life.
And while I lay there, tortured out of death,
Faint waves of cold, as if the dead were breathing,
Came over me and through me; and I felt
Quick fearful tears of anguish on my face
And in my throat. But soon, and in the distance,
Concealed, importunate, there was a sound

Of coming steps,—and I was not afraid;
No, I was not afraid then, I was glad;
For I could feel, with every thought, the Man,
The Mystery, the Child, a footfall nearer.
Then, when he stood before me, there was no
Surprise, there was no questioning: I knew him,
As I had known him always; and he smiled.
'Why are you here?' he asked; and reaching down,
He took up my dull blades and rubbed his thumb
Across the edges of them and then smiled
Once more.—'I was a carpenter,' I said,
'But there was nothing in the world to do.'—
'Nothing?' said he.—'No, nothing,' I replied.—
'But are you sure,' he asked, 'that you have skill?
And are you sure that you have learned your trade?
No, you are not.'—He looked at me and laughed
As he said that; but I did not laugh then,
Although I might have laughed.—'They are dull,' said he;
'They were not very sharp if they were ground;
But they are what you have, and they will earn
What you have not. So take them as they are,
Grind them and clean them, put new handles to them,
And then go learn your trade in Nazareth.
Only be sure that you find Nazareth.'—
'But if I starve—what then?' said I.—He smiled.

"Now I call that as curious a dream
As ever Meleager's mother had,—
Æneas, Alcibiades, or Jacob.
I'll not except the scientist who dreamed
That he was Adam and that he was Eve
At the same time; or yet that other man
Who dreamed that he was Æschylus, reborn
To clutch, combine, compensate, and adjust
The plunging and unfathomable chorus

CAPTAIN CRAIG

Wherein we catch, like a bacchanale through thunder,
The chanting of the new Eumenides,
Implacable, renascent, farcical,
Triumphant, and American. He did it,
But did it in a dream. When he awoke
One phrase of it remained; one verse of it
Went singing through the remnant of his life
Like a bag-pipe through a mad-house.—He died young,
And if I ponder the small history
That I have gleaned of him by scattered roads,
The more do I rejoice that he died young.
That measure would have chased him all his days,
Defeated him, deposed him, wasted him,
And shrewdly ruined him—though in that ruin
There would have lived, as always it has lived,
In ruin as in failure, the supreme
Fulfilment unexpressed, the rhythm of God
That beats unheard through songs of shattered men
Who dream but cannot sound it.—He declined,
From all that I have ever learned of him,
With absolute good-humor. No complaint,
No groaning at the burden which is light,
No brain-waste of impatience—'Never mind,'
He whispered, 'for I might have written Odes.'

"Speaking of odes now makes me think of ballads.
Your admirable Mr. Killigrew
Has latterly committed what he calls
A Ballad of London—London 'Town,' of course—
And he has wished that I pass judgment on it.
He says there is a 'generosity'
About it, and a 'sympathetic insight;'
And there are strong lines in it, so he says.
But who am I that he should make of me
A judge? You are his friend, and you know best

The measure of his jingle. I am old,
And you are young. Be sure, I may go back
To squeak for you the tunes of yesterday
On my old fiddle—or what's left of it—
And give you as I'm able a young sound;
But all the while I do it I remain
One of Apollo's pensioners (and yours),
An usher in the Palace of the Sun,
A candidate for mattocks and trombones
(The brass-band will be indispensable),
A patron of high science, but no critic.
So I shall have to tell him, I suppose,
That I read nothing now but Wordsworth, Pope,
Lucretius, Robert Burns, and William Shakespeare.
Now this is Mr. Killigrew's performance:

"'Say, do you go to London Town,
    You with the golden feather?'—
'And if I go to London Town
    With my golden feather?'—
'These autumn roads are bright and brown,
   The season wears a russet crown;
   And if you go to London Town,
    We'll go down together.'

"I cannot say for certain, but I think
The brown bright nightingale was half assuaged
Before your Mr. Killigrew was born.
If I have erred in my chronology,
No matter,—for the feathered man sings now:

"'Yes, I go to London Town'
    (Merrily waved the feather),
'And if you go to London Town,
    Yes, we'll go together.'

CAPTAIN CRAIG

So in the autumn bright and brown,
Just as the year began to frown,
All the way to London Town
    Rode the two together.

"*'I go to marry a fair maid'*
    (Lightly swung the feather)—
'Pardie, a true and loyal maid'
    (Oh, the swinging feather!)—
'For us the wedding gold is weighed,
For us the feast will soon be laid;
We'll make a gallant show,' he said,—
    'She and I together.'

"The feathered man may do a thousand things,
And all go smiling; but the feathered man
May do too much. Now mark how he continues:

"*'And you—you go to London Town?'*
    (Breezes waved the feather)—
'Yes, I go to London Town.'
    (Ah, the stinging feather!)—
'Why do you go, my merry blade?
Like me, to marry a fair maid?'—
'Why do I go? . . . God knows,' he said;
    And on they rode together.

"Now you have read·it through, and you know best
What worth it has. We fellows with gray hair
Who march with sticks to music that is gray
Judge not your vanguard fifing. You are one
To judge; and you will tell me what you think.
Barring the Town, the Fair Maid, and the Feather,
The dialogue and those parentheses,

You cherish it, undoubtedly. 'Pardie!'
You call it; with a few conservative
Allowances, an excellent small thing
For patient inexperience to do:
Derivative, you say,—still rather pretty.
But what is wrong with Mr. Killigrew?
Is he in love, or has he read Rossetti?—
Forgive me! I am old and garrulous . . .
When are you coming back to Tilbury Town?"

III

I FOUND the old man sitting in his bed,
Propped up and uncomplaining. On a chair
Beside him was a dreary bowl of broth,
A magazine, some glasses, and a pipe.
"I do not light it nowadays," he said,
"But keep it for an antique influence
That it exerts, an aura that it sheds—
Like hautboys, or Provence. You understand:
The charred memorial defeats us yet,
But think you not for always. We are young,
And we are friends of time. Time that made smoke
Will drive away the smoke, and we shall know
The work that we are doing. We shall build
With embers of all shrines one pyramid,
And we shall have the most resplendent flame
From earth to heaven, as the old words go,
And we shall need no smoke . . . Why don't you laugh?"

I gazed into those calm, half-lighted eyes
And smiled at them with grim obedience.
He told me that I did it very well,
But added that I should undoubtedly
Do better in the future: "There is nothing,"

CAPTAIN CRAIG

He said, "so beneficial in a sick-room
As a well-bred spontaneity of manner.
Your sympathetic scowl obtrudes itself,
And is indeed surprising. After death,
Were you to take it with you to your coffin
An unimaginative man might think
That you had lost your life in worrying
To find out what it was that worried you.
The ways of unimaginative men
Are singularly fierce . . . Why do you stand?
Sit here and watch me while I take this soup.
The doctor likes it, therefore it is good.

"The man who wrote the decalogue," pursued
The Captain, having swallowed four or five
Heroic spoonfuls of his lukewarm broth,
"Forgot the doctors. And I think sometimes
The man of Galilee (or, if you choose,
The men who made the sayings of the man)
Like Buddha, and the others who have seen,
Was to men's loss the Poet—though it be
The Poet only of him we revere,
The Poet we remember. We have put
The prose of him so far away from us,
The fear of him so crudely over us,
That I have wondered—wondered."—Cautiously,
But yet as one were cautious in a dream,
He set the bowl down on the chair again,
Crossed his thin fingers, looked me in the face,
And looking smiled a little. "Go away,"
He said at last, "and let me go to sleep.
I told you I should eat, but I shall not.
To-morrow I shall eat; and I shall read
Some clauses of a jocund instrument
That I have been preparing here of late

For you and for the rest, assuredly.
'Attend the testament of Captain Craig:
Good citizens, good fathers and your sons,
Good mothers and your daughters.' I should say so.
Now go away and let me go to sleep."

I stood before him and held out my hand,
He took it, pressed it; and I felt again
The sick soft closing on it. He would not
Let go, but lay there, looking up to me
With eyes that had a sheen of water on them
And a faint wet spark within them. So he clung,
Tenaciously, with fingers icy warm,
And eyes too full to keep the sheen unbroken.
I looked at him. The fingers closed hard once,
And then fell down.—I should have left him then.

But when we found him the next afternoon,
My first thought was that he had made his eyes
Miraculously smaller. They were sharp
And hard and dry, and the spark in them was dry.
For a glance it all but seemed as if the man
Had artfully forsworn the brimming gaze
Of yesterday, and with a wizard strength
Inveigled in, reduced, and vitalized
The straw-shine of October; and had that
Been truth, we should have humored him no less,
Albeit he had fooled us,—for he said
That we had made him glad by coming to him.
And he was glad: the manner of his words
Revealed the source of them; and the gray smile
Which lingered like a twilight on his face
Told of its own slow fading that it held
The promise of the sun. Cadaverous,
God knows it was; and we knew it was honest.

CAPTAIN CRAIG

"So you have come to hear the old man read
To you from his last will and testament:
Well, it will not be long—not very long—
So listen." He brought out from underneath
His pillow a new manuscript, and said,
"You have done well to come and hear me read
My testament. There are men in the world
Who say of me, if they remember me,
That I am poor;—and I believe the ways
Of certain men who never find things out
Are stranger than the way Lord Bacon wrote
Leviticus, and *Faust."* He fixed his eyes
Abstractedly on something far from us,
And with a look that I remembered well
Gazed hard the while we waited. But at length
He found himself and soon began to chant,
With a fitful shift at thin sonorousness
The jocund instrument; and had he been
Definitively parceling to us
All Kimberley and half of Ballarat,
The lordly quaver of his poor old words
Could not have been the more magniloquent.
No promise of dead carbon or of gold,
However, flashed in ambush to corrupt us:

"I, Captain Craig, abhorred iconoclast,
Sage-errant, favored of the Mysteries,
And self-reputed humorist at large,
Do now, confessed of my world-worshiping,
Time-questioning, sun-fearing, and heart-yielding,
Approve and unreservedly devise
To you and your assigns for evermore,
God's universe and yours. If I had won
What first I sought, I might have made you beam
By giving less; but now I make you laugh

By giving more than what had made you beam,
And it is well. No man has ever done
The deed of humor that God promises,
But now and then we know tragedians
Reform, and in denial too divine
For sacrifice, too firm for ecstasy,
Record in letters, or in books they write,
What fragment of God's humor they have caught,
What earnest of its rhythm; and I believe
That I, in having somewhat recognized
The formal measure of it, have endured
The discord of infirmity no less
Through fortune than by failure. What men lose,
Man gains; and what man gains reports itself
In losses we but vaguely deprecate,
So they be not for us;—and this is right,
Except that when the devil in the sun
Misguides us we go darkly where the shine
Misleads us, and we know not what we see:
We know not if we climb or if we fall;
And if we fly, we know not where we fly.

"And here do I insert an urging clause
For climbers and up-fliers of all sorts,
Cliff-climbers and high-fliers: Phaethon,
Bellerophon, and Icarus did each
Go gloriously up, and each in turn
Did famously come down—as you have read
In poems and elsewhere; but other men
Have mounted where no fame has followed them,
And we have had no sight, no news of them,
And we have heard no crash. The crash may count,
Undoubtedly, and earth be fairer for it;
Yet none save creatures out of harmony
Have ever, in their fealty to the flesh,

CAPTAIN CRAIG

Made crashing an ideal. It is the flesh
That ails us, for the spirit knows no qualm,
No failure, no down-falling: so climb high,
And having set your steps regard not much
The downward laughter clinging at your feet,
Nor overmuch the warning; only know,
As well as you know dawn from lantern-light,
That far above you, for you, and within you,
There burns and shines and lives, unwavering
And always yours, the truth. Take on yourself
But your sincerity, and you take on
Good promise for all climbing: fly for truth,
And hell shall have no storm to crush your flight,
No laughter to vex down your loyalty.

"I think you may be smiling at me now—
And if I make you smile, so much the better;
For I would have you know that I rejoice
Always to see the thing that I would see—
The righteous thing, the wise thing. I rejoice
Always to think that any thought of mine,
Or any word or any deed of mine,
May grant sufficient of what fortifies
Good feeling and the courage of calm joy
To make the joke worth while. Contrariwise,
When I review some faces I have known—
Sad faces, hungry faces—and reflect
On thoughts I might have moulded, human words
I might have said, straightway it saddens me
To feel perforce that had I not been mute
And actionless, I might have made them bright
Somehow, though only for the moment. Yes,
Howbeit I may confess the vanities,
It saddens me; and sadness, of all things
Miscounted wisdom, and the most of all

When warmed with old illusions and regrets,
I mark the selfishest, and on like lines
The shrewdest. For your sadness makes you climb
With dragging footsteps, and it makes you groan;
It hinders you when most you would be free,
And there are many days it wearies you
Beyond the toil itself. And if the load
It lays on you may not be shaken off
Till you have known what now you do not know—
Meanwhile you climb; and he climbs best who sees
Above him truth burn faithfulest, and feels
Within him truth burn purest. Climb or fall,
One road remains and one firm guidance always;
One way that shall be taken, climb or fall.

"But 'falling, falling, falling.' There's your song,
The cradle-song that sings you to the grave.
What is it your bewildered poet says?—

" *'The toiling ocean thunders of unrest*
And aching desolation; the still sea
Paints but an outward calm that mocks itself
To the final and irrefragable sleep
That owns no shifting fury; and the shoals
Of ages are but records of regret
Where Time, the sun's arch-phantom, writes on sand
The prelude of his ancient nothingness.'

" 'T is easy to compound a dirge like that,
And it is easy to be deceived
And alienated by the fleshless note
Of half-world yearning in it; but the truth
To which we all are tending,—charlatans
And architects alike, artificers
In tinsel as in gold, evangelists

CAPTAIN CRAIG

Of ruin and redemption, all alike,—
The truth we seek and equally the truth
We do not seek, but yet may not escape,
Was never found alone through flesh contempt
Or through flesh reverence. Look east and west
And we may read the story: where the light
Shone first the shade now darkens; where the shade
Clung first, the light fights westward—though the shade
Still feeds, and there is yet the Orient.

"But there is this to be remembered always:
Whatever be the altitude you reach,
You do not rise alone; nor do you fall
But you drag others down to more or less
Than your preferred abasement. God forbid
That ever I should preach, and in my zeal
Forget that I was born an humorist;
But now, for once, before I go away,
I beg of you to be magnanimous
A moment, while I speak to please myself:

"Though I have heard it variously sung
That even in the fury and the clash
Of battles, and the closer fights of men
When silence gives the knowing world no sign,
One flower there is, though crushed and cursed it be,
Keeps rooted through all tumult and all scorn,—
Still do I find, when I look sharply down,
There's yet another flower that grows well
And has the most unconscionable roots
Of any weed on earth. Perennial
It grows, and has the name of Selfishness;
No doubt you call it Love. In either case,
You propagate it with a diligence
That hardly were outmeasured had its leaf

The very juice in it of that famed herb
Which gave back breath to Glaucus; and I know
That in the twilight, after the day's work,
You take your little children in your arms,
Or lead them by their credulous frail hands
Benignly out and through the garden-gate
And show them there the things that you have raised;
Not everything, perchance, but always one
Miraculously rooted flower plot
Which is your pride, their pattern. Socrates,
Could he be with you there at such a time,
Would have some unsolicited shrewd words
To say that you might hearken to; but I
Say nothing, for I am not Socrates.—
So much, good friends, for flowers; and I thank you.

"There was a poet once who would have roared
Away the world and had an end of stars.
Where was he when I quoted him?—oh, yes:
'T is easy for a man to link loud words
With woeful pomp and unschooled emphasis
And add one thundered contribution more
To the dirges of all-hollowness, I said;
But here again I find the question set
Before me, after turning books on books
And looking soulward through man after man,
If there indeed be more determining
Play-service in remotely sounding down
The world's one-sidedness. If I judge right,
Your pounding protestations, echoing
Their burden of unfraught futility,
Surge back to mute forgetfulness at last
And have a kind of sunny, sullen end,
Like any cold north storm.—But there are few
Still seas that have no life to profit them,

CAPTAIN CRAIG

And even in such currents of the mind
As have no tide-rush in them, but are drowsed,
Crude thoughts may dart in armor and upspring
With waking sound, when all is dim with peace,
Like sturgeons in the twilight out of Lethe;
And though they be discordant, hard, grotesque,
And all unwelcome to the lethargy
That you think means repose, you know as well
As if your names were shouted when they leap,
And when they leap you listen.—Ah! friends, friends,
There are these things we do not like to know:
They trouble us, they make us hesitate,
They touch us, and we try to put them off.
We banish one another and then say
That we are left alone: the midnight leaf
That rattles where it hangs above the snow—
Gaunt, fluttering, forlorn—scarcely may seem
So cold in all its palsied loneliness
As we, we frozen brothers, who have yet
Profoundly and severely to find out
That there is more of unpermitted love
In most men's reticence than most men think.

"Once, when I made it out fond-headedness
To say that we should ever be apprised
Of our deserts and their emolument
At all but in the specious way of words,
The wisdom of a warm thought woke within me
And I could read the sun. Then did I turn
My long-defeated face full to the world,
And through the clouded warfare of it all
Discern the light. Through dusk that hindered it,
I found the truth, and for the first whole time
Knew then that we were climbing. Not as one
Who mounts along with his experience

Bound on him like an Old Man of the Sea—
Not as a moral pedant who drags chains
Of his unearned ideals after him
And always to the lead-like thud they make
Attunes a cold inhospitable chant
Of All Things Easy to the Non-Attached,—
But as a man, a scarred man among men,
I knew it, and I felt the strings of thought
Between us to pull tight the while I strove;
And if a curse came ringing now and then
To my defended ears, how could I know
The light that burned above me and within me,
And at the same time put on cap-and-bells
For such as yet were groping?"

                              Killigrew
Made there as if to stifle a small cough.
I might have kicked him, but regret forbade
The subtle admonition; and indeed
When afterwards I reprimanded him,
The fellow never knew quite what I meant.
I may have been unjust.—The Captain read
Right on, without a chuckle or a pause,
As if he had heard nothing:

                        "How, forsooth,
Shall any man, by curses or by groans,
Or by the laugh-jarred stillness of all hell,
Be so drawn down to servitude again
That on some backward level of lost laws
And undivined relations, he may know
No longer Love's imperative resource,
Firm once and his, well treasured then, but now
Too fondly thrown away? And if there come
But once on all his journey, singing down

CAPTAIN CRAIG

To find him, the gold-throated forward call,
What way but one, what but the forward way,
Shall after that call guide him? When his ears
Have earned an inward skill to methodize
The clash of all crossed voices and all noises,
How shall he grope to be confused again,
As he has been, by discord? When his eyes
Have read the book of wisdom in the sun,
And after dark deciphered it on earth,
How shall he turn them back to scan some huge
Blood-lettered protest of bewildered men
That hunger while he feeds where they would starve
And all absurdly perish?"

       Killigrew
Looked hard for a subtile object on the wall,
And, having found it, sighed. The Captain paused:
If he grew tedious, most assuredly
Did he crave pardon of us; he had feared
Beforehand that he might be wearisome,
But there was not much more of it, he said,—
No more than just enough. And we rejoiced
That he should look so kindly on us then.
("Commend me to a dying man's grimace
For absolute humor, always," Killigrew
Maintains; but I know better.)

       "Work for them,
You tell me? Work the folly out of them?
Go back to them and teach them how to climb,
While you teach caterpillars how to fly?
You tell me that Alnaschar is a fool
Because he dreams? And what is this you ask?
I make him wise? I teach him to be still?
While you go polishing the Pyramids,

I hold Alnaschar's feet? And while you have
The ghost of Memnon's image all day singing,
I sit with aching arms and hardly catch
A few spilled echoes of the song of songs—
The song that I should have as utterly
For mine as other men should once have had
The sweetest a glad shepherd ever trilled
In Sharon, long ago? Is this the way
For me to do good climbing any more
Than Phaethon's? Do you think the golden tone
Of that far-singing call you all have heard
Means any more for you than you should be
Wise-heartedly, glad-heartedly yourselves?
Do this, there is no more for you to do;
And you have no dread left, no shame, no scorn.
And while you have your wisdom and your gold,
Songs calling, and the Princess in your arms,
Remember, if you like, from time to time,
Down yonder where the clouded millions go,
Your bloody-knuckled scullions are not slaves,
Your children of Alnaschar are not fools.

"Nor are they quite so foreign or far down
As you may think to see them. What you take
To be the cursedest mean thing that crawls
On earth is nearer to you than you know:
You may not ever crush him but you lose,
You may not ever shield him but you gain—
As he, with all his crookedness, gains with you.
Your preaching and your teaching, your achieving,
Your lifting up and your discovering,
Are more than often—more than you have dreamed—
The world-refracted evidence of what
Your dream denies. You cannot hide yourselves
In any multitude or solitude,

CAPTAIN CRAIG

Or mask yourselves in any studied guise
Of hardness or of old humility,
But soon by some discriminating man—
Some humorist at large, like Socrates—
You get yourselves found out.—Now I should be
Found out without an effort. For example:
When I go riding, trimmed and shaved again,
Consistent, adequate, respectable,—
Some citizen, for curiosity,
Will ask of a good neighbor, 'What is this?'—
'It is the funeral of Captain Craig,'
Will be the neighbor's word.—'And who, good man,
Was Captain Craig?'—'He was an humorist;
And we are told that there is nothing more
For any man alive to say of him.'—
'There is nothing very strange in that,' says A;
'But the brass band? What has he done to be
Blown through like this by cornets and trombones?
And here you have this incompatible dirge—
Where are the jokes in that?'—Then B should say:
'Maintained his humor: nothing more or less.
The story goes that on the day before
He died—some say a week, but that's a trifle—
He said, with a subdued facetiousness,
"Play Handel, not Chopin; assuredly not
Chopin." '—He was indeed an humorist."

He made the paper fall down at arm's length;
And with a tension of half-quizzical
Benignity that made it hard for us,
He looked up—first at Morgan, then at me—
Almost, I thought, as if his eyes would ask
If we were satisfied; and as he looked,
The tremor of an old heart's weariness
Was on his mouth. He gazed at each of us,

But spoke no further word that afternoon.
He put away the paper, closed his eyes,
And went to sleep with his lips flickering;
And after that we left him.—At midnight
Plunket and I looked in; but he still slept,
And everything was going as it should.
The watchman yawned, rattled his newspaper,
And wondered what it was that ailed his lamp.

Next day we found the Captain wide awake,
Propped up, and searching dimly with a spoon
Through another dreary dish of chicken-broth,
Which he raised up to me, at my approach,
So fervently and so unconsciously,
That one could only laugh. He looked again
At each of us, and as he looked he frowned;
And there was something in that frown of his
That none of us had ever seen before.
"Kind friends," he said, "be sure that I rejoice
To know that you have come to visit me;
Be sure I speak with undisguised words
And earnest, when I say that I rejoice."—
"But what the devil!" whispered Killigrew.
I kicked him, for I thought I understood.
The old man's eyes had glimmered wearily
At first, but now they glittered like to those
Of a glad fish. "Beyond a doubt," said he,
"My dream this morning was more singular
Than any other I have ever known.
Give me that I might live ten thousand years,
And all those years do nothing but have dreams,
I doubt me much if any one of them
Could be so quaint or so fantastical,
So pregnant, as a dream of mine this morning.
You may not think it any more than odd;

CAPTAIN CRAIG

You may not feel—you cannot wholly feel—
How droll it was:—I dreamed that I found Hamlet—
Found him at work, drenched with an angry sweat,
Predestined, he declared with emphasis,
To root out a large weed on Lethe wharf;
And after I had watched him for some time,
I laughed at him and told him that no root
Would ever come the while he talked like that:
The power was not in him, I explained,
For such compound accomplishment. He glared
At me, of course,—next moment laughed at me,
And finally laughed with me. I was right,
And we had eisel on the strength of it:—
'They tell me that this water is not good,'
Said Hamlet, and you should have seen him smile.
Conceited? Pelion and Ossa?—pah . . .

"But anon comes in a crocodile. We stepped
Adroitly down upon the back of him,
And away we went to an undiscovered country—
A fertile place, but in more ways than one
So like the region we had started from,
That Hamlet straightway found another weed
And there began to tug. I laughed again,
Till he cried out on me and on my mirth,
Protesting all he knew: 'The Fates,' he said,
'Have ordered it that I shall have these roots.'
But all at once a dreadful hunger seized him,
And it was then we killed the crocodile—
Killed him and ate him. Washed with eisel down
That luckless reptile was, to the last morsel;
And there we were with flag-fens all around us,—
And there was Hamlet, at his task again,
Ridiculous. And while I watched his work,
The drollest of all changes came to pass.

The weed had snapped off just above the root,
Not warning him, and I was left alone.
The bubbles rose, and I laughed heartily
To think of him; I laughed when I woke up;
And when my soup came in I laughed again;
I think I may have laughed a little—no?—
Not when you came? . . . Why do you look like that?
You don't believe me? Crocodiles—why not?
Who knows what he has eaten in his life?
Who knows but I have eaten Atropos? . . .
'Briar and oak for a soldier's crown,' you say?
Provence? Oh, no . . . Had I been Socrates,
Count Pretzel would have been the King of Spain."

Now of all casual things we might have said
To make the matter smooth at such a time,
There may have been a few that we had found
Sufficient. Recollection fails, however,
To say that we said anything. We looked.
Had he been Carmichael, we might have stood
Like faithful hypocrites and laughed at him;
But the Captain was not Carmichael at all,
For the Captain had no frogs: he had the sun.
So there we waited, hungry for the word,—
Tormented, unsophisticated, stretched—
Till, with a drawl, to save us, Killigrew
Good-humoredly spoke out. The Captain fixed
His eyes on him with some severity.

"That was a funny dream, beyond a doubt,"
Said Killigrew;—"too funny to be laughed at;
Too humorous, we mean."—"Too humorous?"
The Captain answered; "I approve of that.
Proceed."—We were not glad for Killigrew.
"Well," he went on, "'t was only this. You see

CAPTAIN CRAIG

My dream this morning was a droll one too:
I dreamed that a sad man was in my room,
Sitting, as I do now, beside the bed.
I questioned him, but he made no reply,—
Said not a word, but sang."—"Said not a word,
But sang," the Captain echoed. "Very good.
Now tell me what it was the sad man sang."
"Now that," said Killigrew, constrainedly,
And with a laugh that might have been left out,
"Is why I know it must have been a dream.
But there he was, and I lay in the bed
Like you; and I could see him just as well
As you see my right hand. And for the songs
He sang to me—there's where the dream part comes."

"You don't remember them?" the Captain said,
With a weary little chuckle; "very well,
I might have guessed it. Never mind your dream,
But let me go to sleep."—For a moment then
There was a frown on Killigrew's good face,
And then there was a smile. "Not quite," said he;
"The songs that he sang first were sorrowful,
And they were stranger than the man himself—
And he was very strange; but I found out,
Through all the gloom of him and of his music,
That a—say, well, say mystic cheerfulness,
Pervaded him; for slowly, as he sang,
There came a change, and I began to know
The method of it all. Song after song
Was ended; and when I had listened there
For hours—I mean for dream-hours—hearing him,
And always glad that I was hearing him,
There came another change—a great one. Tears
Rolled out at last like bullets from his eyes,
And I could hear them fall down on the floor

Like shoes; and they were always marking time
For the song that he was singing. I have lost
The greater number of his verses now,
But there are some, like these, that I remember:

> *"'Ten men from Zanzibar,*
> *Black as iron hammers are,*
> *Riding on a cable-car*
> *Down to Crowley's theatre.'* . . .

"Ten men?" the Captain interrupted there—
"Ten men, my Euthyphron? That is beautiful.
But never mind, I wish to go to sleep:
Tell Cebes that I wish to go to sleep. . . .
O ye of little faith, your golden plumes
Are like to drag . . . par-dee!"—We may have smiled
In after days to think how Killigrew
Had sacrificed himself to fight that silence,
But we were grateful to him, none the less;
And if we smiled, that may have been the reason.
But the good Captain for a long time then
Said nothing: he lay quiet—fast asleep,
For all that we could see. We waited there
Till each of us, I fancy, must have made
The paper on the wall begin to squirm,
And then got up to leave. My friends went out,
And I was going, when the old man cried:
"You leave me now—now it has come to this?
What have I done to make you go? Come back!
Come back!"

There was a quaver in his cry
That we shall not forget—reproachful, kind,
Indignant, piteous. It seemed as one
Marooned on treacherous tide-feeding sand

CAPTAIN CRAIG

Were darkly calling over the still straits
Between him and irrevocable shores
Where now there was no lamp to fade for him,
No call to give him answer. We were there
Before him, but his eyes were not much turned
On us; nor was it very much to us
That he began to speak the broken words,
The scattered words, that he had left in him.

"So it has come to this? And what is this?
Death, do you call it? Death? And what is death?
Why do you look like that at me again?
Why do you shrink your brows and shut your lips?
If it be fear, then I can do no more
Than hope for all of you that you may find
Your promise of the sun; if it be grief
You feel, to think that this old face of mine
May never look at you and laugh again,
Then tell me why it is that you have gone
So long with me, and followed me so far,
And had me to believe you took my words
For more than ever misers did their gold?"

He listened, but his eyes were far from us—
Too far to make us turn to Killigrew,
Or search the futile shelves of our own thoughts
For golden-labeled insincerities
To make placebos of. The marrowy sense
Of slow November rain that splashed against
The shingles and the glass reminded us
That we had brought umbrellas. He continued:
"Oh, can it be that I, too credulous,
Have made myself believe that you believe
Yourselves to be the men that you are not?
I prove and I prize well your friendliness,

165

But I would have that your last look at me
Be not like this; for I would scan to-day
Strong thoughts on all your faces—no regret,
No still commiseration—oh, not that!—
No doubt, no fear. A man may be as brave
As Ajax in the fury of his arms,
And in the midmost warfare of his thoughts
Be frail as Paris . . . For the love, therefore,
That brothered us when we stood back that day
From Delium—the love that holds us now
More than it held us at Amphipolis—
Forget you not that he who in his work
Would mount from these low roads of measured shame
To tread the leagueless highway must fling first
And fling forevermore beyond his reach
The shackles of a slave who doubts the sun.
There is no servitude so fraudulent
As of a sun-shut mind; for 't is the mind
That makes you craven or invincible,
Diseased or puissant. The mind will pay
Ten thousand fold and be the richer then
To grant new service; but the world pays hard,
And accurately sickens till in years
The dole has eked its end and there is left
What all of you are noting on all days
In these Athenian streets, where squandered men
Drag ruins of half-warriors to the grave—
Or to Hippocrates."

      His head fell back,
And he lay still with wearied eyes half-closed.
We waited, but a few faint words yet stayed:
"Kind friends," he said, "friends I have known so long,
Though I have jested with you in time past,
Though I have stung your pride with epithets

CAPTAIN CRAIG

Not all forbearing,—still, when I am gone,
Say Socrates wrought always for the best
And for the wisest end . . . Give me the cup!
The truth is yours, God's universe is yours . . .
Good-by . . . good citizens . . . give me the cup" . . .
Again we waited; and this time we knew
Those lips of his that would not flicker down
Had yet some fettered message for us there.
We waited, and we watched him. All at once,
With a faint flash, the clouded eyes grew clear,
And then we knew the man was coming back.
We watched him, and I listened. The man smiled
And looked about him—not regretfully,
Not anxiously; and when at last he spoke,
Before the long drowse came to give him peace,
One word was all he said. "Trombones," he said.

That evening, at "The Chrysalis" again,
We smoked and looked at one another's eyes,
And we were glad. The world had scattered ways
For us to take, we knew; but for the time
That one snug room where big beech logs roared smooth
Defiance to the cold rough rain outside
Sufficed. There were no scattered ways for us
That we could see just then, and we were glad:
We were glad to be on earth, and we rejoiced
No less for Captain Craig that he was gone.
We might, for his dead benefit, have run
The gamut of all human weaknesses
And uttered after-platitudes enough—
Wrecked on his own abstractions, and all such—
To drive away Gambrinus and the bead
From Bernard's ale; and I suppose we might
Have praised, accordingly, the Lord of Hosts

For letting us believe that we were not
The least and idlest of His handiwork.

So Plunket, who had knowledge of all sorts,
Yet hardly ever spoke, began to plink
O tu, Palermo!—quaintly, with his nails,—
On Morgan's fiddle, and at once got seized,
As if he were some small thing, by the neck.
Then the consummate Morgan, having told
Explicitly what hardship might accrue
To Plunket if he did that any more,
Made roaring chords and acrobatic runs—
And then, with his kind eyes on Killigrew,
Struck up the schoolgirls' march in *Lohengrin,*
So Killigrew might smile and stretch himself
And have to light his pipe. When that was done
We knew that Morgan, by the looks of him,
Was in the mood for almost anything
From Bach to Offenbach; and of all times
That he has ever played, that one somehow—
That evening of the day the Captain died—
Stands out like one great verse of a good song,
One strain that sings itself beyond the rest
For magic and a glamour that it has.

The ways have scattered for us, and all things
Have changed; and we have wisdom, I doubt not,
More fit for the world's work than we had then;
But neither parted roads nor cent per cent
May starve quite out the child that lives in us—
The Child that is the Man, the Mystery,
The Phœnix of the World. So, now and then,
That evening of the day the Captain died
Returns to us; and there comes always with it
The storm, the warm restraint, the fellowship,

ISAAC AND ARCHIBALD

The friendship and the firelight, and the fiddle.
So too there comes a day that followed it—
A windy, dreary day with a cold white shine,
Which only gummed the tumbled frozen ruts
That made us ache. The road was hard and long,
But we had what we knew to comfort us,
And we had the large humor of the thing
To make it advantageous; for men stopped
And eyed us on that road from time to time,
And on that road the children followed us;
And all along that road the Tilbury Band
Blared indiscreetly the Dead March in Saul.

ISAAC AND ARCHIBALD

(To Mrs. Henry Richards)

Isaac and Archibald were two old men.
I knew them, and I may have laughed at them
A little; but I must have honored them
For they were old, and they were good to me.

I do not think of either of them now,
Without remembering, infallibly,
A journey that I made one afternoon
With Isaac to find out what Archibald
Was doing with his oats. It was high time
Those oats were cut, said Isaac; and he feared
That Archibald—well, he could never feel
Quite sure of Archibald. Accordingly
The good old man invited me—that is,
Permitted me—to go along with him;
And I, with a small boy's adhesiveness
To competent old age, got up and went.

I do not know that I cared overmuch
For Archibald's or anybody's oats,
But Archibald was quite another thing,
And Isaac yet another; and the world
Was wide, and there was gladness everywhere.
We walked together down the River Road
With all the warmth and wonder of the land
Around us, and the wayside flash of leaves,—
And Isaac said the day was glorious;
But somewhere at the end of the first mile
I found that I was figuring to find
How long those ancient legs of his would keep
The pace that he had set for them. The sun
Was hot, and I was ready to sweat blood;
But Isaac, for aught I could make of him,
Was cool to his hat-band. So I said then
With a dry gasp of affable despair,
Something about the scorching days we have
In August without knowing it sometimes;
But Isaac said the day was like a dream,
And praised the Lord, and talked about the breeze.
I made a fair confession of the breeze,
And crowded casually on his thought
The nearness of a profitable nook
That I could see. First I was half inclined
To caution him that he was growing old,
But something that was not compassion soon
Made plain the folly of all subterfuge.
Isaac was old, but not so old as that.

So I proposed, without an overture,
That we be seated in the shade a while,
And Isaac made no murmur. Soon the talk
Was turned on Archibald, and I began
To feel some premonitions of a kind

ISAAC AND ARCHIBALD

That only childhood knows; for the old man
Had looked at me and clutched me with his eye,
And asked if I had ever noticed things.
I told him that I could not think of them,
And I knew then, by the frown that left his face
Unsatisfied, that I had injured him.
"My good young friend," he said, "you cannot feel
What I have seen so long. You have the eyes—
Oh, yes—but you have not the other things:
The sight within that never will deceive,
You do not know—you have no right to know;
The twilight warning of experience,
The singular idea of loneliness,—
These are not yours. But they have long been mine,
And they have shown me now for seven years
That Archibald is changing. It is not
So much that he should come to his last hand,
And leave the game, and go the old way down;
But I have known him in and out so long,
And I have seen so much of good in him
That other men have shared and have not seen,
And I have gone so far through thick and thin,
Through cold and fire with him, that now it brings
To this old heart of mine an ache that you
Have not yet lived enough to know about.
But even unto you, and your boy's faith,
Your freedom, and your untried confidence,
A time will come to find out what it means
To know that you are losing what was yours,
To know that you are being left behind;
And then the long contempt of innocence—
God bless you, boy!—don't think the worse of it
Because an old man chatters in the shade—
Will all be like a story you have read
In childhood and remembered for the pictures.

And when the best friend of your life goes down,
When first you know in him the slackening
That comes, and coming always tells the end,—
Now in a common word that would have passed
Uncaught from any other lips than his,
Now in some trivial act of every day,
Done as he might have done it all along
But for a twinging little difference
That nips you like a squirrel's teeth—oh, yes,
Then you will understand it well enough.
But oftener it comes in other ways;
It comes without your knowing when it comes;
You know that he is changing, and you know
That he is going—just as I know now
That Archibald is going, and that I
Am staying. . . . Look at me, my boy,
And when the time shall come for you to see
That I must follow after him, try then
To think of me, to bring me back again,
Just as I was to-day. Think of the place
Where we are sitting now, and think of me—
Think of old Isaac as you knew him then,
When you set out with him in August once
To see old Archibald."—The words come back
Almost as Isaac must have uttered them,
And there comes with them a dry memory
Of something in my throat that would not move.

If you had asked me then to tell just why
I made so much of Isaac and the things
He said, I should have gone far for an answer;
For I knew it was not sorrow that I felt,
Whatever I may have wished it, or tried then
To make myself believe. My mouth was full
Of words, and they would have been comforting

ISAAC AND ARCHIBALD

To Isaac, spite of my twelve years, I think;
But there was not in me the willingness
To speak them out. Therefore I watched the ground;
And I was wondering what made the Lord
Create a thing so nervous as an ant,
When Isaac, with commendable unrest,
Ordained that we should take the road again—
For it was yet three miles to Archibald's,
And one to the first pump. I felt relieved
All over when the old man told me that;
I felt that he had stilled a fear of mine
That those extremities of heat and cold
Which he had long gone through with Archibald
Had made the man impervious to both;
But Isaac had a desert somewhere in him,
And at the pump he thanked God for all things
That He had put on earth for men to drink,
And he drank well,—so well that I proposed
That we go slowly lest I learn too soon
The bitterness of being left behind,
And all those other things. That was a joke
To Isaac, and it pleased him very much;
And that pleased me—for I was twelve years old.

At the end of an hour's walking after that
The cottage of old Archibald appeared.
Little and white and high on a smooth round hill
It stood, with hackmatacks and apple-trees
Before it, and a big barn-roof beyond;
And over the place—trees, house, fields and all—
Hovered an air of still simplicity
And a fragrance of old summers—the old style
That lives the while it passes. I dare say
That I was lightly conscious of all this
When Isaac, of a sudden, stopped himself,

And for the long first quarter of a minute
Gazed with incredulous eyes, forgetful quite
Of breezes and of me and of all else
Under the scorching sun but a smooth-cut field,
Faint yellow in the distance. I was young,
But there were a few things that I could see,
And this was one of them.—"Well, well!" said he;
And "Archibald will be surprised, I think,"
Said I. But all my childhood subtlety
Was lost on Isaac, for he strode along
Like something out of Homer—powerful
And awful on the wayside, so I thought.
Also I thought how good it was to be
So near the end of my short-legged endeavor
To keep the pace with Isaac for five miles.

Hardly had we turned in from the main road
When Archibald, with one hand on his back
And the other clutching his huge-headed cane,
Came limping down to meet us.—"Well! well! well!"
Said he; and then he looked at my red face,
All streaked with dust and sweat, and shook my hand,
And said it must have been a right smart walk
That we had had that day from Tilbury Town.—
"Magnificent," said Isaac; and he told
About the beautiful west wind there was
Which cooled and clarified the atmosphere.
"You must have made it with your legs, I guess,"
Said Archibald; and Isaac humored him
With one of those infrequent smiles of his
Which he kept in reserve, apparently,
For Archibald alone. "But why," said he,
"Should Providence have cider in the world
If not for such an afternoon as this?"
And Archibald, with a soft light in his eyes,

ISAAC AND ARCHIBALD

Replied that if he chose to go down cellar,
There he would find eight barrels—one of which
Was newly tapped, he said, and to his taste
An honor to the fruit. Isaac approved
Most heartily of that, and guided us
Forthwith, as if his venerable feet
Were measuring the turf in his own door-yard,
Straight to the open rollway. Down we went,
Out of the fiery sunshine to the gloom,
Grateful and half sepulchral, where we found
The barrels, like eight potent sentinels,
Close ranged along the wall. From one of them
A bright pine spile stuck out alluringly,
And on the black flat stone, just under it,
Glimmered a late-spilled proof that Archibald
Had spoken from unfeigned experience.
There was a fluted antique water-glass
Close by, and in it, prisoned, or at rest,
There was a cricket, of the brown soft sort
That feeds on darkness. Isaac turned him out,
And touched him with his thumb to make him jump,
And then composedly pulled out the plug
With such a practised hand that scarce a drop
Did even touch his fingers. Then he drank
And smacked his lips with a slow patronage
And looked along the line of barrels there
With a pride that may have been forgetfulness
That they were Archibald's and not his own.
"I never twist a spigot nowadays,"
He said, and raised the glass up to the light,
"But I thank God for orchards." And that glass
Was filled repeatedly for the same hand
Before I thought it worth while to discern
Again that I was young, and that old age,
With all his woes, had some advantages.

"Now, Archibald," said Isaac, when we stood
Outside again, "I have it in my mind
That I shall take a sort of little walk—
To stretch my legs and see what you are doing.
You stay and rest your back and tell the boy
A story: Tell him all about the time
In Stafford's cabin forty years ago,
When four of us were snowed up for ten days
With only one dried haddock. Tell him all
About it, and be wary of your back.
Now I will go along."—I looked up then
At Archibald, and as I looked I saw
Just how his nostrils widened once or twice
And then grew narrow. I can hear to-day
The way the old man chuckled to himself—
Not wholesomely, not wholly to convince
Another of his mirth,—as I can hear
The lonely sigh that followed.—But at length
He said: "The orchard now's the place for us;
We may find something like an apple there,
And we shall have the shade, at any rate."
So there we went and there we laid ourselves
Where the sun could not reach us; and I champed
A dozen of worm-blighted astrakhans
While Archibald said nothing—merely told
The tale of Stafford's cabin, which was good,
Though "master chilly"—after his own phrase—
Even for a day like that. But other thoughts
Were moving in his mind, imperative,
And writhing to be spoken: I could see
The glimmer of them in a glance or two,
Cautious, or else unconscious, that he gave
Over his shoulder: . . . "Stafford and the rest—
But that's an old song now, and Archibald
And Isaac are old men. Remember, boy,

ISAAC AND ARCHIBALD

That we are old. Whatever we have gained,
Or lost, or thrown away, we are old men.
You look before you and we look behind,
And we are playing life out in the shadow—
But that's not all of it. The sunshine lights
A good road yet before us if we look,
And we are doing that when least we know it;
For both of us are children of the sun,
Like you, and like the weed there at your feet.
The shadow calls us, and it frightens us—
We think; but there's a light behind the stars
And we old fellows who have dared to live,
We see it—and we see the other things,
The other things . . . Yes, I have seen it come
These eight years, and these ten years, and I know
Now that it cannot be for very long
That Isaac will be Isaac. You have seen—
Young as you are, you must have seen the strange
Uncomfortable habit of the man?
He'll take my nerves and tie them in a knot
Sometimes, and that's not Isaac. I know that—
And I know what it is: I get it here
A little, in my knees, and Isaac—here."
The old man shook his head regretfully
And laid his knuckles three times on his forehead.
"That's what it is: Isaac is not quite right.
You see it, but you don't know what it means:
The thousand little differences—no,
You do not know them, and it's well you don't;
You'll know them soon enough—God bless you, boy!—
You'll know them, but not all of them—not all.
So think of them as little as you can:
There's nothing in them for you, or for me—
But I am old and I must think of them;
I'm in the shadow, but I don't forget

The light, my boy,—the light behind the stars.
Remember that: remember that I said it;
And when the time that you think far away
Shall come for you to say it—say it, boy;
Let there be no confusion or distrust
In you, no snarling of a life half lived,
Nor any cursing over broken things
That your complaint has been the ruin of.
Live to see clearly and the light will come
To you, and as you need it.—But there, there,
I'm going it again, as Isaac says,
And I'll stop now before you go to sleep.—
Only be sure that you growl cautiously,
And always where the shadow may not reach you."

Never shall I forget, long as I live,
The quaint thin crack in Archibald's voice,
The lonely twinkle in his little eyes,
Or the way it made me feel to be with him.
I know I lay and looked for a long time
Down through the orchard and across the road,
Across the river and the sun-scorched hills
That ceased in a blue forest, where the world
Ceased with it. Now and then my fancy caught
A flying glimpse of a good life beyond—
Something of ships and sunlight, streets and singing,
Troy falling, and the ages coming back,
And ages coming forward: Archibald
And Isaac were good fellows in old clothes,
And Agamemnon was a friend of mine;
Ulysses coming home again to shoot
With bows and feathered arrows made another,
And all was as it should be. I was young.

So I lay dreaming of what things I would,
Calm and incorrigibly satisfied

ISAAC AND ARCHIBALD

With apples and romance and ignorance,
And the still smoke from Archibald's clay pipe.
There was a stillness over everything,
As if the spirit of heat had laid its hand
Upon the world and hushed it; and I felt
Within the mightiness of the white sun
That smote the land around us and wrought out
A fragrance from the trees, a vital warmth
And fullness for the time that was to come,
And a glory for the world beyond the forest.
The present and the future and the past,
Isaac and Archibald, the burning bush,
The Trojans and the walls of Jericho,
Were beautifully fused; and all went well
Till Archibald began to fret for Isaac
And said it was a master day for sunstroke.
That was enough to make a mummy smile,
I thought; and I remained hilarious,
In face of all precedence and respect,
Till Isaac (who had come to us unheard)
Found he had no tobacco, looked at me
Peculiarly, and asked of Archibald
What ailed the boy to make him chirrup so.
From that he told us what a blessed world
The Lord had given us.—"But, Archibald,"
He added, with a sweet severity
That made me think of peach-skins and goose-flesh,
"I'm half afraid you cut those oats of yours
A day or two before they were well set."
"They were set well enough," said Archibald,—
And I remarked the process of his nose
Before the words came out. "But never mind
Your neighbor's oats: you stay here in the shade
And rest yourself while I go find the cards.
We'll have a little game of seven-up

And let the boy keep count."—"We'll have the game,
Assuredly," said Isaac; "and I think
That I will have a drop of cider, also."

They marched away together towards the house
And left me to my childish ruminations
Upon the ways of men. I followed them
Down cellar with my fancy, and then left them
For a fairer vision of all things at once
That was anon to be destroyed again
By the sound of voices and of heavy feet—
One of the sounds of life that I remember,
Though I forget so many that rang first
As if they were thrown down to me from Sinai.

So I remember, even to this day,
Just how they sounded, how they placed themselves,
And how the game went on while I made marks
And crossed them out, and meanwhile made some Trojans.
Likewise I made Ulysses, after Isaac,
And a little after Flaxman. Archibald
Was injured when he found himself left out,
But he had no heroics, and I said so:
I told him that his white beard was too long
And too straight down to be like things in Homer.
"Quite so," said Isaac.—"Low," said Archibald;
And he threw down a deuce with a deep grin
That showed his yellow teeth and made me happy.
So they played on till a bell rang from the door,
And Archibald said, "Supper."—After that
The old men smoked while I sat watching them
And wondered with all comfort what might come
To me, and what might never come to me;
And when the time came for the long walk home
With Isaac in the twilight, I could see

THE RETURN OF MORGAN AND FINGAL

The forest and the sunset and the sky-line,
No matter where it was that I was looking:
The flame beyond the boundary, the music,
The foam and the white ships, and two old men
Were things that would not leave me.—And that night
There came to me a dream—a shining one,
With two old angels in it. They had wings,
And they were sitting where a silver light
Suffused them, face to face. The wings of one
Began to palpitate as I approached,
But I was yet unseen when a dry voice
Cried thinly, with unpatronizing triumph,
"I've got you, Isaac; high, low, jack, and the game."

Isaac and Archibald have gone their way
To the silence of the loved and well-forgotten.
I knew them, and I may have laughed at them;
But there's a laughing that has honor in it,
And I have no regret for light words now.
Rather I think sometimes they may have made
Their sport of me;—but they would not do that,
They were too old for that. They were old men,
And I may laugh at them because I knew them.

THE RETURN OF MORGAN AND FINGAL

And there we were together again—
    Together again, we three:
Morgan, Fingal, fiddle, and all,
    They had come for the night with me.

The spirit of joy was in Morgan's wrist,
    There were songs in Fingal's throat;
And secure outside, for the spray to drench,
    Was a tossed and empty boat.

And there were the pipes, and there was the punch,
    And somewhere were twelve years;
So it came, in the manner of things unsought,
    That a quick knock vexed our ears.

The night wind hovered and shrieked and snarled,
    And I heard Fingal swear;
Then I opened the door—but I found no more
    Than a chalk-skinned woman there.

I looked, and at last, "What is it?" I said—
    "What is it that we can do?"
But never a word could I get from her
    But "You—you three—it is you!"

Now the sense of a crazy speech like that
    Was more than a man could make;
So I said, "But we—we are what, we three?"
    And I saw the creature shake.

"Be quick!" she cried, "for I left her dead—
    And I was afraid to come;
But you, you three—God made it be—
    Will ferry the dead girl home.

"Be quick! be quick!—but listen to that
    Who is that makes it?—hark!"
But I heard no more than a knocking splash
    And a wind that shook the dark.

"It is only the wind that blows," I said,
    "And the boat that rocks outside."
And I watched her there, and I pitied her there—
    "Be quick! be quick!" she cried.

THE RETURN OF MORGAN AND FINGAL

She cried so loud that her voice went in
    To find where my two friends were;
So Morgan came, and Fingal came,
    And out we went with her.

'T was a lonely way for a man to take
    And a fearsome way for three;
And over the water, and all day long,
    They had come for the night with me.

But the girl was dead, as the woman had said,
    And the best we could see to do
Was to lay her aboard. The north wind roared,
    And into the night we flew.

Four of us living and one for a ghost,
    Furrowing crest and swell,
Through the surge and the dark, for that faint far spark,
    We ploughed with Azrael.

Three of us ruffled and one gone mad,
    Crashing to south we went;
And three of us there were too spattered to care
    What this late sailing meant.

So down we steered and along we tore
    Through the flash of the midnight foam:
Silent enough to be ghosts on guard.
    We ferried the dead girl home.

We ferried her down to the voiceless wharf,
    And we carried her up to the light;
And we left the two to the father there,
    Who counted the coals that night.

Then back we steered through the foam again,
  But our thoughts were fast and few;
And all we did was to crowd the surge
  And to measure the life we knew;—

Till at last we came where a dancing gleam
  Skipped out to us, we three,—
And the dark wet mooring pointed home
  Like a finger from the sea.

Then out we pushed the teetering skiff
  And in we drew to the stairs;
And up we went, each man content
  With a life that fed no cares.

Fingers were cold and feet were cold,
  And the tide was cold and rough;
But the light was warm, and the room was warm,
  And the world was good enough.

And there were the pipes, and there was the punch,
  More shrewd than Satan's tears:
Fingal had fashioned it, all by himself,
  With a craft that comes of years.

And there we were together again—
  Together again, we three:
Morgan, Fingal, fiddle, and all,
  They were there for the night with me.

AUNT IMOGEN

AUNT IMOGEN was coming, and therefore
The children—Jane, Sylvester, and Young George—
Were eyes and ears; for there was only one
Aunt Imogen to them in the whole world,

AUNT IMOGEN

And she was in it only for four weeks
In fifty-two. But those great bites of time
Made all September a Queen's Festival;
And they would strive, informally, to make
The most of them.—The mother understood,
And wisely stepped away. Aunt Imogen
Was there for only one month in the year,
While she, the mother,—she was always there;
And that was what made all the difference.
She knew it must be so, for Jane had once
Expounded it to her so learnedly
That she had looked away from the child's eyes
And thought; and she had thought of many things.

There was a demonstration every time
Aunt Imogen appeared, and there was more
Than one this time. And she was at a loss
Just how to name the meaning of it all:
It puzzled her to think that she could be
So much to any crazy thing alive—
Even to her sister's little savages
Who knew no better than to be themselves;
But in the midst of her glad wonderment
She found herself besieged and overcome
By two tight arms and one tumultuous head,
And therewith half bewildered and half pained
By the joy she felt and by the sudden love
That proved itself in childhood's honest noise.
Jane, by the wings of sex, had reached her first;
And while she strangled her, approvingly,
Sylvester thumped his drum and Young George howled.
But finally, when all was rectified,
And she had stilled the clamor of Young George
By giving him a long ride on her shoulders,
They went together into the old room

That looked across the fields; and Imogen
Gazed out with a girl's gladness in her eyes,
Happy to know that she was back once more
Where there were those who knew her, and at last
Had gloriously got away again
From cabs and clattered asphalt for a while;
And there she sat and talked and looked and laughed
And made the mother and the children laugh.
Aunt Imogen made everybody laugh.

There was the feminine paradox—that she
Who had so little sunshine for herself
Should have so much for others. How it was
That she could make, and feel for making it,
So much of joy for them, and all along
Be covering, like a scar, and while she smiled,
That hungering incompleteness and regret—
That passionate ache for something of her own,
For something of herself—she never knew.
She knew that she could seem to make them all
Believe there was no other part of her
Than her persistent happiness; but the why
And how she did not know. Still none of them
Could have a thought that she was living down—
Almost as if regret were criminal,
So proud it was and yet so profitless—
The penance of a dream, and that was good.
Her sister Jane—the mother of little Jane,
Sylvester, and Young George—might make herself
Believe she knew, for she—well, she was Jane.

Young George, however, did not yield himself
To nourish the false hunger of a ghost
That made no good return. He saw too much:
The accumulated wisdom of his years

AUNT IMOGEN

Had so conclusively made plain to him
The permanent profusion of a world
Where everybody might have everything
To do, and almost everything to eat,
That he was jubilantly satisfied
And all unthwarted by adversity.
Young George knew things. The world, he had found out,
Was a good place, and life was a good game—
Particularly when Aunt Imogen
Was in it. And one day it came to pass—
One rainy day when she was holding him
And rocking him—that he, in his own right,
Took it upon himself to tell her so;
And something in his way of telling it—
The language, or the tone, or something else—
Gripped like insidious fingers on her throat,
And then went foraging as if to make
A plaything of her heart. Such undeserved
And unsophisticated confidence
Went mercilessly home; and had she sat
Before a looking glass, the deeps of it
Could not have shown more clearly to her then
Than one thought-mirrored little glimpse had shown,
The pang that wrenched her face and filled her eyes
With anguish and intolerable mist.
The blow that she had vaguely thrust aside
Like fright so many times had found her now:
Clean-thrust and final it had come to her
From a child's lips at last, as it had come
Never before, and as it might be felt
Never again. Some grief, like some delight,
Stings hard but once: to custom after that
The rapture or the pain submits itself,
And we are wiser than we were before.
And Imogen was wiser; though at first

Her dream-defeating wisdom was indeed
A thankless heritage: there was no sweet,
No bitter now; nor was there anything
To make a daily meaning for her life—
Till truth, like Harlequin, leapt out somehow
From ambush and threw sudden savor to it—
But the blank taste of time. There were no dreams,
No phantoms in her future any more:
One clinching revelation of what was
One by-flash of irrevocable chance,
Had acridly but honestly foretold
The mystical fulfilment of a life
That might have once . . . But that was all gone by:
There was no need of reaching back for that:
The triumph was not hers: there was no love
Save borrowed love: there was no might have been.

But there was yet Young George—and he had gone
Conveniently to sleep, like a good boy;
And there was yet Sylvester with his drum,
And there was frowzle-headed little Jane;
And there was Jane the sister, and the mother,—
Her sister, and the mother of them all.
They were not hers, not even one of them:
She was not born to be so much as that,
For she was born to be Aunt Imogen.
Now she could see the truth and look at it;
Now she could make stars out where once had palled
A future's emptiness; now she could share
With others—ah, the others!—to the end
The largess of a woman who could smile;
Now it was hers to dance the folly down,
And all the murmuring; now it was hers
To be Aunt Imogen.—So, when Young George
Woke up and blinked at her with his big eyes,

THE KLONDIKE

And smiled to see the way she blinked at him,
'T was only in old concord with the stars
That she took hold of him and held him close,
Close to herself, and crushed him till he laughed.

THE KLONDIKE

Never mind the day we left, or the day the women clung to us;
All we need now is the last way they looked at us.
Never mind the twelve men there amid the cheering—
Twelve men or one man, 't will soon be all the same;
For this is what we know: we are five men together,
Five left o' twelve men to find the golden river.

Far we came to find it out, but the place was here for all of us;
Far, far we came, and here we have the last of us.
We that were the front men, we that would be early,
We that had the faith, and the triumph in our eyes:
We that had the wrong road, twelve men together,—
Singing when the devil sang to find the golden river.

Say the gleam was not for us, but never say we doubted it;
Say the wrong road was right before we followed it.
We that were the front men, fit for all forage,—
Say that while we dwindle we are front men still;
For this is what we know to-night: we're starving here together—
Starving on the wrong road to find the golden river.

Wrong, we say, but wait a little: hear him in the corner there;
He knows more than we, and he'll tell us if we listen there—
He that fought the snow-sleep less than all the others
Stays awhile yet, and he knows where he stays:
Foot and hand a frozen clout, brain a freezing feather,
Still he's here to talk with us and to the golden river.

"Flow," he says, "and flow along, but you cannot flow away
    from us;
All the world's ice will never keep you far from us;
Every man that heeds your call takes the way that leads him—
The one way that's his way, and lives his own life:
Starve or laugh, the game goes on, and on goes the river;
Gold or no, they go their way—twelve men together.

"Twelve," he says, "who sold their shame for a lure you call too
    fair for them—
You that laugh and flow to the same word that urges them:
Twelve who left the old town shining in the sunset,
Left the weary street and the small safe days:
Twelve who knew but one way out, wide the way or narrow:
Twelve who took the frozen chance and laid their lives on yellow.

"Flow by night and flow by day, nor ever once be seen by them;
Flow, freeze, and flow, till time shall hide the bones of them;
Laugh and wash their names away, leave them all forgotten,
Leave the old town to crumble where it sleeps;
Leave it there as they have left it, shining in the valley,—
Leave the town to crumble down and let the women marry.

"Twelve of us or five," he says, "we know the night is on us now:
Five while we last, and we may as well be thinking now:
Thinking each his own thought, knowing, when the light comes,
Five left or none left, the game will not be lost.
Crouch or sleep, we go the way, the last way together:
Five or none, the game goes on, and on goes the river.

"For after all that we have done and all that we have failed
    to do,
Life will be life and a world will have its work to do:
Every man who follows us will heed in his own fashion
The calling and the warning and the friends who do not know:

THE GROWTH OF "LORRAINE"

Each will hold an icy knife to punish his heart's lover,
And each will go the frozen way to find the golden river."

There you hear him, all he says, and the last we'll ever get from
    him.
Now he wants to sleep, and that will be the best for him.
Let him have his own way—no, you needn't shake him—
Your own turn will come, so let the man sleep.
For this is what we know: we are stalled here together—
Hands and feet and hearts of us, to find the golden river.

And there's a quicker way than sleep? . . . Never mind the
    looks of him:
All he needs now is a finger on the eyes of him.
You there on the left hand, reach a little over—
Shut the stars away, or he'll see them all night:
He'll see them all night and he'll see them all to-morrow,
Crawling down the frozen sky, cold and hard and yellow.

Won't you move an inch or two—to keep the stars away from
    him?
—No, he won't move, and there's no need of asking him.
Never mind the twelve men, never mind the women;
Three while we last, we'll let them all go;
And we'll hold our thoughts north while we starve here together,
Looking each his own way to find the golden river.

THE GROWTH OF "LORRAINE"

I

WHILE I stood listening, discreetly dumb,
Lorraine was having the last word with me:
"I know," she said, "I know it, but you see
Some creatures are born fortunate, and some

Are born to be found out and overcome,—
Born to be slaves, to let the rest go free;
And if I'm one of them (and I must be)
You may as well forget me and go home.

"You tell me not to say these things, I know,
But I should never try to be content:
I've gone too far; the life would be too slow.
Some could have done it—some girls have the stuff;
But I can't do it: I don't know enough.
I'm going to the devil."—And she went.

II

I DID not half believe her when she said
That I should never hear from her again;
Nor when I found a letter from Lorraine,
Was I surprised or grieved at what I read:
"Dear friend, when you find this, I shall be dead.
You are too far away to make me stop.
They say that one drop—think of it, one drop!—
Will be enough,—but I'll take five instead.

"You do not frown because I call you friend,
For I would have you glad that I still keep
Your memory, and even at the end—
Impenitent, sick, shattered—cannot curse
The love that flings, for better or for worse,
This worn-out, cast-out flesh of mine to sleep."

THE SAGE

FOREGUARDED and unfevered and serene,
Back to the perilous gates of Truth he went—
Back to fierce wisdom and the Orient,
To the Dawn that is, that shall be, and has been:

ERASMUS

Previsioned of the madness and the mean,
He stood where Asia, crowned with ravishment,
The curtain of Love's inner shrine had rent,
And after had gone scarred by the Unseen.

There at his touch there was a treasure chest,
And in it was a gleam, but not of gold;
And on it, like a flame, these words were scrolled:
"I keep the mintage of Eternity.
Who comes to take one coin may take the rest,
And all may come—but not without the key."

ERASMUS

When he protested, not too solemnly,
That for a world's achieving maintenance
The crust of overdone divinity
Lacked aliment, they called it recreance;
And when he chose through his own glass to scan
Sick Europe, and reduced, unyieldingly,
The monk within the cassock to the man
Within the monk, they called it heresy.

And when he made so perilously bold
As to be scattered forth in black and white,
Good fathers looked askance at him and rolled
Their inward eyes in anguish and affright;
There were some of them did shake at what was told,
And they shook best who knew that he was right.

THE WOMAN AND THE WIFE

I—The Explanation

"You thought we knew," she said, "but we were wrong.
This we can say, the rest we do not say;
Nor do I let you throw yourself away
Because you love me. Let us both be strong,
And we shall find in sorrow, before long,
Only the price Love ruled that we should pay:
The dark is at the end of every day,
And silence is the end of every song.

"You ask me for one proof that I speak right,
But I can answer only what I know;
You look for just one lie to make black white,
But I can tell you only what is true—
God never made me for the wife of you.
This we can say,—believe me! . . . Tell me so!"

II—The Anniversary

"Give me the truth, whatever it may be.
You thought we knew, now tell me what you miss:
You are the one to tell me what it is—
You are a man, and you have married me.
What is it worth to-night that you can see
More marriage in the dream of one dead kiss
Than in a thousand years of life like this?
Passion has turned the lock, Pride keeps the key.

"Whatever I have said or left unsaid,
Whatever I have done or left undone,—
Tell me. Tell me the truth. . . . Are you afraid?
Do you think that Love was ever fed with lies
But hunger lived thereafter in his eyes?
Do you ask me to take moonlight for the sun?"

THE BOOK OF ANNANDALE

I

PARTLY to think, more to be left alone,
George Annandale said something to his friends—
A word or two, brusque, but yet smoothed enough
To suit their funeral gaze—and went upstairs;
And there, in the one room that he could call
His own, he found a sort of meaningless
Annoyance in the mute familiar things
That filled it; for the grate's monotonous gleam
Was not the gleam that he had known before,
The books were not the books that used to be,
The place was not the place. There was a lack
Of something; and the certitude of death
Itself, as with a furtive questioning,
Hovered, and he could not yet understand.
He knew that she was gone—there was no need
Of any argued proof to tell him that,
For they had buried her that afternoon,
Under the leaves and snow; and still there was
A doubt, a pitiless doubt, a plunging doubt,
That struck him, and upstartled when it struck,
The vision, the old thought in him. There was
A lack, and one that wrenched him; but it was
Not that—not that. There was a present sense
Of something indeterminably near—
The soul-clutch of a prescient emptiness
That would not be foreboding. And if not,
What then?—or was it anything at all?
Yes, it was something—it was everything—
But what was everything? or anything?

COLLECTED POEMS

Tired of time, bewildered, he sat down;
But in his chair he kept on wondering
That he should feel so desolately strange
And yet—for all he knew that he had lost
More of the world than most men ever win—
So curiously calm. And he was left
Unanswered and unsatisfied: there came
No clearer meaning to him than had come
Before; the old abstraction was the best
That he could find, the farthest he could go;
To that was no beginning and no end—
No end that he could reach. So he must learn
To live the surest and the largest life
Attainable in him, would he divine
The meaning of the dream and of the words
That he had written, without knowing why,
On sheets that he had bound up like a book
And covered with red leather. There it was—
There in his desk, the record he had made,
The spiritual plaything of his life:
There were the words no eyes had ever seen
Save his; there were the words that were not made
For glory or for gold. The pretty wife
Whom he had loved and lost had not so much
As heard of them. They were not made for her.
His love had been so much the life of her,
And hers had been so much the life of him,
That any wayward phrasing on his part
Would have had no moment. Neither had lived enough
To know the book, albeit one of them
Had grown enough to write it. There it was,
However, though he knew not why it was:
There was the book, but it was not for her,
For she was dead. And yet, there was the book.

THE BOOK OF ANNANDALE

Thus would his fancy circle out and out,
And out and in again, till he would make
As if with a large freedom to crush down
Those under-thoughts. He covered with his hands
His tired eyes, and waited: he could hear—
Or partly feel and hear, mechanically—
The sound of talk, with now and then the steps
And skirts of some one scudding on the stairs,
Forgetful of the nerveless funeral feet
That she had brought with her; and more than once
There came to him a call as of a voice—
A voice of love returning—but not hers.
Whose he knew not, nor dreamed; nor did he know,
Nor did he dream, in his blurred loneliness
Of thought, what all the rest might think of him.

For it had come at last, and she was gone
With all the vanished women of old time,—
And she was never coming back again.
Yes, they had buried her that afternoon,
Under the frozen leaves and the cold earth,
Under the leaves and snow. The flickering week,
The sharp and certain day, and the long drowse
Were over, and the man was left alone.
He knew the loss—therefore it puzzled him
That he should sit so long there as he did,
And bring the whole thing back—the love, the trust,
The pallor, the poor face, and the faint way
She last had looked at him—and yet not weep,
Or even choose to look about the room
To see how sad it was; and once or twice
He winked and pinched his eyes against the flame
And hoped there might be tears. But hope was all,
And all to him was nothing: he was lost.
And yet he was not lost: he was astray—

Out of his life and in another life;
And in the stillness of this other life
He wondered and he drowsed. He wondered when
It was, and wondered if it ever was
On earth that he had known the other face—
The searching face, the eloquent, strange face—
That with a sightless beauty looked at him
And with a speechless promise uttered words
That were not the world's words, or any kind
That he had known before. What was it, then?
What was it held him—fascinated him?
Why should he not be human? He could sigh,
And he could even groan,—but what of that?
There was no grief left in him. Was he glad?

Yet how could he be glad, or reconciled,
Or anything but wretched and undone?
How could he be so frigid and inert—
So like a man with water in his veins
Where blood had been a little while before?
How could he sit shut in there like a snail?
What ailed him? What was on him? Was he glad?
Over and over again the question came,
Unanswered and unchanged,—and there he was.
But what in heaven's name did it all mean?
If he had lived as other men had lived,
If home had ever shown itself to be
The counterfeit that others had called home,
Then to this undivined resource of his
There were some key; but now . . . Philosophy?
Yes, he could reason in a kind of way
That he was glad for Miriam's release—
Much as he might be glad to see his friends
Laid out around him with their grave-clothes on,
And this life done for them; but something else

THE BOOK OF ANNANDALE

There was that foundered reason, overwhelmed it,
And with a chilled, intuitive rebuff
Beat back the self-cajoling sophistries
That his half-tutored thought would half-project.

What was it, then? Had he become transformed
And hardened through long watches and long grief
Into a loveless, feelingless dead thing
That brooded like a man, breathed like a man,—
Did everything but ache? And was a day
To come some time when feeling should return
Forever to drive off that other face—
The lineless, indistinguishable face—
That once had thrilled itself between his own
And hers there on the pillow,—and again
Between him and the coffin-lid had flashed
Like fate before it closed,—and at the last
Had come, as it should seem, to stay with him,
Bidden or not?. He were a stranger then,
Foredrowsed awhile by some deceiving draught
Of poppied anguish, to the covert grief
And the stark loneliness that waited him,
And for the time were cursedly endowed
With a dull trust that shammed indifference
To knowing there would be no touch again
Of her small hand on his, no silencing
Of her quick lips on his, no feminine
Completeness and love-fragrance in the house,
No sound of some one singing any more,
No smoothing of slow fingers on his hair,
No shimmer of pink slippers on brown tiles.

But there was nothing, nothing, in all that:
He had not fooled himself so much as that;
He might be dreaming or he might be sick,

But not like that. There was no place for fear,
No reason for remorse. There was the book
That he had made, though. . . . It might be the book;
Perhaps he might find something in the book;
But no, there could be nothing there at all—
He knew it word for word; but what it meant—
He was not sure that he had written it
For what it meant; and he was not quite sure
That he had written it;—more likely it
Was all a paper ghost. . . . But the dead wife
Was real: he knew all that, for he had been
To see them bury her; and he had seen
The flowers and the snow and the stripped limbs
Of trees; and he had heard the preacher pray;
And he was back again, and he was glad.
Was he a brute? No, he was not a brute:
He was a man—like any other man:
He had loved and married his wife Miriam,
They had lived a little while in paradise
And she was gone; and that was all of it.

But no, not all of it—not all of it:
There was the book again; something in that
Pursued him, overpowered him, put out
The futile strength of all his whys and wheres,
And left him unintelligibly numb—
Too numb to care for anything but rest.
It must have been a curious kind of book
That he had made it: it was a drowsy book
At any rate. The very thought of it
Was like the taste of some impossible drink—
A taste that had no taste, but for all that
Had mixed with it a strange thought-cordial,
So potent that it somehow killed in him
The ultimate need of doubting any more—

THE BOOK OF ANNANDALE

Of asking any more. Did he but live
The life that he must live, there were no more
To seek.—The rest of it was on the way.

Still there was nothing, nothing, in all this—
Nothing that he cared now to reconcile
With reason or with sorrow. All he knew
For certain was that he was tired out:
His flesh was heavy and his blood beat small;
Something supreme had been wrenched out of him
As if to make vague room for something else.
He had been through too much. Yes, he would stay
There where he was and rest.—And there he stayed;
The daylight became twilight, and he stayed;
The flame and the face faded, and he slept.
And they had buried her that afternoon,
Under the tight-screwed lid of a long box,
Under the earth, under the leaves and snow.

II

Look where she would, feed conscience how she might,
There was but one way now for Damaris—
One straight way that was hers, hers to defend,
At hand, imperious. But the nearness of it,
The flesh-bewildering simplicity,
And the plain strangeness of it, thrilled again
That wretched little quivering single string
Which yielded not, but held her to the place
Where now for five triumphant years had slept
The flameless dust of Argan.—He was gone,
The good man she had married long ago;
And she had lived, and living she had learned,
And surely there was nothing to regret:
Much happiness had been for each of them,

And they had been like lovers to the last:
And after that, and long, long after that,
Her tears had washed out more of widowed grief
Than smiles had ever told of other joy.—
But could she, looking back, find anything
That should return to her in the new time,
And with relentless magic uncreate
This temple of new love where she had thrown
Dead sorrow on the altar of new life?
Only one thing, only one thread was left;
When she broke that, when reason snapped it off,
And once for all, baffled, the grave let go
The trivial hideous hold it had on her,—
Then she were free, free to be what she would,
Free to be what she was.—And yet she stayed,
Leashed, as it were, and with a cobweb strand,
Close to a tombstone—maybe to starve there.

But why to starve? And why stay there at all?
Why not make one good leap and then be done
Forever and at once with Argan's ghost
And all such outworn churchyard servitude?
For it was Argan's ghost that held the string,
And her sick fancy that held Argan's ghost—
Held it and pitied it. She laughed, almost,
There for the moment; but her strained eyes filled
With tears, and she was angry for those tears—
Angry at first, then proud, then sorry for them.
So she grew calm; and after a vain chase
For thoughts more vain, she questioned of herself
What measure of primeval doubts and fears
Were still to be gone through that she might win
Persuasion of her strength and of herself
To be what she could see that she must be,
No matter where the ghost was.—And the more

THE BOOK OF ANNANDALE

She lived, the more she came to recognize
That something out of her thrilled ignorance
Was luminously, proudly being born,
And thereby proving, thought by forward thought,
The prowess of its image; and she learned
At length to look right on to the long days
Before her without fearing. She could watch
The coming course of them as if they were
No more than birds, that slowly, silently,
And irretrievably should wing themselves
Uncounted out of sight. And when he came
Again, she might be free—she would be free.
Else, when he looked at her she must look down,
Defeated, and malignly dispossessed
Of what was hers to prove and in the proving
Wisely to consecrate. And if the plague
Of that perverse defeat should come to be—
If at that sickening end she were to find
Herself to be the same poor prisoner
That he had found at first—then she must lose
All sight and sound of him, she must abjure
All possible thought of him; for he would go
So far and for so long from her that love—
Yes, even a love like his, exiled enough,
Might for another's touch be born again—
Born to be lost and starved for and not found;
Or, at the next, the second wretchedest,
It might go mutely flickering down and out,
And on some incomplete and piteous day,
Some perilous day to come, she might at last
Learn, with a noxious freedom, what it is
To be at peace with ghosts. Then were the blow
Thrice deadlier than any kind of death
Could ever be: to know that she had won
The truth too late—there were the dregs indeed

Of wisdom, and of love the final thrust
Unmerciful; and there where now did lie
So plain before her the straight radiance
Of what was her appointed way to take,
Were only the bleak ruts of an old road
That stretched ahead and faded and lay far
Through deserts of unconscionable years.

But vampire thoughts like these confessed the doubt
That love denied; and once, if never again,
They should be turned away. They might come back—
More craftily, perchance, they might come back—
And with a spirit-thirst insatiable
Finish the strength of her; but now, to-day
She would have none of them. She knew that love
Was true, that he was true, that she was true;
And should a death-bed snare that she had made
So long ago be stretched inexorably
Through all her life, only to be unspun
With her last breathing? And were bats and threads,
Accursedly devised with watered gules,
To be Love's heraldry? What were it worth
To live and to find out that life were life
But for an unrequited incubus
Of outlawed shame that would not be thrown down
Till she had thrown down fear and overcome
The woman that was yet so much of her
That she might yet go mad? What were it worth
To live, to linger, and to be condemned
In her submission to a common thought
That clogged itself and made of its first faith
Its last impediment? What augured it,
Now in this quick beginning of new life,
To clutch the sunlight and be feeling back,
Back with a scared fantastic fearfulness,

THE BOOK OF ANNANDALE

To touch, not knowing why, the vexed-up ghost
Of what was gone?

                    Yes, there was Argan's face,
Pallid and pinched and ruinously marked
With big pathetic bones; there were his eyes,
Quiet and large, fixed wistfully on hers;
And there, close-pressed again within her own,
Quivered his cold thin fingers. And, ah! yes,
There were the words, those dying words again,
And hers that answered when she promised him.
Promised him? . . . yes. And had she known the truth
Of what she felt that he should ask her that,
And had she known the love that was to be,
God knew that she could not have told him then.
But then she knew it not, nor thought of it;
There was no need of it; nor was there need
Of any problematical support
Whereto to cling while she convinced herself
That love's intuitive utility,
Inexorably merciful, had proved
That what was human was unpermanent
And what was flesh was ashes. She had told
Him then that she would love no other man,
That there was not another man on earth
Whom she could ever love, or who could make
So much as a love thought go through her brain;
And he had smiled. And just before he died
His lips had made as if to say something—
Something that passed unwhispered with his breath,
Out of her reach, out of all quest of it.
And then, could she have known enough to know
The meaning of her grief, the folly of it,
The faithlessness and the proud anguish of it,
There might be now no threads to punish her,

No vampire thoughts to suck the coward blood,
The life, the very soul of her.

                              Yes, Yes,
They might come back. . . . But why should they come back?
Why was it she had suffered? Why had she
Struggled and grown these years to demonstrate
That close without those hovering clouds of gloom
And through them here and there forever gleamed
The Light itself, the life, the love, the glory,
Which was of its own radiance good proof
That all the rest was darkness and blind sight?
And who was *she?* The woman she had known—
The woman she had petted and called "I"—
The woman she had pitied, and at last
Commiserated for the most abject
And persecuted of all womankind,—
Could it be she that had sought out the way
To measure and thereby to quench in her
The woman's fear—the fear of her not fearing?
A nervous little laugh that lost itself,
Like logic in a dream, fluttered her thoughts
An instant there that ever she should ask
What she might then have told so easily—
So easily that Annandale had frowned,
Had he been given wholly to be told
The truth of what had never been before
So passionately, so inevitably
Confessed.

                For she could see from where she sat
The sheets that he had bound up like a book
And covered with red leather; and her eyes
Could see between the pages of the book,
Though her eyes, like them, were closed. And she could read

THE BOOK OF ANNANDALE

As well as if she had them in her hand,
What he had written on them long ago,—
Six years ago, when he was waiting for her.
She might as well have said that she could see
The man himself, as once he would have looked
Had she been there to watch him while he wrote
Those words, and all for her. . . . For her whose face
Had flashed itself, prophetic and unseen,
But not unspirited, between the life
That would have been without her and the life
That he had gathered up like frozen roots
Out of a grave-clod lying at his feet,
Unconsciously, and as unconsciously
Transplanted and revived. He did not know
The kind of life that he had found, nor did
He doubt, not knowing it; but well he knew
That it was life—new life, and that the old
Might then with unimprisoned wings go free,
Onward and all along to its own light,
Through the appointed shadow.

       While she gazed
Upon it there she felt within herself
The growing of a newer consciousness—
The pride of something fairer than her first
Outclamoring of interdicted thought
Had ever quite foretold; and all at once
There quivered and requivered through her flesh,
Like music, like the sound of an old song,
Triumphant, love-remembered murmurings
Of what for passion's innocence had been
Too mightily, too perilously hers,
Ever to be reclaimed and realized
Until to-day. To-day she could throw off
The burden that had held her down so long,

And she could stand upright, and she could see
The way to take, with eyes that had in them
No gleam but of the spirit. Day or night,
No matter; she could see what was to see—
All that had been till now shut out from her,
The service, the fulfillment, and the truth,
And thus the cruel wiseness of it all.

So Damaris, more like than anything
To one long prisoned in a twilight cave
With hovering bats for all companionship,
And after time set free to fight the sun,
Laughed out, so glad she was to recognize
The test of what had been, through all her folly,
The courage of her conscience; for she knew,
Now on a late-flushed autumn afternoon
That else had been too bodeful of dead things
To be endured with aught but the same old
Inert, self-contradicted martyrdom
Which she had known so long, that she could look
Right forward through the years, nor any more
Shrink with a cringing prescience to behold
The glitter of dead summer on the grass,
Or the brown-glimmered crimson of still trees
Across the intervale where flashed along,
Black-silvered, the cold river. She had found,
As if by some transcendent freakishness
Of reason, the glad life that she had sought
Where naught but obvious clouds could ever be—
Clouds to put out the sunlight from her eyes,
And to put out the love-light from her soul.
But they were gone—now they were all gone;
And with a whimsied pathos, like the mist
Of grief that clings to new-found happiness
Hard wrought, she might have pity for the small

THE BOOK OF ANNANDALE

Defeated quest of them that brushed her sight
Like flying lint—lint that had once been thread. . . .

Yes, like an anodyne, the voice of him,
There were the words that he had made for her,
For her alone. The more she thought of them
The more she lived them, and the more she knew
The life-grip and the pulse of warm strength in them.
They were the first and last of words to her,
And there was in them a far questioning
That had for long been variously at work,
Divinely and elusively at work,
With her, and with the grave that had been hers;
They were eternal words, and they diffused
A flame of meaning that men's lexicons
Had never kindled; they were choral words
That harmonized with love's enduring chords
Like wisdom with release; triumphant words
That rang like elemental orisons
Through ages out of ages; words that fed
Love's hunger in the spirit; words that smote;
Thrilled words that echoed, and barbed words that clung;—
And every one of them was like a friend
Whose obstinate fidelity, well tried,
Had found at last and irresistibly
The way to her close conscience, and thereby
Revealed the unsubstantial Nemesis
That she had clutched and shuddered at so long;
And every one of them was like a real
And ringing voice, clear toned and absolute,
But of a love-subdued authority
That uttered thrice the plain significance
Of what had else been generously vague
And indolently true. It may have been
The triumph and the magic of the soul,

Unspeakably revealed, that finally
Had reconciled the grim probationing
Of wisdom with unalterable faith,
But she could feel—not knowing what it was,
For the sheer freedom of it—a new joy
That humanized the latent wizardry
Of his prophetic voice and put for it
The man within the music.

                              So it came
To pass, like many a long-compelled emprise
That with its first accomplishment almost
Annihilates its own severity,
That she could find, whenever she might look,
The certified achievement of a love
That had endured, self-guarded and supreme,
To the glad end of all that wavering;
And she could see that now the flickering world
Of autumn was awake with sudden bloom,
New-born, perforce, of a slow bourgeoning.
And she had found what more than half had been
The grave-deluded, flesh-bewildered fear
Which men and women struggle to call faith,
To be the paid progression to an end
Whereat she knew the foresight and the strength
To glorify the gift of what was hers,
To vindicate the truth of what she was.
And had it come to her so suddenly?
There was a pity and a weariness
In asking that, and a great needlessness;
For now there were no wretched quivering strings
That held her to the churchyard any more:
There were no thoughts that flapped themselves like bats
Around her any more. The shield of love
Was clean, and she had paid enough to learn

SAINTE-NITOUCHE

How it had always been so. And the truth,
Like silence after some far victory,
Had come to her, and she had found it out
As if it were a vision, a thing born
So suddenly!—just as a flower is born,
Or as a world is born—so suddenly.

SAINTE-NITOUCHE

Though not for common praise of him,
  Nor yet for pride or charity,
Still would I make to Vanderberg
  One tribute for his memory:

One honest warrant of a friend
  Who found with him that flesh was grass—
Who neither blamed him in defect
  Nor marveled how it came to pass;

Or why it ever was that he—
  That Vanderberg, of all good men,
Should lose himself to find himself,
  Straightway to lose himself again.

For we had buried Sainte-Nitouche,
  And he had said to me that night:
"Yes, we have laid her in the earth,
  But what of that?" And he was right.

And he had said: "We have a wife,
  We have a child, we have a church;
'T would be a scurrilous way out
  If we should leave them in the lurch.

"That's why I have you here with me
    To-night: you know a talk may take
The place of bromide, cyanide,
    Et cetera. For heaven's sake,

"Why do you look at me like that?
    What have I done to freeze you so?
Dear man, you see where friendship means
    A few things yet that you don't know;

"And you see partly why it is
    That I am glad for what is gone:
For Sainte-Nitouche and for the world
    In me that followed. What lives on—

"Well, here you have it: here at home—
    For even home will yet return.
You know the truth is on my side,
    And that will make the embers burn.

"I see them brighten while I speak,
    I see them flash,—and they are mine!
You do not know them, but I do:
    I know the way they used to shine.

"And I know more than I have told
    Of other life that is to be:
I shall have earned it when it comes,
    And when it comes I shall be free.

"Not as I was before she came,
    But farther on for having been
The servitor, the slave of her—
    The fool, you think. But there's your sin—

SAINTE-NITOUCHE

"Forgive me!—and your ignorance:
    Could you but have the vision here
That I have, you would understand
    As I do that all ways are clear

"For those who dare to follow them
    With earnest eyes and honest feet.
But Sainte-Nitouche has made the way
    For me, and I shall find it sweet.

"Sweet with a bitter sting left?—Yes,
    Bitter enough, God knows, at first;
But there are more steep ways than one
    To make the best look like the worst;

"And here is mine—the dark and hard,
    For me to follow, trust, and hold:
And worship, so that I may leave
    No broken story to be told.

"Therefore I welcome what may come,
    Glad for the days, the nights, the years."—
An upward flash of ember-flame
    Revealed the gladness in his tears.

"You see them, but you know," said he,
    "Too much to be incredulous:
You know the day that makes us wise,
    The moment that makes fools of us.

"So I shall follow from now on
    The road that she has found for me:
The dark and starry way that leads
    Right upward, and eternally.

"Stumble at first? I may do that;
   And I may grope, and hate the night;
But there's a guidance for the man
   Who stumbles upward for the light,

"And I shall have it all from her,
   The foam-born child of innocence.
I feel you smiling while I speak,
   But that's of little consequence;

"For when we learn that we may find
   The truth where others miss the mark,
What is it worth for us to know
   That friends are smiling in the dark?

"Could we but share the lonely pride
   Of knowing, all would then be well;
But knowledge often writes itself
   In flaming words we cannot spell.

"And I, who have my work to do,
   Look forward; and I dare to see,
Far stretching and all mountainous,
   God's pathway through the gloom for me."

I found so little to say then
   That I said nothing.—"Say good-night,"
Said Vanderberg; "and when we meet
   To-morrow, tell me I was right.

"Forget the dozen other things
   That you have not the faith to say;
For now I know as well as you
   That you are glad to go away."

SAINTE-NITOUCHE

I could have blessed the man for that,
    And he could read me with a smile:
"You doubt," said he, "but if we live
    You'll know me in a little while."

He lived; and all as he foretold,
    I knew him—better than he thought:
My fancy did not wholly dig
    The pit where I believed him caught.

But yet he lived and laughed, and preached,
    And worked—as only players can:
He scoured the shrine that once was home
    And kept himself a clergyman.

The clockwork of his cold routine
    Put friends far off that once were near;
The five staccatos in his laugh
    Were too defensive and too clear;

The glacial sermons that he preached
    Were longer than they should have been;
And, like the man who fashioned them,
    The best were too divinely thin.

But still he lived, and moved, and had
    The sort of being that was his,
Till on a day the shrine of home
    For him was in the Mysteries:—

"My friend, there's one thing yet," said he,
    "And one that I have never shared
With any man that I have met;
    But you—you know me." And he stared

For a slow moment at me then
  With conscious eyes that had the gleam,
The shine, before the stroke:—"You know
  The ways of us, the way we dream:

"You know the glory we have won,
  You know the glamour we have lost;
You see me now, you look at me,—
  And yes, you pity me, almost;

"But never mind the pity—no,
  Confess the faith you can't conceal;
And if you frown, be not like one
  Of those who frown before they feel.

"For there is truth, and half truth,—yes,
  And there's a quarter truth, no doubt;
But mine was more than half. . . . You smile?
  You understand? You bear me out?

"You always knew that I was right—
  You are my friend—and I have tried
Your faith—your love."—The gleam grew small,
  The stroke was easy, and he died.

I saw the dim look change itself
  To one that never will be dim;
I saw the dead flesh to the grave,
  But that was not the last of him.

For what was his to live lives yet:
  Truth, quarter truth, death cannot reach;
Nor is it always what we know
  That we are fittest here to teach.

SAINTE-NITOUCHE

The fight goes on when fields are still,
  The triumph clings when arms are down;
The jewels of all coronets
  Are pebbles of the unseen crown;

The specious weight of loud reproof
  Sinks where a still conviction floats;
And on God's ocean after storm
  Time's wreckage is half pilot-boats;

And what wet faces wash to sight
  Thereafter feed the common moan:—
But Vanderberg no pilot had,
  Nor could have: he was all alone.

Unchallenged by the larger light
  The starry quest was his to make;
And of all ways that are for men,
  The starry way was his to take.

We grant him idle names enough
  To-day, but even while we frown
The fight goes on, the triumph clings,
  And there is yet the unseen crown

But was it his? Did Vanderberg
  Find half truth to be passion's thrall,
Or as we met him day by day,
  Was love triumphant, after all?

I do not know so much as that;
  I only know that he died right:
Saint Anthony nor Sainte-Nitouche
  Had ever smiled as he did—quite.

AS A WORLD WOULD HAVE IT

Alcestis

Shall I never make him look at me again?
I look at him, I look my life at him,
I tell him all I know the way to tell,
    But there he stays the same.

Shall I never make him speak one word to me?
Shall I never make him say enough to show
My heart if he be glad? Be glad? . . . ah! God,
    Why did they bring me back?

I wonder, if I go to him again,
If I take him by those two cold hands again,
Shall I get one look of him at last, or feel
    One sign—or anything?

Or will he still sit there in the same way,
Without an answer for me from his lips,
Or from his eyes,—or even with a touch
    Of his hand on my hand? . . .

"Will you look down this once—look down at me?
Speak once—and if you never speak again,
Tell me enough—tell me enough to make
    Me know that you are glad!

"You are my King, and once my King would speak:
You were Admetus once, you loved me once:
Life was a dream of heaven for us once—
    And has the dream gone by?

AS A WORLD WOULD HAVE IT

"Do I cling to shadows when I call you Life?
Do you love me still, or are the shadows all?
Or is it I that love you in the grave,
    And you that mourn for me?

"If it be that, then do not mourn for me;
Be glad that I have loved you, and be King.
But if it be not that—if it be true . . .
    Tell me if it be true!"

Then with a choking answer the King spoke;
But never touched his hand on hers, or fixed
His eyes on hers, or on the face of her:
    "Yes, it is true," he said.

"You are alive, and you are with me now;
And you are reaching up to me that I—
That I may take you—I that am a King—
    I that was once a man."

So then she knew. She might have known before;
Truly, she thought, she must have known it long
Before: she must have known it when she came
    From that great sleep of hers.

She knew the truth, but not yet all of it:
He loved her, but he would not let his eyes
Prove that he loved her; and he would not hold
    His wife there in his arms.

So, like a slave, she waited at his knees,
And waited. She was not unhappy now.
She quivered, but she knew that he would speak
    Again—and he did speak.

And while she felt the tremor of his words,
He told her all there was for him to tell;
And then he turned his face to meet her face,
　　That she might look at him.

She looked; and all her trust was in that look,
And all her faith was in it, and her love;
And when his answer to that look came back,
　　It flashed back through his tears.

So then she put her arms around his neck,
And kissed him on his forehead and his lips;
And there she clung, fast in his arms again,
　　Triumphant, with closed eyes.

At last, half whispering, she spoke once more:
"Why was it that you suffered for so long?
Why could you not believe me—trust in me?
　　Was I so strange as that?

"We suffer when we do not understand;
And you have suffered—you that love me now—
Because you are a man. . . . There is one thing
　　No man can understand.

"I would have given everything?—gone down
To Tartarus—to silence? Was it that?
I would have died? I would have let you live?—
　　And was it very strange?"

THE CORRIDOR

It may have been the pride in me for aught
I know, or just a patronizing whim;
But call it freak or fancy, or what not,
I cannot hide that hungry face of him.

CORTEGE

I keep a scant half-dozen words he said,
And every now and then I lose his name;
He may be living or he may be dead,
But I must have him with me all the same.

I knew it, and I knew it all along,—
And felt it once or twice, or thought I did;
But only as a glad man feels a song
That sounds around a stranger's coffin lid.

I knew it, and he knew it, I believe,
But silence held us alien to the end;
And I have now no magic to retrieve
That year, to stop that hunger for a friend.

CORTÈGE

FOUR o'clock this afternoon,
Fifteen hundred miles away:
So it goes, the crazy tune,
So it pounds and hums all day

Four o'clock this afternoon,
Earth will hide them far away:
Best they go to go so soon,
Best for them the grave to-day.

Had she gone but half so soon,
Half the world had passed away.
Four o'clock this afternoon,
Best for them they go to-day.

Four o'clock this afternoon
Love will hide them deep, they say;
Love that made the grave so soon,
Fifteen hundred miles away.

Four o'clock this afternoon—
Ah, but they go slow to-day:
Slow to suit my crazy tune,
Past the need of all we say.

Best it came to come so soon,
Best for them they go to-day:
Four o'clock this afternoon,
Fifteen hundred miles away.

PARTNERSHIP

YES, you have it; I can see.
Beautiful? . . . Dear, look at me!
Look and let my shame confess
Triumph after weariness.
Beautiful? Ah, yes.

Lift it where the beams are bright;
Hold it where the western light,
Shining in above my bed,
Throws a glory on your head.
Now it is all said.

All there was for me to say
From the first until to-day.
Long denied and long deferred,
Now I say it in one word—
Now; and you have heard.

Life would have its way with us,
And I've called it glorious:
For I know the glory now
And I read it on your brow.
You have shown me how.

TWILIGHT SONG

I can feel your cheeks all wet,
But your eyes will not forget:
In the frown you cannot hide
I can read where faith and pride
Are not satisfied.

But the word was, two should live:
Two should suffer—and forgive:
By the steep and weary way,
For the glory of the clay,
Two should have their day.

We have toiled and we have wept
For the gift the gods have kept:
Clashing and unreconciled
When we might as well have smiled,
We have played the child.

But the clashing is all past,
And the gift is yours at last.
Lift it—hold it high again! . . .
Did I doubt you now and then?
Well, we are not men.

Never mind; we know the way,—
And I do not need to stay.
Let us have it well confessed:
You to triumph, I to rest.
That will be the best.

TWILIGHT SONG

Through the shine, through the rain
We have shared the day's load;
To the old march again
We have tramped the long road;

We have laughed, we have cried,
And we've tossed the King's crown;
We have fought, we have died,
And we've trod the day down.
So it's lift the old song
Ere the night flies again,
Where the road leads along
Through the shine, through the rain.

Long ago, far away,
Came a sign from the skies;
And we feared then to pray
For the new sun to rise:
With the King there at hand,
Not a child stepped or stirred—
Where the light filled the land
And the light brought the word;
For we knew then the gleam
Though we feared then the day,
And the dawn smote the dream
Long ago, far away.

But the road leads us all,
For the King now is dead;
And we know, stand or fall,
We have shared the day's bread.
We may laugh down the dream,
For the dream breaks and flies;
And we trust now the gleam,
For the gleam never dies;—
So it's off now the load,
For we know the night's call,
And we know now the road
And the road leads us all.

VARIATIONS OF GREEK THEMES

Through the shine, through the rain,
We have wrought the day's quest;
To the old march again
We have earned the day's rest;
We have laughed, we have cried,
And we've heard the King's groans;
We have fought, we have died,
And we've burned the King's bones,
And we lift the old song
Ere the night flies again,
Where the road leads along
Through the shine, through the rain.

VARIATIONS OF GREEK THEMES

I

A Happy Man

(Carphyllides)

When these graven lines you see,
Traveler, do not pity me;
Though I be among the dead,
Let no mournful word be said.

Children that I leave behind,
And their children, all were kind;
Near to them and to my wife,
I was happy all my life.

My three sons I married right,
And their sons I rocked at night;
Death nor sorrow ever brought
Cause for one unhappy thought.

Now, and with no need of tears,
Here they leave me, full of years,—
Leave me to my quiet rest
In the region of the blest.

II

A Mighty Runner

(Nicarchus)

The day when Charmus ran with five
In Arcady, as I'm alive,
He came in seventh.—"Five and one
Make seven, you say? It can't be done."—
Well, if you think it needs a note,
A friend in a fur overcoat
Ran with him, crying all the while,
"You'll beat 'em, Charmus, by a mile!"
And so he came in seventh.
Therefore, good Zoilus, you see
The thing is plain as plain can be;
And with four more for company,
He would have been eleventh.

III

The Raven

(Nicarchus)

The gloom of death is on the raven's wing,
  The song of death is in the raven's cries:
But when Demophilus begins to sing,
  The raven dies.

VARIATIONS OF GREEK THEMES

IV

EUTYCHIDES

(Lucilius)

EUTYCHIDES, who wrote the songs,
Is going down where he belongs.
O you unhappy ones, beware:
Eutychides will soon be there!
For he is coming with twelve lyres,
And with more than twice twelve quires
Of the stuff that he has done
In the world from which he's gone.
Ah, now must you know death indeed,
For he is coming with all speed;
And with Eutychides in Hell,
Where's a poor tortured soul to dwell?

V

DORICHA

(Posidippus)

So now the very bones of you are gone
Where they were dust and ashes long ago;
And there was the last ribbon you tied on
To bind your hair, and that is dust also;
And somewhere there is dust that was of old
A soft and scented garment that you wore—
The same that once till dawn did closely fold
You in with fair Charaxus, fair no more.

But Sappho, and the white leaves of her song,
Will make your name a word for all to learn,
And all to love thereafter, even while

COLLECTED POEMS

It's but a name; and this will be as long
As there are distant ships that will return
Again to your Naucratis and the Nile.

VI

THE DUST OF TIMAS

(Sappho)

THIS dust was Timas; and they say
That almost on her wedding day
She found her bridal home to be
The dark house of Persephone.

And many maidens, knowing then
That she would not come back again,
Unbound their curls; and all in tears,
They cut them off with sharpened shears.

VII

ARETEMIAS

(Antipater of Sidon)

I'M sure I see it all now as it was,
When first you set your foot upon the shore
Where dim Cocytus flows for evermore,
And how it came to pass
That all those Dorian women who are there
In Hades, and still fair,
Came up to you, so young, and wept and smiled
When they beheld you and your little child.
And then, I'm sure, with tears upon your face
To be in that sad place,

VARIATIONS OF GREEK THEMES

You told of the two children you had borne,
And then of Euphron, whom you leave to mourn.
"One stays with him," you said,
"And this one I bring with me to the dead."

VIII

The Old Story

(Marcus Argentarius)

Like many a one, when you had gold
Love met you smiling, we are told;
But now that all your gold is gone,
Love leaves you hungry and alone.

And women, who have called you more
Sweet names than ever were before,
Will ask another now to tell
What man you are and where you dwell.

Was ever anyone but you
So long in learning what is true?
Must you find only at the end
That who has nothing has no friend?

IX

To-morrow

(Macedonius)

To-morrow? Then your one word left is always now the same;
And that's a word that names a day that has no more a name.
To-morrow, I have learned at last, is all you have to give:

The rest will be another's now, as long as I may live.
You will see me in the evening?—And what evening has there been,
Since time began with women, but old age and wrinkled skin?

X

Lais to Aphrodite

(*Plato*)

When I, poor Lais, with my crown
Of beauty could laugh Hellas down,
Young lovers crowded at my door,
Where now my lovers come no more.

So, Goddess, you will not refuse
A mirror that has now no use;
For what I was I cannot be,
And what I am I will not see.

XI

An Inscription by the Sea

(*Glaucus*)

No dust have I to cover me,
　My grave no man may show;
My tomb is this unending sea,
　And I lie far below.
My fate, O stranger, was to drown;
And where it was the ship went down
　Is what the sea-birds know.

THE FIELD OF GLORY

War shook the land where Levi dwelt,
And fired the dismal wrath he felt,
That such a doom was ever wrought
As his, to toil while others fought;
To toil, to dream—and still to dream,
With one day barren as another;
To consummate, as it would seem,
The dry despair of his old mother.

Far off one afternoon began
The sound of man destroying man;
And Levi, sick with nameless rage,
Condemned again his heritage,
And sighed for scars that might have come,
And would, if once he could have sundered
Those harsh, inhering claims of home
That held him while he cursed and wondered.

Another day, and then there came,
Rough, bloody, ribald, hungry, lame,
But yet themselves, to Levi's door,
Two remnants of the day before.
They laughed at him and what he sought;
They jeered him, and his painful acre;
But Levi knew that they had fought,
And left their manners to their Maker.

That night, for the grim widow's ears,
With hopes that hid themselves in fears,
He told of arms, and fiery deeds,
Whereat one leaps the while he reads,

And said he'd be no more a clown,
While others drew the breath of battle.—
The mother looked him up and down,
And laughed—a scant laugh with a rattle.

She told him what she found to tell,
And Levi listened, and heard well
Some admonitions of a voice
That left him no cause to rejoice.—
He sought a friend, and found the stars,
And prayed aloud that they should aid him;
But they said not a word of wars,
Or of a reason why God made him.

And who's of this or that estate
We do not wholly calculate,
When baffling shades that shift and cling
Are not without their glimmering;
When even Levi, tired of faith,
Beloved of none, forgot by many,
Dismissed as an inferior wraith,
Reborn may be as great as any.

MERLIN
(1917)
To George Burnham

MERLIN

I

"Gawaine, Gawaine, what look ye for to see,
So far beyond the faint edge of the world?
D'ye look to see the lady Vivian,
Pursued by divers ominous vile demons
That have another king more fierce than ours?
Or think ye that if ye look far enough
And hard enough into the feathery west
Ye'll have a glimmer of the Grail itself?
And if ye look for neither Grail nor lady,
What look ye for to see, Gawaine, Gawaine?"

So Dagonet, whom Arthur made a knight
Because he loved him as he laughed at him,
Intoned his idle presence on a day
To Gawaine, who had thought himself alone,
Had there been in him thought of anything
Save what was murmured now in Camelot
Of Merlin's hushed and all but unconfirmed
Appearance out of Brittany. It was heard
At first there was a ghost in Arthur's palace,
But soon among the scullions and anon
Among the knights a firmer credit held
All tongues from uttering what all glances told—
Though not for long. Gawaine, this afternoon,
Fearing he might say more to Lancelot

Of Merlin's rumor-laden resurrection
Than Lancelot would have an ear to cherish,
Had sauntered off with his imagination
To Merlin's Rock, where now there was no Merlin
To meditate upon a whispering town
Below him in the silence.—Once he said
To Gawaine: "You are young; and that being so,
Behold the shining city of our dreams
And of our King."—"Long live the King," said Gawaine.—
"Long live the King," said Merlin after him;
"Better for me that I shall not be King;
Wherefore I say again, Long live the King,
And add, God save him, also, and all kings—
All kings and queens. I speak in general.
Kings have I known that were but weary men
With no stout appetite for more than peace
That was not made for them."—"Nor were they made
For kings," Gawaine said, laughing.—"You are young,
Gawaine, and you may one day hold the world
Between your fingers, knowing not what it is
That you are holding. Better for you and me,
I think, that we shall not be kings."

                                              Gawaine,
Remembering Merlin's words of long ago,
Frowned as he thought, and having frowned again,
He smiled and threw an acorn at a lizard:
"There's more afoot and in the air to-day
Than what is good for Camelot. Merlin
May or may not know all, but he said well
To say to me that he would not be King.
Nor more would I be King." Far down he gazed
On Camelot, until he made of it
A phantom town of many stillnesses,

MERLIN

Not reared for men to dwell in, or for kings
To reign in, without omens and obscure
Familiars to bring terror to their days;
For though a knight, and one as hard at arms
As any, save the fate-begotten few
That all acknowledged or in envy loathed,
He felt a foreign sort of creeping up
And down him, as of moist things in the dark,—
When Dagonet, coming on him unawares,
Presuming on his title of Sir Fool,
Addressed him and crooned on till he was done:
"What look ye for to see, Gawaine, Gawaine?"

"Sir Dagonet, you best and wariest
Of all dishonest men, I look through Time,
For sight of what it is that is to be.
I look to see it, though I see it not.
I see a town down there that holds a king,
And over it I see a few small clouds—
Like feathers in the west, as you observe;
And I shall see no more this afternoon
Than what there is around us every day,
Unless you have a skill that I have not
To ferret the invisible for rats."

"If you see what's around us every day,
You need no other showing to go mad.
Remember that and take it home with you;
And say tonight, 'I had it of a fool—
With no immediate obliquity
For this one or for that one, or for me.' "
Gawaine, having risen, eyed the fool curiously:
"I'll not forget I had it of a knight,
Whose only folly is to fool himself;
And as for making other men to laugh,

And so forget their sins and selves a little,
There's no great folly there. So keep it up,
As long as you've a legend or a song,
And have whatever sport of us you like
Till havoc is the word and we fall howling.
For I've a guess there may not be so loud
A sound of laughing here in Camelot
When Merlin goes again to his gay grave
In Brittany. To mention lesser terrors,
Men say his beard is gone."

"Do men say that?"
A twitch of an impatient weariness
Played for a moment over the lean face
Of Dagonet, who reasoned inwardly:
"The friendly zeal of this inquiring knight
Will overtake his tact and leave it squealing,
One of these days."—Gawaine looked hard at him:
"If I be too familiar with a fool,
I'm on the way to be another fool,"
He mused, and owned a rueful qualm within him:
"Yes, Dagonet," he ventured, with a laugh,
"Men tell me that his beard has vanished wholly,
And that he shines now as the Lord's anointed,
And wears the valiance of an ageless youth
Crowned with a glory of eternal peace."

Dagonet, smiling strangely, shook his head:
"I grant your valiance of a kind of youth
To Merlin, but your crown of peace I question;
For, though I know no more than any churl
Who pinches any chambermaid soever
In the King's palace, I look not to Merlin
For peace, when out of his peculiar tomb
He comes again to Camelot. Time swings

MERLIN

A mighty scythe, and some day all your peace
Goes down before its edge like so much clover.
No, it is not for peace that Merlin comes,
Without a trumpet—and without a beard,
If what you say men say of him be true—
Nor yet for sudden war."

                        Gawaine, for a moment,
Met then the ambiguous gaze of Dagonet,
And, making nothing of it, looked abroad
As if at something cheerful on all sides,
And back again to the fool's unasking eyes:
"Well, Dagonet, if Merlin would have peace,
Let Merlin stay away from Brittany,"
Said he, with admiration for the man
Whom Folly called a fool: "And we have known him;
We knew him once when he knew everything."

"He knew as much as God would let him know
Until he met the lady Vivian.
I tell you that, for the world knows all that;
Also it knows he told the King one day
That he was to be buried, and alive,
In Brittany; and that the King should see
The face of him no more. Then Merlin sailed
Away to Vivian in Broceliande,
Where now she crowns him and herself with flowers
And feeds him fruits and wines and many foods
Of many savors, and sweet ortolans.
Wise books of every lore of every land
Are there to fill his days, if he require them,
And there are players of all instruments—
Flutes, hautboys, drums, and viols; and she sings
To Merlin, till he trembles in her arms

And there forgets that any town alive
Had ever such a name as Camelot.
So Vivian holds him with her love, they say,
And he, who has no age, has not grown old.
I swear to nothing, but that's what they say.
That's being buried in Broceliande
For too much wisdom and clairvoyancy.
But you and all who live, Gawaine, have heard
This tale, or many like it, more than once;
And you must know that Love, when Love invites
Philosophy to play, plays high and wins,
Or low and loses. And you say to me,
'If Merlin would have peace, let Merlin stay
Away from Brittany.' Gawaine, you are young,
And Merlin's in his grave."

                                "Merlin said once
That I was young, and it's a joy for me
That I am here to listen while you say it.
Young or not young, if that be burial,
May I be buried long before I die.
I might be worse than young; I might be old."—
Dagonet answered, and without a smile:
"Somehow I fancy Merlin saying that;
A fancy—a mere fancy." Then he smiled:
"And such a doom as his may be for you,
Gawaine, should your untiring divination
Delve in the veiled eternal mysteries
Too far to be a pleasure for the Lord.
And when you stake your wisdom for a woman,
Compute the woman to be worth a grave,
As Merlin did, and say no more about it.
But Vivian, she played high. Oh, very high!
Flutes, hautboys, drums, and viols,—and her love.
Gawaine, farewell."

MERLIN

                    "Farewell, Sir Dagonet,
And may the devil take you presently."
He followed with a vexed and envious eye,
And with an arid laugh, Sir Dagonet's
Departure, till his gaunt obscurity
Was cloaked and lost amid the glimmering trees.
"Poor fool!" he murmured. "Or am I the fool?
With all my fast ascendency in arms,
That ominous clown is nearer to the King
Than I am—yet; and God knows what he knows,
And what his wits infer from what he sees
And feels and hears. I wonder what he knows
Of Lancelot, or what I might know now,
Could I have sunk myself to sound a fool
To springe a friend. . . . No, I like not this day.
There's a cloud coming over Camelot
Larger than any that is in the sky,—
Or Merlin would be still in Brittany,
With Vivian and the viols. It's all too strange."

And later, when descending to the city,
Through unavailing casements he could hear
The roaring of a mighty voice within,
Confirming fervidly his own conviction:
"It's all too strange, and half the world's half crazy!"—
He scowled: "Well, I agree with Lamorak."
He frowned, and passed: "And I like not this day."

II

SIR LAMORAK, the man of oak and iron,
Had with him now, as a care-laden guest,
Sir Bedivere, a man whom Arthur loved
As he had loved no man save Lancelot.

Like one whose late-flown shaft of argument
Had glanced and fallen afield innocuously,
He turned upon his host a sudden eye
That met from Lamorak's an even shaft
Of native and unused authority;
And each man held the other till at length
Each turned away, shutting his heavy jaws
Again together, prisoning thus two tongues
That might forget and might not be forgiven.
Then Bedivere, to find a plain way out,
Said, "Lamorak, let us drink to some one here,
And end this dryness. Who shall it be—the King,
The Queen, or Lancelot?"—"Merlin," Lamorak growled;
And then there were more wrinkles round his eyes
Than Bedivere had said were possible.
"There's no refusal in me now for that,"
The guest replied; "so, 'Merlin' let it be.
We've not yet seen him, but if he be here,
And even if he should not be here, say 'Merlin.'"
They drank to the unseen from two new tankards,
And fell straightway to sighing for the past,
And what was yet before them. Silence laid
A cogent finger on the lips of each
Impatient veteran, whose hard hands lay clenched
And restless on his midriff, until words
Were stronger than strong Lamorak:

"Bedivere,"

Began the solid host, "you may as well
Say now as at another time hereafter
That all your certainties have bruises on 'em,
And all your pestilent asseverations
Will never make a man a salamander—
Who's born, as we are told, so fire won't bite him,—
Or a slippery queen a nun who counts and burns

MERLIN

Herself to nothing with her beads and candles.
There's nature, and what's in us, to be sifted
Before we know ourselves, or any man
Or woman that God suffers to be born.
That's how I speak; and while you strain your mazard,
Like Father Jove, big with a new Minerva,
We'll say, to pass the time, that I speak well.
God's fish! The King had eyes; and Lancelot
Won't ride home to his mother, for she's dead.
The story is that Merlin warned the King
Of what's come now to pass; and I believe it
And Arthur, he being Arthur and a king,
Has made a more pernicious mess than one,
We're told, for being so great and amorous:
It's that unwholesome and inclement cub
Young Modred I'd see first in hell before
I'd hang too high the Queen or Lancelot;
The King, if one may say it, set the pace,
And we've two strapping bastards here to prove it.
Young Borre, he's well enough; but as for Modred,
I squirm as often as I look at him.
And there again did Merlin warn the King,
The story goes abroad; and I believe it."

Sir Bedivere, as one who caught no more
Than what he would of Lamorak's outpouring,
Inclined his grizzled head and closed his eyes
Before he sighed and rubbed his beard and spoke:
"For all I know to make it otherwise,
The Queen may be a nun some day or other;
I'd pray to God for such a thing to be,
If prayer for that were not a mockery.
We're late now for much praying, Lamorak,
When you and I can feel upon our faces
A wind that has been blowing over ruins

That we had said were castles and high towers—
Till Merlin, or the spirit of him, came
As the dead come in dreams. I saw the King
This morning, and I saw his face. Therefore,
I tell you, if a state shall have a king,
The king must have the state, and be the state;
Or then shall we have neither king nor state,
But bones and ashes, and high towers all fallen:
And we shall have, where late there was a kingdom,
A dusty wreck of what was once a glory—
A wilderness whereon to crouch and mourn
And moralize, or else to build once more
For something better or for something worse.
Therefore again, I say that Lancelot
Has wrought a potent wrong upon the King,
And all who serve and recognize the King,
And all who follow him and all who love him.
Whatever the stormy faults he may have had,
To look on him today is to forget them;
And if it be too late for sorrow now
To save him—for it was a broken man
I saw this morning, and a broken king—
The God who sets a day for desolation
Will not forsake him in Avilion,
Or whatsoever shadowy land there be
Where peace awaits him on its healing shores."

Sir Lamorak, shifting in his oaken chair,
Growled like a dog and shook himself like one:
"For the stone-chested, helmet-cracking knight
That you are known to be from Lyonnesse
To northward, Bedivere, you fol-de-rol
When days are rancid, and you fiddle-faddle
More like a woman than a man with hands
Fit for the smiting of a crazy giant

MERLIN

With armor an inch thick, as we all know
You are, when you're not sermonizing at us.
As for the King, I say the King, no doubt,
Is angry, sorry, and all sorts of things,
For Lancelot, and for his easy Queen,
Whom he took knowing she'd thrown sparks already
On that same piece of tinder, Lancelot,
Who fetched her with him from Leodogran
Because the King—God save poor human reason!—
Would prove to Merlin, who knew everything
Worth knowing in those days, that he was wrong.
I'll drink now and be quiet,—but, by God,
I'll have to tell you, Brother Bedivere,
Once more, to make you listen properly,
That crowns and orders, and high palaces,
And all the manifold ingredients
Of this good solid kingdom, where we sit
And spit now at each other with our eyes,
Will not go rolling down to hell just yet
Because a pretty woman is a fool.
And here's Kay coming with his fiddle face
As long now as two fiddles. Sit ye down,
Sir Man, and tell us everything you know
Of Merlin—or his ghost without a beard.
What mostly is it?"

                          Sir Kay, the seneschal,
Sat wearily while he gazed upon the two:
"To you it mostly is, if I err not,
That what you hear of Merlin's coming back
Is nothing more or less than heavy truth.
But ask me nothing of the Queen, I say,
For I know nothing. All I know of her
Is what her eyes have told the silences
That now attend her; and that her estate

Is one for less complacent execration
Than quips and innuendoes of the city
Would augur for her sin—if there be sin—
Or for her name—if now she have a name.
And where, I say, is this to lead the King,
And after him, the kingdom and ourselves?
Here be we, three men of a certain strength
And some confessed intelligence, who know
That Merlin has come out of Brittany—
Out of his grave, as he would say it for us—
Because the King has now a desperation
More strong upon him than a woman's net
Was over Merlin—for now Merlin's here,
And two of us who knew him know how well
His wisdom, if he have it any longer,
Will by this hour have sounded and appraised
The grief and wrath and anguish of the King,
Requiring mercy and inspiring fear
Lest he forego the vigil now most urgent,
And leave unwatched a cranny where some worm
Or serpent may come in to speculate."

"I know your worm, and his worm's name is Modred—
Albeit the streets are not yet saying so,"
Said Lamorak, as he lowered his wrath and laughed
A sort of poisonous apology
To Kay: "And in the meantime, I'll be gyved!
Here's Bedivere a-wailing for the King,
And you, Kay, with a moist eye for the Queen.
I think I'll blow a horn for Lancelot;
For by my soul a man's in sorry case
When Guineveres are out with eyes to scorch him:
I'm not so ancient or so frozen certain
That I'd ride horses down to skeletons

MERLIN

If she were after me. Has Merlin seen him—
This Lancelot, this Queen-fed friend of ours?"

Kay answered sighing, with a lonely scowl:
"The picture that I conjure leaves him out;
The King and Merlin are this hour together,
And I can say no more; for I know nothing.
But how the King persuaded or beguiled
The stricken wizard from across the water
Outriddles my poor wits. It's all too strange."

"It's all too strange, and half the world's half crazy!"
Roared Lamorak, forgetting once again
The devastating carriage of his voice.
"Is the King sick?" he said, more quietly;
"Is he to let one damned scratch be enough
To paralyze the force that heretofore
Would operate a way through hell and iron,
And iron already slimy with his blood?
Is the King blind—with Modred watching him?
Does he forget the crown for Lancelot?
Does he forget that every woman mewing
Shall some day be a handful of small ashes?"

"You speak as one for whom the god of Love
Has yet a mighty trap in preparation.
We know you, Lamorak," said Bedivere:
"We know you for a short man, Lamorak,—
In deeds, if not in inches or in words;
But there are fens and heights and distances
That your capricious ranging has not yet
Essayed in this weird region of man's love.
Forgive me, Lamorak, but your words are words.
Your deeds are what they are; and ages hence
Will men remember your illustriousness,

247

If there be gratitude in history.
For me, I see the shadow of the end,
Wherein to serve King Arthur to the end,
And, if God have it so, to see the Grail
Before I die."

                              But Lamorak shook his head:
"See what you will, or what you may. For me,
I see no other than a stinking mess—
With Modred stirring it, and Agravaine
Spattering Camelot with as much of it
As he can throw. The Devil got somehow
Into God's workshop once upon a time,
And out of the red clay that he found there
He made a shape like Modred, and another
As like as eyes are to this Agravaine.
'I never made 'em,' said the good Lord God,
'But let 'em go, and see what comes of 'em.'
And that's what we're to do. As for the Grail,
I've never worried it, and so the Grail
Has never worried me."

                              Kay sighed. "I see
With Bedivere the coming of the end,"
He murmured; "for the King I saw today
Was not, nor shall he ever be again,
The King we knew. I say the King is dead;
The man is living, but the King is dead.
The wheel is broken."

                                    "Faugh!" said Lamorak;
"There are no dead kings yet in Camelot;
But there is Modred who is hatching ruin,—
And when it hatches I may not be here.
There's Gawaine too, and he does not forget

MERLIN

My father, who killed his. King Arthur's house
Has more divisions in it than I like
In houses; and if Modred's aim be good
For backs like mine, I'm not long for the scene."

III

KING ARTHUR, as he paced a lonely floor
That rolled a muffled echo, as he fancied,
All through the palace and out through the world,
Might now have wondered hard, could he have heard
Sir Lamorak's apathetic disregard
Of what Fate's knocking made so manifest
And ominous to others near the King—
If any, indeed, were near him at this hour
Save Merlin, once the wisest of all men,
And weary Dagonet, whom he had made
A knight for love of him and his abused
Integrity. He might have wondered hard
And wondered much; and after wondering,
He might have summoned, with as little heart
As he had now for crowns, the fond, lost Merlin,
Whose Nemesis had made of him a slave,
A man of dalliance, and a sybarite.

"Men change in Brittany, Merlin," said the King;
And even his grief had strife to freeze again
A dreary smile for the transmuted seer
Now robed in heavy wealth of purple silk,
With frogs and foreign tassels. On his face,
Too smooth now for a wizard or a sage,
Lay written, for the King's remembering eyes,
A pathos of a lost authority
Long faded, and unconscionably gone;
And on the King's heart lay a sudden cold:

"I might as well have left him in his grave,
As he would say it, saying what was true,—
As death is true. This Merlin is not mine,
But Vivian's. My crown is less than hers,
And I am less than woman to this man."

Then Merlin, as one reading Arthur's words
On viewless tablets in the air before him:
"Now, Arthur, since you are a child of mine—
A foster-child, and that's a kind of child—
Be not from hearsay or despair too eager
To dash your meat with bitter seasoning,
So none that are more famished than yourself
Shall have what you refuse. For you are King,
And if you starve yourself, you starve the state;
And then by sundry looks and silences
Of those you loved, and by the lax regard
Of those you knew for fawning enemies,
You may learn soon that you are King no more,
But a slack, blasted, and sad-fronted man,
Made sadder with a crown. No other friend
Than I could say this to you, and say more;
And if you bid me say no more, so be it."

The King, who sat with folded arms, now bowed
His head and felt, unfought and all aflame
Like immanent hell-fire, the wretchedness
That only those who are to lead may feel—
And only they when they are maimed and worn
Too sore to covet without shuddering
The fixed impending eminence where death
Itself were victory, could they but lead
Unbitten by the serpents they had fed.
Turning, he spoke: "Merlin, you say the truth:
There is no man who could say more to me

MERLIN

Today, or say so much to me, and live.
But you are Merlin still, or part of him;
I did you wrong when I thought otherwise,
And I am sorry now. Say what you will.
We are alone, and I shall be alone
As long as Time shall hide a reason here
For me to stay in this infested world
Where I have sinned and erred and heeded not
Your counsel; and where you yourself—God save us!—
Have gone down smiling to the smaller life
That you and your incongruous laughter called
Your living grave. God save us all, Merlin,
When you, the seer, the founder, and the prophet,
May throw the gold of your immortal treasure
Back to the God that gave it, and then laugh
Because a woman has you in her arms . . .
Why do you sting me now with a small hive
Of words that are all poison? I do not ask
Much honey; but why poison me for nothing,
And with a venom that I know already
As I know crowns and wars? Why tell a king—
A poor, foiled, flouted, miserable king—
That if he lets rats eat his fingers off
He'll have no fingers to fight battles with?
I know as much as that, for I am still
A king—who thought himself a little less
Than God; a king who built him palaces
On sand and mud, and hears them crumbling now,
And sees them tottering, as he knew they must.
You are the man who made me to be King—
Therefore, say anything."

                          Merlin, stricken deep
With pity that was old, being born of old
Foreshadowings, made answer to the King:

"This coil of Lancelot and Guinevere
Is not for any mortal to undo,
Or to deny, or to make otherwise;
But your most violent years are on their way
To days, and to a sounding of loud hours
That are to strike for war. Let not the time
Between this hour and then be lost in fears,
Or told in obscurations and vain faith
In what has been your long security;
For should your force be slower then than hate,
And your regret be sharper than your sight,
And your remorse fall heavier than your sword,—
Then say farewell to Camelot, and the crown.
But say not you have lost, or failed in aught
Your golden horoscope of imperfection
Has held in starry words that I have read.
I see no farther now than I saw then,
For no man shall be given of everything
Together in one life; yet I may say
The time is imminent when he shall come
For whom I founded the Siege Perilous;
And he shall be too much a living part
Of what he brings, and what he burns away in,
To be for long a vexed inhabitant
Of this mad realm of stains and lower trials.
And here the ways of God again are mixed:
For this new knight who is to find the Grail
For you, and for the least who pray for you
In such lost coombs and hollows of the world
As you have never entered, is to be
The son of him you trusted—Lancelot,
Of all who ever jeopardized a throne
Sure the most evil-fated, saving one,
Your son, begotten, though you knew not then
Your leman was your sister, of Morgause;

MERLIN

For it is Modred now, not Lancelot,
Whose native hate plans your annihilation—
Though he may smile till he be sick, and swear
Allegiance to an unforgiven father
Until at last he shake an empty tongue
Talked out with too much lying—though his lies
Will have a truth to steer them. Trust him not,
For unto you the father, he the son
Is like enough to be the last of terrors—
If in a field of time that looms to you
Far larger than it is you fail to plant
And harvest the old seeds of what I say,
And so be nourished and adept again
For what may come to be. But Lancelot
Will have you first; and you need starve no more
For the Queen's love, the love that never was.
Your Queen is now your Kingdom, and hereafter
Let no man take it from you, or you die.
Let no man take it from you for a day;
For days are long when we are far from what
We love, and mischief's other name is distance.
Let that be all, for I can say no more;
Not even to Blaise the Hermit, were he living,
Could I say more than I have given you now
To hear; and he alone was my confessor."

The King arose and paced the floor again.
"I get gray comfort of dark words," he said;
"But tell me not that you can say no more:
You can, for I can hear you saying it.
Yet I'll not ask for more. I have enough—
Until my new knight comes to prove and find
The promise and the glory of the Grail,
Though I shall see no Grail. For I have built
On sand and mud, and I shall see no Grail."—

"Nor I," said Merlin. "Once I dreamed of it,
But I was buried. I shall see no Grail,
Nor would I have it otherwise. I saw
Too much, and that was never good for man.
The man who goes alone too far goes mad—
In one way or another. God knew best,
And he knows what is coming yet for me.
I do not ask. Like you, I have enough."

That night King Arthur's apprehension found
In Merlin an obscure and restive guest,
Whose only thought was on the hour of dawn,
When he should see the last of Camelot
And ride again for Brittany; and what words
Were said before the King was left alone
Were only darker for reiteration.
They parted, all provision made secure
For Merlin's early convoy to the coast,
And Arthur tramped the past. The loneliness
Of kings, around him like the unseen dead,
Lay everywhere; and he was loath to move,
As if in fear to meet with his cold hand
The touch of something colder. Then a whim,
Begotten of intolerable doubt,
Seized him and stung him until he was asking
If any longer lived among his knights
A man to trust as once he trusted all,
And Lancelot more than all. "And it is he
Who is to have me first," so Merlin says,—
"As if he had me not in hell already.
Lancelot! Lancelot!" He cursed the tears
That cooled his misery, and then he asked
Himself again if he had one to trust
Among his knights, till even Bedivere,
Tor, Bors, and Percival, rough Lamorak,

MERLIN

Griflet, and Gareth, and gay Gawaine, all
Were dubious knaves,—or they were like to be,
For cause to make them so; and he had made
Himself to be the cause. "God set me right,
Before this folly carry me on farther,"
He murmured; and he smiled unhappily,
Though fondly, as he thought: "Yes, there is one
Whom I may trust with even my soul's last shred;
And Dagonet will sing for me tonight
An old song, not too merry or too sad."

When Dagonet, having entered, stood before
The King as one affrighted, the King smiled:
"You think because I call for you so late
That I am angry, Dagonet? Why so?
Have you been saying what I say to you,
And telling men that you brought Merlin here?
No? So I fancied; and if you report
No syllable of anything I speak,
You will have no regrets, and I no anger.
What word of Merlin was abroad today?"

"Today have I heard no man save Gawaine,
And to him I said only what all men
Are saying to their neighbors. They believe
That you have Merlin here, and that his coming
Denotes no good. Gawaine was curious,
But ever mindful of your majesty.
He pressed me not, and we made light of it."

"Gawaine, I fear, makes light of everything,"
The King said, looking down. "Sometimes I wish
I had a full Round Table of Gawaines.
But that's a freak of midnight,—never mind it.
Sing me a song—one of those endless things

255

That Merlin liked of old, when men were younger
And there were more stars twinkling in the sky.
I see no stars that are alive tonight,
And I am not the king of sleep. So then,
Sing me an old song."

                                       Dagonet's quick eye
Caught sorrow in the King's; and he knew more,
In a fool's way, than even the King himself
Of what was hovering over Camelot.
"O King," he said, "I cannot sing tonight.
If you command me I shall try to sing,
But I shall fail; for there are no songs now
In my old throat, or even in these poor strings
That I can hardly follow with my fingers.
Forgive me—kill me—but I cannot sing."
Dagonet fell down then on both his knees
And shook there while he clutched the King's cold hand
And wept for what he knew.

                                    "There, Dagonet;
I shall not kill my knight, or make him sing.
No more; get up, and get you off to bed.
There'll be another time for you to sing,
So get you to your covers and sleep well."
Alone again, the King said, bitterly:
"Yes, I have one friend left, and they who know
As much of him as of themselves believe
That he's a fool. Poor Dagonet's a fool.
And if he be a fool, what else am I
Than one fool more to make the world complete?
'The love that never was!' . . . Fool, fool, fool, fool!"

The King was long awake. No covenant
With peace was his tonight; and he knew sleep

MERLIN

As he knew the cold eyes of Guinevere
That yesterday had stabbed him, having first
On Lancelot's name struck fire, and left him then
As now they left him—with a wounded heart,
A wounded pride, and a sickening pang worse yet
Of lost possession. He thought wearily
Of watchers by the dead, late wayfarers,
Rough-handed mariners on ships at sea,
Lone-yawning sentries, wastrels, and all others
Who might be saying somewhere to themselves,
"The King is now asleep in Camelot;
God save the King."—"God save the King, indeed,
If there be now a king to save," he said.
Then he saw giants rising in the dark,
Born horribly of memories and new fears
That in the gray-lit irony of dawn
Were partly to fade out and be forgotten;
And then there might be sleep, and for a time
There might again be peace. His head was hot
And throbbing; but the rest of him was cold,
As he lay staring hard where nothing stood,
And hearing what was not, even while he saw
And heard, like dust and thunder far away,
The coming confirmation of the words
Of him who saw so much and feared so little
Of all that was to be. No spoken doom
That ever chilled the last night of a felon
Prepared a dragging anguish more profound
And absolute than Arthur, in these hours,
Made out of darkness and of Merlin's words;
No tide that ever crashed on Lyonnesse
Drove echoes inland that were lonelier
For widowed ears among the fisher-folk,
Than for the King were memories tonight
Of old illusions that were dead for ever.

IV

The tortured King—seeing Merlin wholly meshed
In his defection, even to indifference,
And all the while attended and exalted
By some unfathomable obscurity
Of divination, where the Grail, unseen,
Broke yet the darkness where a king saw nothing—
Feared now the lady Vivian more than Fate;
For now he knew that Modred, Lancelot,
The Queen, the King, the Kingdom, and the World,
Were less to Merlin, who had made him King,
Than one small woman in Broceliande.
Whereas the lady Vivian, seeing Merlin
Acclaimed and tempted and allured again
To service in his old magnificence,
Feared now King Arthur more than storms and robbers;
For Merlin, though he knew himself immune
To no least whispered little wish of hers
That might afflict his ear with ecstasy,
Had yet sufficient of his old command
Of all around him to invest an eye
With quiet lightning, and a spoken word
With easy thunder, so accomplishing
A profit and a pastime for himself—
And for the lady Vivian, when her guile
Outlived at intervals her graciousness;
And this equipment of uncertainty,
Which now had gone away with him to Britain
With Dagonet, so plagued her memory
That soon a phantom brood of goblin doubts
Inhabited his absence, which had else
Been empty waiting and a few brave fears,
And a few more, she knew, that were not brave,
Or long to be disowned, or manageable.

MERLIN

She thought of him as he had looked at her
When first he had acquainted her alarm
At sight of the King's letter with its import;
And she remembered now his very words:
"The King believes today as in his boyhood
That I am Fate," he said; and when they parted
She had not even asked him not to go;
She might as well, she thought, have bid the wind
Throw no more clouds across a lonely sky
Between her and the moon,—so great he seemed
In his oppressed solemnity, and she,
In her excess of wrong imagining,
So trivial in an hour, and, after all
A creature of a smaller consequence
Than kings to Merlin, who made kings and kingdoms
And had them as a father; and so she feared
King Arthur more than robbers while she waited
For Merlin's promise to fulfil itself,
And for the rest that was to follow after:
"He said he would come back, and so he will.
He will because he must, and he is Merlin,
The master of the world—or so he was;
And he is coming back again to me
Because he must and I am Vivian.
It's all as easy as two added numbers:
Some day I'll hear him ringing at the gate,
As he rang on that morning in the spring,
Ten years ago; and I shall have him then
For ever. He shall never go away
Though kings come walking on their hands and knees
To take him on their backs." When Merlin came,
She told him that, and laughed; and he said strangely:
"Be glad or sorry, but no kings are coming.
Not Arthur, surely; for now Arthur knows
That I am less than Fate."

                                            Ten years ago
The King had heard, with unbelieving ears
At first, what Merlin said would be the last
Reiteration of his going down
To find a living grave in Brittany:
"Buried alive I told you I should be,
By love made little and by woman shorn,
Like Samson, of my glory; and the time
Is now at hand. I follow in the morning
Where I am led. I see behind me now
The last of crossways, and I see before me
A straight and final highway to the end
Of all my divination. You are King,
And in your kingdom I am what I was.
Wherever I have warned you, see as far
As I have seen; for I have shown the worst
There is to see. Require no more of me,
For I can be no more than what I was."
So, on the morrow, the King said farewell;
And he was never more to Merlin's eye
The King than at that hour; for Merlin knew
How much was going out of Arthur's life
With him, as he went southward to the sea.

Over the waves and into Brittany
Went Merlin, to Broceliande. Gay birds
Were singing high to greet him all along
A broad and sanded woodland avenue
That led him on forever, so he thought,
Until at last there was an end of it;
And at the end there was a gate of iron,
Wrought heavily and invidiously barred.
He pulled a cord that rang somewhere a bell
Of many echoes, and sat down to rest,
Outside the keeper's house, upon a bench

MERLIN

Of carven stone that might for centuries
Have waited there in silence to receive him.
The birds were singing still; leaves flashed and swung
Before him in the sunlight; a soft breeze
Made intermittent whisperings around him
Of love and fate and danger, and faint waves
Of many sweetly-stinging fragile odors
Broke lightly as they touched him; cherry-boughs
Above him snowed white petals down upon him,
And under their slow falling Merlin smiled
Contentedly, as one who contemplates
No longer fear, confusion, or regret,
May smile at ruin or at revelation.

A stately fellow with a forest air
Now hailed him from within, with searching words
And curious looks, till Merlin's glowing eye
Transfixed him and he flinched: "My compliments
And homage to the lady Vivian.
Say Merlin from King Arthur's Court is here,
A pilgrim and a stranger in appearance,
Though in effect her friend and humble servant.
Convey to her my speech as I have said it,
Without abbreviation or delay,
And so deserve my gratitude forever."
"But Merlin?" the man stammered; "Merlin? Merlin?"—
"One Merlin is enough. I know no other.
Now go you to the lady Vivian
And bring to me her word, for I am weary."
Still smiling at the cherry-blossoms falling
Down on him and around him in the sunlight,
He waited, never moving, never glancing
This way or that, until his messenger
Came jingling into vision, weighed with keys,
And inly shaken with much wondering

At this great wizard's coming unannounced
And unattended. When the way was open
The stately messenger, now bowing low
In reverence and awe, bade Merlin enter;
And Merlin, having entered, heard the gate
Clang back behind him; and he swore no gate
Like that had ever clanged in Camelot,
Or any other place if not in hell.
"I may be dead; and this good fellow here,
With all his keys," he thought, "may be the Devil,—
Though I were loath to say so, for the keys
Would make him rather more akin to Peter;
And that's fair reasoning for this fair weather."

"The lady Vivian says you are most welcome,"
Said now the stately-favored servitor,
"And are to follow me. She said, 'Say Merlin—
A pilgrim and a stranger in appearance,
Though in effect my friend and humble servant—
Is welcome for himself, and for the sound
Of his great name that echoes everywhere.'"—
"I like you and I like your memory,"
Said Merlin, curiously, "but not your gate.
Why forge for this elysian wilderness
A thing so vicious with unholy noise?"—
"There's a way out of every wilderness
For those who dare or care enough to find it,"
The guide said: and they moved along together,
Down shaded ways, through open ways with hedgerows.
And into shade again more deep than ever,
But edged anon with rays of broken sunshine
In which a fountain, raining crystal music,
Made faery magic of it through green leafage,
Till Merlin's eyes were dim with preparation
For sight now of the lady Vivian.

MERLIN

He saw at first a bit of living green
That might have been a part of all the green
Around the tinkling fountain where she gazed
Upon the circling pool as if her thoughts
Were not so much on Merlin—whose advance
Betrayed through his enormity of hair
The cheeks and eyes of youth—as on the fishes.
But soon she turned and found him, now alone,
And held him while her beauty and her grace
Made passing trash of empires, and his eyes
Told hers of what a splendid emptiness
Her tedious world had been without him in it
Whose love and service were to be her school,
Her triumph, and her history: "This is Merlin,"
She thought; "and I shall dream of him no more.
And he has come, he thinks, to frighten me
With beards and robes and his immortal fame;
Or is it I who think so? I know not.
I'm frightened, sure enough, but if I show it,
I'll be no more the Vivian for whose love
He tossed away his glory, or the Vivian
Who saw no man alive to make her love him
Till she saw Merlin once in Camelot,
And seeing him, saw no other. In an age
That has no plan for me that I can read
Without him, shall he tell me what I am,
And why I am, I wonder?" While she thought,
And feared the man whom her perverse negation
Must overcome somehow to soothe her fancy,
She smiled and welcomed him; and so they stood,
Each finding in the other's eyes a gleam
Of what eternity had hidden there.

"Are you always all in green, as you are now?"
Said Merlin, more employed with her complexion,

Where blood and olive made wild harmony
With eyes and wayward hair that were too dark
For peace if they were not subordinated;
"If so you are, then so you make yourself
A danger in a world of many dangers.
If I were young, God knows if I were safe
Concerning you in green, like a slim cedar,
As you are now, to say my life was mine:
Were you to say to me that I should end it,
Longevity for me were jeopardized.
Have you your green on always and all over?"

"Come here, and I will tell you about that,"
Said Vivian, leading Merlin with a laugh
To an arbored seat where they made opposites:
"If you are Merlin—and I know you are,
For I remember you in Camelot,—
You know that I am Vivian, as I am;
And if I go in green, why, let me go so,
And say at once why you have come to me
Cloaked over like a monk, and with a beard
As long as Jeremiah's. I don't like it.
I'll never like a man with hair like that
While I can feed a carp with little frogs.
I'm rather sure to hate you if you keep it,
And when I hate a man I poison him."

"You've never fed a carp with little frogs,"
Said Merlin; "I can see it in your eyes."—
"I might then, if I haven't," said the lady;
"For I'm a savage, and I love no man
As I have seen him yet. I'm here alone,
With some three hundred others, all of whom
Are ready, I dare say, to die for me;
I'm cruel and I'm cold, and I like snakes;

MERLIN

And some have said my mother was a fairy,
Though I believe it not."

                          "Why not believe it?"
Said Merlin; "I believe it. I believe
Also that you divine, as I had wished,
In my surviving ornament of office
A needless imposition on your wits,
If not yet on the scope of your regard.
Even so, you cannot say how old I am,
Or yet how young. I'm willing cheerfully
To fight, left-handed, Hell's three headed hound
If you but whistle him up from where he lives;
I'm cheerful and I'm fierce, and I've made kings;
And some have said my father was the Devil,
Though I believe it not. Whatever I am,
I have not lived in Time until to-day."
A moment's worth of wisdom there escaped him,
But Vivian seized it, and it was not lost.

Embroidering doom with many levities,
Till now the fountain's crystal silver, fading,
Became a splash and a mere chilliness,
They mocked their fate with easy pleasantries
That were too false and small to be forgotten,
And with ingenious insincerities
That had no repetition or revival.
At last the lady Vivian arose,
And with a crying of how late it was
Took Merlin's hand and led him like a child
Along a dusky way between tall cones
Of tight green cedars: "Am I like one of these?
You said I was, though I deny it wholly."—
"Very," said Merlin, to his bearded lips
Uplifting her small fingers.—"O, that hair!"

265

She moaned, as if in sorrow: "Must it be?
Must every prophet and important wizard
Be clouded so that nothing but his nose
And eyes, and intimations of his ears,
Are there to make us know him when we see him?
Praise heaven I'm not a prophet! Are you glad?"—

He did not say that he was glad or sorry;
For suddenly came flashing into vision
A thing that was a manor and a castle,
With walls and roofs that had a flaming sky
Behind them, like a sky that he remembered,
And one that had from his rock-sheltered haunt
Above the roofs of his forsaken city
Made flame as if all Camelot were on fire.
The glow brought with it a brief memory
Of Arthur as he left him, and the pain
That fought in Arthur's eyes for losing him,
And must have overflowed when he had vanished.
But now the eyes that looked hard into his
Were Vivian's, not the King's; and he could see,
Or so he thought, a shade of sorrow in them.
She took his two hands: "You are sad," she said.—
He smiled: "Your western lights bring memories
Of Camelot. We all have memories—
Prophets, and women who are like slim cedars;
But you are wrong to say that I am sad."—
"Would you go back to Camelot?" she asked,
Her fingers tightening. Merlin shook his head.
"Then listen while I tell you that I'm glad,"
She purred, as if assured that he would listen:
"At your first warning, much too long ago,
Of this quaint pilgrimage of yours to see
'The fairest and most orgulous of ladies'—
No language for a prophet, I am sure—

MERLIN

Said I, 'When this great Merlin comes to me,
My task and avocation for some time
Will be to make him willing, if I can,
To teach and feed me with an ounce of wisdom.'
For I have eaten to an empty shell,
After a weary feast of observation
Among the glories of a tinsel world
That had for me no glory till you came,
A life that is no life. Would you go back
To Camelot?"—Merlin shook his head again,
And the two smiled together in the sunset.

They moved along in silence to the door,
Where Merlin said: "Of your three hundred here
There is but one I know, and him I favor;
I mean the stately one who shakes the keys
Of that most evil sounding gate of yours,
Which has a clang as if it shut forever."—
"If there be need, I'll shut the gate myself,"
She said. "And you like Blaise? Then you shall have him.
He was not born to serve, but serve he must,
It seems, and be enamoured of my shadow.
He cherishes the taint of some high folly
That haunts him with a name he cannot know,
And I could fear his wits are paying for it.
Forgive his tongue, and humor it a little."—
"I knew another one whose name was Blaise,"
He said; and she said lightly, "Well, what of it?"—
"And he was nigh the learnedest of hermits;
His home was far away from everywhere,
And he was all alone there when he died."—
"Now be a pleasant Merlin," Vivian said,
Patting his arm, "and have no more of that;
For I'll not hear of dead men far away,
Or dead men anywhere this afternoon.

There'll be a trifle in the way of supper
This evening, but the dead shall not have any.
Blaise and this man will tell you all there is
For you to know. Then you'll know everything."
She laughed, and vanished like a humming-bird.

V

THE sun went down, and the dark after it
Starred Merlin's new abode with many a sconced
And many a moving candle, in whose light
The prisoned wizard, mirrored in amazement,
Saw fronting him a stranger, falcon-eyed,
Firm-featured, of a negligible age,
And fair enough to look upon, he fancied,
Though not a warrior born, nor more a courtier.
A native humor resting in his long
And solemn jaws now stirred, and Merlin smiled
To see himself in purple, touched with gold,
And fledged with snowy lace.—The careful Blaise,
Having drawn some time before from Merlin's wallet
The sable raiment of a royal scholar,
Had eyed it with a long mistrust and said:
"The lady Vivian would be vexed, I fear,
To meet you vested in these learned weeds
Of gravity and death; for she abhors
Mortality in all its hues and emblems—
Black wear, long argument, and all the cold
And solemn things that appertain to graves."—
And Merlin, listening, to himself had said,
"This fellow has a freedom, yet I like him;"
And then aloud: "I trust you. Deck me out,
However, with a temperate regard
For what your candid eye may find in me
Of inward coloring. Let them reap my beard,

268

MERLIN

Moreover, with a sort of reverence,
For I shall never look on it again.
And though your lady frown her face away
To think of me in black, for God's indulgence,
Array me not in scarlet or in yellow."—
And so it came to pass that Merlin sat
At ease in purple, even though his chin
Reproached him as he pinched it, and seemed yet
A little fearful of its nakedness.
He might have sat and scanned himself for ever
Had not the careful Blaise, regarding him,
Remarked again that in his proper judgment,
And on the valid word of his attendants,
No more was to be done. "Then do no more,"
Said Merlin, with a last look at his chin;
"Never do more when there's no more to do,
And you may shun thereby the bitter taste
Of many disillusions and regrets.
God's pity on us that our words have wings
And leave our deeds to crawl so far below them;
For we have all two heights, we men who dream,
Whether we lead or follow, rule or serve."—
"God's pity on us anyhow," Blaise answered,
"Or most of us. Meanwhile, I have to say,
As long as you are here, and I'm alive,
Your summons will assure the loyalty
Of all my diligence and expedition.
The gong that you hear singing in the distance
Was rung for your attention and your presence."—
"I wonder at this fellow, yet I like him,"
Said Merlin; and he rose to follow him.

The lady Vivian in a fragile sheath
Of crimson, dimmed and veiled ineffably
By the flame-shaken gloom wherein she sat,

And twinkled if she moved, heard Merlin coming,
And smiled as if to make herself believe
Her joy was all a triumph; yet her blood
Confessed a tingling of more wonderment
Than all her five and twenty worldly years
Of waiting for this triumph could remember;
And when she knew and felt the slower tread
Of his unseen advance among the shadows
To the small haven of uncertain light
That held her in it as a torch-lit shoal
Might hold a smooth red fish, her listening skin
Responded with a creeping underneath it,
And a crinkling that was incident alike
To darkness, love, and mice. When he was there,
She looked up at him in a whirl of mirth
And wonder, as in childhood she had gazed
Wide-eyed on royal mountebanks who made
So brief a shift of the impossible
That kings and queens would laugh and shake themselves;
Then rising slowly on her little feet,
Like a slim creature lifted, she thrust out
Her two small hands as if to push him back—
Whereon he seized them. "Go away," she said;
"I never saw you in my life before."—
"You say the truth," he answered; "when I met
Myself an hour ago, my words were yours.
God made the man you see for you to like,
If possible. If otherwise, turn down
These two prodigious and remorseless thumbs
And leave your lions to annihilate him."—

"I have no other lion than yourself,"
She said; "and since you cannot eat yourself,
Pray do a lonely woman, who is, you say,
More like a tree than any other thing

MERLIN

In your discrimination, the large honor
Of sharing with her a small kind of supper."—
"Yes, you are like a tree,—or like a flower;
More like a flower to-night." He bowed his head
And kissed the ten small fingers he was holding,
As calmly as if each had been a son;
Although his heart was leaping and his eyes
Had sight for nothing save a swimming crimson
Between two glimmering arms. "More like a flower
To-night," he said, as now he scanned again
The immemorial meaning of her face
And drew it nearer to his eyes. It seemed
A flower of wonder with a crimson stem
Came leaning slowly and regretfully
To meet his will—a flower of change and peril
That had a clinging blossom of warm olive
Half stifled with a tyranny of black,
And held the wayward fragrance of a rose
Made woman by delirious alchemy.
She raised her face and yoked his willing neck
With half her weight; and with hot lips that left
The world with only one philosophy
For Merlin or for Anaxagoras,
Called his to meet them and in one long hush
Of capture to surrender and make hers
The last of anything that might remain
Of what was now their beardless wizardry.
Then slowly she began to push herself
Away, and slowly Merlin let her go
As far from him as his outreaching hands
Could hold her fingers while his eyes had all
The beauty of the woodland and the world
Before him in the firelight, like a nymph
Of cities, or a queen a little weary
Of inland stillness and immortal trees.

"Are you to let me go again sometime,"
She said,—"before I starve to death, I wonder?
If not, I'll have to bite the lion's paws,
And make him roar. He cannot shake his mane,
For now the lion has no mane to shake;
The lion hardly knows himself without it,
And thinks he has no face, but there's a lady
Who says he had no face until he lost it.
So there we are. And there's a flute somewhere,
Playing a strange old tune. You know the words:
'The Lion and the Lady are both hungry.'"

Fatigue and hunger—tempered leisurely
With food that some devout magician's oven
Might after many failures have delivered,
And wine that had for decades in the dark
Of Merlin's grave been slowly quickening,
And with half-heard, dream-weaving interludes
Of distant flutes and viols, made more distant
By far, nostalgic hautboys blown from nowhere,—
Were tempered not so leisurely, may be,
With Vivian's inextinguishable eyes
Between two shining silver candlesticks
That lifted each a trembling flame to make
The rest of her a dusky loveliness
Against a bank of shadow. Merlin made,
As well as he was able while he ate,
A fair division of the fealty due
To food and beauty, albeit more times than one
Was he at odds with his urbanity
In honoring too long the grosser viand.
"The best invention in Broceliande
Has not been over-taxed in vain, I see,"
She told him, with her chin propped on her fingers
And her eyes flashing blindness into his:

MERLIN

"I put myself out cruelly to please you,
And you, for that, forget almost at once
The name and image of me altogether.
You needn't, for when all is analyzed,
It's only a bird-pie that you are eating."

"I know not what you call it," Merlin said;
"Nor more do I forget your name and image,
Though I do eat; and if I did not eat,
Your sending out of ships and caravans
To get whatever 'tis that's in this thing
Would be a sorrow for you all your days;
And my great love, which you have seen by now,
Might look to you a lie; and like as not
You'd actuate some sinewed mercenary
To carry me away to God knows where
And seal me in a fearsome hole to starve,
Because I made of this insidious picking
An idle circumstance. My dear fair lady—
And there is not another under heaven
So fair as you are as I see you now—
I cannot look at you too much and eat;
And I must eat, or be untimely ashes,
Whereon the light of your celestial gaze
Would fall, I fear me, for no longer time
Than on the solemn dust of Jeremiah—
Whose beard you likened once, in heathen jest,
To mine that now is no man's."

                                  "Are you sorry?"
Said Vivian, filling Merlin's empty goblet;
"If you are sorry for the loss of it,
Drink more of this and you may tell me lies
Enough to make me sure that you are glad;
But if your love is what you say it is,

Be never sorry that my love took off
That horrid hair to make your face at last
A human fact. Since I have had your name
To dream of and say over to myself,
The visitations of that awful beard
Have been a terror for my nights and days—
For twenty years. I've seen it like an ocean,
Blown seven ways at once and wrecking ships,
With men and women screaming for their lives;
I've seen it woven into shining ladders
That ran up out of sight and so to heaven,
All covered with white ghosts with hanging robes
Like folded wings,—and there were millions of them,
Climbing, climbing, climbing, all the time;
And all the time that I was watching them
I thought how far above me Merlin was,
And wondered always what his face was like.
But even then, as a child, I knew the day
Would come some time when I should see his face
And hear his voice, and have him in my house
Till he should care no more to stay in it,
And go away to found another kingdom."—
"Not that," he said; and, sighing, drank more wine;
"One kingdom for one Merlin is enough."—
"One Merlin for one Vivian is enough,"
She said. "If you care much, remember that;
But the Lord knows how many Vivians
One Merlin's entertaining eye might favor,
Indifferently well and all at once,
If they were all at hand. Praise heaven they're not."

"If they were in the world—praise heaven they're not—
And if one Merlin's entertaining eye
Saw two of them, there might be left him then
The sight of no eye to see anything—

MERLIN

Not even the Vivian who is everything,
She being Beauty, Beauty being She,
She being Vivian, and so on for ever."—
"I'm glad you don't see two of me," she said;
"For there's a whole world yet for you to eat
And drink and say to me before I know
The sort of creature that you see in me.
I'm withering for a little more attention,
But, being woman, I can wait. These cups
That you see coming are for the last there is
Of what my father gave to kings alone,
And far from always. You are more than kings
To me; therefore I give it all to you,
Imploring you to spare no more of it
Than a small cockle-shell would hold for me
To pledge your love and mine in. Take the rest,
That I may see tonight the end of it.
I'll have no living remnant of the dead
Annoying me until it fades and sours
Of too long cherishing; for Time enjoys
The look that's on our faces when we scowl
On unexpected ruins, and thrift itself
May be a sort of slow unwholesome fire
That eats away to dust the life that feeds it.
You smile, I see, but I said what I said.
One hardly has to live a thousand years
To contemplate a lost economy;
So let us drink it while it's yet alive
And you and I are not untimely ashes.
My last words are your own, and I don't like 'em."—
A sudden laughter scattered from her eyes
A threatening wisdom. He smiled and let her laugh,
Then looked into the dark where there was nothing:
"There's more in this than I have seen," he thought,
"Though I shall see it."—"Drink," she said again;

"There's only this much in the world of it,
And I am near to giving all to you
Because you are so great and I so little."

With a long-kindling gaze that caught from hers
A laughing flame, and with a hand that shook
Like Arthur's kingdom, Merlin slowly raised
A golden cup that for a golden moment
Was twinned in air with hers; and Vivian,
Who smiled at him across their gleaming rims,
From eyes that made a fuel of the night
Surrounding her, shot glory over gold
At Merlin, while their cups touched and his trembled.
He drank, not knowing what, nor caring much
For kings who might have cared less for themselves,
He thought, had all the darkness and wild light
That fell together to make Vivian
Been there before them then to flower anew
Through sheathing crimson into candle-light
With each new leer of their loose, liquorish eyes.
Again he drank, and he cursed every king
Who might have touched her even in her cradle;
For what were kings to such as he, who made them
And saw them totter—for the world to see,
And heed, if the world would? He drank again,
And yet again—to make himself assured
No manner of king should have the last of it—
The cup that Vivian filled unfailingly
Until she poured for nothing. "At the end
Of this incomparable flowing gold,"
She prattled on to Merlin, who observed
Her solemnly, "I fear there may be specks."—
He sighed aloud, whereat she laughed at him
And pushed the golden cup a little nearer.
He scanned it with a sad anxiety,

MERLIN

And then her face likewise, and shook his head
As if at her concern for such a matter:
"Specks? What are specks? Are you afraid of them?"
He murmured slowly, with a drowsy tongue;
"There are specks everywhere. I fear them not.
If I were king in Camelot, I might
Fear more than specks. But now I fear them not.
You are too strange a lady to fear specks."

He stared a long time at the cup of gold
Before him but he drank no more. There came
Between him and the world a crumbling sky
Of black and crimson, with a crimson cloud
That held a far off town of many towers.
All swayed and shaken, till at last they fell,
And there was nothing but a crimson cloud
That crumbled into nothing, like the sky
That vanished with it, carrying away
The world, the woman, and all memory of them,
Until a slow light of another sky
Made gray an open casement, showing him
Faint shapes of an exotic furniture
That glimmered with a dim magnificence,
And letting in the sound of many birds
That were, as he lay there remembering,
The only occupation of his ears
Until it seemed they shared a fainter sound,
As if a sleeping child with a black head
Beside him drew the breath of innocence.

One shining afternoon around the fountain,
As on the shining day of his arrival,
The sunlight was alive with flying silver
That had for Merlin a more dazzling flash
Than jewels rained in dreams, and a richer sound

Than harps, and all the morning stars together,—
When jewels and harps and stars and everything
That flashed and sang and was not Vivian,
Seemed less than echoes of her least of words—
For she was coming. Suddenly, somewhere
Behind him, she was coming; that was all
He knew until she came and took his hand
And held it while she talked about the fishes.
When she looked up he thought a softer light
Was in her eyes than once he had found there;
And had there been left yet for dusky women
A beauty that was heretofore not hers,
He told himself he must have seen it then
Before him in the face at which he smiled
And trembled. "Many men have called me wise,"
He said, "but you are wiser than all wisdom
If you know what you are."—"I don't," she said;
"I know that you and I are here together;
I know that I have known for twenty years
That life would be almost a constant yawning
Until you came; and now that you are here,
I know that you are not to go away
Until you tell me that I'm hideous;
I know that I like fishes, ferns, and snakes,—
Maybe because I liked them when the world
Was young and you and I were salamanders;
I know, too, a cool place not far from here,
Where there are ferns that are like marching men
Who never march away. Come now and see them,
And do as they do—never march away.
When they are gone, some others, crisp and green,
Will have their place, but never march away."—
He smoothed her silky fingers, one by one:
"Some other Merlin, also, do you think,
Will have his place—and never march away?"—

MERLIN

Then Vivian laid a finger on his lips
And shook her head at him before she laughed:
"There is no other Merlin than yourself,
And you are never going to be old."

Oblivious of a world that made of him
A jest, a legend, and a long regret,
And with a more commanding wizardry
Than his to rule a kingdom where the king
Was Love and the queen Vivian, Merlin found
His queen without the blemish of a word
That was more rough than honey from her lips,
Or the first adumbration of a frown
To cloud the night-wild fire that in her eyes
Had yet a smoky friendliness of home,
And a foreknowing care for mighty trifles.
"There are miles and miles for you to wander in,"
She told him once: "Your prison yard is large,
And I would rather take my two ears off
And feed them to the fishes in the fountain
Than buzz like an incorrigible bee
For always around yours, and have you hate
The sound of me; for some day then, for certain,
Your philosophic rage would see in me
A bee in earnest, and your hand would smite
My life away. And what would you do then?
I know: for years and years you'd sit alone
Upon my grave, and be the grieving image
Of lean remorse, and suffer miserably;
And often, all day long, you'd only shake
Your celebrated head and all it holds,
Or beat it with your fist the while you groaned
Aloud and went on saying to yourself:
'Never should I have killed her, or believed
She was a bee that buzzed herself to death,

First having made me crazy, had there been
Judicious distance and wise absences
To keep the two of us inquisitive.' "—
"I fear you bow your unoffending head
Before a load that should be mine," said he;
"If so, you led me on by listening.
You should have shrieked and jumped, and then fled yelling;
That's the best way when a man talks too long.
God's pity on me if I love your feet
More now than I could ever love the face
Of any one of all those Vivians
You summoned out of nothing on the night
When I saw towers. I'll wander and amend."—
At that she flung the noose of her soft arms
Around his neck and kissed him instantly:
"You are the wisest man that ever was,
And I've a prayer to make: May all you say
To Vivian be a part of what you knew
Before the curse of her unquiet head
Was on your shoulder, as you have it now,
To punish you for knowing beyond knowledge.
You are the only one who sees enough
To make me see how far away I am
From all that I have seen and have not been;
You are the only thing there is alive
Between me as I am and as I was
When Merlin was a dream. You are to listen
When I say now to you that I'm alone.
Like you, I saw too much; and unlike you
I made no kingdom out of what I saw—
Or none save this one here that you must rule,
Believing you are ruled. I see too far
To rule myself. Time's way with you and me
Is our way, in that we are out of Time
And out of tune with Time. We have this place,

MERLIN

And you must hold us in it or we die.
Look at me now and say if what I say
Be folly or not; for my unquiet head
Is no conceit of mine. I had it first
When I was born; and I shall have it with me
Till my unquiet soul is on its way
To be, I hope, where souls are quieter.
So let the first and last activity
Of what you say so often is your love
Be always to remember that our lyres
Are not strung for Today. On you it falls
To keep them in accord here with each other,
For you have wisdom, I have only sight
For distant things—and you. And you are Merlin.
Poor wizard! Vivian is your punishment
For making kings of men who are not kings;
And you are mine, by the same reasoning,
For living out of Time and out of tune
With anything but you. No other man
Could make me say so much of what I know
As I say now to you. And you are Merlin!"

She looked up at him till his way was lost
Again in the familiar wilderness
Of night that love made for him in her eyes,
And there he wandered as he said he would;
He wandered also in his prison-yard,
And, when he found her coming after him,
Beguiled her with her own admonishing
And frowned upon her with a fierce reproof
That many a time in the old world outside
Had set the mark of silence on strong men—
Whereat she laughed, not always wholly sure,
Nor always wholly glad, that he who played
So lightly was the wizard of her dreams:

"No matter—if only Merlin keep the world
Away," she thought. "Our lyres have many strings,
But he must know them all, for he is Merlin."

And so for years, till ten of them were gone,—
Ten years, ten seasons, or ten flying ages—
Fate made Broceliande a paradise,
By none invaded, until Dagonet,
Like a discordant, awkward bird of doom,
Flew in with Arthur's message. For the King,
In sorrow cleaving to simplicity,
And having in his love a quick remembrance
Of Merlin's old affection for the fellow,
Had for this vain, reluctant enterprise
Appointed him—the knight who made men laugh,
And was a fool because he played the fool.

"The King believes today, as in his boyhood,
That I am Fate; and I can do no more
Than show again what in his heart he knows,"
Said Merlin to himself and Vivian:
"This time I go because I made him King,
Thereby to be a mirror for the world;
This time I go, but never after this,
For I can be no more than what I was,
And I can do no more than I have done."
He took her slowly in his arms and felt
Her body throbbing like a bird against him:
"This time I go; I go because I must."

And in the morning, when he rode away
With Dagonet and Blaise through the same gate
That once had clanged as if to shut for ever,
She had not even asked him not to go;
For it was then that in his lonely gaze

MERLIN

Of helpless love and sad authority
She found the gleam of his imprisoned power
That Fate withheld; and, pitying herself,
She pitied the fond Merlin she had changed,
And saw the Merlin who had changed the world.

VI

"No kings are coming on their hands and knees,
Nor yet on horses or in chariots,
To carry me away from you again,"
Said Merlin, winding around Vivian's ear
A shred of her black hair. "King Arthur knows
That I have done with kings, and that I speak
No more their crafty language. Once I knew it,
But now the only language I have left
Is one that I must never let you hear
Too long, or know too well. When towering deeds
Once done shall only out of dust and words
Be done again, the doer may then be wary
Lest in the complement of his new fabric
There be more words than dust."

"Why tell me so?"
Said Vivian; and a singular thin laugh
Came after her thin question. "Do you think
That I'm so far away from history
That I require, even of the wisest man
Who ever said the wrong thing to a woman,
So large a light on what I know already—
When all I seek is here before me now
In your new eyes that you have brought for me
From Camelot? The eyes you took away
Were sad and old; and I could see in them
A Merlin who remembered all the kings

He ever saw, and wished himself, almost,
Away from Vivian, to make other kings,
And shake the world again in the old manner.
I saw myself no bigger than a beetle
For several days, and wondered if your love
Were large enough to make me any larger
When you came back. Am I a beetle still?"
She stood up on her toes and held her cheek
For some time against his, and let him go.

"I fear the time has come for me to wander
A little in my prison-yard," he said.—
"No, tell me everything that you have seen
And heard and done, and seen done, and heard done,
Since you deserted me. And tell me first
What the King thinks of me."—"The King believes
That you are almost what you are," he told her:
"The beauty of all ages that are vanished,
Reborn to be the wonder of one woman."—
"I knew he hated me. What else of him?"—
"And all that I have seen and heard and done,
Which is not much, would make a weary telling;
And all your part of it would be to sleep,
And dream that Merlin had his beard again."—
"Then tell me more about your good fool knight,
Sir Dagonet. If Blaise were not half-mad
Already with his pondering on the name
And shield of his unshielding nameless father,
I'd make a fool of him. I'd call him Ajax;
I'd have him shake his fist at thunder-storms,
And dance a jig as long as there was lightning,
And so till I forgot myself entirely.
Not even your love may do so much as that."—
"Thunder and lightning are no friends of mine,"
Said Merlin slowly, "more than they are yours;

MERLIN

They bring me nearer to the elements
From which I came than I care now to be."—
"You owe a service to those elements;
For by their service you outwitted age
And made the world a kingdom of your will."—
He touched her hand, smiling: "Whatever service
Of mine awaits them will not be forgotten,"
He said; and the smile faded on his face.—
"Now of all graceless and ungrateful wizards—"
But there she ceased, for she found in his eyes
The first of a new fear. "The wrong word rules
Today," she said; "and we'll have no more journeys."

Although he wandered rather more than ever
Since he had come again to Brittany
From Camelot, Merlin found eternally
Before him a new loneliness that made
Of garden, park, and woodland, all alike,
A desolation and a changelessness
Defying reason, without Vivian
Beside him, like a child with a black head,
Or moving on before him, or somewhere
So near him that, although he saw it not
With eyes, he felt the picture of her beauty
And shivered at the nearness of her being.
Without her now there was no past or future,
And a vague, soul-consuming premonition
He found the only tenant of the present;
He wondered, when she was away from him,
If his avenging injured intellect
Might shine with Arthur's kingdom a twin mirror,
Fate's plaything, for new ages without eyes
To see therein themselves and their declension.
Love made his hours a martyrdom without her;
The world was like an empty house without her,

Where Merlin was a prisoner of love
Confined within himself by too much freedom,
Repeating an unending exploration
Of many solitary silent rooms,
And only in a way remembering now
That once their very solitude and silence
Had by the magic of expectancy
Made sure what now he doubted—though his doubts,
Day after day, were founded on a shadow.

For now to Merlin, in his paradise,
Had come an unseen angel with a sword
Unseen, the touch of which was a long fear
For longer sorrow that had never come,
Yet might if he compelled it. He discovered,
One golden day in autumn as he wandered,
That he had made the radiance of two years
A misty twilight when he might as well
Have had no mist between him and the sun,
The sun being Vivian. On his coming then
To find her all in green against a wall
Of green and yellow leaves, and crumbling bread
For birds around the fountain while she sang
And the birds ate the bread, he told himself
That everything today was as it was
At first, and for a minute he believed it.
"I'd have you always all in green out here,"
He said, "if I had much to say about it."—
She clapped her crumbs away and laughed at him:
"I've covered up my bones with every color
That I can carry on them without screaming,
And you have liked them all—or made me think so."—
"I must have liked them if you thought I did,"
He answered, sighing; "but the sight of you

MERLIN

Today as on the day I saw you first,
All green, all wonderful" . . . He tore a leaf
To pieces with a melancholy care
That made her smile.—"Why pause at 'wonderful'?
You've hardly been yourself since you came back
From Camelot, where that unpleasant King
Said things that you have never said to me."—
He looked upon her with a worn reproach:
"The King said nothing that I keep from you."—
"What is it then?" she asked, imploringly;
"You man of moods and miracles, what is it?"—
He shook his head and tore another leaf:
"There is no need of asking what it is;
Whatever you or I may choose to name it,
The name of it is Fate, who played with me
And gave me eyes to read of the unwritten
More lines than I have read. I see no more
Today than yesterday, but I remember.
My ways are not the ways of other men;
My memories go forward. It was you
Who said that we were not in tune with Time;
It was not I who said it."—"But you knew it;
What matter then who said it?"—"It was you
Who said that Merlin was your punishment
For being in tune with him and not with Time—
With Time or with the world; and it was you
Who said you were alone, even here with Merlin;
It was not I who said it. It is I
Who tell you now my inmost thoughts." He laughed
As if at hidden pain around his heart,
But there was not much laughing in his eyes.
They walked, and for a season they were silent:
"I shall know what you mean by that," she said,
"When you have told me. Here's an oak you like,
And here's a place that fits me wondrous well

To sit in. You sit there. I've seen you there
Before; and I have spoiled your noble thoughts
By walking all my fingers up and down
Your countenance, as if they were the feet
Of a small animal with no great claws.
Tell me a story now about the world,
And the men in it, what they do in it,
And why it is they do it all so badly."—
"I've told you every story that I know,
Almost," he said.—"O, don't begin like that."—
"Well, once upon a time there was a King."—
"That has a more commendable address;
Go on, and tell me all about the King;
I'll bet the King had warts or carbuncles,
Or something wrong in his divine insides,
To make him wish that Adam had died young."

Merlin observed her slowly with a frown
Of saddened wonder. She laughed rather lightly,
And at his heart he felt again the sword
Whose touch was a long fear for longer sorrow.
"Well, once upon a time there was a king,"
He said again, but now in a dry voice
That wavered and betrayed a venturing.
He paused, and would have hesitated longer,
But something in him that was not himself
Compelled an utterance that his tongue obeyed,
As an unwilling child obeys a father
Who might be richer for obedience
If he obeyed the child: "There was a king
Who would have made his reign a monument
For kings and peoples of the waiting ages
To reverence and remember, and to this end
He coveted and won, with no ado
To make a story of, a neighbor queen

MERLIN

Who limed him with her smile and had of him,
In token of their sin, what he found soon
To be a sort of mongrel son and nephew—
And a most precious reptile in addition—
To ornament his court and carry arms,
And latterly to be the darker half
Of ruin. Also the king, who made of love
More than he made of life and death together,
Forgot the world and his example in it
For yet another woman—one of many—
And this one he made Queen, albeit he knew
That her unsworn allegiance to the knight
That he had loved the best of all his order
Must one day bring along the coming end
Of love and honor and of everything;
And with a kingdom builded on two pits
Of living sin,—so founded by the will
Of one wise counsellor who loved the king,
And loved the world and therefore made him king
To be a mirror for it,—the king reigned well
For certain years, awaiting a sure doom;
For certain years he waved across the world
A royal banner with a Dragon on it;
And men of every land fell worshipping
The Dragon as it were the living God,
And not the living sin."

      She rose at that,
And after a calm yawn, she looked at Merlin:
"Why all this new insistence upon sin?"
She said; "I wonder if I understand
This king of yours, with all his pits and dragons;
I know I do not like him." A thinner light
Was in her eyes than he had found in them
Since he became the willing prisoner

That she had made of him; and on her mouth
Lay now a colder line of irony
Than all his fears or nightmares could have drawn
Before today: "What reason do you know
For me to listen to this king of yours?
What reading has a man of woman's days,
Even though the man be Merlin and a prophet?"

"I know no call for you to love the king,"
Said Merlin, driven ruinously along
By the vindictive urging of his fate;
"I know no call for you to love the king,
Although you serve him, knowing not yet the king
You serve. There is no man, or any woman,
For whom the story of the living king
Is not the story of the living sin.
I thought my story was the common one,
For common recognition and regard."

"Then let us have no more of it," she said;
"For we are not so common, I believe,
That we need kings and pits and flags and dragons
To make us know that we have let the world
Go by us. Have you missed the world so much
That you must have it in with all its clots
And wounds and bristles on to make us happy—
Like Blaise, with shouts and horns and seven men
Triumphant with a most unlovely boar?
Is there no other story in the world
Than this one of a man that you made king
To be a moral for the speckled ages?
You said once long ago, if you remember,
'You are too strange a lady to fear specks';
And it was you, you said, who feared them not.
Why do you look at me as at a snake

MERLIN

All coiled to spring at you and strike you dead?
I am not going to spring at you, or bite you;
I'm going home. And you, if you are kind,
Will have no fear to wander for an hour.
I'm sure the time has come for you to wander;
And there may come a time for you to say
What most you think it is that we need here
To make of this Broceliande a refuge
Where two disheartened sinners may forget
A world that has today no place for them."

A melancholy wave of revelation
Broke over Merlin like a rising sea,
Long viewed unwillingly and long denied.
He saw what he had seen, but would not feel,
Till now the bitterness of what he felt
Was in his throat, and all the coldness of it
Was on him and around him like a flood
Of lonelier memories than he had said
Were memories, although he knew them now
For what they were—for what his eyes had seen,
For what his ears had heard and what his heart
Had felt, with him not knowing what it felt.
But now he knew that his cold angel's name
Was Change, and that a mightier will than his
Or Vivian's had ordained that he be there.
To Vivian he could not say anything
But words that had no more of hope in them
Than anguish had of peace: "I meant the world . . .
I meant the world," he groaned; "not you—not me."

Again the frózen line of irony
Was on her mouth. He looked up once at it.
And then away—too fearful of her eyes
To see what he could hear now in her laugh

That melted slowly into what she said,
Like snow in icy water: "This world of yours
Will surely be the end of us. And why not?
I'm overmuch afraid we're part of it,—
Or why do we build walls up all around us,
With gates of iron that make us think the day
Of judgment's coming when they clang behind us?
And yet you tell me that you fear no specks!
With you I never cared for them enough
To think of them. I was too strange a lady.
And your return is now a speckled king
And something that you call a living sin—
That's like an uninvited poor relation
Who comes without a welcome, rather late,
And on a foundered horse."

"Specks? What are specks?"
He gazed at her in a forlorn wonderment
That made her say: "You said, 'I fear them not.'
'If I were king in Camelot,' you said,
'I might fear more than specks.' Have you forgotten?
Don't tell me, Merlin, you are growing old.
Why don't you make somehow a queen of me,
And give me half the world? I'd wager thrushes
That I should reign, with you to turn the wheel,
As well as any king that ever was.
The curse on me is that I cannot serve
A ruler who forgets that he is king."

In his bewildered misery Merlin then
Stared hard at Vivian's face, more like a slave
Who sought for common mercy than like Merlin:
"You speak a language that was never mine,
Or I have lost my wits. Why do you seize
The flimsiest of opportunities

MERLIN

To make of what I said another thing
Than love or reason could have let me say,
Or let me fancy? Why do you keep the truth
So far away from me, when all your gates
Will open at your word and let me go
To some place where no fear or weariness
Of yours need ever dwell? Why does a woman,
Made otherwise a miracle of love
And loveliness, and of immortal beauty,
Tear one word by the roots out of a thousand,
And worry it, and torture it, and shake it,
Like a small dog that has a rag to play with?
What coil of an ingenious destiny
Is this that makes of what I never meant
A meaning as remote as hell from heaven?"

"I don't know," Vivian said reluctantly,
And half as if in pain; "I'm going home.
I'm going home and leave you here to wander,
Pray take your kings and sins away somewhere
And bury them, and bury the Queen in also.
I know this king; he lives in Camelot,
And I shall never like him. There are specks
Almost all over him. Long live the king,
But not the king who lives in Camelot,
With Modred, Lancelot, and Guinevere—
And all four speckled like a merry nest
Of addled eggs together. You made him King
Because you loved the world and saw in him
From infancy a mirror for the millions.
The world will see itself in him, and then
The world will say its prayers and wash its face,
And build for some new king a new foundation.
Long live the King! . . . But now I apprehend
A time for me to shudder and grow old

And garrulous—and so become a fright
For Blaise to take out walking in warm weather—
Should I give way to long considering
Of worlds you may have lost while prisoned here
With me and my light mind. I contemplate
Another name for this forbidden place,
And one more fitting. Tell me, if you find it,
Some fitter name than Eden. We have had
A man and woman in it for some time,
And now, it seems, we have a Tree of Knowledge."
She looked up at the branches overhead
And shrugged her shoulders. Then she went away;
And what was left of Merlin's happiness,
Like a disloyal phantom, followed her.

He felt the sword of his cold angel thrust
And twisted in his heart, as if the end
Were coming next, but the cold angel passed
Invisibly and left him desolate,
With misty brow and eyes. "The man who sees
May see too far, and he may see too late
The path he takes unseen," he told himself
When he found thought again. "The man who sees
May go on seeing till the immortal flame
That lights and lures him folds him in its heart,
And leaves of what there was of him to die
An item of inhospitable dust
That love and hate alike must hide away;
Or there may still be charted for his feet
A dimmer faring, where the touch of time
Were like the passing of a twilight moth
From flower to flower into oblivion,
If there were not somewhere a barren end
Of moths and flowers, and glimmering far away
Beyond a desert where the flowerless days

MERLIN

Are told in slow defeats and agonies,
The guiding of a nameless light that once
Had made him see too much—and has by now
Revealed in death, to the undying child
Of Lancelot, the Grail. For this pure light
Has many rays to throw, for many men
To follow; and the wise are not all pure,
Nor are the pure all wise who follow it.
There are more rays than men. But let the man
Who saw too much, and was to drive himself
From paradise, play too lightly or too long
Among the moths and flowers, he finds at last
There is a dim way out; and he shall grope
Where pleasant shadows lead him to the plain
That has no shadow save his own behind him.
And there, with no complaint, nor much regret,
Shall he plod on, with death between him now
And the far light that guides him, till he falls
And has an empty thought of empty rest;
Then Fate will put a mattock in his hands
And lash him while he digs himself the grave
That is to be the pallet and the shroud
Of his poor blundering bones. The man who saw
Too much must have an eye to see at last
Where Fate has marked the clay; and he shall delve,
Although his hand may slacken, and his knees
May rock without a method as he toils;
For there's a delving that is to be done—
If not for God, for man. I see the light,
But I shall fall before I come to it;
For I am old. I was young yesterday.
Time's hand that I have held away so long
Grips hard now on my shoulder. Time has won.
Tomorrow I shall say to Vivian

That I am old and gaunt and garrulous,
And tell her one more story: I am old."

There were long hours for Merlin after that,
And much long wandering in his prison-yard,
Where now the progress of each heavy step
Confirmed a stillness of impending change
And imminent farewell. To Vivian's ear
There came for many days no other story
Than Merlin's iteration of his love
And his departure from Broceliande,
Where Merlin still remained. In Vivian's eye,
There was a quiet kindness, and at times
A smoky flash of incredulity
That faded into pain. Was this the Merlin—
This incarnation of idolatry
And all but supplicating deference—
This bowed and reverential contradiction
Of all her dreams and her realities—
Was this the Merlin who for years and years
Before she found him had so made her love him
That kings and princes, thrones and diadems,
And honorable men who drowned themselves
For love, were less to her than melon-shells?
Was this the Merlin whom her fate had sent
One spring day to come ringing at her gate,
Bewildering her love with happy terror
That later was to be all happiness?
Was this the Merlin who had made the world
Half over, and then left it with a laugh
To be the youngest, oldest, weirdest, gayest,
And wisest, and sometimes the foolishest
Of all the men of her consideration?
Was this the man who had made other men
As ordinary as arithmetic?

MERLIN

Was this man Merlin who came now so slowly
Towards the fountain where she stood again
In shimmering green? Trembling, he took her hands
And pressed them fondly, one upon the other,
Between his:

           "I was wrong that other day,
For I have one more story. I am old."
He waited like one hungry for the word
Not said; and she found in his eyes a light
As patient as a candle in a window
That looks upon the sea and is a mark
For ships that have gone down. "Tomorrow," he said;
"Tomorrow I shall go away again
To Camelot; and I shall see the King
Once more; and I may come to you again
Once more; and I shall go away again
For ever. There is now no more than that
For me to do; and I shall do no more.
I saw too much when I saw Camelot;
And I saw farther backward into Time,
And forward, than a man may see and live,
When I made Arthur king. I saw too far,
But not so far as this. Fate played with me
As I have played with Time; and Time, like me,
Being less than Fate, will have on me his vengeance.
On Fate there is no vengeance, even for God."
He drew her slowly into his embrace
And held her there, but when he kissed her lips
They were as cold as leaves and had no answer;
For Time had given him then, to prove his words,
A frozen moment of a woman's life.

When Merlin the next morning came again
In the same pilgrim robe that he had worn

While he sat waiting where the cherry-blossoms
Outside the gate fell on him and around him
Grief came to Vivian at the sight of him;
And like a flash of a swift ugly knife,
A blinding fear came with it. "Are you going?"
She said, more with her lips than with her voice;
And he said, "I am going. Blaise and I
Are going down together to the shore,
And Blaise is coming back. For this one day
Be good enough to spare him, for I like him.
I tell you now, as once I told the King,
That I can be no more than what I was,
And I can say no more than I have said.
Sometimes you told me that I spoke too long
And sent me off to wander. That was good.
I go now for another wandering,
And I pray God that all be well with you."

For long there was a whining in her ears
Of distant wheels departing. When it ceased,
She closed the gate again so quietly
That Merlin could have heard no sound of it.

VII

By Merlin's Rock, where Dagonet the fool
Was given through many a dying afternoon
To sit and meditate on human ways
And ways divine, Gawaine and Bedivere
Stood silent, gazing down on Camelot.
The two had risen and were going home:
"It hits me sore, Gawaine," said Bedivere,
"To think on all the tumult and affliction
Down there, and all the noise and preparation

MERLIN

That hums of coming death, and, if my fears
Be born of reason, of what's more than death.
Wherefore, I say to you again, Gawaine,—
To you—that this late hour is not too late
For you to change yourself and change the King:
For though the King may love me with a love
More tried, and older, and more sure, may be,
Than for another, for such a time as this
The friend who turns him to the world again
Shall have a tongue more gracious and an eye
More shrewd than mine. For such a time as this
The King must have a glamour to persuade him."

"The King shall have a glamour, and anon,"
Gawaine said, and he shot death from his eyes;
"If you were King, as Arthur is—or was—
And Lancelot had carried off your Queen,
And killed a score or so of your best knights—
Not mentioning my two brothers, whom he slew
Unarmored and unarmed—God save your wits!
Two stewards with skewers could have done as much,
And you and I might now be rotting for it."

"But Lancelot's men were crowded,—they were crushed;
And there was nothing for them but to strike
Or die, not seeing where they struck. Think you
They would have slain Gareth and Gaheris,
And Tor, and all those other friends of theirs?
God's mercy for the world he made, I say,
And for the blood that writes the story of it.
Gareth and Gaheris, Tor and Lamorak,—
All dead, with all the others that are dead!
These years have made me turn to Lamorak
For counsel—and now Lamorak is dead."

"Why do you fling those two names in my face?
'Twas Modred made an end of Lamorak,
Not I; and Lancelot now has done for Tor.
I'll urge no king on after Lancelot
For such a two as Tor and Lamorak:
Their father killed my father, and their friend
Was Lancelot, not I. I'll own my fault—
I'm living; and while I've a tongue can talk,
I'll say this to the King: 'Burn Lancelot
By inches till he give you back the Queen;
Then hang him—drown him—or do anything
To rid the world of him.' He killed my brothers,
And he was once my friend. Now damn the soul
Of him who killed my brothers! There you have me."

"You are a strong man, Gawaine, and your strength
Goes ill where foes are. You may cleave their limbs
And heads off, but you cannot damn their souls;
What you may do now is to save their souls,
And bodies too, and like enough your own.
Remember that King Arthur is a king,
And where there is a king there is a kingdom.
Is not the kingdom any more to you
Than one brief enemy? Would you see it fall
And the King with it, for one mortal hate
That burns out reason? Gawaine, you are king
Today. Another day may see no king
But Havoc, if you have no other word
For Arthur now than hate for Lancelot.
Is not the world as large as Lancelot?
Is Lancelot, because one woman's eyes
Are brighter when they look on him, to sluice
The world with angry blood? Poor flesh! Poor flesh!
And you, Gawaine,—are you so gaffed with hate
You cannot leave it and so plunge away

MERLIN

To stiller places and there see, for once,
What hangs on this pernicious expedition
The King in his insane forgetfulness
Would undertake—with you to drum him on?
Are you as mad as he and Lancelot
Made ravening into one man twice as mad
As either? Is the kingdom of the world,
Now rocking, to go down in sound and blood
And ashes and sick ruin, and for the sake
Of three men and a woman? If it be so,
God's mercy for the world he made, I say,—
And say again to Dagonet. Sir Fool,
Your throne is empty, and you may as well
Sit on it and be ruler of the world
From now till supper-time."

                         Sir Dagonet,
Appearing, made reply to Bedivere's
Dry welcome with a famished look of pain,
On which he built a smile: "If I were King,
You, Bedivere, should be my counsellor;
And we should have no more wars over women.
I'll sit me down and meditate on that."
Gawaine, for all his anger, laughed a little,
And clapped the fool's lean shoulder; for he loved him
And was with Arthur when he made him knight.
Then Dagonet said on to Bedivere,
As if his tongue would make a jest of sorrow:
"Sometime I'll tell you what I might have done
Had I been Lancelot and you King Arthur—
Each having in himself the vicious essence
That now lives in the other and makes war.
When all men are like you and me, my lord,
When all are rational or rickety,
There may be no more war. But what's here now?

Lancelot loves the Queen, and he makes war
Of love; the King, being bitten to the soul
By love and hate that work in him together,
Makes war of madness; Gawaine hates Lancelot,
And he, to be in tune, makes war of hate;
Modred hates everything, yet he can see
With one damned illegitimate small eye
His father's crown, and with another like it
He sees the beauty of the Queen herself;
He needs the two for his ambitious pleasure,
And therefore he makes war of his ambition;
And somewhere in the middle of all this
There's a squeezed world that elbows for attention.
Poor Merlin, buried in Broceliande!
He must have had an academic eye
For woman when he founded Arthur's kingdom,
And in Broceliande he may be sorry.
Flutes, hautboys, drums, and viols. God be with him!
I'm glad they tell me there's another world,
For this one's a disease without a doctor."

"No, not so bad as that," said Bedivere;
The doctor, like ourselves, may now be learning;
And Merlin may have gauged his enterprise
Whatever the cost he may have paid for knowing.
We pass, but many are to follow us,
And what they build may stay; though I believe
Another age will have another Merlin,
Another Camelot, and another King.
Sir Dagonet, farewell."

                    "Farewell, Sir Knight,
And you, Sir Knight: Gawaine, you have the world
Now in your fingers—an uncommon toy,
Albeit a small persuasion in the balance

MERLIN

With one man's hate. I'm glad you're not a fool,
For then you might be rickety, as I am,
And rational as Bedivere. Farewell.
I'll sit here and be king. God save the King!"

But Gawaine scowled and frowned and answered nothing
As he went slowly down with Bedivere
To Camelot, where Arthur's army waited
The King's word for the melancholy march
To Joyous Gard, where Lancelot hid the Queen
And armed his host, and there was now no joy,
As there was now no joy for Dagonet
While he sat brooding, with his wan cheek-bones
Hooked with his bony fingers: "Go, Gawaine,"
He mumbled: "Go your way, and drag the world
Along down with you. What's a world or so
To you if you can hide an ell of iron
Somewhere in Lancelot, and hear him wheeze
And sputter once or twice before he goes
Wherever the Queen sends him? There's a man
Who should have been a king, and would have been,
Had he been born so. So should I have been
A king, had I been born so, fool or no:
King Dagonet, or Dagonet the King;
King-Fool, Fool-King; 'twere not impossible.
I'll meditate on that and pray for Arthur,
Who made me all I am, except a fool.
Now he goes mad for love, as I might go
Had I been born a king and not a fool.
Today I think I'd rather be a fool;
Today the world is less than one scared woman—
Wherefore a field of waving men may soon
Be shorn by Time's indifferent scythe, because
The King is mad. The seeds of history
Are small, but given a few gouts of warm blood

For quickening, they sprout out wondrously
And have a leaping growth whereof no man
May shun such harvesting of change or death,
Or life, as may fall on him to be borne
When I am still alive and rickety,
And Bedivere's alive and rational—
If he come out of this, and there's a doubt,—
The King, Gawaine, Modred, and Lancelot
May all be lying underneath a weight
Of bloody sheaves too heavy for their shoulders
All spent, and all dishonored, and all dead;
And if it come to be that this be so,
And it be true that Merlin saw the truth,
Such harvest were the best. Your fool sees not
So far as Merlin sees: yet if he saw
The truth—why then, such harvest were the best.
I'll pray for Arthur; I can do no more."

"Why not for Merlin? Or do you count him,
In this extreme, so foreign to salvation
That prayer would be a stranger to his name?"

Poor Dagonet, with terror shaking him,
Stood up and saw before him an old face
Made older with an inch of silver beard,
And faded eyes more eloquent of pain
And ruin than all the faded eyes of age
Till now had ever been, although in them
There was a mystic and intrinsic peace
Of one who sees where men of nearer sight
See nothing. On their way to Camelot,
Gawaine and Bedivere had passed him by,
With lax attention for the pilgrim cloak
They passed, and what it hid: yet Merlin saw

MERLIN

Their faces, and he saw the tale was true
That he had lately drawn from solemn strangers.

"Well, Dagonet, and by your leave," he said,
"I'll rest my lonely relics for a while
On this rock that was mine and now is yours.
I favor the succession; for you know
Far more than many doctors, though your doubt
Is your peculiar poison. I foresaw
Long since, and I have latterly been told
What moves in this commotion down below
To show men what it means. It means the end—
If men whose tongues had less to say to me
Than had their shoulders are adept enough
To know; and you may pray for me or not,
Sir Friend, Sir Dagonet."

               "Sir fool, you mean,"
Dagonet said, and gazed on Merlin sadly:
"I'll never pray again for anything,
And last of all for this that you behold—
The smouldering faggot of unlovely bones
That God has given to me to call Myself.
When Merlin comes to Dagonet for prayer,
It is indeed the end."

               "And in the end
Are more beginnings, Dagonet, than men
Shall name or know today. It was the end
Of Arthur's insubstantial majesty
When to him and his knights the Grail foreshowed
The quest of life that was to be the death
Of many, and the slow discouraging
Of many more. Or do I err in this?"

"No," Dagonet replied; "there was a Light;
And Galahad, in the Siege Perilous,
Alone of all on whom it fell, was calm;
There was a Light wherein men saw themselves
In one another as they might become—
Or so they dreamed. There was a long to-do,
And Gawaine, of all forlorn ineligibles,
Rose up the first, and cried more lustily
Than any after him that he should find
The Grail, or die for it,—though he did neither;
For he came back as living and as fit
For new and old iniquity as ever.
Then Lancelot came back, and Bors came back,—
Like men who had seen more than men should see,
And still come back. They told of Percival
Who saw too much to make of this worn life
A long necessity, and of Galahad,
Who died and is alive. They all saw Something.
God knows the meaning or the end of it,
But they saw Something. And if I've an eye,
Small joy has the Queen been to Lancelot
Since he came back from seeing what he saw;
For though his passion hold him like hot claws,
He's neither in the world nor out of it.
Gawaine is king, though Arthur wears the crown;
And Gawaine's hate for Lancelot is the sword
That hangs by one of Merlin's fragile hairs
Above the world. Were you to see the King,
The frenzy that has overthrown his wisdom,
Instead of him and his upheaving empire,
Might have an end."

                        "I came to see the King,"
Said Merlin, like a man who labors hard
And long with an importunate confession.

MERLIN

"No, Dagonet, you cannot tell me why,
Although your tongue is eager with wild hope
To tell me more than I may tell myself
About myself. All this that was to be
Might show to man how vain it were to wreck
The world for self if it were all in vain.
When I began with Arthur I could see
In each bewildered man who dots the earth
A moment with his days a groping thought
Of an eternal will, strangely endowed
With merciful illusions whereby self
Becomes the will itself and each man swells
In fond accordance with his agency.
Now Arthur, Modred, Lancelot, and Gawaine
Are swollen thoughts of this eternal will
Which have no other way to find the way
That leads them on to their inheritance
Than by the time-infuriating flame
Of a wrecked empire, lighted by the torch
Of woman, who, together with the light
That Galahad found, is yet to light the world."

A wan smile crept across the weary face
Of Dagonet the fool: "If you knew that
Before your burial in Broceliande,
No wonder your eternal will accords
With all your dreams of what the world requires.
My master, I may say this unto you
Because I am a fool, and fear no man;
My fear is that I've been a groping thought
That never swelled enough. You say the torch
Of woman and the light that Galahad found
Are some day to illuminate the world?
I'll meditate on that. The world is done
For me; and I have been. to make men laugh,

A lean thing of no shape and many capers.
I made them laugh, and I could laugh anon
Myself to see them killing one another
Because a woman with corn-colored hair
Has pranked a man with horns. 'Twas but a flash
Of chance, and Lancelot, the other day
That saved this pleasing sinner from the fire
That she may spread for thousands. Were she now
The cinder the King willed, or were you now
To see the King, the fire might yet go out;
But the eternal will says otherwise.
So be it; I'll assemble certain gold
That I may say is mine and get myself
Away from this accurst unhappy court,
And in some quiet place where shepherd clowns
And cowherds may have more respondent ears
Than kings and kingdom-builders, I shall troll
Old men to easy graves and be a child
Again among the children of the earth.
I'll have no more kings, even though I loved
King Arthur, who is mad, as I could love
No other man save Merlin, who is dead."

"Not wholly dead, but old. Merlin is old."
The wizard shivered as he spoke, and stared
Away into the sunset where he saw
Once more, as through a cracked and cloudy glass,
A crumbling sky that held a crimson cloud
Wherein there was a town of many towers
All swayed and shaken, in a woman's hand
This time, till out of it there spilled and flashed
And tumbled, like loose jewels, town, towers, and walls,
And there was nothing but a crumbling sky
That made anon of black and red and ruin
A wild and final rain on Camelot.

MERLIN

He bowed, and pressed his eyes: "Now by my soul,
I have seen this before—all black and red—
Like that—like that—like Vivian—black and red;
Like Vivian, when her eyes looked into mine
Across the cups of gold. A flute was playing—
Then all was black and red."

                              Another smile
Crept over the wan face of Dagonet,
Who shivered in his turn. "The torch of woman,"
He muttered, "and the light that Galahad found,
Will some day save us all, as they saved Merlin.
Forgive my shivering wits, but I am cold,
And it will soon be dark. Will you go down
With me to see the King, or will you not?
If not, I go tomorrow to the shepherds.
The world is mad, and I'm a groping thought
Of your eternal will; the world and I
Are strangers, and I'll have no more of it—
Except you go with me to see the King."

"No, Dagonet, you cannot leave me now,"
Said Merlin, sadly. "You and I are old;
And, as you say, we fear no man. God knows
I would not have the love that once you had
For me be fear of me, for I am past
All fearing now. But Fate may send a fly
Sometimes, and he may sting us to the grave,
So driven to test our faith in what we see.
Are you, now I am coming to an end,
As Arthur's days are coming to an end,
To sting me like a fly? I do not ask
Of you to say that you see what I see,
Where you see nothing; nor do I require
Of any man more vision than is his;

Yet I could wish for you a larger part
For your last entrance here than this you play
Tonight of a sad insect stinging Merlin.
The more you sting, the more he pities you;
And you were never overfond of pity.
Had you been so, I doubt if Arthur's love,
Or Gawaine's, would have made of you a knight.
No, Dagonet, you cannot leave me now,
Nor would you if you could. You call yourself
A fool, because the world and you are strangers.
You are a proud man, Dagonet; you have suffered
What I alone have seen. You are no fool;
And surely you are not a fly to sting
My love to last regret. Believe or not
What I have seen, or what I say to you,
But say no more to me that I am dead
Because the King is mad, and you are old,
And I am older. In Broceliande
Time overtook me as I knew he must;
And I, with a fond overplus of words,
Had warned the lady Vivian already,
Before these wrinkles and this hesitancy
Inhibiting my joints oppressed her sight
With age and dissolution. She said once
That she was cold and cruel; but she meant
That she was warm and kind, and over-wise
For woman in a world where men see not
Beyond themselves. She saw beyond them all,
As I did; and she waited, as I did,
The coming of a day when cherry-blossoms
Were to fall down all over me like snow
In springtime. I was far from Camelot
That afternoon; and I am farther now
From her. I see no more for me to do
Than to leave her and Arthur and the world

MERLIN

Behind me, and to pray that all be well
With Vivian, whose unquiet heart is hungry
For what is not, and what shall never be
Without her, in a world that men are making,
Knowing not how, nor caring yet to know
How slowly and how grievously they do it,—
Though Vivian, in her golden shell of exile,
Knows now and cares, not knowing that she cares,
Nor caring that she knows. In time to be,
The like of her shall have another name
Than Vivian, and her laugh shall be a fire,
Not shining only to consume itself
With what it burns. She knows not yet the name
Of what she is, for now there is no name;
Some day there shall be. Time has many names,
Unwritten yet, for what we say is old
Because we are so young that it seems old.
And this is all a part of what I saw
Before you saw King Arthur. When we parted.
I told her I should see the King again,
And, having seen him, might go back again
To see her face once more. But I shall see
No more the lady Vivian. Let her love
What man she may, no other love than mine
Shall be an index of her memories.
I fear no man who may come after me,
And I see none. I see her, still in green,
Beside the fountain. I shall not go back.
We pay for going back; and all we get
Is one more needless ounce of weary wisdom
To bring away with us. If I come not,
The lady Vivian will remember me,
And say: 'I knew him when his heart was young,
Though I have lost him now. Time called him home,

And that was as it was; for much is lost
Between Broceliande and Camelot.'"

He stared away into the west again,
Where now no crimson cloud or phantom town
Deceived his eyes. Above a living town
There were gray clouds and ultimate suspense,
And a cold wind was coming. Dagonet,
Now crouched at Merlin's feet in his dejection,
Saw multiplying lights far down below,
Where lay the fevered streets. At length he felt
On his lean shoulder Merlin's tragic hand
And trembled, knowing that a few more days
Would see the last of Arthur and the first
Of Modred, whose dark patience had attained
To one precarious half of what he sought:
"And even the Queen herself may fall to him,"
Dagonet murmured.—"The Queen fall to Modred?
Is that your only fear tonight?" said Merlin;
"She may, but not for long."—"No, not my fear;
For I fear nothing. But I wish no fate
Like that for any woman the King loves,
Although she be the scourge and the end of him
That you saw coming, as I see it now."
Dagonet shook, but he would have no tears,
He swore, for any king, queen, knave, or wizard—
Albeit he was a stranger among those
Who laughed at him because he was a fool.
"You said the truth, I cannot leave you now,"
He stammered, and was angry for the tears
That mocked his will and choked him.

         Merlin smiled,
Faintly, and for the moment: "Dagonet,
I need your word as one of Arthur's knights

MERLIN

That you will go on with me to the end
Of my short way, and say unto no man
Or woman that you found or saw me here.
No good would follow, for a doubt would live
Unstifled of my loyalty to him
Whose deeds are wrought for those who are to come;
And many who see not what I have seen,
Or what you see tonight, would prattle on
For ever, and their children after them,
Of what might once have been had I gone down
With you to Camelot to see the King.
I came to see the King,—but why see kings?
All this that was to be is what I saw
Before there was an Arthur to be king,
And so to be a mirror wherein men
May see themselves, and pause. If they see not,
Or if they do see and they ponder not,—
I saw; but I was neither Fate nor God.
I saw too much; and this would be the end,
Were there to be an end. I saw myself—
A sight no other man has ever seen;
And through the dark that lay beyond myself
I saw two fires that are to light the world."

On Dagonet the silent hand of Merlin
Weighed now as living iron that held him down
With a primeval power. Doubt, wonderment,
Impatience, and a self-accusing sorrow
Born of an ancient love, possessed and held him
Until his love was more than he could name,
And he was Merlin's fool, not Arthur's now:
"Say what you will, I say that I'm the fool
Of Merlin, King of Nowhere; which is Here.
With you for king and me for court, what else
Have we to sigh for but a place to sleep?

I know a tavern that will take us in;
And on the morrow I shall follow you
Until I die for you. And when I die . . ."—
"Well, Dagonet, the King is listening."—
And Dagonet answered, hearing in the words
Of Merlin a grave humor and a sound
Of graver pity, "I shall die a fool."
He heard what might have been a father's laugh,
Faintly behind him; and the living weight
Of Merlin's hand was lifted. They arose,
And, saying nothing, found a groping way
Down through the gloom together. Fiercer now,
The wind was like a flying animal
That beat the two of them incessantly
With icy wings, and bit them as they went.
The rock above them was an empty place
Where neither seer nor fool should view again
The stricken city. Colder blew the wind
Across the world, and on it heavier lay
The shadow and the burden of the night;
And there was darkness over Camelot.

THE TOWN DOWN THE RIVER
(1910)
To Theodore Roosevelt

THE TOWN DOWN THE RIVER
(1910)
To Theodore Roosevelt

THE MASTER *

(Lincoln)

A FLYING word from here and there
Had sown the name at which we sneered,
But soon the name was everywhere,
To be reviled and then revered:
A presence to be loved and feared,
We cannot hide it, or deny
That we, the gentlemen who jeered,
May be forgotten by and by.

He came when days were perilous
And hearts of men were sore beguiled;
And having made his note of us,
He pondered and was reconciled.
Was ever master yet so mild
As he, and so untamable?
We doubted, even when he smiled,
Not knowing what he knew so well.

He knew that undeceiving fate
Would shame us whom he served unsought;
He knew that he must wince and wait—
The jest of those for whom he fought;

* Supposed to have been written not long after the Civil War.

He knew devoutly what he thought
Of us and of our ridicule;
He knew that we must all be taught
Like little children in a school.

We gave a glamour to the task
That he encountered and saw through,
But little of us did he ask,
And little did we ever do.
And what appears if we review
The season when we railed and chaffed?
It is the face of one who knew
That we were learning while we laughed.

The face that in our vision feels
Again the venom that we flung,
Transfigured to the world reveals
The vigilance to which we clung.
Shrewd, hallowed, harassed, and among
The mysteries that are untold,
The face we see was never young
Nor could it wholly have been old.

For he, to whom we had applied
Our shopman's test of age and worth,
Was elemental when he died,
As he was ancient at his birth:
The saddest among kings of earth,
Bowed with a galling crown, this man
Met rancor with a cryptic mirth,
Laconic—and Olympian.

The love, the grandeur, and the fame
Are bounded by the world alone;

THE TOWN DOWN THE RIVER

The calm, the smouldering, and the flame
Of awful patience were his own:
With him they are forever flown
Past all our fond self-shadowings,
Wherewith we cumber the Unknown
As with inept, Icarian wings.

For we were not as other men:
'Twas ours to soar and his to see;
But we are coming down again,
And we shall come down pleasantly;
Nor shall we longer disagree
On what it is to be sublime,
But flourish in our perigee
And have one Titan at a time.

THE TOWN DOWN THE RIVER

I

SAID the Watcher by the Way
To the young and the unladen,
To the boy and to the maiden,
"God be with you both to-day.
First your song came ringing,
Now you come, you two,—
Knowing naught of what you do,
Or of what your dreams are bringing.

"O you children who go singing
To the Town down the River,
Where the millions cringe and shiver,
Tell me what you know to-day;
Tell me how far you are going,

Tell me how you find your way.
O you children who go dreaming,
Tell me what you dream to-day."

"He is old and we have heard him,"
Said the boy then to the maiden;
"He is old and heavy laden
With a load we throw away.
Care may come to find us,
Age may lay us low;
Still, we seek the light we know,
And the dead we leave behind us.

"Did he think that he would blind us
Into such a small believing
As to live without achieving,
When the lights have led so far?
Let him watch or let him wither,—
Shall he tell us where we are?
We know best who go together,
Downward, onward, and so far."

II

SAID the Watcher by the Way
To the fiery folk that hastened,
To the loud and the unchastened,
"You are strong, I see, to-day.
Strength and hope may lead you
To the journey's end,—
Each to be the other's friend
If the Town should fail to need you.

"And are ravens there to feed you
In the Town down the River,

THE TOWN DOWN THE RIVER

Where the gift appalls the giver
And youth hardens day by day?
O you brave and you unshaken,
Are you truly on your way?
And are sirens in the River,
That you come so far to-day?"

"You are old, and we have listened,"
Said the voice of one who halted;
"You are sage and self-exalted,
But your way is not our way.
You that cannot aid us
Give us words to eat.
Be assured that they are sweet,
And that we are as God made us.

"Not in vain have you delayed us,
Though the River still be calling
Through the twilight that is falling
And the Town be still so far.
By the whirlwind of your wisdom
Leagues are lifted as leaves are;
But a king without a kingdom
Fails us, who have come so far."

III

SAID the Watcher by the Way
To the slower folk who stumbled,
To the weak and the world-humbled,
"Tell me how you fare to-day.
Some with ardor shaken,
All with honor scarred,
Do you falter, finding hard
The far chance that you have taken?

"Or, do you at length awaken
To an antic retribution,
Goading to a new confusion
The drugged hopes of yesterday?
O you poor mad men that hobble,
Will you not return, or stay?
Do you trust, you broken people,
To a dawn without the day?"

"You speak well of what you know not,"
Muttered one; and then a second:
"You have begged and you have beckoned,
But you see us on our way.
Who are you to scold us,
Knowing what we know?
Jeremiah, long ago,
Said as much as you have told us.

"As we are, then, you behold us:
Derelicts of all conditions,
Poets, rogues, and sick physicians,
Plodding forward from afar;
Forward now into the darkness
Where the men before us are;
Forward, onward, out of grayness,
To the light that shone so far."

IV

Said the Watcher by the Way
To some aged ones who lingered,
To the shrunken, the claw-fingered,
"So you come for me to-day."—
"Yes, to give you warning;
You are old," one said;

AN ISLAND

"You have old hairs on your head,
Fit for laurel, not for scorning.

"From the first of early morning
We have toiled along to find you;
We, as others, have maligned you,
But we need your scorn to-day.
By the light that we saw shining,
Let us not be lured alway;
Let us hear no River calling
When to-morrow is to-day."

"But your lanterns are unlighted
And the Town is far before you:
Let us hasten, I implore you,"
Said the Watcher by the Way.
"Long have I waited,
Longer have I known
That the Town would have its own,
And the call be for the fated.

"In the name of all created,
Let us hear no more, my brothers;
Are we older than all others?
Are the planets in our way?"—
"Hark," said one; "I hear the River,
Calling always, night and day."—
"Forward, then! The lights are shining,"
Said the Watcher by the Way.

AN ISLAND

(Saint Helena, 1821)

TAKE it away, and swallow it yourself.
Ha! Look you, there's a rat.

Last night there were a dozen on that shelf,
And two of them were living in my hat.
Look! Now he goes, but he'll come back—
Ha? But he will, I say . .
*Il reviendra-z-à Pâques,
Ou à la Trinité* . . .
Be very sure that he'll return again;
For said the Lord: Imprimis, we have rats,
And having rats, we have rain.—
So on the seventh day
He rested, and made Pain.
—Man, if you love the Lord, and if the Lord
Love liars, I will have you at your word
And swallow it. *Voilà.* Bah!

Where do I say it is
That I have lain so long?
Where do I count myself among the dead,
As once above the living and the strong?
And what is this that comes and goes,
Fades and swells and overflows,
Like music underneath and overhead?
What is it in me now that rings and roars
Like fever-laden wine?
What ruinous tavern-shine
Is this that lights me far from worlds and wars
And women that were mine?
Where do I say it is
That Time has made my bed?
What lowering outland hostelry is this
For one the stars have disinherited?

An island, I have said:
A peak, where fiery dreams and far desires
Are rained on, like old fires:

AN ISLAND

A vermin region by the stars abhorred,
Where falls the flaming word
By which I consecrate with unsuccess
An acreage of God's forgetfulness,
Left here above the foam and long ago
Made right for my duress;
Where soon the sea,
My foaming and long-clamoring enemy,
Will have within the cryptic, old embrace
Of her triumphant arms—a memory.
Why then, the place?
What forage of the sky or of the shore
Will make it any more,
To me, than my award of what was left
Of number, time, and space?

And what is on me now that I should heed
The durance or the silence or the scorn?
I was the gardener who had the seed
Which holds within its heart the food and fire
That gives to man a glimpse of his desire;
And I have tilled, indeed,
Much land, where men may say that I have planted
Unsparingly my corn—
For a world harvest-haunted
And for a world unborn.

Meanwhile, am I to view, as at a play,
Through smoke the funeral flames of yesterday,
And think them far away?
Am I to doubt and yet be given to know
That where my demon guides me, there I go?—
An island? Be it so.
For islands, after all is said and done,
Tell but a wilder game that was begun,

When Fate, the mistress of iniquities,
The mad Queen-spinner of all discrepancies,
Beguiled the dyers of the dawn that day,
And even in such a curst and sodden way
Made my three colors one.
—So be it, and the way be as of old:
So be the weary truth again retold
Of great kings overthrown
Because they would be kings, and lastly kings alone.
Fling to each dog his bone.

Flags that are vanished, flags that are soiled and furled,
Say what will be the word when I am gone:
What learned little acrid archive men
Will burrow to find me out and burrow again,—
But all for naught, unless
To find there was another Island. . . . Yes,
There are too many islands in this world,
There are too many rats, and there is too much rain.
So three things are made plain
Between the sea and sky:
Three separate parts of one thing, which is Pain . . .
Bah, what a way to die!—
To leave my Queen still spinning there on high,
Still wondering, I dare say,
To see me in this way . . .
Madame à sa tour monte
Si haut qu'elle peut monter—
Like one of our Commissioners . . . *ai! ai!*
Prometheus and the women have to cry,
But no, not I . . .
Faugh, what a way to die!

But who are these that come and go
Before me, shaking laurel as they pass?

AN ISLAND

Laurel, to make me know
For certain what they mean:
That now my Fate, my Queen,
Having found that she, by way of right reward,
Will after madness go remembering,
And laurel be as grass,—
Remembers the one thing
That she has left to bring.
The floor about me now is like a sward
Grown royally. Now it is like a sea
That heaves with laurel heavily,
Surrendering an outworn enmity
For what has come to be.

But not for you, returning with your curled
And haggish lips. And why are you alone?
Why do you stay when all the rest are gone?
Why do you bring those treacherous eyes that reek
With venom and hate the while you seek
To make me understand?—
Laurel from every land,
Laurel, but not the world?

Fury, or perjured Fate, or whatsoever,
Tell me the bloodshot word that is your name
And I will pledge remembrance of the same
That shall be crossed out never;
Whereby posterity
May know, being told, that you have come to me,
You and your tongueless train without a sound,
With covetous hands and eyes and laurel all around,
Foreshowing your endeavor
To mirror me the demon of my days,
To make me doubt him, loathe him, face to face.
Bowed with unwilling glory from the quest

That was ordained and manifest,
You shake it off and wish me joy of it?
Laurel from every place,
Laurel, but not the rest?
Such are the words in you that I divine,
Such are the words of men.
So be it, and what then?
Poor, tottering counterfeit,
Are you a thing to tell me what is mine?

Grant we the demon sees
An inch beyond the line,
What comes of mine and thine?
A thousand here and there may shriek and freeze,
Or they may starve in fine.
The Old Physician has a crimson cure
For such as these,
And ages after ages will endure
The minims of it that are victories.
The wreath may go from brow to brow,
The state may flourish, flame, and cease;
But through the fury and the flood somehow
The demons are acquainted and at ease,
And somewhat hard to please.
Mine, I believe, is laughing at me now
In his primordial way,
Quite as he laughed of old at Hannibal,
Or rather at Alexander, let us say.
Therefore, be what you may,
Time has no further need
Of you, or of your breed.
My demon, irretrievably astray,
Has ruined the last chorus of a play
That will, so he avers, be played again some day;
And you, poor glowering ghost,

AN ISLAND

Have staggered under laurel here to boast
Above me, dying, while you lean
In triumph awkward and unclean,
About some words of his that you have read?
Thing, do I not know them all?
He tells me how the storied leaves that fall
Are tramped on, being dead?
They are sometimes: with a storm foul enough
They are seized alive and they are blown far off
To mould on islands.—What else have you read?
He tells me that great kings look very small
When they are put to bed;
And this being said,
He tells me that the battles I have won
Are not my own,
But his—howbeit fame will yet atone
For all defect, and sheave the mystery:
The follies and the slaughters I have done
Are mine alone,
And so far History.
So be the tale again retold
And leaf by clinging leaf unrolled
Where I have written in the dawn,
With ink that fades anon,
Like Cæsar's, and the way be as of old.

Ho, is it you? I thought you were a ghost.
Is it time for you to poison me again?
Well, here's our friend the rain,—
Mironton, mironton, mirontaine . . .
Man, I could murder you almost,
You with your pills and toast.
Take it away and eat it, and shoot rats.
Ha! there he comes. Your rat will never fail,
My punctual assassin, to prevail—

While he has power to crawl,
Or teeth to gnaw withal—
Where kings are caged. Why has a king no cats?
You say that I'll achieve it if I try?
Swallow it?—No, not I . . .
God, what a way to die!

CALVERLY'S

We go no more to Calverly's,
For there the lights are few and low;
And who are there to see by them,
Or what they see, we do not know.
Poor strangers of another tongue
May now creep in from anywhere,
And we, forgotten, be no more
Than twilight on a ruin there.

We two, the remnant. All the rest
Are cold and quiet. You nor I,
Nor fiddle now, nor flagon-lid,
May ring them back from where they lie.
No fame delays oblivion
For them, but something yet survives:
A record written fair, could we
But read the book of scattered lives.

There'll be a page for Leffingwell,
And one for Lingard, the Moon-calf;
And who knows what for Clavering,
Who died because he couldn't laugh?
Who knows or cares? No sign is here,
No face, no voice, no memory;

LEFFINGWELL

No Lingard with his eerie joy,
No Clavering, no Calverly.

We cannot have them here with us
To say where their light lives are gone,
Or if they be of other stuff
Than are the moons of Ilion.
So, be their place of one estate
With ashes, echoes, and old wars,—
Or ever we be of the night,
Or we be lost among the stars.

LEFFINGWELL

I—The Lure

No, no,—forget your Cricket and your Ant,
For I shall never set my name to theirs
That now bespeak the very sons and heirs
Incarnate of Queen Gossip and King Cant.
The case of Leffingwell is mixed, I grant,
And futile seems the burden that he bears;
But are we sounding his forlorn affairs
Who brand him parasite and sycophant?

I tell you, Leffingwell was more than these;
And if he prove a rather sorry knight,
What quiverings in the distance of what light
May not have lured him with high promises,
And then gone down?—He may have been deceived;
He may have lied,—he did; and he believed.

II—The Quickstep

The dirge is over, the good work is done,
All as he would have had it, and we go;

And we who leave him say we do not know
How much is ended or how much begun.
So men have said before of many a one;
So men may say of us when Time shall throw
Such earth as may be needful to bestow
On you and me the covering hush we shun.

Well hated, better loved, he played and lost,
And left us; and we smile at his arrears;
And who are we to know what it all cost,
Or what we may have wrung from him, the buyer?
The pageant of his failure-laden years
Told ruin of high price. The place was higher.

III—Requiescat

We never knew the sorrow or the pain
Within him, for he seemed as one asleep—
Until he faced us with a dying leap,
And with a blast of paramount, profane,
And vehement valediction did explain
To each of us, in words that we shall keep,
Why we were not to wonder or to weep,
Or ever dare to wish him back again.

He may be now an amiable shade,
With merry fellow-phantoms unafraid
Around him—but we do not ask. We know
That he would rise and haunt us horribly,
And be with us o' nights of a certainty.
Did we not hear him when he told us so?

CLAVERING

I say no more for Clavering
  Than I should say of him who fails
To bring his wounded vessel home
  When reft of rudder and of sails;

I say no more than I should say
  Of any other one who sees
Too far for guidance of to-day,
  Too near for the eternities.

I think of him as I should think
  Of one who for scant wages played,
And faintly, a flawed instrument
  That fell while it was being made;

I think of him as one who fared,
  Unfaltering and undeceived,
Amid mirages of renown
  And urgings of the unachieved;

I think of him as one who gave
  To Lingard leave to be amused,
And listened with a patient grace
  That we, the wise ones, had refused;

I think of metres that he wrote
  For Cubit, the ophidian guest:
"What Lilith, or Dark Lady" . . . Well,
  Time swallows Cubit with the rest.

I think of last words that he said
  One midnight over Calverly:
"Good-by—good man." He was not good;
  So Clavering was wrong, you see.

I wonder what had come to pass
  Could he have borrowed for a spell
The fiery-frantic indolence
  That made a ghost of Leffingwell;

I wonder if he pitied us
  Who cautioned him till he was gray
To build his house with ours on earth
  And have an end of yesterday;

I wonder what it was we saw
  To make us think that we were strong;
I wonder if he saw too much,
  Or if he looked one way too long.

But when were thoughts or wonderings
  To ferret out the man within?
Why prate of what he seemed to be,
  And all that he might not have been?

He clung to phantoms and to friends,
  And never came to anything.
He left a wreath on Cubit's grave.
  I say no more for Clavering.

LINGARD AND THE STARS

THE table hurled itself, to our surprise,
At Lingard, and anon rapped eagerly:
"When earth is cold and there is no more sea,
There will be what was Lingard. Otherwise,
Why lure the race to ruin through the skies?
And why have Leffingwell, or Calverly?"—

PASA THALASSA THALASSA

"I wish the ghost would give his name," said he;
And searching gratitude was in his eyes.

He stood then by the window for a time,
And only after the last midnight chime
Smote the day dead did he say anything:
"Come out, my little one, the stars are bright;
Come out, you lælaps, and inhale the night."
And so he went away with Clavering.

PASA THALASSA THALASSA

"The sea is everywhere the sea."

I

GONE—faded out of the story, the sea-faring friend I remember?
Gone for a decade, they say: never a word or a sign.
Gone with his hard red face that only his laughter could wrinkle,
Down where men go to be still, by the old way of the sea.

Never again will he come, with rings in his ears like a pirate,
Back to be living and seen, here with his roses and vines;
Here where the tenants are shadows and echoes of years uneventful,
Memory meets the event, told from afar by the sea.

Smoke that floated and rolled in the twilight away from the chimney
Floats and rolls no more. Wheeling and falling, instead,
Down with a twittering flash go the smooth and inscrutable swallows,
Down to the place made theirs by the cold work of the sea.

Roses have had their day, and the dusk is on yarrow and wormwood—
Dusk that is over the grass, drenched with memorial dew;

Trellises lie like bones in a ruin that once was a garden,
Swallows have lingered and ceased, shadows and echoes are all.

II

Where is he lying to-night, as I turn away down to the valley,
Down where the lamps of men tell me the streets are alive?
Where shall I ask, and of whom, in the town or on land or on water,
News of a time and a place buried alike and with him?

Few now remain who may care, nor may they be wiser for caring,
Where or what manner the doom, whether by day or by night;
Whether in Indian deeps or on flood-laden fields of Atlantis,
Or by the roaring Horn, shrouded in silence he lies.

Few now remain who return by the weed-weary path to his cottage,
Drawn by the scene as it was—met by the chill and the change;
Few are alive who report, and few are alive who remember,
More of him now than a name carved somewhere on the sea.

"Where is he lying?" I ask, and the lights in the valley are nearer;
Down to the streets I go, down to the murmur of men.
Down to the roar of the sea in a ship may be well for another—
Down where he lies to-night, silent, and under the storms.

MOMUS

"Where's the need of singing now?"—
Smooth your brow,
Momus, and be reconciled,
For King Kronos is a child—

UNCLE ANANIAS

Child and father,
Or god rather,
And all gods are wild.

"Who reads Byron any more?"—
Shut the door,
Momus, for I feel a draught;
Shut it quick, for some one laughed.—
"What's become of
Browning? Some of
Wordsworth lumbers like a raft?

"What are poets to find here?"—
Have no fear:
When the stars are shining blue
There will yet be left a few
Themes availing—
And these failing,
Momus, there'll be you.

UNCLE ANANIAS

His words were magic and his heart was true,
    And everywhere he wandered he was blessed.
Out of all ancient men my childhood knew
    I choose him and I mark him for the best.
Of all authoritative liars, too,
    I crown him loveliest.

How fondly I remember the delight
    That always glorified him in the spring;
The joyous courage and the benedight
    Profusion of his faith in everything!

He was a good old man, and it was right
    That he should have his fling.

And often, underneath the apple-trees,
    When we surprised him in the summer time,
With what superb magnificence and ease
    He sinned enough to make the day sublime!
And if he liked us there about his knees,
    Truly it was no crime.

All summer long we loved him for the same
    Perennial inspiration of his lies;
And when the russet wealth of autumn came,
    There flew but fairer visions to our eyes—
Multiple, tropical, winged with a feathery flame,
    Like birds of paradise.

So to the sheltered end of many a year
    He charmed the seasons out with pageantry
Wearing upon his forehead, with no fear,
    The laurel of approved iniquity.
And every child who knew him, far or near,
    Did love him faithfully.

THE WHIP

The doubt you fought so long
The cynic net you cast,
The tyranny, the wrong,
The ruin, they are past;
And here you are at last,
Your blood no longer vexed.
The coffin has you fast,
The clod will have you next.

THE WHIP

But fear you not the clod,
Nor ever doubt the grave:
The roses and the sod
Will not forswear the wave.
The gift the river gave
Is now but theirs to cover:
The mistress and the slave
Are gone now, and the lover.

You left the two to find
Their own way to the brink
Then—shall I call you blind?—
You chose to plunge and sink.
God knows the gall we drink
Is not the mead we cry for,
Nor was it, I should think—
For you—a thing to die for.

Could we have done the same,
Had we been in your place?—
This funeral of your name
Throws no light on the case.
Could we have made the chase,
And felt then as you felt?—
But what's this on your face,
Blue, curious, like a welt?

There were some ropes of sand
Recorded long ago,
But none, I understand,
Of water. Is it so?
And she—she struck the blow,
You but a neck behind. . .
You saw the river flow—
Still, shall I call you blind?

THE WHITE LIGHTS

(BROADWAY, 1906)

When in from Delos came the gold
That held the dream of Pericles,
When first Athenian ears were told
The tumult of Euripides,
When men met Aristophanes,
Who fledged them with immortal quills—
Here, where the time knew none of these,
There were some islands and some hills.

When Rome went ravening to see
The sons of mothers end their days,
When Flaccus bade Leuconoë
To banish her Chaldean ways,
When first the pearled, alembic phrase
Of Maro into music ran—
Here there was neither blame nor praise
For Rome, or for the Mantuan.

When Avon, like a faery floor,
Lay freighted, for the eyes of One,
With galleons laden long before
By moonlit wharves in Avalon—
Here, where the white lights have begun
To seethe a way for something fair,
No prophet knew, from what was done,
That there was triumph in the air.

EXIT

For what we owe to other days,
Before we poisoned him with praise,

THE WISE BROTHERS

May we who shrank to find him weak
Remember that he cannot speak.

For envy that we may recall,
And for our faith before the fall,
May we who are alive be slow
To tell what we shall never know.

For penance he would not confess,
And for the fateful emptiness
Of early triumph undermined,
May we now venture to be kind.

LEONORA

They have made for Leonora this low dwelling in the ground,
And with cedar they have woven the four walls round.
Like a little dryad hiding she'll be wrapped all in green,
Better kept and longer valued than by ways that would have been.

They will come with many roses in the early afternoon,
They will come with pinks and lilies and with Leonora soon;
And as long as beauty's garments over beauty's limbs are thrown,
There'll be lilies that are liars, and the rose will have its own.

There will be a wondrous quiet in the house that they have made,
And to-night will be a darkness in the place where she'll be laid;
But the builders, looking forward into time, could only see
Darker nights for Leonora than to-night shall ever be.

THE WISE BROTHERS

First Voice

So long adrift, so fast aground,
What foam and ruin have we found—

We, the Wise Brothers?
Could heaven and earth be framed amiss,
That we should land in fine like this—
    We, and no others?

Second Voice

Convoyed by what accursèd thing
Made we this evil reckoning—
    We, the Wise Brothers?
And if the failure be complete,
Why look we forward from defeat—
    We, and what others?

Third Voice

Blown far from harbors once in sight,
May we not, going far, go right,—
    We, the Wise Brothers?
Companioned by the whirling spheres,
Have we no more than what appears—
    We, and all others?

BUT FOR THE GRACE OF GOD

"There, but for the grace of God, goes . . ."

THERE is a question that I ask,
    And ask again:
What hunger was half-hidden by the mask
    That he wore then?

There was a word for me to say
    That I said not;
And in the past there was another day
    That I forgot:

BUT FOR THE GRACE OF GOD

A dreary, cold, unwholesome day,
    Racked overhead,—
As if the world were turning the wrong way,
    And the sun dead:

A day that comes back well enough
    Now he is gone.
What then? Has memory no other stuff
    To seize upon?

Wherever he may wander now
    In his despair,
Would he be more contented in the slough
    If all were there?

And yet he brought a kind of light
    Into the room;
And when he left, a tinge of something bright
    Survived the gloom.

Why will he not be where he is,
    And not with me?
The hours that are my life are mine, not his,—
    Or used to be.

What numerous imps invisible
    Has he at hand,
Far-flying and forlorn as what they tell
    At his command?

What hold of weirdness or of worth
    Can he possess,
That he may speak from anywhere on earth
    His loneliness?

Shall I be caught and held again
  In the old net?—
He brought a sorry sunbeam with him then,
  But it beams yet.

FOR ARVIA

On Her Fifth Birthday

You Eyes, you large and all-inquiring Eyes,
That look so dubiously into me,
And are not satisfied with what you see,
Tell me the worst and let us have no lies:
Tell me the meaning of your scrutinies.
And of myself. Am I a Mystery?
Am I a Boojum—or just Company?
What do you say? What do you think, You Eyes?

You say not; but you think, beyond a doubt;
And you have the whole world to think about,
With very little time for little things.
So let it be; and let it all be fair—
For you, and for the rest who cannot share
Your gold of unrevealed awakenings.

THE SUNKEN CROWN

Nothing will hold him longer—let him go;
Let him go down where others have gone down;
Little he cares whether we smile or frown,
Or if we know, or if we think we know.

SHADRACH O'LEARY

The call is on him for his overthrow,
Say we; so let him rise, or let him drown.
Poor fool! He plunges for the sunken crown,
And we—we wait for what the plunge may show.

Well, we are safe enough. Why linger, then?
The watery chance was his, not ours. Poor fool!
Poor truant, poor Narcissus out of school;
Poor jest of Ascalon; poor king of men.—
The crown, if he be wearing it, may cool
His arrogance, and he may sleep again.

DOCTOR OF BILLIARDS

Of all among the fallen from on high,
We count you last and leave you to regain
Your born dominion of a life made vain
By three spheres of insidious ivory.
You dwindle to the lesser tragedy—
Content, you say. We call, but you remain.
Nothing alive gone wrong could be so plain,
Or quite so blasted with absurdity.

You click away the kingdom that is yours,
And you click off your crown for cap and bells;
You smile, who are still master of the feast,
And for your smile we credit you the least;
But when your false, unhallowed laugh occurs,
We seem to think there may be something else.

SHADRACH O'LEARY

O'Leary was a poet—for a while:
He sang of many ladies frail and fair,

The rolling glory of their golden hair,
And emperors extinguished with a smile.
They foiled his years with many an ancient wile,
And if they limped, O'Leary didn't care:
He turned them loose and had them everywhere,
Undoing saints and senates with their guile.

But this was not the end. A year ago
I met him—and to meet was to admire:
Forgotten were the ladies and the lyre,
And the small, ink-fed Eros of his dream.
By questioning I found a man to know—
A failure spared, a Shadrach of the Gleam.

HOW ANNANDALE WENT OUT

"They called it Annandale—and I was there
To flourish, to find words, and to attend:
Liar, physician, hypocrite, and friend,
I watched him; and the sight was not so fair
As one or two that I have seen elsewhere:
An apparatus not for me to mend—
A wreck, with hell between him and the end,
Remained of Annandale; and I was there.

"I knew the ruin as I knew the man;
So put the two together, if you can,
Remembering the worst you know of me.
Now view yourself as I was, on the spot—
With a slight kind of engine. Do you see?
Like this . . . You wouldn't hang me? I thought not."

ALMA MATER

He knocked, and I beheld him at the door—
A vision for the gods to verify.

MINIVER CHEEVY

"What battered ancientry is this," thought I,
"And when, if ever, did we meet before?"
But ask him as I might, I got no more
For answer than a moaning and a cry:
Too late to parley, but in time to die,
He staggered, and lay shapeless on the floor.

When had I known him? And what brought him here?
Love, warning, malediction, hunger, fear?
Surely I never thwarted such as he?—
Again, what soiled obscurity was this:
Out of what scum, and up from what abyss,
Had they arrived—these rags of memory?

MINIVER CHEEVY

MINIVER CHEEVY, child of scorn,
    Grew lean while he assailed the seasons;
He wept that he was ever born,
    And he had reasons.

Miniver loved the days of old
    When swords were bright and steeds were prancing;
The vision of a warrior bold
    Would set him dancing.

Miniver sighed for what was not,
    And dreamed, and rested from his labors;
He dreamed of Thebes and Camelot,
    And Priam's neighbors.

Miniver mourned the ripe renown
    That made so many a name so fragrant;
He mourned Romance, now on the town,
    And Art, a vagrant.

Miniver loved the Medici,
  Albeit he had never seen one;
He would have sinned incessantly
  Could he have been one.

Miniver cursed the commonplace
  And eyed a khaki suit with loathing;
He missed the mediæval grace
  Of iron clothing.

Miniver scorned the gold he sought,
  But sore annoyed was he without it;
Miniver thought, and thought, and thought,
  And thought about it.

Miniver Cheevy, born too late,
  Scratched his head and kept on thinking;
Miniver coughed, and called it fate,
  And kept on drinking.

THE PILOT

From the Past and Unavailing
Out of cloudland we are steering:
After groping, after fearing,
Into starlight we come trailing,
And we find the stars are true.
Still, O comrade, what of you?
You are gone, but we are sailing,
And the old ways are all new.

For the Lost and Unreturning
We have drifted, we have waited;
Uncommanded and unrated,

VICKERY'S MOUNTAIN

We have tossed and wandered, yearning
For a charm that comes no more
From the old lights by the shore:
We have shamed ourselves in learning
What you knew so long before.

For the Breed of the Far-going
Who are strangers, and all brothers,
May forget no more than others
Who looked seaward with eyes flowing.
But are brothers to bewail
One who fought so foul a gale?
You have won beyond our knowing,
You are gone, but yet we sail.

VICKERY'S MOUNTAIN

Blue in the west the mountain stands,
    And through the long twilight
Vickery sits with folded hands,
    And Vickery's eyes are bright.

Bright, for he knows what no man else
    On earth as yet may know:
There's a golden word that he never tells,
    And a gift that he will not show.

He dreams of honor and wealth and fame,
    He smiles, and well he may;
For to Vickery once a sick man came
    Who did not go away.

The day before the day to be,
    "Vickery," said the guest,
"You know as you live what's left of me—
    And you shall know the rest.

"You know as you live that I have come
  To this we call the end.
No doubt you have found me troublesome,
  But you've also found a friend;

"For we shall give and you shall take
  The gold that is in view;
The mountain there and I shall make
  A golden man of you.

"And you shall leave a friend behind
  Who neither frets nor feels;
And you shall move among your kind
  With hundreds at your heels.

"Now this that I have written here
  Tells all that need be told;
So, Vickery, take the way that's clear.
  And be a man of gold."

Vickery turned his eyes again
  To the far mountain-side,
And wept a tear for worthy men
  Defeated and defied.

Since then a crafty score of years
  Have come, and they have gone;
But Vickery counts no lost arrears:
  He lingers and lives on.

Blue in the west the mountain stands,
  Familiar as a face.
Blue, but Vickery knows what sards
  Are golden at its base.

BON VOYAGE

He dreams and lives upon the day
  When he shall walk with kings.
Vickery smiles—and well he may.
  The life-caged linnet sings.

Vickery thinks the time will come
  To go for what is his;
But hovering, unseen hands at home
  Will hold him where he is.

There's a golden word that he never tells
  And a gift that he will not show.
All to be given to some one else—
  And Vickery not to know.

BON VOYAGE

CHILD of a line accurst
  And old as Troy,
Bringer of best and worst
  In wild alloy—
Light, like a linnet first,
  He sang for joy.

Thrall to the gilded ease
  Of every day,
Mocker of all degrees
  And always gay,
Child of the Cyclades
  And of Broadway—

Laughing and half divine
  The boy began,
Drunk with a woodland wine
  Thessalian:
But there was rue to twine
  The pipes of Pan.

Therefore he skipped and flew
  The more along,
Vivid and always new
  And always wrong,
Knowing his only clew
  A siren song.

Careless of each and all
  He gave and spent:
Feast or a funeral
  He laughed and went,
Laughing to be so small
  In the event.

Told of his own deceit
  By many a tongue,
Flayed for his long defeat
  By being young,
Lured by the fateful sweet
  Of songs unsung—

Knowing it in his heart,
  But knowing not
The secret of an art
  That few forgot,
He played the twinkling part
  That was his lot.

And when the twinkle died,
  As twinkles do,
He pushed himself aside
  And out of view:
Out with the wind and tide,
  Before we knew.

ATHERTON'S GAMBIT

THE COMPANION

Let him answer as he will,
Or be lightsome as he may,
Now nor after shall he say
Worn-out words enough to kill,
Or to lull down by their craft,
Doubt, that was born yesterday,
When he lied and when she laughed.

Let him find another name
For the starlight on the snow,
Let him teach her till she know
That all seasons are the same,
And all sheltered ways are fair,—
Still, wherever she may go,
Doubt will have a dwelling there.

ATHERTON'S GAMBIT

The master played the bishop's pawn,
For jest, while Atherton looked on;
The master played this way and that,
And Atherton, amazed thereat,
Said "Now I have a thing in view
That will enlighten one or two,
And make a difference or so
In what it is they do not know."

The morning stars together sang
And forth a mighty music rang—

Not heard by many, save as told
Again through magic manifold
By such a few as have to play
For others, in the Master's way,
The music that the Master made
When all the morning stars obeyed.

Atherton played the bishop's pawn
While more than one or two looked on;
Atherton played this way and that,
And many a friend, amused thereat,
Went on about his business
Nor cared for Atherton the less;
A few stood longer by the game,
With Atherton to them the same.

The morning stars are singing still,
To crown, to challenge, and to kill;
And if perforce there falls a voice
On pious ears that have no choice
Except to urge an erring hand
To wreak its homage on the land,
Who of us that is worth his while
Will, if he listen, more than smile?

Who of us, being what he is,
May scoff at others' ecstasies?
However we may shine to-day,
More-shining ones are on the way;
And so it were not wholly well
To be at odds with Azrael,—
Nor were it kind of any one
To sing the end of Atherton.

TWO GARDENS IN LINNDALE

FOR A DEAD LADY

No more with overflowing light
Shall fill the eyes that now are faded,
Nor shall another's fringe with night
Their woman-hidden world as they did.
No more shall quiver down the days
The flowing wonder of her ways,
Whereof no language may requite
The shifting and the many-shaded.

The grace, divine, definitive,
Clings only as a faint forestalling;
The laugh that love could not forgive
Is hushed, and answers to no calling;
The forehead and the little ears
Have gone where Saturn keeps the years;
The breast where roses could not live
Has done with rising and with falling.

The beauty, shattered by the laws
That have creation in their keeping,
No longer trembles at applause,
Or over children that are sleeping;
And we who delve in beauty's lore
Know all that we have known before
Of what inexorable cause
Makes Time so vicious in his reaping.

TWO GARDENS IN LINNDALE

Two brothers, Oakes and Oliver,
Two gentle men as ever were,
Would roam no longer, but abide
In Linndale, where their fathers died,
And each would be a gardener.

"Now first we fence the garden through,
With this for me and that for you,"
Said Oliver.—"Divine!" said Oakes,
"And I, while I raise artichokes,
Will do what I was born to do."

"But this is not the soil, you know,"
Said Oliver, "to make them grow:
The parent of us, who is dead,
Compassionately shook his head
Once on a time and told me so."

"I hear you, gentle Oliver,"
Said Oakes, "and in your character
I find as fair a thing indeed
As ever bloomed and ran to seed
Since Adam was a gardener.

"Still, whatsoever I find there,
Forgive me if I do not share
The knowing gloom that you take on
Of one who doubted and is done:
For chemistry meets every prayer."

"Sometimes a rock will meet a plough,"
Said Oliver; "but anyhow
'Tis here we are, 'tis here we live,
With each to take and each to give:
There's no room for a quarrel now.

"I leave you in all gentleness
To science and a ripe success.
Now God be with you, brother Oakes,
With you and with your artichokes:
You have the vision, more or less."

TWO GARDENS IN LINNDALE

"By fate, that gives to me no choice,
I have the vision and the voice:
Dear Oliver, believe in me,
And we shall see what we shall see;
Henceforward let us both rejoice."

"But first, while we have joy to spare
We'll plant a little here and there;
And if you be not in the wrong,
We'll sing together such a song
As no man yet sings anywhere."

They planted and with fruitful eyes
Attended each his enterprise.
"Now days will come and days will go,
And many a way be found, we know,"
Said Oakes, "and we shall sing, likewise."

"The days will go, the years will go,
And many a song be sung, we know,"
Said Oliver; "and if there be
Good harvesting for you and me,
Who cares if we sing loud or low?"

They planted once, and twice, and thrice,
Like amateurs in paradise;
And every spring, fond, foiled, elate,
Said Oakes, "We are in tune with Fate:
One season longer will suffice."

Year after year 'twas all the same:
With none to envy, none to blame,
They lived along in innocence,
Nor ever once forgot the fence,
Till on a day the Stranger came.

He came to greet them where they were,
And he too was a Gardener:
He stood between these gentle men,
He stayed a little while, and then
The land was all for Oliver.

'Tis Oliver who tills alone
Two gardens that are now his own;
'Tis Oliver who sows and reaps
And listens, while the other sleeps,
For songs undreamed of and unknown.

'Tis he, the gentle anchorite,
Who listens for them day and night;
But most he hears them in the dawn,
When from his trees across the lawn
Birds ring the chorus of the light.

He cannot sing without the voice,
But he may worship and rejoice
For patience in him to remain,
The chosen heir of age and pain,
Instead of Oakes—who had no choice.

'Tis Oliver who sits beside
The other's grave at eventide,
And smokes, and wonders what new race
Will have two gardens, by God's grace,
In Linndale, where their fathers died.

And often, while he sits and smokes,
He sees the ghost of gentle Oakes
Uprooting, with a restless hand,
Soft, shadowy flowers in a land
Of asphodels and artichokes.

THE REVEALER

(Roosevelt)

He turned aside to see the carcase of the lion: and behold, there was a swarm of bees and honey in the carcase of the lion. . . . And the men of the city said unto him, What is sweeter than honey? and what is stronger than a lion?—*Judges*, 14.

THE palms of Mammon have disowned
The gift of our complacency;
The bells of ages have intoned
Again their rhythmic irony;
And from the shadow, suddenly,
'Mid echoes of decrepit rage,
The seer of our necessity
Confronts a Tyrian heritage.

Equipped with unobscured intent
He smiles with lions at the gate,
Acknowledging the compliment
Like one familiar with his fate;
The lions, having time to wait,
Perceive a small cloud in the skies,
Whereon they look, disconsolate,
With scared, reactionary eyes.

A shadow falls upon the land,—
They sniff, and they are like to roar;
For they will never understand
What they have never seen before.
They march in order to the door,
Not knowing the best thing to seek,
Nor caring if the gods restore
The lost composite of the Greek.

The shadow fades, the light arrives,
And ills that were concealed are seen;
The combs of long-defended hives
Now drip dishonored and unclean;
No Nazarite or Nazarene
Compels our questioning to prove
The difference that is between
Dead lions—or the sweet thereof.

But not for lions, live or dead,
Except as we are all as one,
Is he the world's accredited
Revealer of what we have done;
What You and I and Anderson
Are still to do is his reward;
If we go back when he is gone—
There is an Angel with a Sword.

He cannot close again the doors
That now are shattered for our sake;
He cannot answer for the floors
We crowd on, or for walls that shake;
He cannot wholly undertake
The cure of our immunity;
He cannot hold the stars, or make
Of seven years a century.

So Time will give us what we earn
Who flaunt the handful for the whole,
And leave us all that we may learn
Who read the surface for the soul;
And we'll be steering to the goal,
For we have said so to our sons:
When we who ride can pay the toll,
Time humors the far-seeing ones.

THE REVEALER

Down to our nose's very end
We see, and are invincible,—
Too vigilant to comprehend
The scope of what we cannot sell;
But while we seem to know as well
As we know dollars, or our skins,
The Titan may not always tell
Just where the boundary begins.

LANCELOT
(1920)
To Lewis M. Isaacs

LANCELOT

(1920)

To Laura M. Feuster

LANCELOT

I

Gawaine, aware again of Lancelot
In the King's garden, coughed and followed him;
Whereat he turned and stood with folded arms
And weary-waiting eyes, cold and half-closed—
Hard eyes, where doubts at war with memories
Fanned a sad wrath. "Why frown upon a friend?
Few live that have too many," Gawaine said,
And wished unsaid, so thinly came the light
Between the narrowing lids at which he gazed.
"And who of us are they that name their friends?"
Lancelot said. "They live that have not any.
Why do they live, Gawaine? Ask why, and answer."

Two men of an elected eminence,
They stood for a time silent. Then Gawaine,
Acknowledging the ghost of what was gone,
Put out his hand: "Rather, I say, why ask?
If I be not the friend of Lancelot,
May I be nailed alive along the ground
And emmets eat me dead. If I be not
The friend of Lancelot, may I be fried
With other liars in the pans of hell.
What item otherwise of immolation
Your Darkness may invent, be it mine to endure
And yours to gloat on. For the time between,
Consider this thing you see that is my hand.
If once, it has been yours a thousand times;

Why not again? Gawaine has never lied
To Lancelot; and this, of all wrong days—
This day before the day when you go south
To God knows what accomplishment of exile—
Were surely an ill day for lies to find
An issue or a cause or an occasion.
King Ban your father and King Lot my father,
Were they alive, would shake their heads in sorrow
To see us as we are, and I shake mine
In wonder. Will you take my hand, or no?
Strong as I am, I do not hold it out
For ever and on air. You see—my hand."
Lancelot gave his hand there to Gawaine,
Who took it, held it, and then let it go,
Chagrined with its indifference.

                               "Yes, Gawaine,
I go tomorrow, and I wish you well;
You and your brothers, Gareth, Gaheris,—
And Agravaine; yes, even Agravaine,
Whose tongue has told all Camelot and all Britain
More lies than yet have hatched of Modred's envy.
You say that you have never lied to me,
And I believe it so. Let it be so.
For now and always. Gawaine, I wish you well.
Tomorrow I go south, as Merlin went,
But not for Merlin's end. I go, Gawaine,
And leave you to your ways. There are ways left."

"There are three ways I know, three famous ways,
And all in Holy Writ," Gawaine said, smiling:
"The snake's way and the eagle's way are two,
And then we have a man's way with a maid—
Or with a woman who is not a maid.
Your late way is to send all women scudding,
To the last flash of the last cramoisy,

LANCELOT

While you go south to find the fires of God.
Since we came back again to Camelot
From our immortal Quest—I came back first—
No man has known you for the man you were
Before you saw whatever 't was you saw,
To make so little of kings and queens and friends
Thereafter. Modred? Agravaine? My brothers?
And what if they be brothers? What are brothers,
If they be not our friends, your friends and mine?
You turn away, and my words are no mark
On you affection or your memory?
So be it then, if so it is to be.
God save you, Lancelot; for by Saint Stephen,
You are no more than man to save yourself."

"Gawaine, I do not say that you are wrong,
Or that you are ill-seasoned in your lightness;
You say that all you know is what you saw,
And on your own averment you saw nothing.
Your spoken word, Gawaine, I have not weighed
In those unhappy scales of inference
That have no beam but one made out of hates
And fears, and venomous conjecturings;
Your tongue is not the sword that urges me
Now out of Camelot. Two other swords
There are that are awake, and in their scabbards
Are parching for the blood of Lancelot.
Yet I go not away for fear of them,
But for a sharper care. You say the truth,
But not when you contend the fires of God
Are my one fear,—for there is one fear more.
Therefore I go. Gawaine, I wish you well."

"Well-wishing in a way is well enough;
So, in a way, is caution; so, in a way,

Are leeches, neatherds, and astrologers.
Lancelot, listen. Sit you down and listen:
You talk of swords and fears and banishment.
Two swords, you say; Modred and Agravaine,
You mean. Had you meant Gaheris and Gareth,
Or willed an evil on them, I should welcome
And hasten your farewell. But Agravaine
Hears little what I say; his ears are Modred's.
The King is Modred's father, and the Queen
A prepossession of Modred's lunacy.
So much for my two brothers whom you fear,
Not fearing for yourself. I say to you,
Fear not for anything—and so be wise
And amiable again as heretofore;
Let Modred have his humor, and Agravaine
His tongue. The two of them have done their worst,
And having done their worst, what have they done?
A whisper now and then, a chirrup or so
In corners,—and what else? Ask what, and answer."

Still with a frown that had no faith in it,
Lancelot, pitying Gawaine's lost endeavour
To make an evil jest of evidence,
Sat fronting him with a remote forbearance—
Whether for Gawaine blind or Gawaine false,
Or both, or neither, he could not say yet,
If ever; and to himself he said no more
Than he said now aloud: "What else, Gawaine?
What else, am I to say? Then ruin, I say;
Destruction, dissolution, desolation,
I say,—should I compound with jeopardy now.
For there are more than whispers here, Gawaine:
The way that we have gone so long together
Has underneath our feet, without our will,
Become a twofold faring. Yours, I trust,

LANCELOT

May lead you always on, as it has led you,
To praise and to much joy. Mine, I believe,
Leads off to battles that are not yet fought,
And to the Light that once had blinded me.
When I came back from seeing what I saw,
I saw no place for me in Camelot.
There is no place for me in Camelot.
There is no place for me save where the Light
May lead me; and to that place I shall go.
Meanwhile I lay upon your soul no load
Of counsel or of empty admonition;
Only I ask of you, should strife arise
In Camelot, to remember, if you may,
That you've an ardor that outruns your reason,
Also a glamour that outshines your guile;
And you are a strange hater. I know that;
And I'm in fortune that you hate not me.
Yet while we have our sins to dream about,
Time has done worse for time than in our making;
Albeit there may be sundry falterings
And falls against us in the Book of Man."

"Praise Adam, you are mellowing at last!
I've always liked this world, and would so still;
And if it is your new Light leads you on
To such an admirable gait, for God's sake,
Follow it, follow it, follow it, Lancelot;
Follow it as you never followed glory.
Once I believed that I was on the way
That you call yours, but I came home again
To Camelot—and Camelot was right,
For the world knows its own that knows not you;
You are a thing too vaporous to be sharing
The carnal feast of life. You mow down men
Like elder-stems, and you leave women sighing

For one more sight of you; but they do wrong.
You are a man of mist, and have no shadow.
God save you, Lancelot. If I laugh at you,
I laugh in envy and in admiration."

The joyless evanescence of a smile,
Discovered on the face of Lancelot
By Gawaine's unrelenting vigilance,
Wavered, and with a sullen change went out;
And then there was the music of a woman
Laughing behind them, and a woman spoke:
"Gawaine, you said 'God save you, Lancelot.'
Why should He save him any more to-day
Than on another day? What has he done,
Gawaine, that God should save him?" Guinevere,
With many questions in her dark blue eyes
And one gay jewel in her golden hair,
Had come upon the two of them unseen,
Till now she was a russet apparition
At which the two arose—one with a dash
Of easy leisure in his courtliness,
One with a stately calm that might have pleased
The Queen of a strange land indifferently.
The firm incisive languor of her speech,
Heard once, was heard through battles: "Lancelot,
What have you done to-day that God should save you?
What has he done, Gawaine, that God should save him?
I grieve that you two pinks of chivalry
Should be so near me in my desolation,
And I, poor soul alone, know nothing of it.
What has he done, Gawaine?"

                        With all her poise,
To Gawaine's undeceived urbanity
She was less queen than woman for the nonce,

LANCELOT

And in her eyes there was a flickering
Of a still fear that would not be veiled wholly
With any mask of mannered nonchalance.
"What has he done? Madam, attend your nephew;
And learn from him, in your incertitude,
That this inordinate man Lancelot,
This engine of renown, this hewer down daily
Of potent men by scores in our late warfare,
Has now inside his head a foreign fever
That urges him away to the last edge
Of everything, there to efface himself
In ecstasy, and so be done with us.
Hereafter, peradventure certain birds
Will perch in meditation on his bones,
Quite as if they were some poor sailor's bones,
Or felon's jettisoned, or fisherman's,
Or fowler's bones, or Mark of Cornwall's bones.
In fine, this flower of men that was our comrade
Shall be for us no more, from this day on,
Than a much remembered Frenchman far away.
Magnanimously I leave you now to prize
Your final sight of him; and leaving you,
I leave the sun to shine for him alone,
Whiles I grope on to gloom. Madam, farewell;
And you, contrarious Lancelot, farewell."

II

The flash of oak leaves over Guinevere
That afternoon, with the sun going down,
Made memories there for Lancelot, although
The woman who in silence looked at him
Now seemed his inventory of the world
That he must lose, or suffer to be lost
For love of her who sat there in the shade,

With oak leaves flashing in a golden light
Over her face and over her golden hair.
"Gawaine has all the graces, yet he knows;
He knows enough to be the end of us,
If so he would," she said. "He knows and laughs
And we are at the mercy of a man
Who, if the stars went out, would only laugh."
She looked away at a small swinging blossom,
And then she looked intently at her fingers,
While a frown gathered slowly round her eyes,
And wrinkled her white forehead.

                                      Lancelot,
Scarce knowing whether to himself he spoke
Or to the Queen, said emptily: "As for Gawaine,
My question is, if any curious hind
Or knight that is alive in Britain breathing,
Or prince, or king, knows more of us, or less,
Than Gawaine, in his gay complacency,
Knows or believes he knows. There's over much
Of knowing in this realm of many tongues,
Where deeds are less to those who tell of them
Than are the words they sow; and you and I
Are like to yield a granary of such words,
For God knows what next harvesting. Gawain
I fear no more than Gareth, or Colgrevance;
So far as it is his to be the friend
Of any man, so far is he my friend—
Till I have crossed him in some enterprise
Unlikely and unborn. So fear not Gawaine
But let your primal care be now for one
Whose name is yours."

                      The Queen, with her blue eyes
Too bright for joy, still gazed on Lancelot,

LANCELOT

Who stared as if in angry malediction
Upon the shorn grass growing at his feet.
"Why do you speak as if the grass had ears
And I had none? What are you saying now,
So darkly to the grass, of knights and hinds?
Are you the Lancelot who rode, long since,
Away from me on that unearthly Quest,
Which left no man the same who followed it—
Or none save Gawaine, who came back so soon
That we had hardly missed him?" Faintly then
She smiled a little, more in her defence,
He knew, than for misprision of a man
Whom yet she feared: "Why do you set this day—
This golden day, when all are not so golden—
To tell me, with your eyes upon the ground,
That idle words have been for idle tongues
And ears a moment's idle entertainment?
Have I become, and all at once, a thing
So new to courts, and to the buzz they make,
That I should hear no murmur, see no sign?
Where malice and ambition dwell with envy,
They go the farthest who believe the least;
So let them,—while I ask of you again,
Why this day for all this? Was yesterday
A day of ouphes and omens? Was it Friday?
I don't remember. Days are all alike
When I have you to look on; when you go,
There are no days but hours. You might say now
What Gawaine said, and say it in our language."
The sharp light still was in her eyes, alive
And anxious with a reminiscent fear.

Lancelot, like a strong man stricken hard
With pain, looked up at her unhappily;
And slowly, on a low and final note,

Said: "Gawaine laughs alike at what he knows,
And at the loose convenience of his fancy;
He sees in others what his humor needs
To nourish it, and lives a merry life.
Sometimes a random shaft of his will hit
Nearer the mark than one a wise man aims
With infinite address and reservation;
So has it come to pass this afternoon."

Blood left the quivering cheeks of Guinevere
As color leaves a cloud; and where white was
Before, there was a ghostliness not white,
But gray; and over it her shining hair
Coiled heavily its mocking weight of gold.
The pride of her forlorn light-heartedness
Fled like a storm-blown feather; and her fear,
Possessing her, was all that she possessed.
She sought for Lancelot, but he seemed gone.
There was a strong man glowering in a chair
Before her, but he was not Lancelot,
Or he would look at her and say to her
That Gawaine's words were less than chaff in the wind—
A nonsense about exile, birds, and bones,
Born of an indolence of empty breath.
"Say what has come to pass this afternoon,"
She said, "or I shall hear you all my life,
Not hearing what it was you might have told."

He felt the trembling of her slow last words,
And his were trembling as he answered them:
"Why this day, why no other? So you ask,
And so must I in honor tell you more—
For what end, I have yet no braver guess
Than Modred has of immortality,
Or you of Gawaine. Could I have him alone

LANCELOT

Between me and the peace I cannot know,
My life were like the sound of golden bells
Over still fields at sunset, where no storm
Should ever blast the sky with fire again,
Or thunder follow ruin for you and me,—
As like it will, if I for one more day,
Assume that I see not what I have seen,
See now, and shall see. There are no more lies
Left anywhere now for me to tell myself
That I have not already told myself,
And overtold, until today I seem
To taste them as I might the poisoned fruit
That Patrise had of Mador, and so died.
And that same apple of death was to be food
For Gawaine; but he left it and lives on,
To make his joy of living your confusion.
His life is his religion; he loves life
With such a manifold exuberance
That poison shuns him and seeks out a way
To wreak its evil upon innocence.
There may be chance in this, there may be '
Be what there be, I do not fear Gawaine."

The Queen, with an indignant little foot,
Struck viciously the unoffending grass
And said: "Why not let Gawaine go his way?
I'll think of him no more, fear him no more,
And hear of him no more. I'll hear no more
Of any now save one who is, or was,
All men to me. And he said once to me
That he would say why this day, of all days,
Was more mysteriously felicitous
For solemn commination than another."
Again she smiled, but her blue eyes were telling
No more their story of old happiness.

"For me today is not as other days,"
He said, "because it is the first, I find,
That has empowered my will to say to you
What most it is that you must hear and heed.
When Arthur, with a faith unfortified,
Sent me alone, of all he might have sent,
That May-day to Leodogran your father,
I went away from him with a sore heart;
For in my heart I knew that I should fail
My King, who trusted me too far beyond
The mortal outpost of experience.
And this was after Merlin's admonition,
Which Arthur, in his passion, took for less
Than his inviolable majesty.
When I rode in between your father's guards
And heard his trumpets blown for my loud honor,
I sent my memory back to Camelot,
And said once to myself, 'God save the king!'
But the words tore my throat and were like blood
Upon my tongue. Then a great shout went up
From shining men around me everywhere;
And I remember more fair women's eyes
Than there are stars in autumn, all of them
Thrown on me for a glimpse of that high knight
Sir Lancelot—Sir Lancelot of the Lake.
I saw their faces and I saw not one
To sever a tendril of my integrity;
But I thought once again, to make myself
Believe a silent lie, 'God save the King' . . .
I saw your face, and there were no more kings."

The sharp light softened in the Queen's blue eyes,
And for a moment there was joy in them:
"Was I so menacing to the peace, I wonder,
Of anyone else alive? But why go back?

LANCELOT

I tell you that I fear Gawaine no more;
And if you fear him not, and I fear not
What you fear not, what have we then to fear?"
Fatigued a little with her reasoning,
She waited longer than a woman waits,
Without a cloudy sign, for Lancelot's
Unhurried answer: "Whether or not you fear,
Know always that I fear for me no stroke
Maturing for the joy of any knave
Who sees the world, with me alive in it,
A place too crowded for the furtherance
Of his inflammatory preparations.
But Lot of Orkney had a wife, a dark one;
And rumor says no man who gazed at her,
Attentively, might say his prayers again
Without a penance or an absolution.
I know not about that; but the world knows
That Arthur prayed in vain once, if he prayed,
Or we should have no Modred watching us.
Know then that what you fear to call my fear
Is all for you; and what is all for you
Is all for love, which were the same to me
As life—had I not seen what I have seen.
But first I am to tell you what I see,
And what I mean by fear. It is yourself
That I see now; and if I saw you only,
I might forego again all other service,
And leave to Time, who is Love's almoner,
The benefaction of what years or days
Remaining might be found unchronicled
For two that have not always watched or seen
The sands of gold that flow for golden hours.
If I saw you alone! But I know now
That you are never more to be alone.
The shape of one infernal foul attendant

Will be for ever prowling after you,
To leer at me like a damned thing whipped out
Of the last cave in hell. You know his name.
Over your shoulder I could see him now,
Adventuring his misbegotten patience
For one destroying word in the King's ear—
The word he cannot whisper there quite yet,
Not having it yet to say. If he should say it,
Then all this would be over, and our days
Of life, your days and mine, be over with it.
No day of mine that were to be for you
Your last, would light for me a longer span
Than for yourself; and there would be no twilight."

The Queen's implacable calm eyes betrayed
The doubt that had as yet for what he said
No healing answer: "If I fear no more
Gawaine, I fear your Modred even less.
Your fear, you say, is for an end outside
Your safety; and as much as that I grant you.
And I believe in your belief, moreover,
That some far-off unheard-of retribution
Hangs over Camelot, even as this oak-bough,
That I may almost reach, hangs overhead,
All dark now. Only a small time ago
The light was falling through it, and on me.
Another light, a longer time ago,
Was living in your eyes, and we were happy.
Yet there was Modred then as he is now,
As much a danger then as he is now,
And quite as much a nuisance. Let his eyes
Have all the darkness in them they may hold,
And there will be less left of it outside
For fear to grope and thrive in. Lancelot,
I say the dark is not what you fear most.

LANCELOT

There is a Light that you fear more today
Than all the darkness that has ever been;
Yet I doubt not that your Light will burn on
For some time yet without your ministration.
I'm glad for Modred,—though I hate his eyes,—
That he should hold me nearer to your thoughts
Than I should hold myself, I fear, without him;
I'm glad for Gawaine, also,—who, you tell me,
Misled my fancy with his joy of living."

Incredulous of her voice and of her lightness,
He saw now in the patience of her smile
A shining quiet of expectancy
That made as much of his determination
As he had made of giants and Sir Peris.
"But I have more to say than you have heard,"
He faltered—"though God knows what you have heard
Should be enough."

          "I see it now," she said;
"I see it now as always women must
Who cannot hold what holds them any more.
If Modred's hate were now the only hazard—
The only shadow between you and me—
How long should I be saying all this to you,
Or you be listening? No, Lancelot,—no.
I knew it coming for a longer time
Than you fared for the Grail. You told yourself,
When first that wild light came to make men mad
Round Arthur's Table—as Gawaine told himself,
And many another tired man told himself—
That it was God, not something new, that called you.
Well, God was something new to most of them,
And so they went away. But you were changing
Long before you, or Bors, or Percival,

Or Galahad rode away—or poor Gawaine,
Who came back presently; and for a time
Before you went—albeit for no long time—
I may have made for your too loyal patience
A jealous exhibition of my folly—
All for those two Elaines; and one of them
Is dead, poor child, for you. How do you feel,
You men, when women die for you? They do,
Sometimes, you know. Not often, but sometimes."

Discomfiture, beginning with a scowl
And ending in a melancholy smile,
Crept over Lancelot's face the while he stared,
More like a child than like the man he was,
At Guinevere's demure serenity
Before him in the shadow, soon to change
Into the darkness of a darker night
Than yet had been since Arthur was a king.
"What seizure of an unrelated rambling
Do you suppose it was that had you then?"
He said; and with a frown that had no smile
Behind it, he sat brooding.

                             The Queen laughed,
And looked at him again with lucent eyes
That had no sharpness in them; they were soft now,
And a blue light, made wet with happiness,
Distilled from pain into abandonment,
Shone out of them and held him while she smiled,
Although they trembled with a questioning
Of what his gloom foretold: "All that I saw
Was true, and I have paid for what I saw—
More than a man may know. Hear me, and listen:
You cannot put me or the truth aside,
With half-told words that I could only wish

LANCELOT

No man had said to me; not you, of all men.
If there were only Modred in the way,
Should I see now, from here and in this light,
So many furrows over your changed eyes?
Why do you fear for me when all my fears
Are for the needless burden you take on?
To put me far away, and your fears with me,
Were surely no long toil, had you the will
To say what you have known and I have known
Longer than I dare guess. Have little fear:
Never shall I become for you a curse
Laid on your conscience to be borne for ever;
Nor shall I be a weight for you to drag
On always after you, as a poor slave
Drags iron at his heels. Therefore, today,
These ominous reassurances of mine
Would seem to me to be a waste of life,
And more than life."

      Lancelot's memory wandered
Into the blue and wistful distances
That her soft eyes unveiled. He knew their trick,
As he knew the great love that fostered it,
And the wild passionate fate that hid itself
In all the perilous calm of white and gold
That was her face and hair, and might as well
Have been of gold and marble for the world,
And for the King. Before he knew, she stood
Behind him with her warm hands on his cheeks,
And her lips on his lips; and though he heard
Not half of what she told, he heard enough
To make as much of it, or so it seemed,
As man was ever told, or should be told,
Or need be, until everything was told,
And all the mystic silence of the stars

Had nothing more to keep or to reveal.
"If there were only Modred in the way,"
She murmured, "would you come to me tonight?
The King goes to Carleon or Carlisle,
Or some place where there's hunting. Would you come,
If there were only Modred in the way?"
She felt his hand on hers and laid her cheek
Upon his forehead, where the furrows were:
"All these must go away, and so must I—
Before there are more shadows. You will come,
And you may tell me everything you must
That I must hear you tell me—if I must—
Of bones and horrors and of horrid waves
That break for ever on the world's last edge."

III

LANCELOT looked about him, but he saw
No Guinevere. The place where she had sat
Was now an empty chair that might have been
The shadowy throne of an abandoned world,
But for the living fragrance of a kiss
That he remembered, and a living voice
That hovered when he saw that she was gone.
There was too much remembering while he felt
Upon his cheek the warm sound of her words;
There was too much regret; there was too much
Remorse. Regret was there for what had gone,
Remorse for what had come. Yet there was time,
That had not wholly come. There was time enough
Between him and the night—as there were shoals
Enough, no doubt, that in the sea somewhere
Were not yet hidden by the drowning tide.
"So there is here between me and the dark
Some twilight left," he said. He sighed, and said

LANCELOT

Again, "Time, tide, and twilight—and the dark;
And then, for me, the Light. But what for her?
I do not think of anything but life
That I may give to her by going now;
And if I look into her eyes again,
Or feel her breath upon my face again,
God knows if I may give so much as life;
Or if the durance of her loneliness
Would have it for the asking. What am I?
What have I seen that I must leave behind
So much of heaven and earth to burn itself
Away in white and gold, until in time
There shall be no more white and no more gold?
I cannot think of such a time as that;
I cannot—yet I must; for I am he
That shall have hastened it and hurried on
To dissolution all that wonderment—
That envy of all women who have said
She was a child of ice and ivory;
And of all men, save one. And who is he?
Who is this Lancelot that has betrayed
His King, and served him with a cankered honor?
Who is this Lancelot that sees the Light
And waits now in the shadow for the dark?
Who is this King, this Arthur, who believes
That what has been, and is, will be for ever,—
Who has no eye for what he will not see,
And will see nothing but what's passing here
In Camelot, which is passing? Why are we here?
What are we doing—kings, queens, Camelots,
And Lancelots? And what is this dim world
That I would leave, and cannot leave tonight
Because a Queen is in it and a King
Has gone away to some place where there's hunting—
Carleon or Carlisle! Who is this Queen,

This pale witch-wonder of white fire and gold,
This Guinevere that I brought back with me
From Cameliard for Arthur, who knew then
What Merlin told, as he forgets it now
And rides away from her—God watch the world!—
To some place where there's hunting! What are kings?
And how much longer are there to be kings?
When are the millions who are now like worms
To know that kings are worms, if they are worms?
When are the women who make toys of men
To know that they themselves are less than toys
When Time has laid upon their skins the touch
Of his all-shrivelling fingers? When are they
To know that men must have an end of them
When men have seen the Light and left the world
That I am leaving now. Yet, here I am,
And all because a king has gone a-hunting. . . .
Carleon or Carlisle!"

                                So Lancelot
Fed with a sullen rancor, which he knew
To be as false as he was to the King,
The passion and the fear that now in him
Were burning like two slow infernal fires
That only flight and exile far away
From Camelot should ever cool again.
"Yet here I am," he said,—"and here I am.
Time, tide, and twilight; and there is no twilight—
And there is not much time. But there's enough
To eat and drink in; and there may be time
For me to frame a jest or two to prove
How merry a man may be who sees the Light.
And I must get me up and go along,
Before the shadows blot out everything,
And leave me stumbling among skeletons.

LANCELOT

God, what a rain of ashes falls on him
Who sees the new and cannot leave the old!"

He rose and looked away into the south
Where a gate was, by which he might go out,
Now, if he would, while Time was yet there with him—
Time that was tearing minutes out of life
While he stood shivering in his loneliness,
And while the silver lights of memory
Shone faintly on a far-off eastern shore
Where he had seen on earth for the last time
The triumph and the sadness in the face
Of Galahad, for whom the Light was waiting.
Now he could see the face of him again,
He fancied; and his flickering will adjured him
To follow it and be free. He followed it
Until it faded and there was no face,
And there was no more light. Yet there was time
That had not come, though he could hear it now
Like ruining feet of marching conquerors
That would be coming soon and were not men.
Forlornly and unwillingly he came back
To find the two dim chairs. In one of them
Was Guinevere, and on her phantom face
There fell a golden light that might have been
The changing gleam of an unchanging gold
That was her golden hair. He sprang to touch
The wonder of it, but she too was gone,
Like Galahad; he was alone again
With shadows, and one face that he still saw.
The world had no more faces now than one
That for a moment, with a flash of pain,
Had shown him what it is that may be seen
In embers that break slowly into dust,
Where for a time was fire. He saw it there

Before him, and he knew it was not good
That he should learn so late, and of this hour,
What men may leave behind them in the eyes
Of women who have nothing more to give,
And may not follow after. Once again
He gazed away to southward, but the face
Of Galahad was not there. He turned, and saw
Before him, in the distance, many lights
In Arthur's palace; for the dark had come
To Camelot, while Time had come and gone.

IV

NOT having viewed Carleon or Carlisle,
The King came home to Camelot after midnight,
Feigning an ill not feigned; and his return
Brought Bedivere, and after him Gawaine,
To the King's inner chamber, where they waited
Through the grim light of dawn. Sir Bedivere,
By nature stern to see, though not so bleak
Within as to be frozen out of mercy,
Sat with arms crossed and with his head weighed low
In heavy meditation. Once or twice
His eyes were lifted for a careful glimpse
Of Gawaine at the window, where he stood
Twisting his fingers feverishly behind him,
Like one distinguishing indignantly,
For swift eclipse and for offence not his,
The towers and roofs and the sad majesty
Of Camelot in the dawn, for the last time.

Sir Bedivere, at last, with a long sigh
That said less of his pain than of his pity,
Addressed the younger knight who turned and heard
His elder, but with no large eagerness:

LANCELOT

"So it has come, Gawaine; and we are here.
I find when I see backward something farther,
By grace of time, than you are given to see—
Though you, past any doubt, see much that I
See not—I find that what the colder speech
Of reason most repeated says to us
Of what is in a way to come to us
Is like enough to come. And we are here.
Before the unseeing sun is here to mock us,
Or the King here to prove us, we are here.
We are the two, it seems, that are to make
Of words and of our presences a veil
Between him and the sight of what he does.
Little have I to say that I may tell him:
For what I know is what the city knows,
Not what it says,—for it says everything.
The city says the first of all who met
The sword of Lancelot was Colgrevance,
Who fell dead while he wept—a brave machine,
Cranked only for the rudiments of war.
But some of us are born to serve and shift,
And that's not well. The city says, also,
That you and Lancelot were in the garden,
Before the sun went down."

       "Yes," Gawaine groaned;
"Yes, we were there together in the garden,
Before the sun went down; and I conceive
A place among the possibilities
For me with other causes unforeseen
Of what may shake down soon to grief and ashes
This kingdom and this empire. Bedivere,
Could I have given a decent seriousness
To Lancelot while he said things to me
That pulled his heart half out of him by the roots,

And left him, I see now, half sick with pity
For my poor uselessness to serve a need
That I had never known, we might be now
Asleep and easy in our beds at home,
And we might hear no murmurs after sunrise
Of what we are to hear. A few right words
Of mine, if said well, might have been enough.
That shall I never know. I shall know only
That it was I who laughed at Lancelot
When he said what lay heaviest on his heart.
By now he might be far away from here,
And farther from the world. But the Queen came;
The Queen came, and I left them there together;
And I laughed as I left them. After dark
I met with Modred and said what I could,
When I had heard him, to discourage him.
His mother was my mother. I told Bors,
And he told Lancelot; though as for that,
My story would have been the same as his,
And would have had the same acknowledgment:
'Thanks, but no matter'—or to that effect.
The Queen, of course, had fished him for his word,
And had it on the hook when she went home;
And after that, an army of red devils
Could not have held the man away from her.
And I'm to live as long as I'm to wonder
What might have been, had I not been—myself.
I heard him, and I laughed. Then the Queen came."

"Recriminations are not remedies,
Gawaine; and though you cast them at yourself,
And hurt yourself, you cannot end or swerve
The flowing of these minutes that leave hours
Behind us, as we leave our faded selves
And yesterdays. The surest-visioned of us

LANCELOT

Are creatures of our dreams and inferences,
And though it look to us a few go far
For seeing far, the fewest and the farthest
Of all we know go not beyond themselves.
No, Gawaine, you are not the cause of this;
And I have many doubts if all you said,
Or in your lightness may have left unsaid,
Would have unarmed the Queen. The Queen was there."—
Gawaine looked up, and then looked down again:
"Good God, if I had only said—said something!"

"Say nothing now, Gawaine." Bedivere sighed,
And shook his head: "Morning is not in the west.
The sun is rising and the King is coming;
Now you may hear him in the corridor,
Like a sick landlord shuffling to the light
For one last look-out on his mortgaged hills.
But hills and valleys are not what he sees;
He sees with us the fire—the sign—the law.
The King that is the father of the law
Is weaker than his child, except he slay it.
Not long ago, Gawaine, I had a dream
Of a sword over kings, and of a world
Without them."—"Dreams, dreams."—"Hush, Gawaine."

King Arthur
Came slowly on till in the darkened entrance
He stared and shivered like a sleep-walker,
Brought suddenly awake where a cliff's edge
Is all he sees between another step
And his annihilation. Bedivere rose,
And Gawaine rose; and with instinctive arms
They partly guided, partly carried him,
To the King's chair.

                              "I thank you, gentlemen,
Though I am not so shaken, I dare say,
As you would have me. This is not the hour
When kings who do not sleep are at their best;
And had I slept this night that now is over,
No man should ever call me King again."
He pulled his heavy robe around him closer,
And laid upon his forehead a cold hand
That came down warm and wet. "You, Bedivere,
And you, Gawaine, are shaken with events
Incredible yesterday,—but kings are men.
Take off their crowns and tear away their colors
And let them see with my eyes what I see—
Yes, they are men, indeed! If there's a slave
In Britain with a reptile at his heart
Like mine that with his claws of ice and fire
Tears out of me the fevered roots of mercy,
Find him, and I will make a king of him!
And then, so that his happiness may swell
Tenfold, I'll sift the beauty of all courts
And capitals, to fetch the fairest woman
That evil has in hiding; after that,
That he may know the sovran one man living
To be his friend, I'll prune all chivalry
To one sure knight. In this wise our new king
Will have his queen to love, as I had mine,—
His friend that he may trust, as I had mine,—
And he will be as gay, if all goes well,
As I have been: as fortunate in his love,
And in his friend as fortunate—as I am!
And what am I? . . . And what are you—you two!
If you are men, why don't you say I'm dreaming?
I know men when I see them, I know daylight;
And I see now the gray shine of our dreams.
I tell you I'm asleep and in my bed! . . .

LANCELOT

But no—no . . . I remember. You are men.
You are no dreams—but God, God, if you were!
If I were strong enough to make you vanish
And have you back again with yesterday—
Before I lent myself to that false hunting,
Which yet may stalk the hours of many more
Than Lancelot's unhappy twelve who died,—
With a misguided Colgrevance to lead them,
And Agravaine to follow and fall next,—
Then should I know at last that I was King,
And I should then be King. But kings are men,
And I have gleaned enough these two years gone
To know that queens are women. Merlin told me:
'The love that never was.' Two years ago
He told me that: 'The love that never was!'
I saw—but I saw nothing. Like the bird
That hides his head, I made myself see nothing.
But yesterday I saw—and I saw fire.
I think I saw it first in Modred's eyes;
Yet he said only truth—and fire is right.
It is—it must be fire. The law says fire.
And I, the King who made the law, say fire!
What have I done—what folly have I said,
Since I came here, of dreaming? Dreaming? Ha!
I wonder if the Queen and Lancelot
Are dreaming! . . . Lancelot! Have they found him yet?
He slashed a way into the outer night—
Somewhere with Bors. We'll have him here anon,
And we shall feed him also to the fire.
There are too many faggots lying cold
That might as well be cleansing, for our good,
A few deferred infections of our state
That honor should no longer look upon.
Thank heaven, I man my drifting wits again!

Gawaine, your brothers, Gareth and Gaheris,
Are by our royal order there to see
And to report. They went unwillingly,
For they are new to law and young to justice;
But what they are to see will harden them
With wholesome admiration of a realm
Where treason's end is ashes. Ashes. Ashes!
Now this is better. I am King again.
Forget, I pray, my drowsy temporizing,
For I was not then properly awake. . . .
What? Hark! Whose crass insanity is that!
If I be King, go find the fellow and hang him
Who beats into the morning on that bell
Before there is a morning! This is dawn!
What! Bedivere? Gawaine? You shake your heads?
I tell you this is dawn! . . . What have I done?
What have I said so lately that I flinch
To think on! What have I sent those boys to see?
I'll put clouts on my eyes, and I'll not see it!
Her face, and hands, and little small white feet,
And all her shining hair and her warm body—
No—for the love of God, no!—it's alive!
She's all alive, and they are burning her—
The Queen—the love—the love that never was!
Gawaine! Bedivere! Gawaine!—Where is Gawaine!
Is he there in the shadow? Is he dead?
Are we all dead? Are we in hell?—Gawaine! . . .
I cannot see her now in the smoke. Her eyes
Are what I see—and her white body is burning!
She never did enough to make me see her
Like that—to make her look at me like that!
There's not room in the world for so much evil
As I see clamoring in her poor white face
For pity. Pity her, God! God! . . . Lancelot!"

LANCELOT

V

GAWAINE, his body trembling and his heart
Pounding as if he were a boy in battle,
Sat crouched as far away from everything
As walls would give him distance. Bedivere
Stood like a man of stone with folded arms,
And wept in stony silence. The King moved
His pallid lips and uttered fitfully
Low fragments of a prayer that was half sad,
Half savage, and was ended in a crash
Of distant sound that anguish lifted near
To those who heard it. Gawaine sprang again
To the same casement where the towers and roofs
Had glimmered faintly a long hour ago,
But saw no terrors yet—though now he heard
A fiercer discord than allegiance rings
To rouse a mourning city: blows, groans, cries,
Loud iron struck on iron, horses trampling,
Death-yells and imprecations, and at last
A moaning silence. Then a murmuring
Of eager fearfulness, which had a note
Of exultation and astonishment,
Came nearer, till a tumult of hard feet
Filled the long corridor where late the King
Had made a softer progress.

"Well then, Lucan,"
The King said, urging an indignity
To qualify suspense: "For what arrears
Of grace are we in debt for this attention?
Why all this early stirring of our sentries,
And their somewhat unseasoned innovation,
To bring you at this unappointed hour?

Are we at war with someone or another,
Without our sanction or intelligence?
Are Lucius and the Romans here to greet us,
Or was it Lucius we saw dead?"

                                    Sir Lucan
Bowed humbly in amazed acknowledgment
Of his intrusion, meanwhile having scanned
What three grief-harrowed faces were revealing:
"Praise God, sir, there are tears in the King's eyes,
And in his friends'. Having regarded them,
And having ventured an abrupt appraisal
Of what I translate. . . ."

                          "Lucan," the King said,
"No matter what procedure or persuasion
Gave you an entrance—tell us what it is
That you have come to tell us, and no more.
There was a most uncivil sound abroad
Before you came. Who riots in the city?"

"Sir, will your patience with a clement ear,
Attend the confirmation of events,
I will, with all available precision,
Say what this morning has inaugurated.
No preface or prolonged exordium
Need aggravate the narrative, I venture.
The man of God, requiring of the Queen
A last assoiling prayer for her salvation,
Heard what none else did hear save God the Father.
Then a great hush descended on a scene
Where stronger men than I fell on their knees,
And wet with tears their mail of shining iron
That soon was to be cleft unconscionably
Beneath a blast of anguish as intense
And fabulous in ardor and effect

LANCELOT

As Jove's is in his lightning. To be short,
They led the Queen—and she went bravely to it,
Or so she was configured in the picture—
A brief way more; and we who did see that,
Believed we saw the last of all her sharing
In this conglomerate and perplexed existence.
But no—and here the prodigy comes in—
The penal flame had hardly bit the faggot,
When, like an onslaught out of Erebus,
There came a crash of horses, and a flash
Of axes, and a hewing down of heroes,
Not like to any in its harsh, profound,
Unholy, and uneven execution.
I felt the breath of one horse on my neck,
And of a sword that all but left a chasm
Where still, praise be to God, I have intact
A face, if not a fair one. I achieved
My flight, I trust, with honorable zeal,
Not having arms, or mail, or preservation
In any phase of necessary iron.
I found a refuge; and there saw the Queen,
All white, and in a swound of woe uplifted
By Lionel, while a dozen fought about him,
And Lancelot, who seized her while he struck,
And with his insane army galloped away,
Before the living, whom he left amazed,
Were sure they were alive among the dead.
Not even in the legendary mist
Of wars that none today may verify,
Did ever men annihilate their kind
With a more vicious inhumanity,
Or a more skilful frenzy. Lancelot
And all his heated adjuncts are by now
Too far, I fear, for such immediate
Reprisal as your majesty perchance . . ."

"O' God's name, Lucan," the King cried, "be still!"
He gripped with either sodden hand an arm
Of his unyielding chair, while his eyes blazed
In anger, wonder, and fierce hesitation.
Then with a sigh that may have told unheard
Of an unwilling gratitude, he gazed
Upon his friends who gazed again at him;
But neither King nor friend said anything
Until the King turned once more to Sir Lucan:
"Be still, or publish with a shorter tongue
The names of our companions who are dead.
Well, were you there? Or did you run so fast
That you were never there? You must have eyes,
Or you could not have run to find us here."

Then Lucan, with a melancholy glance
At Gawaine, who stood glaring his impatience,
Addressed again the King: "I will be short, sir;
Too brief to measure with finality
The scope of what I saw with indistinct
Amazement and incredulous concern.
Sir Tor, Sir Griflet, and Sir Aglovale
Are dead. Sir Gillimer, he is dead. Sir—Sir—
But should a living error be detailed
In my account, how should I meet your wrath
For such a false addition to your sorrow?"
He turned again to Gawaine, who shook now
As if the fear in him were more than fury.—
The King, observing Gawaine, beat his foot
In fearful hesitancy on the floor:
"No, Lucan; if so kind an error lives
In your dead record, you need have no fear.
My sorrow has already, in the weight
Of this you tell, too gross a task for that."

LANCELOT

"Then I must offer you cold naked words,
Without the covering warmth of even one
Forlorn alternative," said Lucan, slowly:
"Sir Gareth, and Sir Gaheris—are dead."

The rage of a fulfilled expectancy,
Long tortured on a rack of endless moments,
Flashed out of Gawaine's overflowing eyes
While he flew forward, seizing Lucan's arms,
And hurled him while he held him.—"Stop, Gawaine,"
The King said grimly. "Now is no time for that.
If Lucan, in a too bewildered heat
Of observation or sad reckoning,
Has added life to death, our joy therefor
Will be the larger. You have lost yourself."

"More than myself it is that I have lost,"
Gawaine said, with a choking voice that faltered:
"Forgive me, Lucan; I was a little mad.
Gareth?—and Gaheris? Do you say their names,
And then say they are dead! They had no arms—
No armor. They were like you—and you live!
Why do you live when they are dead! You ran,
You say? Well, why were they not running—
If they ran only for a pike to die with?
I knew my brothers, and I know your tale
Is not all told. Gareth?—and Gaheris?
Would they stay there to die like silly children?
Did they believe the King would have them die
For nothing? There are dregs of reason, Lucan,
In lunacy itself. My brothers, Lucan,
Were murdered like two dogs. Who murdered them?"

Lucan looked helplessly at Bedivere,
The changeless man of stone, and then at Gawaine:

397

"I cannot use the word that you have used,
Though yours must have an answer. Your two brothers
Would not have squandered or destroyed themselves
In a vain show of action. I pronounce it,
If only for their known obedience
To the King's instant wish. Know then your brothers
Were caught and crowded, this way and then that,
With men and horses raging all around them;
And there were swords and axes everywhere
That heads of men were. Armored and unarmored,
They knew the iron alike. In so great press,
Discrimination would have had no pause
To name itself; and therefore Lancelot
Saw not—or seeing, he may have seen too late—
On whom his axes fell."

"Why do you flood
The name of Lancelot with words enough
To drown him and his army—and his axes! . . .
His axes?—or his axe! Which, Lucan? Speak!
Speak, or by God you'll never speak again! . . .
Forgive me, Lucan; I was a little mad.
You, sir, forgive me; and you, Bedivere.
There are too many currents in this ocean
Where I'm adrift, and I see no land yet.
Men tell of a great whirlpool in the north
Where ships go round until the men aboard
Go dizzy, and are dizzy when they're drowning.
But whether I'm to drown or find the shore,
There is one thing—and only one thing now—
For me to know. . . . His axes? or his axe!
Say, Lucan, or I—O Lucan, speak—speak—speak!
Lucan, did Lancelot kill my two brothers?"

"I say again that in all human chance
He knew not upon whom his axe was falling."

LANCELOT

"So! Then it was his axe and not his axes.
It was his hell-begotten self that did it,
And it was not his men. Gareth! Gaheris!
You came too soon. There was no place for you
Where there was Lancelot. My folly it was,
Not yours, to take for true the inhuman glamour
Of his high-shining fame for that which most
Was not the man. The truth we see too late
Hides half its evil in our stupidity;
And we gape while we groan for what we learn.
An hour ago and I was all but eager
To mourn with Bedivere for grief I had
That I did not say something to this villain—
To this true, gracious, murderous friend of mine—
To comfort him and urge him out of this,
While I was half a fool and half believed
That he was going. Well, there is this to say:
The world that has him will not have him long.
You see how calm I am, now I have said it?
And you, sir, do you see how calm I am?
And it was I who told of shipwrecks—whirlpools—
Drowning! I must have been a little mad,
Not having occupation. Now I have one.
And I have now a tongue as many-phrased
As Lucan's. Gauge it, Lucan, if you will;
Or take my word. It's all one thing to me—
All one, all one! There's only one thing left . . .
Gareth and Gaheris! Gareth! . . . Lancelot!"

"Look, Bedivere," the King said: "look to Gawaine.
Now lead him, you and Lucan, to a chair—
As you and Gawaine led me to this chair
Where I am sitting. We may all be led,
If there be coming on for Camelot
Another day like this. Now leave me here,

Alone with Gawaine. When a strong man goes
Like that, it makes him sick to see his friends
Around him. Leave us, and go now. Sometimes
I'll scarce remember that he's not my son,
So near he seems. I thank you, gentlemen."

The King, alone with Gawaine, who said nothing,
Had yet no heart for news of Lancelot
Or Guinevere. He saw them on their way
To Joyous Gard, where Tristram and Isolt
Had islanded of old their stolen love,
While Mark of Cornwall entertained a vengeance
Envisaging an ending of all that;
And he could see the two of them together
As Mark had seen Isolt there, and her knight,—
Though not, like Mark, with murder in his eyes.
He saw them as if they were there already,
And he were a lost thought long out of mind;
He saw them lying in each other's arms,
Oblivious of the living and the dead
They left in Camelot. Then he saw the dead
That lay so quiet outside the city walls,
And wept, and left the Queen to Lancelot—
Or would have left her, had the will been his
To leave or take; for now he could acknowledge
An inrush of a desolate thanksgiving
That she, with death around her, had not died.
The vision of a peace that humbled him,
And yet might save the world that he had won,
Came slowly into view like something soft
And ominous on all-fours, without a spirit
To make it stand upright. "Better be that,
Even that, than blood," he sighed, "if that be peace."
But looking down on Gawaine, who said nothing,
He shook his head: "The King has had his world,

LANCELOT

And he shall have no peace. With Modred here,
And Agravaine with Gareth, who is dead
With Gaheris, Gawaine will have no peace.
Gawaine or Modred—Gawaine with his hate,
Or Modred with his anger for his birth,
And the black malady of his ambition—
Will make of my Round Table, where was drawn
The circle of a world, a thing of wreck
And yesterday—a furniture forgotten;
And I, who loved the world as Merlin did,
May lose it as he lost it, for a love
That was not peace, and therefore was not love."

VI

THE dark of Modred's hour not yet availing,
Gawaine it was who gave the King no peace;
Gawaine it was who goaded him and drove him
To Joyous Gard, where now for long his army,
Disheartened with unprofitable slaughter,
Fought for their weary King and wearily
Died fighting. Only Gawaine's hate it was
That held the King's knights and his warrior slaves
Close-hived in exile, dreaming of old scenes
Where Sorrow, and her demon sister Fear,
Now shared the dusty food of loneliness,
From Orkney to Cornwall. There was no peace,
Nor could there be, so Gawaine told the King,
And so the King in anguish told himself,
Until there was an end of one of them—
Of Gawaine or the King, or Lancelot,
Who might have had an end, as either knew,
Long since of Arthur and of Gawaine with him.
One evening in the moonlight Lancelot
And Bors, his kinsman, and the loyalest,

If least assured, of all who followed him,
Sat gazing from an ivy-cornered casement
In angry silence upon Arthur's horde,
Who in the silver distance, without sound,
Were dimly burying dead men. Sir Bors,
Reiterating vainly what was told
As wholesome hearing for unhearing ears,
Said now to Lancelot: "And though it be
For no more now than always, let me speak:
You have a pity for the King, you say,
That is not hate; and for Gawaine you have
A grief that is not hate. Pity and grief!
And the Queen all but shrieking out her soul
That morning when we snatched her from the faggots
That were already crackling when we came!
Why, Lancelot, if in you is an answer,
Have you so vast a charity for the King,
And so enlarged a grief for his gay nephew,
Whose tireless hate for you has only one
Disastrous appetite? You know for what—
For your slow blood. I knew you, Lancelot,
When all this would have been a merry fable
For smiling men to yawn at and forget,
As they forget their physic. Pity and grief
Are in your eyes. I see them well enough;
And I saw once with you, in a far land,
The glimmering of a Light that you saw nearer—
Too near for your salvation or advantage,
If you be what you seem. What I saw then
Made life a wilder mystery than ever,
And earth a new illusion. You, maybe,
Saw pity and grief. What I saw was a Gleam,
To fight for or to die for—till we know
Too much to fight or die. Tonight you turn
A page whereon your deeds are to engross

LANCELOT

Inexorably their story of tomorrow;
And then tomorrow. How many of these tomorrows
Are coming to ask unanswered why this war
Was fought and fought for the vain sake of slaughter?
Why carve a compost of a multitude,
When only two, discriminately despatched,
Would sum the end of what you know is ending
And leave to you the scorch of no more blood
Upon your blistered soul? The Light you saw
Was not for this poor crumbling realm of Arthur,
Nor more for Rome; but for another state
That shall be neither Rome nor Camelot,
Nor one that we may name. Why longer, then,
Are you and Gawaine to anoint with war,
That even in hell would be superfluous,
A reign already dying, and ripe to die?
I leave you to your last interpretation
Of what may be the pleasure of your madness."

Meanwhile a mist was hiding the dim work
Of Arthur's men; and like another mist,
All gray, came Guinevere to Lancelot,
Whom Bors had left, not having had of him
The largess of a word. She laid her hands
Upon his hair, vexing him to brief speech:
"And you—are you like Bors?"

"I may be so,"
She said; and she saw faintly where she gazed,
Like distant insects of a shadowy world,
Dim clusters here and there of shadowy men
Whose occupation was her long abhorrence:
"If he came here and went away again,
And all for nothing, I may be like Bors.
Be glad, at least, that I am not like Mark

Of Cornwall, who stood once behind a man
And slew him without saying he was there.
Not Arthur, I believe, nor yet Gawaine,
Would have done quite like that; though only God
May say what there's to come before this war
Shall have an end—unless you are to see,
As I have seen so long, a way to end it."

He frowned, and watched again the coming mist
That hid with a cold veil of augury
The stillness of an empire that was dying:
"And are you here to say that if I kill
Gawaine and Arthur we shall both be happy?"

"Is there still such a word as happiness?
I come to tell you nothing, Lancelot,
That folly and waste have not already told you.
Were you another man than Lancelot,
I might say folly and fear. But no,—no fear,
As I know fear, was yet composed and wrought,
By man, for your delay and your undoing.
God knows how cruelly and how truly now
You might say, that of all who breathe and suffer
There may be others who are not so near
To you as I am, and so might say better
What I say only with a tongue not apt
Or guarded for much argument. A woman,
As men have known since Adam heard the first
Of Eve's interpreting of how it was
In Paradise, may see but one side only—
Where maybe there are two, to say no more.
Yet here, for you and me, and so for all
Caught with us in this lamentable net,
I see but one deliverance: I see none,
Unless you cut for us a clean way out,

LANCELOT

So rending these hate-woven webs of horror
Before they mesh the world. And if the world
Or Arthur's name be now a dying glory,
Why bleed it for the sparing of a man
Who hates you, and a King that hates himself?
If war be war—and I make only blood
Of your red writing—why dishonor Time
For torture longer drawn in your slow game
Of empty slaughter? Tomorrow it will be
The King's move, I suppose, and we shall have
One more magnificent waste of nameless pawns,
And of a few more knights. God, how you love
This game!—to make so loud a shambles of it,
When you have only twice to lift your finger
To signal peace, and give to this poor drenched
And clotted earth a time to heal itself.
Twice over I say to you, if war be war,
Why play with it? Why look a thousand ways
Away from what it is, only to find
A few stale memories left that would requite
Your tears with your destruction? Tears, I say,
For I have seen your tears; I see them now,
Although the moon is dimmer than it was
Before I came. I wonder if I dimmed it.
I wonder if I brought this fog here with me
To make you chillier even than you are
When I am not so near you. . . . Lancelot,
There must be glimmering yet somewhere within you
The last spark of a little willingness
To tell me why it is this war goes on.
Once I believed you told me everything;
And what you may have hidden was no matter,
For what you told was all I needed then.
But crumbs that are a festival for joy
Make a dry fare for sorrow; and the few

Spared words that were enough to nourish faith,
Are for our lonely fears a frugal poison.
So, Lancelot, if only to bring back
For once the ghost of a forgotten mercy,
Say now, even though you strike me to the floor
When you have said it, for what untold end
All this goes on. Am I not anything now?
Is Gawaine, who would feed you to wild swine,
And laugh to see them tear you, more than I am?
Is Arthur, at whose word I was dragged out
To wear for you the fiery crown itself
Of human torture, more to you than I am?
Am I, because you saw death touch me once,
Too gross a trifle to be longer prized?
Not many days ago, when you lay hurt
And aching on your bed, and I cried out
Aloud on heaven that I should bring you there,
You said you would have paid the price of hell
To save me that foul morning from the fire.
You paid enough: yet when you told me that,
With death going on outside the while you said it,
I heard the woman in me asking why.
Nor do I wholly find an answer now
In any shine of any far-off Light
You may have seen. Knowing the world, you know
How surely and how indifferently that Light
Shall burn through many a war that is to be,
To which this war were no more than a smear
On circumstance. The world has not begun.
The Light you saw was not the Light of Rome,
Or Time, though you seem battling here for time,
While you are still at war with Arthur's host
And Gawaine's hate. How many thousand men
Are going to their death before Gawaine
And Arthur go to theirs—and I to mine?"

LANCELOT

Lancelot, looking off into the fog,
In which his fancy found the watery light
Of a dissolving moon, sighed without hope
Of saying what the Queen would have him say:
"I fear, my lady, my fair nephew Bors,
Whose tongue affords a random wealth of sound,
May lately have been scattering on the air
For you a music less oracular
Than to your liking. . . . Say, then, you had split
The uncovered heads of two men with an axe,
Not knowing whose heads—if that's a palliation—
And seen their brains fly out and splash the ground
As they were common offal, and then learned
That you had butchered Gaheris and Gareth—
Gareth, who had for me a greater love
Than any that has ever trod the ways
Of a gross world that early would have crushed him,—
Even you, in your quick fever of dispatch,
Might hesitate before you drew the blood
Of him that was their brother, and my friend.
Yes, he was more my friend, was I to know,
Than I had said or guessed; for it was Gawaine
Who gave to Bors the word that might have saved us,
And Arthur's fading empire, for the time
Till Modred had in his dark wormy way
Crawled into light again with a new ruin
At work in that occult snake's brain of his.
And even in your prompt obliteration
Of Arthur from a changing world that rocks
Itself into a dizziness around him,
A moment of attendant reminiscence
Were possible, if not likely. Had he made
A knight of you, scrolling your name with his
Among the first of men—and in his love
Inveterately the first—and had you then

Betrayed his fame and honor to the dust
That now is choking him, you might in time—
You might, I say—to my degree succumb.
Forgive me, if my lean words are for yours
Too bare an answer, and ascribe to them
No tinge of allegation or reproach.
What I said once to you I said for ever—
That I would pay the price of hell to save you.
As for the Light, leave that for me alone;
Or leave as much of it as yet for me
May shine. Should I, through any unforeseen
Remote effect of awkwardness or chance,
Be done to death or durance by the King,
I leave some writing wherein I beseech
For you the clemency of afterthought.
Were I to die and he to see me dead,
My living prayer, surviving the cold hand
That wrote, would leave you in his larger prudence,
If I have known the King, free and secure
To bide the summoning of another King
More great than Arthur. But all this is language;
And I know more than words have yet the scope
To show of what's to come. Go now to rest;
And sleep, if there be sleep. There was a moon;
And now there is no sky where the moon was.
Sometimes I wonder if this be the world
We live in, or the world that lives in us."

The new day, with a cleansing crash of rain
That washed and sluiced the soiled and hoof-torn field
Of Joyous Gard, prepared for Lancelot
And his wet men the not unwelcome scene
Of a drenched emptiness without an army.
"Our friend the foe is given to dry fighting,"
Said Lionel, advancing with a shrug,

LANCELOT

To Lancelot, who saw beyond the rain.
And later Lionel said, "What fellows are they,
Who are so thirsty for their morning ride
That swimming horses would have hardly time
To eat before they swam? You, Lancelot,
If I see rather better than a blind man,
Are waiting on three pilgrims who must love you,
To voyage a flood like this. No friend have I,
To whisper not of three, on whom to count
For such a loyal wash. The King himself
Would entertain a kindly qualm or so,
Before he suffered such a burst of heaven
To splash even three musicians."

                              "Good Lionel,
I thank you, but you need afflict your fancy
No longer for my sake. For these who come,
If I be not immoderately deceived,
Are bearing with them the white flower of peace—
Which I could hope might never parch or wither,
Were I a stranger to this ravening world
Where we have mostly a few rags and tags
Between our skins and those that wrap the flesh
Of less familiar brutes we feed upon
That we may feed the more on one another."

"Well, now that we have had your morning grace
Before our morning meat, pray tell to me
The why and whence of this anomalous
Horse-riding offspring of the Fates. Who are they?"

"I do not read their features or their names;
But if I read the King, they are from Rome,
Spurred here by the King's prayer for no delay;

And I pray God aloud that I say true."
And after a long watching, neither speaking,
"You do," said Lionel; "for by my soul,
I see no other than my lord the Bishop,
Who does God's holy work in Rochester.
Since you are here, you may as well abide here,
While I go foraging."

                        Now in the gateway,
The Bishop, who rode something heavily,
Was glad for rest though grim in his refusal
At once of entertainment or refection:
"What else you do, Sir Lancelot, receive me
As one among the honest when I say
That my voluminous thanks were less by cantos
Than my damp manner feels. Nay, hear my voice:
If once I'm off this royal animal,
How o' God's name shall I get on again?
Moreover, the King waits. With your accord,
Sir Lancelot, I'll dry my rainy face,
While you attend what's herein written down,
In language of portentous brevity,
For the King's gracious pleasure and for yours,
Whereof the burden is the word of Rome,
Requiring your deliverance of the Queen
Not more than seven days hence. The King returns
Anon to Camelot; and I go with him,
Praise God, if what he waits now is your will
To end an endless war. No recrudescence,
As you may soon remark, of what is past
Awaits the Queen, or any doubt soever
Of the King's mercy. Have you more to say
Than Rome has written, or do I perceive
Your tranquil acquiescence? Is it so?
Then be it so! Venite. Pax vobiscum."

LANCELOT

"To end an endless war with 'pax vobiscum'
Would seem a ready schedule for a bishop;
Would God that I might see the end of it!"
Lancelot, like a statue in the gateway,
Regarded with a qualified rejoicing
The fading out of his three visitors
Into the cold and swallowing wall of storm
Between him and the battle-wearied King
And the unwearying hatred of Gawaine.
To Bors his nephew, and to Lionel,
He glossed a tale of Roman intercession,
Knowing that for a time, and a long time,
The sweetest fare that he might lay before them
Would hold an evil taste of compromise.
To Guinevere, who questioned him at noon
Of what by then had made of Joyous Gard
A shaken hive of legend-heavy wonder,
He said what most it was the undying Devil,
Who ruled him when he might, would have him say:
"Your confident arrangement of the board
For this day's game was notably not to be;
Today was not for the King's move or mine,
But for the Bishop's; and the board is empty.
The words that I have waited for more days
Than are to now my tallage of gray hairs
Have come at last, and at last you are free.
So, for a time, there will be no more war;
And you are going home to Camelot."

"To Camelot?" . . .
            "To Camelot." But his words
Were said for no queen's hearing. In his arms
He caught her when she fell; and in his arms
He carried her away. The word of Rome
Was in the rain. There was no other sound.

VII

All day the rain came down on Joyous Gard,
Where now there was no joy, and all that night
The rain came down. Shut in for none to find him
Where an unheeded log-fire fought the storm
With upward swords that flashed along the wall
Faint hieroglyphs of doom not his to read,
Lancelot found a refuge where at last
He might see nothing. Glad for sight of nothing,
He saw no more. Now and again he buried
A lonely thought among the coals and ashes
Outside the reaching flame and left it there,
Quite as he left outside in rainy graves
The sacrificial hundreds who had filled them.
"They died, Gawaine," he said, "and you live on,
You and the King, as if there were no dying;
And it was I, Gawaine, who let you live—
You and the King. For what more length of time,
I wonder, may there still be found on earth
Foot-room for four of us? We are too many
For one world, Gawaine; and there may be soon,
For one or other of us, a way out.
As men are listed, we are men for men
To fear; and I fear Modred more than any.
But even the ghost of Modred at the door—
The ghost I should have made him—would employ
For time as hard as this a louder knuckle,
Assuredly now, than that. And I would see
No mortal face till morning. . . . Well, are you well
Again? Are you as well again as ever?"

He led her slowly on with a cold show
Of care that was less heartening for the Queen

LANCELOT

Than anger would have been, into the firelight,
And there he gave her cushions. "Are you warm?"
He said; and she said nothing. "Are you afraid?"
He said again; "are you still afraid of Gawaine?
As often as you think of him and hate him,
Remember too that he betrayed his brothers
To us that he might save us. Well, he saved us;
And Rome, whose name to you was never music,
Saves you again, with heaven alone may tell
What others who might have their time to sleep
In earth out there, with the rain falling on them,
And with no more to fear of wars tonight
Than you need fear of Gawaine or of Arthur.
The way before you is a safer way
For you to follow than when I was in it.
We children who forget the whips of Time,
To live within the hour, are slow to see
That all such hours are passing. They were past
When you came here with me."

         She looked away,
Seeming to read the firelight on the walls
Before she spoke: "When I came here with you,
And found those eyes of yours, I could have wished
And prayed it were the end of hours, and years.
What was it made you save me from the fire,
If only out of memories and forebodings
To build around my life another fire
Of slower faggots? If you had let me die,
Those other faggots would be ashes now,
And all of me that you have ever loved
Would be a few more ashes. If I read
The past as well as you have read the future
You need say nothing of ingratitude,
For I say only lies. My soul, of course,

It was you loved. You told me so yourself.
And that same precious blue-veined cream-white soul
Will soon be safer, if I understand you,
In Camelot, where the King is, than elsewhere
On earth. What more, in faith, have I to ask
Of earth or heaven than that! Although I fell
When you said Camelot, are you to know,
Surely, the stroke you gave me then was not
The measure itself of ecstasy? We women
Are such adept inveterates in our swooning
That we fall down for joy as easily
As we eat one another to show our love.
Even horses, seeing again their absent masters,
Have wept for joy; great dogs have died of it."
Having said as much as that, she frowned and held
Her small white hands out for the fire to warm them.
Forward she leaned, and forward her thoughts went—
To Camelot. But they were not there long,
Her thoughts; for soon she flashed her eyes again,
And he found in them what he wished were tears
Of angry sorrow for what she had said.
"What are you going to do with me?" she asked;
And all her old incisiveness came back,
With a new thrust of malice, which he felt
And feared. "What are you going to do with me?
What does a child do with a worn-out doll?
I was a child once; and I had a father.
He was a king; and, having royal ways,
He made a queen of me—King Arthur's queen.
And if that happened, once upon a time,
Why may it not as well be happening now
That I am not a queen? Was I a queen
When first you brought me here with one torn rag
To cover me? Was I overmuch a queen
When I sat up at last, and in a gear

LANCELOT

That would have made a bishop dance to Cardiff
To see me wearing it? Was I Queen then?"

"You were the Queen of Christendom," he said,
Not smiling at her, "whether now or not
You deem it an unchristian exercise
To vilipend the wearing of the vanished.
The women may have reasoned, insecurely,
That what one queen had worn would please another.
I left them to their ingenuities."

Once more he frowned away a threatening smile,
But soon forgot the memory of all smiling
While he gazed on the glimmering face and hair
Of Guinevere—the glory of white and gold
That had been his, and were, for taking of it,
Still his, to cloud, with an insidious gleam
Of earth, another that was not of earth,
And so to make of him a thing of night—
A moth between a window and a star,
Not wholly lured by one or led by the other.
The more he gazed upon her beauty there,
The longer was he living in two kingdoms,
Not owning in his heart the king of either,
And ruling not himself. There was an end
Of hours, he told her silent face again,
In silence. On the morning when his fury
Wrenched her from that foul fire in Camelot,
Where blood paid irretrievably the toll
Of her release, the whips of Time had fallen
Upon them both. All this to Guinevere
He told in silence and he told in vain.

Observing her ten fingers variously,
She sighed, as in equivocal assent,
"No two queens are alike."

"Is that the flower
Of all your veiled invention?" Lancelot said,
Smiling at last: "If you say, saying all that,
You are not like Isolt—well, you are not.
Isolt was a physician, who cured men
Their wounds, and sent them rowelling for more;
Isolt was too dark, and too versatile;
She was too dark for Mark, if not for Tristram.
Forgive me; I was saying that to myself,
And not to make you shiver. No two queens—
Was that it?—are alike? A longer story
Might have a longer telling and tell less.
Your tale's as brief as Pelleas with his vengeance
On Gawaine, whom he swore that he would slay
At once for stealing of the lady Ettard."

"Treasure my scantling wits, if you enjoy them;
Wonder a little, too, that I conserve them
Through the eternal memory of one morning,
And in these years of days that are the death
Of men who die for me. I should have died.
I should have died for them."

"You are wrong," he said;
"They died because Gawaine went mad with hate
For loss of his two brothers and set the King
On fire with fear, the two of them believing
His fear was vengeance when it was in fact
A royal desperation. They died because
Your world, my world, and Arthur's world is dying,
As Merlin said it would. No blame is yours;
For it was I who led you from the King—
Or rather, to say truth, it was your glory
That led my love to lead you from the King—
By flowery ways, that always end somewhere,

LANCELOT

To fire and fright and exile, and release.
And if you bid your memory now to blot
Your story from the book of what has been,
Your phantom happiness were a ghost indeed,
And I the least of weasels among men,—
Too false to manhood and your sacrifice
To merit a niche in hell. If that were so,
I'd swear there was no light for me to follow,
Save your eyes to the grave; and to the last
I might not know that all hours have an end;
I might be one of those who feed themselves
By grace of God, on hopes dryer than hay,
Enjoying not what they eat, yet always eating.
The Vision shattered, a man's love of living
Becomes at last a trap and a sad habit,
More like an ailing dotard's love of liquor
That ails him, than a man's right love of woman,
Or of his God. There are men enough like that,
And I might come to that. Though I see far
Before me now, could I see, looking back,
A life that you could wish had not been lived,
I might be such a man. Could I believe
Our love was nothing mightier then than we were,
I might be such a man—a living dead man,
One of these days."

                              Guinevere looked at him,
And all that any woman has not said
Was in one look: "Why do you stab me now
With such a needless 'then'? If I am going—
And I suppose I am—are the words all lost
That men have said before to dogs and children
To make them go away? Why use a knife,
When there are words enough without your 'then'
To cut as deep as need be? What I ask you

Is never more to ask me if my life
Be one that I could wish had not been lived—
And that you never torture it again,
To make it bleed and ache as you do now,
Past all indulgence or necessity.
Were you to give a lonely child who loved you
One living thing to keep—a bird, may be—
Before you went away from her forever,
Would you, for surety not to be forgotten,
Maim it and leave it bleeding on her fingers?
And would you leave the child alone with it—
Alone, and too bewildered even to cry,
Till you were out of sight? Are you men never
To know what words are? Do you doubt sometimes
A Vision that lets you see so far away
That you forget so lightly who it was
You must have cared for once to be so kind—
Or seem so kind—when she, and for that only,
Had that been all, would throw down crowns and glories
To share with you the last part of the world?
And even the queen in me would hardly go
So far off as to vanish. If I were patched
And scrapped in what the sorriest fisher-wife
In Orkney might give mumbling to a beggar,
I doubt if oafs and yokels would annoy me
More than I willed they should. Am I so old
And dull, so lean and waning, or what not,
That you must hurry away to grasp and hoard
The small effect of time I might have stolen
From you and from a Light that where it lives
Must live for ever? Where does history tell you
The Lord himself would seem in so great haste
As you for your perfection? If our world—
Your world and mine and Arthur's, as you say—
Is going out now to make way for another,

LANCELOT

Why not before it goes, and I go with it,
Have yet one morsel more of life together,
Before death sweeps the table and our few crumbs
Of love are a few last ashes on a fire
That cannot hurt your Vision, or burn long?
You cannot warm your lonely fingers at it
For a great waste of time when I am dead:
When I am dead you will be on your way,
With maybe not so much as one remembrance
Of all I was, to follow you and torment you.
Some word of Bors may once have given color
To some few that I said, but they were true—
Whether Bors told them first to me, or whether
I told them first to Bors. The Light you saw
Was not the Light of Rome; the word you had
Of Rome was not the word of God—though Rome
Has refuge for the weary and heavy-laden.
Were I to live too long I might seek Rome
Myself, and be the happier when I found it.
Meanwhile, am I to be no more to you
Than a moon-shadow of a lonely stranger
Somewhere in Camelot? And is there no region
In this poor fading world of Arthur's now
Where I may be again what I was once—
Before I die? Should I live to be old,
I shall have been long since too far away
For you to hate me then; and I shall know
How old I am by seeing it in your eyes."
Her misery told itself in a sad laugh,
And in a rueful twisting of her face
That only beauty's perilous privilege
Of injury would have yielded or suborned
As hope's infirm accessory while she prayed
Through Lancelot to heaven for Lancelot.
She looked away: "If I were God," she said,

"I should say, 'Let them be as they have been.
A few more years will heap no vast account
Against eternity, and all their love
Was what I gave them. They brought on the end
Of Arthur's empire, which I wrought through Merlin
For the world's knowing of what kings and queens
Are made for; but they knew not what they did—
Save as a price, and as a fear that love
Might end in fear. It need not end that way,
And they need fear no more for what I gave them;
For it was I who gave them to each other.'
If I were God, I should say that to you."
He saw tears quivering in her pleading eyes,
But through them she could see, with a wild hope,
That he was fighting. When he spoke, he smiled—
Much as he might have smiled at her, she thought,
Had she been Gawaine, Gawaine having given
To Lancelot, who yet would have him live,
An obscure wound that would not heal or kill.

"My life was living backward for the moment,"
He said, still burying in the coals and ashes
Thoughts that he would not think. His tongue was dry,
And each dry word he said was choking him
As he said on: "I cannot ask of you
That you be kind to me, but there's a kindness
That is your proper debt. Would you cajole
Your reason with a weary picturing
On walls or on vain air of what your fancy,
Like firelight, makes of nothing but itself?
Do you not see that I go from you only
Because you go from me?—because our path
Led where at last it had an end in havoc,
As long we knew it must—as Arthur too,
And Merlin knew it must?—as God knew it must?

LANCELOT

A power that I should not have said was mine—
That was not mine, and is not mine—avails me
Strangely tonight, although you are here with me;
And I see much in what has come to pass
That is to be. The Light that I have seen,
As you say true, is not the light of Rome,
Albeit the word of Rome that set you free
Was more than mine or the King's. To flout that word
Would sound the preparation of a terror
To which a late small war on our account
Were a king's pastime and a queen's annoyance;
And that, for the good fortune of a world
As yet not over-fortuned, may not be.
There may be war to come when you are gone,
For I doubt yet Gawaine; but Rome will hold you,
Hold you in Camelot. If there be more war,
No fire of mine shall feed it, nor shall you
Be with me to endure it. You are free;
And free, you are going home to Camelot.
There is no other way than one for you,
Nor is there more than one for me. We have lived,
And we shall die. I thank you for my life.
Forgive me if I say no more tonight."
He rose, half blind with pity that was no longer
The servant of his purpose or his will,
To grope away somewhere among the shadows
For wine to drench his throat and his dry tongue,
That had been saying he knew not what to her
For whom his life-devouring love was now
A scourge of mercy.

      Like a blue-eyed Medea
Of white and gold, broken with grief and fear
And fury that shook her speechless while she waited,
Yet left her calm enough for Lancelot

To see her without seeing, she stood up
To breathe and suffer. Fury could not live long,
With grief and fear like hers and love like hers,
When speech came back: "No other way now than one?
Free? Do you call me free? Do you mean by that
There was never woman alive freer to live
Than I am free to die? Do you call me free
Because you are driven so near to death yourself
With weariness of me, and the sight of me,
That you must use a crueller knife than ever,
And this time at my heart, for me to watch
Before you drive it home? For God's sake, drive it!
Drive it as often as you have the others,
And let the picture of each wound it makes
On me be shown to women and men for ever;
And the good few that know—let them reward you.
I hear them, in such low and pitying words
As only those who know, and are not many,
Are used to say: 'The good knight Lancelot
It was who drove the knife home to her heart,
Rather than drive her home to Camelot.'
Home! Free! Would you let me go there again—
To be at home?—be free? To be his wife?
To live in his arms always, and so hate him
That I could heap around him the same faggots
That you put out with blood? Go home, you say?
Home?—where I saw the black post waiting for me
That morning?—saw those good men die for me—
Gareth and Gaheris, Lamorak's brother Tor,
And all the rest? Are men to die for me
For ever? Is there water enough, do you think,
Between this place and that for me to drown in?"

"There is time enough, I think, between this hour
And some wise hour tomorrow, for you to sleep in.

422

LANCELOT

When you are safe again in Camelot,
The King will not molest you or pursue you;
The King will be a suave and chastened man.
In Camelot you shall have no more to dread
Than you shall hear then of this rain that roars
Tonight as if it would be roaring always.
I do not ask you to forgive the faggots,
Though I would have you do so for your peace.
Only the wise who know may do so much,
And they, as you say truly, are not many.
And I would say no more of this tonight."

"Then do not ask me for the one last thing
That I shall give to God! I thought I died
That morning. Why am I alive again,
To die again? Are you all done with me?
Is there no longer something left of me
That made you need me? Have I lost myself
So fast that what a mirror says I am
Is not what is, but only what was once?
Does half a year do that with us, I wonder,
Or do I still have something that was mine
That afternoon when I was in the sunset,
Under the oak, and you were looking at me?
Your look was not all sorrow for your going
To find the Light and leave me in the dark—
But I am the daughter of Leodogran,
And you are Lancelot,—and have a tongue
To say what I may not. . . . Why must I go
To Camelot when your kinsmen hold all France?
Why is there not some nook in some old house
Where I might hide myself—with you or not?
Is there no castle, or cabin, or cave in the woods?
Yes, I could love the bats and owls, in France,
A lifetime sooner than I could the King

That I shall see in Camelot, waiting there
For me to cringe and beg of him again
The dust of mercy, calling it holy bread.
I wronged him, but he bought me with a name
Too large for my king-father to relinquish—
Though I prayed him, and I prayed God aloud,
To spare that crown. I called it crown enough
To be my father's child—until you came.
And then there were no crowns or kings or fathers
Under the sky. I saw nothing but you.
And you would whip me back to bury myself
In Camelot, with a few slave maids and lackeys
To be my grovelling court; and even their faces
Would not hide half the story. Take me to France—
To France or Egypt,—anywhere else on earth
Than Camelot! Is there not room in France
For two more dots of mortals?—or for one?—
For me alone? Let Lionel go with me—
Or Bors. Let Bors go with me into France,
And leave me there. And when you think of me,
Say Guinevere is in France, where she is happy;
And you may say no more of her than that . . .
Why do you not say something to me now—
Before I go? Why do you look—and look?
Why do you frown as if you thought me mad?
I am not mad—but I shall soon be mad,
If I go back to Camelot where the King is.
Lancelot! . . . Is there nothing left of me?
Nothing of what you called your white and gold,
And made so much of? Has it all gone by?
He must have been a lonely God who made
Man in his image and then made only a woman!
Poor fool she was! Poor Queen! Poor Guinevere!
There were kings and bishops once, under her window
Like children, and all scrambling for a flower.

LANCELOT

Time was!—God help me, what am I saying now!
Does a Queen's memory wither away to that?
Am I so dry as that? Am I a shell?
Have I become so cheap as this? . . . I wonder
Why the King cared!" She fell down on her knees
Crying, and held his knees with hungry fear.

Over his folded arms, as over the ledge
Of a storm-shaken parapet, he could see,
Below him, like a tumbling flood of gold,
The Queen's hair with a crumpled foam of white
Around it: "Do you ask, as a child would,
For France because it has a name? How long
Do you conceive the Queen of the Christian world
Would hide herself in France were she to go there?
How long should Rome require to find her there?
And how long, Rome or not, would such a flower
As you survive the unrooting and transplanting
That you commend so ingenuously tonight?
And if we shared your cave together, how long,
And in the joy of what obscure seclusion,
If I may say it, were Lancelot of the Lake
And Guinevere an unknown man and woman,
For no eye to see twice? There are ways to France,
But why pursue them for Rome's interdict,
And for a longer war? Your path is now
As open as mine is dark—or would be dark,
Without the Light that once had blinded me
To death, had I seen more. I shall see more,
And I shall not be blind. I pray, moreover,
That you be not so now. You are a Queen,
And you may be no other. You are too brave
And kind and fair for men to cheer with lies.
We cannot make one world of two, nor may we
Count one life more than one. Could we go back

425

To the old garden, we should not stay long;
The fruit that we should find would all be fallen,
And have the taste of earth."

                        When she looked up,
A tear fell on her forehead. "Take me away!"
She cried. "Why do you do this? Why do you say this?
If you are sorry for me, take me away
From Camelot! Send me away—drive me away—
Only away from there! The King is there—
And I may kill him if I see him there.
Take me away—take me away to France!
And if I cannot hide myself in France,
Then let me die in France!"

                            He shook his head,
Slowly, and raised her slowly in his arms,
Holding her there; and they stood long together.
And there was no sound then of anything,
Save a low moaning of a broken woman,
And the cold roaring down of that long rain.

All night the rain came down on Joyous Gard;
And all night, there before the crumbling embers
That faded into feathery death-like dust,
Lancelot sat and heard it. He saw not
The fire that died, but he heard rain that fell
On all those graves around him and those years
Behind him; and when dawn came, he was cold.
At last he rose, and for a time stood seeing
The place where she had been. She was not there;
He was not sure that she had ever been there;
He was not sure there was a Queen, or a King,
Or a world with kingdoms on it. He was cold.
He was not sure of anything but the Light—

LANCELOT

The Light he saw not. "And I shall not see it,"
He thought, "so long as I kill men for Gawaine.
If I kill him, I may as well kill myself;
And I have killed his brothers." He tried to sleep,
But rain had washed the sleep out of his life,
And there was no more sleep. When he awoke,
He did not know that he had been asleep;
And the same rain was falling. At some strange hour
It ceased, and there was light. And seven days after,
With a cavalcade of silent men and women,
The Queen rode into Camelot, where the King was,
And Lancelot rode grimly at her side.

When he rode home again to Joyous Gard,
The storm in Gawaine's eyes and the King's word
Of banishment attended him. "Gawaine
Will give the King no peace," Lionel said;
And Lancelot said after him, "Therefore
The King will have no peace."—And so it was
That Lancelot, with many of Arthur's knights
That were not Arthur's now, sailed out one day
From Cardiff to Bayonne, where soon Gawaine,
The King, and the King's army followed them,
For longer sorrow and for longer war.

VIII

For longer war they came, and with a fury
That only Modred's opportunity,
Seized in the dark of Britain, could have hushed
And ended in a night. For Lancelot,
When he was hurried amazed out of his rest
Of a gray morning to the scarred gray wall
Of Benwick, where he slept and fought, and saw
Not yet the termination of a strife

That irked him out of utterance, found again
Before him a still plain without an army.
What the mist hid between him and the distance
He knew not, but a multitude of doubts
And hopes awoke in him, and one black fear,
At sight of a truce-waving messenger
In whose approach he read, as by the Light
Itself, the last of Arthur. The man reined
His horse outside the gate, and Lancelot,
Above him on the wall, with a sick heart,
Listened: "Sir Gawaine to Sir Lancelot
Sends greeting; and this with it, in his hand.
The King has raised the siege, and you in France
He counts no longer with his enemies.
His toil is now for Britain, and this war
With you, Sir Lancelot, is an old war,
If you will have it so."—"Bring the man in,"
Said Lancelot, "and see that he fares well."

All through the sunrise, and alone, he sat
With Gawaine's letter, looking toward the sea
That flowed somewhere between him and the land
That waited Arthur's coming, but not his.
"King Arthur's war with me is an old war,
If I will have it so," he pondered slowly;
"And Gawaine's hate for me is an old hate,
If I will have it so. But Gawaine's wound
Is not a wound that heals; and there is Modred—
Inevitable as ruin after flood.
The cloud that has been darkening Arthur's empire
May now have burst, with Arthur still in France,
Many hours away from Britain, and a world
Away from me. But I read this in my heart.
If in the blot of Modred's evil shadow,
Conjecture views a cloudier world than is,

LANCELOT

So much the better, then, for clouds and worlds,
And kings. Gawaine says nothing yet of this,
But when he tells me nothing he tells all.
Now he is here, fordone and left behind,
Pursuant of his wish; and there are words
That he would say to me. Had I not struck him
Twice to the earth, unwillingly, for my life,
My best eye then, I fear, were best at work
On what he has not written. As it is,
If I go seek him now, and in good faith,
My faith may dig my grave. If so, then so.
If I know only with my eyes and ears,
I may as well not know."

      Gawaine, having scanned
His words and sent them, found a way to sleep—
And sleeping, to forget. But he remembered
Quickly enough when he woke up to meet
With his the shining gaze of Lancelot
Above him in a shuttered morning gloom,
Seeming at first a darkness that had eyes.
Fear for a moment seized him, and his heart,
Long whipped and driven with fever, paused and flickered,
As like to fail too soon. Fearing to move,
He waited; fearing to speak, he waited; fearing
To see too clearly or too much, he waited;
For what, he wondered—even the while he knew
It was for Lancelot to say something.
And soon he did: "Gawaine, I thought at first
No man was here."

      "No man was, till you came.
Sit down; and for the love of God who made you,
Say nothing to me now of my three brothers.
Gareth and Gaheris and Agravaine

Are gone; and I am going after them;
Of such is our election. When you gave
That ultimate knock on my revengeful head,
You did a piece of work."

"May God forgive,"
Lancelot said, "I did it for my life,
Not yours."

"I know, but I was after yours;
Had I been Lancelot, and you Gawaine,
You might be dead."

"Had you been Lancelot,
And I Gawaine, my life had not been yours—
Not willingly. Your brothers are my debt
That I shall owe to sorrow and to God,
For whatsoever payment there may be.
What I have paid is not a little, Gawaine."

"Why leave me out? A brother more or less
Would hardly be the difference of a shaving.
My loose head would assure you, saying this,
That I have no more venom in me now
On their account than mine, which is not much.
There was a madness feeding on us all,
As we fed on the world. When the world sees,
The world will have in turn another madness;
And so, as I've a glimpse, *ad infinitum*.
But I'm not of the seers: Merlin it was
Who turned a sort of ominous early glimmer
On my profane young life. And after that
He falls himself, so far that he becomes
One of our most potential benefits—
Like Vivian, or the mortal end of Modred.

LANCELOT

Why could you not have taken Modred also,
And had the five of us? You did your best,
We know, yet he's more poisonously alive
Than ever; and he's a brother, of a sort,
Or half of one, and you should not have missed him.
A gloomy curiosity was our Modred,
From his first intimation of existence.
God made him as He made the crocodile,
To prove He was omnipotent. Having done so,
And seeing then that Camelot, of all places
Ripe for annihilation, most required him,
He put him there at once, and there he grew.
And there the King would sit with him for hours,
Admiring Modred's growth; and all the time
His evil it was that grew, the King not seeing
In Modred the Almighty's instrument
Of a world's overthrow. You, Lancelot,
And I, have rendered each a contribution;
And your last hard attention on my skull
Might once have been a benison on the realm,
As I shall be, too late, when I'm laid out
With a clean shroud on—though I'd liefer stay
A while alive with you to see what's coming.
But I was not for that; I may have been
For something, but not that. The King, my uncle,
Has had for all his life so brave a diet
Of miracles, that his new fare before him
Of late has ailed him strangely; and of all
Who loved him once he needs you now the most—
Though he would not so much as whisper this
To me or to my shadow. He goes alone
To Britain, with an army brisk as lead,
To battle with his Modred for a throne
That waits, I fear, for Modred—should your France
Not have it otherwise. And the Queen's in this,

431

For Modred's game and prey. God save the Queen,
If not the King! I've always liked this world;
And I would a deal rather live in it
Than leave it in the middle of all this music.
If you are listening, give me some cold water."

Lancelot, seeing by now in dim detail
What little was around him to be seen,
Found what he sought and held a cooling cup
To Gawaine, who, with both hands clutching it,
Drank like a child. "I should have had that first,"
He said, with a loud breath, "before my tongue
Began to talk. What was it saying? Modred?
All through the growing pains of his ambition
I've watched him; and I might have this and that
To say about him, if my hours were days.
Well, if you love the King and hope to save him,
Remember his many infirmities of virtue—
Considering always what you have in Modred,
For ever unique in his iniquity.
My truth might have a prejudicial savor
To strangers, but we are not strangers now.
Though I have only one spoiled eye that sees,
I see in yours we are not strangers now.
I tell you, as I told you long ago—
When the Queen came to put my candles out
With her gold head and her propinquity—
That all your doubts that you had then of me,
When they were more than various imps and harpies
Of your inflamed invention, were sick doubts:
King Arthur was my uncle, as he is now;
But my Queen-aunt, who loved him something less
Than cats love rain, was not my only care.
Had all the women who came to Camelot
Been aunts of mine, I should have been, long since,

LANCELOT

The chilliest of all unwashed eremites
In a far land alone. For my dead brothers,
Though I would leave them where I go to them,
I read their story as I read my own,
And yours, and—were I given the eyes of God—
As I might yet read Modred's. For the Queen,
May she be safe in London where she's hiding
Now in the Tower. For the King, you only—
And you but hardly—may deliver him yet
From that which Merlin's vision long ago,
If I made anything of Merlin's words,
Foretold of Arthur's end. And for ourselves,
And all who died for us, or now are dying
Like rats around us of their numerous wounds
And ills and evils, only this do I know—
And this you know: The world has paid enough
For Camelot. It is the world's turn now—
Or so it would be if the world were not
The world. 'Another Camelot,' Bedivere says;
'Another Camelot and another King'—
Whatever he means by that. With a lineal twist,
I might be king myself; and then, my lord,
Time would have sung my reign—I say not how.
Had I gone on with you, and seen with you
Your Gleam, and had some ray of it been mine,
I might be seeing more and saying less.
Meanwhile, I liked this world; and what was on
The Lord's mind when He made it is no matter.
Be lenient, Lancelot; I've a light head.
Merlin appraised it once when I was young,
Telling me then that I should have the world
To play with. Well, I've had it, and played with it;
And here I'm with you now where you have sent me
Neatly to bed, with a towel over one eye;
And we were two of the world's ornaments.

433

Praise all you are that Arthur was your King;
You might have had no Gleam had I been King,
Or had the Queen been like some queens I knew.
King Lot, my father—"

                        Lancelot laid a finger
On Gawaine's lips: "You are too tired for that."—
"Not yet," said Gawaine, "though I may be soon.
Think you that I forget this Modred's mother
Was mine as well as Modred's? When I meet
My mother's ghost, what shall I do—forgive?
When I'm a ghost, I'll forgive everything . . .
It makes me cold to think what a ghost knows.
Put out the bonfire burning in my head,
And light one at my feet. When the King thought
The Queen was in the flames, he called on you:
'God, God,' he said, and 'Lancelot.' I was there,
And so I heard him. That was a bad morning
For kings and queens, and there are to be worse.
Bedivere had a dream, once on a time:
'Another Camelot and another King,'
He says when he's awake; but when he dreams,
There are no kings. Tell Bedivere, some day,
That he saw best awake. Say to the King
That I saw nothing vaster than my shadow,
Until it was too late for me to see;
Say that I loved him well, but served him ill—
If you two meet again. Say to the Queen . . .
Say what you may say best. Remember me
To Pelleas, too, and tell him that his lady
Was a vain serpent. He was dying once
For love of her, and had me in his eye
For company along the dusky road
Before me now. But Pelleas lived, and married.
Lord God, how much we know!—What have I done?

LANCELOT

Why do you scowl? Well, well,—so the earth clings
To sons of earth; and it will soon be clinging,
To this one son of earth you deprecate,
Closer than heretofore. I say too much,
Who should be thinking all a man may think
When he has no machine. I say too much—
Always. If I persuade the devil again
That I'm asleep, will you espouse the notion
For a small hour or so? I might be glad—
Not to be here alone." He gave his hand
Slowly, in hesitation. Lancelot shivered,
Knowing the chill of it. "Yes, you say too much,"
He told him, trying to smile. "Now go to sleep;
And if you may, forget what you forgive."

Lancelot, for slow hours that were as long
As leagues were to the King and his worn army,
Sat waiting,—though not long enough to know
From any word of Gawaine, who slept on,
That he was glad not to be there alone.—
"Peace to your soul, Gawaine," Lancelot said,
And would have closed his eyes. But they were closed.

IX

So Lancelot, with a world's weight upon him,
Went heavily to that heaviest of all toil,
Which of itself tells hard in the beginning
Of what the end shall be. He found an army
That would have razed all Britain, and found kings
For generals; and they all went to Dover,
Where the white cliffs were ghostlike in the dawn,
And after dawn were deathlike. For the word
Of the dead King's last battle chilled the sea
Before a sail was down; and all who came

With Lancelot heard soon from little men,
Who clambered overside with larger news,
How ill had fared the great. Arthur was dead,
And Modred with him, each by the other slain;
And there was no knight left of all who fought
On Salisbury field save one, Sir Bedivere,
Of whom the tale was told that he had gone
Darkly away to some far hermitage,
To think and die. There were tales told of a ship.

Anon, by further sounding of more men,
Each with a more delirious involution
Than his before him, he believed at last
The Queen was yet alive—if it were life
To draw now the Queen's breath, or to see Britain
With the Queen's eyes—and that she fared somewhere
To westward out of London, where the Tower
Had held her, as once Joyous Gard had held her,
For dolorous weeks and months a prisoner there,
With Modred not far off, his eyes afire
For her and for the King's avenging throne,
That neither King nor son should see again.
" 'The world had paid enough for Camelot,'
Gawaine said; and the Queen had paid enough,
God knows," said Lancelot. He saw Bors again
And found him angry—angry with his tears,
And with his fate that was a reason for them:
"Could I have died with Modred on my soul,
And had the King lived on, then had I lived
On with him; and this played-out world of ours
Might not be for the dead."

"A played-out world,
Although that world be ours, had best be dead,"
Said Lancelot: "There are worlds enough to follow.

LANCELOT

'Another Camelot and another King,'
Bedivere said. And where is Bedivere now?
And Camelot?"

"There is no Camelot,"
Bors answered. "Are we going back to France,
Or are we to tent here and feed our souls
On memories and on ruins till even our souls
Are dead? Or are we to set free for sport
An idle army for what comes of it?"

"Be idle till you hear from me again,
Or for a fortnight. Then, if you have no word,
Go back; and I may follow you alone,
In my own time, in my own way."

"Your way
Of late, I fear, has been too much your own;
But what has been, has been, and I say nothing.
For there is more than men at work in this;
And I have not your eyes to find the Light,
Here in the dark—though some day I may see it."

"We shall all see it, Bors," Lancelot said,
With his eyes on the earth. He said no more.
Then with a sad farewell, he rode away,
Somewhere into the west. He knew not where.

"We shall all see it, Bors," he said again.
Over and over he said it, still as he rode,
And rode, away to the west, he knew not where,
Until at last he smiled unhappily
At the vain sound of it. "Once I had gone
Where the Light guided me, but the Queen came,
And then there was no Light. We shall all see—"

He bit the words off short, snapping his teeth,
And rode on with his memories before him,
Before him and behind. They were a cloud
For no Light now to pierce. They were a cloud
Made out of what was gone; and what was gone
Had now another lure than once it had,
Before it went so far away from him—
To Camelot. And there was no Camelot now—
Now that no Queen was there, all white and gold,
Under an oaktree with another sunlight
Sifting itself in silence on her glory
Through the dark leaves above her where she sat,
Smiling at what she feared, and fearing least
What most there was to fear. Ages ago
That must have been; for a king's world had faded
Since then, and a king with it. Ages ago,
And yesterday, surely it must have been
That he had held her moaning in the firelight
And heard the roaring down of that long rain,
As if to wash away the walls that held them
Then for that hour together. Ages ago,
And always, it had been that he had seen her,
As now she was, floating along before him,
Too far to touch and too fair not to follow,
Even though to touch her were to die. He closed
His eyes, only to see what he had seen
When they were open; and he found it nearer,
Seeing nothing now but the still white and gold
In a wide field of sable, smiling at him,
But with a smile not hers until today—
A smile to drive no votary from the world
To find the Light. "She is not what it is
That I see now," he said: "No woman alive
And out of hell was ever like that to me.
What have I done to her since I have lost her?

LANCELOT

What have I done to change her? No, it is I—
I who have changed. She is not one who changes.
The Light came, and I did not follow it;
Then she came, knowing not what thing she did,
And she it was I followed. The gods play
Like that, sometimes; and when the gods are playing,
Great men are not so great as the great gods
Had led them once to dream. I see her now
Where now she is alone. We are all alone,
We that are left; and if I look too long
Into her eyes . . . I shall not look too long.
Yet look I must. Into the west, they say,
She went for refuge. I see nuns around her;
But she, with so much history tenanting
Her eyes, and all that gold over her eyes,
Were not yet, I should augur, out of them.
If I do ill to see her, then may God
Forgive me one more trespass. I would leave
The world and not the shadow of it behind me."

Time brought his weary search to a dusty end
One afternoon in Almesbury, where he left,
With a glad sigh, his horse in an innyard;
And while he ate his food and drank his wine,
Thrushes, indifferent in their loyalty
To Arthur dead and to Pan never dead,
Sang as if all were now as all had been.
Lancelot heard them till his thoughts came back
To freeze his heart again under the flood
Of all his icy fears. What should he find?
And what if he should not find anything?
"Words, after all," he said, "are only words;
And I have heard so many in these few days
That half my wits are sick."

                        He found the queen,
But she was not the Queen of white and gold
That he had seen before him for so long.
There was no gold; there was no gold anywhere.
The black hood, and the white face under it,
And the blue frightened eyes, were all he saw—
Until he saw more black, and then more white.
Black was a foreign foe to Guinevere;
And in the glimmering stillness where he found her
Now, it was death; and she Alcestis-like,
Had waited unaware for the one hand
Availing, so he thought, that would have torn
Off and away the last fell shred of doom
That was destroying and dishonoring
All the world held of beauty. His eyes burned
With a sad anger as he gazed at hers
That shone with a sad pity. "No," she said;
"You have not come for this. We are done with this.
For there are no queens here; there is a Mother.
The Queen that was is only a child now,
And you are strong. Remember you are strong,
And that your fingers hurt when they forget
How strong they are."

                        He let her go from him
And while he gazed around him, he frowned hard
And long at the cold walls: "Is this the end
Of Arthur's kingdom and of Camelot?"—
She told him with a motion of her shoulders
All that she knew of Camelot or of kingdoms;
And then said: "We are told of other States
Where there are palaces, if we should need them,
That are not made with hands. I thought you knew."

Dumb, like a man twice banished, Lancelot
Stood gazing down upon the cold stone floor;

LANCELOT

And she, demurely, with a calm regard
That he met once and parried, stood apart,
Appraising him with eyes that were no longer
Those he had seen when first they had seen his.
They were kind eyes, but they were not the eyes
Of his desire; and they were not the eyes
That he had followed all the way from Dover.
"I feared the Light was leading you," she said,
"So far by now from any place like this
That I should have your memory, but no more.
Might not that way have been the wiser way?
There is no Arthur now, no Modred now,—
No Guinevere." She paused, and her voice wandered
Away from her own name: "There is nothing now
That I can see between you and the Light
That I have dimmed so long. If you forgive me,
And I believe you do—though I know all
That I have cost, when I was worth so little—
There is no hazard that I see between you
And all you sought so long, and would have found
Had I not always hindered you. Forgive me—
I could not let you go. God pity men
When women love too much—and women more."
He scowled and with an iron shrug he said:
"Yes, there is that between me and the light."
He glared at her black hood as if to seize it;
Their eyes met, and she smiled: "No, Lancelot;
We are going by two roads to the same end;
Or let us hope, at least, what knowledge hides,
And so believe it. We are going somewhere.
Why the new world is not for you and me,
I cannot say; but only one was ours.
I think we must have lived in our one world
All that earth had for us. You are good to me,
Coming to find me here for the last time;

For I should have been lonely many a night,
Not knowing if you cared. I do know now;
And there is not much else for me to know
That earth may tell me. I found in the Tower,
With Modred watching me, that all you said
That rainy night was true. There was time there
To find out everything. There were long days,
And there were nights that I should not have said
God would have made a woman to endure.
I wonder if a woman lives who knows
All she may do."

       "I wonder if one woman
Knows one thing she may do," Lancelot said,
With a sad passion shining out of him
While he gazed on her beauty, palled with black
That hurt him like a sword. The full blue eyes
And the white face were there, and the red lips
Were there, but there was no gold anywhere.
"What have you done with your gold hair?" he said;
"I saw it shining all the way from Dover,
But here I do not see it. Shall I see it?"—
Faintly again she smiled: "Yes, you may see it
All the way back to Dover; but not here.
There's not much of it here, and what there is
Is not for you to see."

       "Well, if not here,"
He said at last, in a low voice that shook,
"Is there no other place left in the world?"

"There is not even the world left, Lancelot,
For you and me."

     "There is France left," he said.
His face flushed like a boy's, but he stood firm
As a peak in the sea and waited.

LANCELOT

                                  "How many lives
Must a man have in one to make him happy?"
She asked, with a wan smile of recollection
That only made the black that was around
Her calm face more funereal: "Was it you,
Or was it Gawaine who said once to me,
'We cannot make one world of two, nor may we
Count one life more than one. Could we go back
To the old garden' . . . Was it you who said it,
Or was it Bors? He was always saying something.
It may have been Bors." She was not looking then
At Lancelot; she was looking at her fingers
In her old way, as to be sure again
How many of them she had.

                            He looked at her,
Without the power to smile, and for the time
Forgot that he was Lancelot: "Is it fair
For you to drag that back, out of its grave,
And hold it up like this for the small feast
Of a small pride?"

                    "Yes, fair enough for a woman,"
Guinevere said, not seeing his eyes. "How long
Do you conceive the Queen of the Christian world
Would hide herself in France . . ."

                           "Why do you pause?
I said it; I remember when I said it;
And it was not today. Why in the name
Of grief should we hide anywhere? Bells and banners
Are not for our occasion, but in France
There may be sights and silences more fair
Than pageants. There are seas of difference
Between this land and France, albeit to cross them

Were no immortal voyage, had you an eye
For France that you had once."

                                      "I have no eye
Today for France, I shall have none tomorrow;
And you will have no eye for France tomorrow.
Fatigue and loneliness, and your poor dream
Of what I was, have led you to forget.
When you have had your time to think and see
A little more, then you will see as I do;
And if you see France, I shall not be there,
Save as a memory there. We are done, you and I,
With what we were. 'Could we go back again,
The fruit that we should find'—but you know best
What we should find. I am sorry for what I said;
But a light word, though it cut one we love,
May save ourselves the pain of a worse wound.
We are all women. When you see one woman—
When you see me—before you in your fancy,
See me all white and gold, as I was once.
I shall not harm you then; I shall not come
Between you and the Gleam that you must follow,
Whether you will or not. There is no place
For me but where I am; there is no place
For you save where it is that you are going.
If I knew everything as I know that,
I should know more than Merlin, who knew all,
And long ago, that we are to know now.
What more he knew he may not then have told
The King, or anyone,—maybe not even himself;
Though Vivian may know something by this time
That he has told her. Have you wished, I wonder,
That I was more like Vivian, or Isolt?
The dark ones are more devious and more famous,

LANCELOT

And men fall down more numerously before them—
Although I think more men get up again,
And go away again, than away from us.
If I were dark, I might say otherwise.
Try to be glad, even if you are sorry,
That I was not born dark; for I was not.
For me there was no dark until it came
When the King came, and with his heavy shadow
Put out the sun that you made shine again
Before I was to die. So I forgive
The faggots; I can do no more than that—
For you, or God." She looked away from him
And in the casement saw the sunshine dying:
"The time that we have left will soon be gone;
When the bell rings, it rings for you to go,
But not for me to go. It rings for me
To stay—and pray. I, who have not prayed much,
May as well pray now. I have not what you have
To make me see, though I shall have, sometime,
A new light of my own. I saw in the Tower,
When all was darkest and I may have dreamed,
A light that gave to men the eyes of Time
To read themselves in silence. Then it faded,
And the men faded. I was there alone.
I shall not have what you have, or much else—
In this place. I shall see in other places
What is not here. I shall not be alone.
And I shall tell myself that you are seeing
All that I cannot see. For the time now,
What most I see is that I had no choice,
And that you came to me. How many years
Of purgatory shall I pay God for saying
This to you here?" Her words came slowly out,
And her mouth shook.

He took her two small hands
That were so pale and empty, and so cold:
"Poor child, I said too much and heard too little
Of what I said. But when I found you here,
So different, so alone, I would have given
My soul to be a chattel and a gage
For dicing fiends to play for, could so doing
Have brought one summer back."

"When they are gone,"
She said, with grateful sadness in her eyes,
"We do not bring them back, or buy them back,
Even with our souls. I see now it is best
We do not buy them back, even with our souls."

A slow and hollow bell began to sound
Somewhere above them, and the world became
For Lancelot one wan face—Guinevere's face.
"When the bell rings, it rings for you to go,"
She said; "and you are going . . . I am not.
Think of me always as I used to be,
All white and gold—for that was what you called me.
You may see gold again when you are gone;
And I shall not be there."—He drew her nearer
To kiss the quivering lips that were before him
For the last time. "No, not again," she said;
"I might forget that I am not alone . . .
I shall not see you in this world again,
But I am not alone. No, . . . not alone.
We have had all there was, and you were kind—
Even when you tried so hard once to be cruel.
I knew it then . . . or now I do. Good-bye."
He crushed her cold white hands and saw them falling
Away from him like flowers into a grave.

LANCELOT

When she looked up to see him, he was gone;
And that was all she saw till she awoke
In her white cell, where the nuns carried her
With many tears and many whisperings.
"She was the Queen, and he was Lancelot,"
One said. "They were great lovers. It is not good
To know too much of love. We who love God
Alone are happiest. Is it not so, Mother?"—
"We who love God alone, my child, are safest,"
The Mother replied; "and we are not all safe
Until we are all dead. We watch, and pray."

Outside again, Lancelot heard the sound
Of reapers he had seen. With lighter tread
He walked away to them to see them nearer;
He walked and heard again the sound of thrushes
Far off. He saw below him, stilled with yellow,
A world that was not Arthur's, and he saw
The convent roof; and then he could see nothing
But a wan face and two dim lonely hands
That he had left behind. They were down there,
Somewhere, her poor white face and hands, alone.
"No man was ever alone like that," he thought,
Not knowing what last havoc pity and love
Had still to wreak on wisdom. Gradually,
In one long wave it whelmed him, and then broke—
Leaving him like a lone man on a reef,
Staring for what had been with him, but now
Was gone and was a white face under the sea,
Alive there, and alone—always alone.
He closed his eyes, and the white face was there,
But not the gold. The gold would not come back.
There were gold fields of corn that lay around him,
But they were not the gold of Guinevere—
Though men had once, for sake of saying words,

COLLECTED POEMS

Prattled of corn about it. The still face
Was there, and the blue eyes that looked at him
Through all the stillness of all distances;
And he could see her lips, trying to say
Again, "I am not alone." And that was all
His life had said to him that he remembered
While he sat there with his hands over his eyes,
And his heart aching. When he rose again
The reapers had gone home. Over the land
Around him in the twilight there was rest.
There was rest everywhere; and there was none
That found his heart. "Why should I look for peace
When I have made the world a ruin of war?"
He muttered; and a Voice within him said:
"Where the Light falls, death falls; a world has died
For you, that a world may live. There is no peace.
Be glad no man or woman bears for ever
The burden of first days. There is no peace."

A word stronger than his willed him away
From Almesbury. All alone he rode that night,
Under the stars, led by the living Voice
That would not give him peace. Into the dark
He rode, but not for Dover. Under the stars,
Alone, all night he rode, out of a world
That was not his, or the King's; and in the night
He felt a burden lifted as he rode,
While he prayed he might bear it for the sake
Of a still face before him that was fading,
Away in a white loneliness. He made,
Once, with groping hand as if to touch it,
But a black branch of leaves was all he found.

Now the still face was dimmer than before,
And it was not so near him. He gazed hard,

LANCELOT

But through his tears he could not see it now;
And when the tears were gone he could see only
That all he saw was fading, always fading;
And she was there alone. She was the world
That he was losing; and the world he sought
Was all a tale for those who had been living,
And had not lived. Once even he turned his horse,
And would have brought his army back with him
To make her free. They should be free together.
But the Voice within him said: "You are not free.
You have come to the world's end, and it is best
You are not free. Where the Light falls, death falls;
And in the darkness comes the Light." He turned
Again; and he rode on, under the stars,
Out of the world, into he knew not what,
Until a vision chilled him and he saw,
Now as in Camelot, long ago in the garden,
The face of Galahad who had seen and died,
And was alive, now in a mist of gold.
He rode on into the dark, under the stars,
And there were no more faces. There was nothing.
But always in the darkness he rode on,
Alone; and in the darkness came the Light.

THE THREE TAVERNS
(1920)

To
Thomas Sergeant Perry
and Lilla Cabot Perry

THE THREE TAVERNS

(1920)

To
Thomas Sergeant Perry
and Lilla Cabot Perry

THE VALLEY OF THE SHADOW

There were faces to remember in the Valley of the Shadow,
There were faces unregarded, there were faces to forget;
There were fires of grief and fear that are a few forgotten ashes,
There were sparks of recognition that are not forgotten yet.
For at first, with an amazed and overwhelming indignation
At a measureless malfeasance that obscurely willed it thus,
They were lost and unacquainted—till they found themselves in others,
Who had groped as they were groping where dim ways were perilous.

There were lives that were as dark as are the fears and intuitions
Of a child who knows himself and is alone with what he knows;
There were pensioners of dreams and there were debtors of illusions,
All to fail before the triumph of a weed that only grows.
There were thirsting heirs of golden sieves that held not wine or water,
And had no names in traffic or more value there than toys:
There were blighted sons of wonder in the Valley of the Shadow,
Where they suffered and still wondered why their wonder made no noise.

There were slaves who dragged the shackles of a precedent unbroken,
Demonstrating the fulfilment of unalterable schemes,
Which had been, before the cradle, Time's inexorable tenants
Of what were now the dusty ruins of their father's dreams.

There were these, and there were many who had stumbled up
   to manhood,
Where they saw too late the road they should have taken
   long ago:
There were thwarted clerks and fiddlers in the Valley of the
   Shadow,
The commemorative wreckage of what others did not know.

And there were daughters older than the mothers who had
   borne them,
Being older in their wisdom, which is older than the earth;
And they were going forward only farther into darkness,
Unrelieved as were the blasting obligations of their birth;
And among them, giving always what was not for their possession,
There were maidens, very quiet, with no quiet in their eyes;
There were daughters of the silence in the Valley of the Shadow,
Each an isolated item in the family sacrifice.

There were creepers among catacombs where dull regrets were
   torches,
Giving light enough to show them what was there upon the
   shelves—
Where there was more for them to see than pleasure would
   remember
Of something that had been alive and once had been themselves.
There were some who stirred the ruins with a solid imprecation,
While as many fled repentance for the promise of despair:
There were drinkers of wrong waters in the Valley of the
   Shadow,
And all the sparkling ways were dust that once had led them
   there.

There were some who knew the steps of Age incredibly beside
   them,

THE VALLEY OF THE SHADOW

And his fingers upon shoulders that had never felt the wheel;
And their last of empty trophies was a gilded cup of nothing,
Which a contemplating vagabond would not have come to steal.
Long and often had they figured for a larger valuation,
But the size of their addition was the balance of a doubt:
There were gentlemen of leisure in the Valley of the Shadow,
Not allured by retrospection, disenchanted, and played out.

And among the dark endurances of unavowed reprisals
There were silent eyes of envy that saw little but saw well;
And over beauty's aftermath of hazardous ambitions
There were tears for what had vanished as they vanished where they fell.
Not assured of what was theirs, and always hungry for the nameless,
There were some whose only passion was for Time who made them cold:
There were numerous fair women in the Valley of the Shadow,
Dreaming rather less of heaven than of hell when they were old.

Now and then, as if to scorn the common touch of common sorrow,
There were some who gave a few the distant pity of a smile;
And another cloaked a soul as with an ash of human embers,
Having covered thus a treasure that would last him for a while.
There were many by the presence of the many disaffected,
Whose exemption was included in the weight that others bore:
There were seekers after darkness in the Valley of the Shadow,
And they alone were there to find what they were looking for.

So they were, and so they are; and as they came are coming others,
And among them are the fearless and the meek and the unborn;
And a question that has held us heretofore without an answer
May abide without an answer until all have ceased to mourn.

For the children of the dark are more to name than are the wretched,
Or the broken, or the weary, or the baffled, or the shamed:
There are builders of new mansions in the Valley of the Shadow,
And among them are the dying and the blinded and the maimed.

THE WANDERING JEW

I saw by looking in his eyes
That they remembered everything;
And this was how I came to know
That he was here, still wandering.
For though the figure and the scene
Were never to be reconciled,
I knew the man as I had known
His image when I was a child.

With evidence at every turn,
I should have held it safe to guess
That all the newness of New York
Had nothing new in loneliness;
Yet here was one who might be Noah,
Or Nathan, or Abimelech,
Or Lamech, out of ages lost,—
Or, more than all, Melchizedek.

Assured that he was none of these,
I gave them back their names again,
To scan once more those endless eyes
Where all my questions ended then.
I found in them what they revealed
That I shall not live to forget,

THE WANDERING JEW

And wondered if they found in mine
Compassion that I might regret.

Pity, I learned, was not the least
Of time's offending benefits
That had now for so long impugned
The conservation of his wits:
Rather it was that I should yield,
Alone, the fealty that presents
The tribute of a tempered ear
To an untempered eloquence.

Before I pondered long enough
On whence he came and who he was,
I trembled at his ringing wealth
Of manifold anathemas;
I wondered, while he seared the world,
What new defection ailed the race,
And if it mattered how remote
Our fathers were from such a place.

Before there was an hour for me
To contemplate with less concern
The crumbling realm awaiting us
Than his that was beyond return,
A dawning on the dust of years
Had shaped with an elusive light
Mirages of remembered scenes
That were no longer for the sight.

For now the gloom that hid the man
Became a daylight on his wrath,
And one wherein my fancy viewed
New lions ramping in his path.
The old were dead and had no fangs,

Wherefore he loved them—seeing not
They were the same that in their time
Had eaten everything they caught.

The world around him was a gift
Of anguish to his eyes and ears,
And one that he had long reviled
As fit for devils, not for seers.
Where, then, was there a place for him
That on this other side of death
Saw nothing good, as he had seen
No good come out of Nazareth?

Yet here there was a reticence,
And I believe his only one,
That hushed him as if he beheld
A Presence that would not be gone.
In such a silence he confessed
How much there was to be denied;
And he would look at me and live,
As others might have looked and died.

As if at last he knew again
That he had always known, his eyes
Were like to those of one who gazed
On those of One who never dies.
For such a moment he revealed
What life has in it to be lost;
And I could ask if what I saw,
Before me there, was man or ghost.

He may have died so many times
That all there was of him to see
Was pride, that kept itself alive
As too rebellious to be free;

NEIGHBORS

He may have told, when more than once
Humility seemed imminent,
How many a lonely time in vain
The Second Coming came and went.

Whether he still defies or not
The failure of an angry task
That relegates him out of time
To chaos, I can only ask.
But as I knew him, so he was;
And somewhere among men to-day
Those old, unyielding eyes may flash,
And flinch—and look the other way.

NEIGHBORS

As often as we thought of her,
   We thought of a gray life
That made a quaint economist
   Of a wolf-haunted wife;
We made the best of all she bore
   That was not ours to bear,
And honored her for wearing things
   That were not things to wear.

There was a distance in her look
   That made us look again;
And if she smiled, we might believe
   That we had looked in vain.
Rarely she came inside our doors,
   And had not long to stay;
And when she left, it seemed somehow
   That she was far away.

At last, when we had all forgot
  That all is here to change,
A shadow on the commonplace
  Was for a moment strange.
Yet there was nothing for surprise,
  Nor much that need be told:
Love, with his gift of pain, had given
  More than one heart could hold.

THE MILL

The miller's wife had waited long,
  The tea was cold, the fire was dead;
And there might yet be nothing wrong
  In how he went and what he said:
"There are no millers any more,"
  Was all that she heard him say;
And he had lingered at the door
  So long that it seemed yesterday.

Sick with a fear that had no form
  She knew that she was there at last;
And in the mill there was a warm
  And mealy fragrance of the past.
What else there was would only seem
  To say again what he had meant;
And what was hanging from a beam
  Would not have heeded where she went.

And if she thought it followed her,
  She may have reasoned in the dark
That one way of the few there were
  Would hide her and would leave no mark:

THE THREE TAVERNS

Black water, smooth above the weir
　Like starry velvet in the night,
Though ruffled once, would soon appear
　The same as ever to the sight.

THE DARK HILLS

Dark hills at evening in the west,
Where sunset hovers like a sound
Of golden horns that sang to rest
Old bones of warriors under ground,
Far now from all the bannered ways
Where flash the legions of the sun,
You fade—as if the last of days
Were fading, and all wars were done.

THE THREE TAVERNS

When the brethren heard of us, they came to meet us as far as Appii Forum, and The Three Taverns.　　　(*Acts xxviii, 15*)

Herodion, Apelles, Amplias,
And Andronicus? Is it you I see—
At last? And is it you now that are gazing
As if in doubt of me? Was I not saying
That I should come to Rome? I did say that;
And I said furthermore that I should go
On westward, where the gateway of the world
Lets in the central sea. I did say that,
But I say only, now, that I am Paul—

A prisoner of the Law, and of the Lord
A voice made free. If there be time enough
To live, I may have more to tell you then
Of western matters. I go now to Rome,
Where Cæsar waits for me, and I shall wait,
And Cæsar knows how long. In Cæsarea
There was a legend of Agrippa saying
In a light way to Festus, having heard
My deposition, that I might be free,
Had I stayed free of Cæsar; but the word
Of God would have it as you see it is—
And here I am. The cup that I shall drink
Is mine to drink—the moment or the place
Not mine to say. If it be now in Rome,
Be it now in Rome; and if your faith exceed
The shadow cast of hope, say not of me
Too surely or too soon that years and shipwreck,
And all the many deserts I have crossed
That are not named or regioned, have undone
Beyond the brevities of our mortal healing
The part of me that is the least of me.
You see an older man than he who fell
Prone to the earth when he was nigh Damascus,
Where the great light came down; yet I am he
That fell, and he that saw, and he that heard.
And I am here, at last; and if at last
I give myself to make another crumb
For this pernicious feast of time and men—
Well, I have seen too much of time and men
To fear the ravening or the wrath of either.

Yes, it is Paul you see—the Saul of Tarsus
That was a fiery Jew, and had men slain
For saying Something was beyond the Law,
And in ourselves. I fed my suffering soul

THE THREE TAVERNS

Upon the Law till I went famishing,
Not knowing that I starved. How should I know,
More then than any, that the food I had—
What else it may have been—was not for me?
My fathers and their fathers and their fathers
Had found it good, and said there was no other,
And I was of the line. When Stephen fell,
Among the stones that crushed his life away,
There was no place alive that I could see
For such a man. Why should a man be given
To live beyond the Law? So I said then,
As men say now to me. How then do I
Persist in living? Is that what you ask?
If so, let my appearance be for you
No living answer; for Time writes of death
On men before they die, and what you see
Is not the man. The man that you see not—
The man within the man—is most alive;
Though hatred would have ended, long ago,
The bane of his activities. I have lived,
Because the faith within me that is life
Endures to live, and shall, till soon or late,
Death, like a friend unseen, shall say to me
My toil is over and my work begun.

How often, and how many a time again,
Have I said I should be with you in Rome!
He who is always coming never comes,
Or comes too late, you may have told yourselves;
And I may tell you now that after me,
Whether I stay for little or for long,
The wolves are coming. Have an eye for them,
And a more careful ear for their confusion
Than you need have much longer for the sound
Of what I tell you—should I live to say

More than I say to Cæsar. What I know
Is down for you to read in what is written;
And if I cloud a little with my own
Mortality the gleam that is immortal,
I do it only because I am I—
Being on earth and of it, in so far
As time flays yet the remnant. This you know;
And if I sting men, as I do sometimes,
With a sharp word that hurts, it is because
Man's habit is to feel before he sees;
And I am of a race that feels. Moreover,
The world is here for what is not yet here
For more than are a few; and even in Rome,
Where men are so enamored of the Cross
That fame has echoed, and increasingly,
The music of your love and of your faith
To foreign ears that are as far away
As Antioch and Haran, yet I wonder
How much of love you know, and if your faith
Be the shut fruit of words. If so, remember
Words are but shells unfilled. Jews have at least
A Law to make them sorry they were born
If they go long without it; and these Gentiles,
For the first time in shrieking history,
Have love and law together, if so they will,
For their defense and their immunity
In these last days. Rome, if I know the name,
Will have anon a crown of thorns and fire
Made ready for the wreathing of new masters,
Of whom we are appointed, you and I,—
And you are still to be when I am gone,
Should I go presently. Let the word fall,
Meanwhile, upon the dragon-ridden field
Of circumstance, either to live or die;
Concerning which there is a parable,

THE THREE TAVERNS

Made easy for the comfort and attention
Of those who preach, fearing they preach in vain.
You are to plant, and then to plant again
Where you have gathered, gathering as you go;
For you are in the fields that are eternal,
And you have not the burden of the Lord
Upon your mortal shoulders. What you have
Is a light yoke, made lighter by the wearing,
Till it shall have the wonder and the weight
Of a clear jewel, shining with a light
Wherein the sun and all the fiery stars
May soon be fading. When Gamaliel said
That if they be of men these things are nothing
But if they be of God, they are for none
To overthrow, he spoke as a good Jew,
And one who stayed a Jew; and he said all.
And you know, by the temper of your faith,
How far the fire is in you that I felt
Before I knew Damascus. A word here,
Or there, or not there, or not anywhere,
Is not the Word that lives and is the life;
And you, therefore, need weary not yourselves
With jealous aches of others. If the world
Were not a world of aches and innovations,
Attainment would have no more joy of it.
There will be creeds and schisms, creeds in creeds,
And schisms in schisms; myriads will be done
To death because a farthing has two sides,
And is at last a farthing. Telling you this,
I, who bid men to live, appeal to Cæsar.
Once I had said the ways of God were dark,
Meaning by that the dark ways of the Law.
Such is the Glory of our tribulations;
For the Law kills the flesh that kills the Law,
And we are then alive. We have eyes then;

And we have then the Cross between two worlds—
To guide us, or to blind us for a time,
Till we have eyes indeed. The fire that smites
A few on highways, changing all at once,
Is not for all. The power that holds the world
Away from God that holds himself away—
Farther away than all your works and words
Are like to fly without the wings of faith—
Was not, nor ever shall be, a small hazard
Enlivening the ways of easy leisure
Or the cold road of knowledge. When our eyes
Have wisdom, we see more than we remember;
And the old world of our captivities
May then become a smitten glimpse of ruin,
Like one where vanished hewers have had their day
Of wrath on Lebanon. Before we see,
Meanwhile, we suffer; and I come to you,
At last, through many storms and through much night.

Yet whatsoever I have undergone,
My keepers in this instance are not hard.
But for the chance of an ingratitude,
I might indeed be curious of their mercy,
And fearful of their leisure while I wait,
A few leagues out of Rome. Men go to Rome,
Not always to return—but not that now.
Meanwhile, I seem to think you look at me
With eyes that are at last more credulous
Of my identity. You remark in me
No sort of leaping giant, though some words
Of mine to you from Corinth may have leapt
A little through your eyes into your soul.
I trust they were alive, and are alive
Today; for there be none that shall indite
So much of nothing as the man of words

THE THREE TAVERNS

Who writes in the Lord's name for his name's sake
And has not in his blood the fire of time
To warm eternity. Let such a man—
If once the light is in him and endures—
Content himself to be the general man,
Set free to sift the decencies and thereby
To learn, except he be one set aside
For sorrow, more of pleasure than of pain;
Though if his light be not the light indeed,
But a brief shine that never really was,
And fails, leaving him worse than where he was,
Then shall he be of all men destitute.
And here were not an issue for much ink,
Or much offending faction among scribes.

The Kingdom is within us, we are told;
And when I say to you that we possess it
In such a measure as faith makes it ours,
I say it with a sinner's privilege
Of having seen and heard, and seen again,
After a darkness; and if I affirm
To the last hour that faith affords alone
The Kingdom entrance and an entertainment,
I do not see myself as one who says
To man that he shall sit with folded hands
Against the Coming. If I be anything,
I move a driven agent among my kind,
Establishing by the faith of Abraham,
And by the grace of their necessities,
The clamoring word that is the word of life
Nearer than heretofore to the solution
Of their tomb-serving doubts. If I have loosed
A shaft of language that has flown sometimes
A little higher than the hearts and heads
Of nature's minions, it will yet be heard,

Like a new song that waits for distant ears.
I cannot be the man that I am not;
And while I own that earth is my affliction,
I am a man of earth, who says not all
To all alike. That were impossible.
Even as it were so that He should plant
A larger garden first. But you today
Are for the larger sowing; and your seed,
A little mixed, will have, as He foresaw,
The foreign harvest of a wider growth,
And one without an end. Many there are,
And are to be, that shall partake of it,
Though none may share it with an understanding
That is not his alone. We are all alone;
And yet we are all parcelled of one order—
Jew, Gentile, or barbarian in the dark
Of wildernesses that are not so much
As names yet in a book. And there are many,
Finding at last that words are not the Word,
And finding only that, will flourish aloft,
Like heads of captured Pharisees on pikes,
Our contradictions and discrepancies;
And there are many more will hang themselves
Upon the letter, seeing not in the Word
The friend of all who fail, and in their faith
A sword of excellence to cut them down.

As long as there are glasses that are dark—
And there are many—we see darkly through them;
All which have I conceded and set down
In words that have no shadow. What is dark
Is dark, and we may not say otherwise;
Yet what may be as dark as a lost fire
For one of us, may still be for another
A coming gleam across the gulf of ages,

THE THREE TAVERNS

And a way home from shipwreck to the shore;
And so, through pangs and ills and desperations,
There may be light for all. There shall be light.
As much as that, you know. You cannot say
This woman or that man will be the next
On whom it falls; you are not here for that.
You ministration is to be for others
The firing of a rush that may for them
Be soon the fire itself. The few at first
Are fighting for the multitude at last;
Therefore remember what Gamaliel said
Before you, when the sick were lying down
In streets all night for Peter's passing shadow.
Fight, and say what you feel; say more than words.
Give men to know that even their days of earth
To come are more than ages that are gone.
Say what you feel, while you have time to say it.
Eternity will answer for itself,
Without your intercession; yet the way
For many is a long one, and as dark,
Meanwhile, as dreams of hell. See not your toil
Too much, and if I be away from you,
Think of me as a brother to yourselves,
Of many blemishes. Beware of stoics,
And give your left hand to grammarians;
And when you seem, as many a time you may,
To have no other friend than hope, remember
That you are not the first, or yet the last.

The best of life, until we see beyond
The shadows of ourselves (and they are less
Than even the blindest of indignant eyes
Would have them) is in what we do not know.
Make, then, for all your fears a place to sleep
With all your faded sins; nor think yourselves

Egregious and alone for your defects
Of youth and yesterday. I was young once;
And there's a question if you played the fool
With a more fervid and inherent zeal
Than I have in my story to remember,
Or gave your necks to folly's conquering foot,
Or flung yourselves with an unstudied aim,
More frequently than I. Never mind that.
Man's little house of days will hold enough,
Sometimes, to make him wish it were not his,
But it will not hold all. Things that are dead
Are best without it, and they own their death
By virtue of their dying. Let them go,—
But think you not the world is ashes yet,
And you have all the fire. The world is here
Today, and it may not be gone tomorrow;
For there are millions, and there may be more,
To make in turn a various estimation
Of its old ills and ashes, and the traps
Of its apparent wrath. Many with ears
That hear not yet, shall have ears given to them,
And then they shall hear strangely. Many with eyes
That are incredulous of the Mystery
Shall yet be driven to feel, and then to read
Where language has an end and is a veil,
Not woven of our words. Many that hate
Their kind are soon to know that without love
Their faith is but the perjured name of nothing.
I that have done some hating in my time
See now no time for hate; I that have left,
Fading behind me like familiar lights
That are to shine no more for my returning,
Home, friends, and honors,—I that have lost all else
For wisdom, and the wealth of it, say now
To you that out of wisdom has come love,

DEMOS

That measures and is of itself the measure
Of works and hope and faith. Your longest hours
Are not so long that you may torture them
And harass not yourselves; and the last days
Are on the way that you prepare for them,
And was prepared for you, here in a world
Where you have sinned and suffered, striven and seen.
If you be not so hot for counting them
Before they come that you consume yourselves,
Peace may attend you all in these last days—
And me, as well as you. Yes, even in Rome.

Well, I have talked and rested, though I fear
My rest has not been yours; in which event,
Forgive one who is only seven leagues
From Cæsar. When I told you I should come,
I did not see myself the criminal
You contemplate, for seeing beyond the Law
That which the Law saw not. But this, indeed,
Was good of you, and I shall not forget;
No, I shall not forget you came so far
To meet a man so dangerous. Well, farewell.
They come to tell me I am going now—
With them. I hope that we shall meet again,
But none may say what he shall find in Rome.

DEMOS

I

ALL you that are enamored of my name
    And least intent on what most I require,
    Beware; for my design and your desire,
Deplorably, are not as yet the same.

Beware, I say, the failure and the shame
    Of losing that for which you now aspire
    So blindly, and of hazarding entire
The gift that I was bringing when I came.

Give as I will, I cannot give you sight
    Whereby to see that with you there are some
    To lead you, and be led. But they are dumb
Before the wrangling and the shrill delight
    Of your deliverance that has not come,
And shall not, if I fail you—as I might.

II

So little have you seen of what awaits
    Your fevered glimpse of a democracy
    Confused and foiled with an equality
Not equal to the envy it creates,
That you see not how near you are the gates
    Of an old king who listens fearfully
    To you that are outside and are to be
The noisy lords of imminent estates.

Rather be then your prayer that you shall have
    Your kingdom undishonored. Having all,
    See not the great among you for the small,
But hear their silence; for the few shall save
    The many, or the many are to fall—
Still to be wrangling in a noisy grave.

THE FLYING DUTCHMAN

Unyielding in the pride of his defiance,
    Afloat with none to serve or to command,

TACT

Lord of himself at last, and all by Science,
    He seeks the Vanished Land.

Alone, by the one light of his one thought,
    He steers to find the shore from which we came,
Fearless of in what coil he may be caught
    On seas that have no name.

Into the night he sails; and after night
    There is a dawning, though there be no sun;
Wherefore, with nothing but himself in sight,
    Unsighted, he sails on.

At last there is a lifting of the cloud
    Between the flood before him and the sky;
And then—though he may curse the Power aloud
    That has no power to die—

He steers himself away from what is haunted
    By the old ghost of what has been before,—
Abandoning, as always, and undaunted,
    One fog-walled island more.

TACT

Observant of the way she told
    So much of what was true,
No vanity could long withhold
    Regard that was her due:
She spared him the familiar guile,
    So easily achieved,
That only made a man to smile
    And left him undeceived.

Aware that all imagining
   Of more than what she meant
Would urge an end of everything,
   He stayed; and when he went,
They parted with a merry word
   That was to him as light
As any that was ever heard
   Upon a starry night.

She smiled a little, knowing well
   That he would not remark
That ruins of a day that fell
   Around her in the dark:
He saw no ruins anywhere,
   Nor fancied there were scars
On anyone who lingered there,
   Alone below the stars.

ON THE WAY

(Philadelphia, 1794)

Note.—The following imaginary dialogue between Alexander Hamilton and Aaron Burr, which is not based upon any specific incident in American history, may be supposed to have occurred a few months previous to Hamilton's retirement from Washington's Cabinet in 1795 and a few years before the political ingenuities of Burr—who has been characterized, without much exaggeration, as the inventor of American politics—began to be conspicuously formidable to the Federalists. These activities on the part of Burr resulted, as the reader will remember, in the Burr-Jefferson tie for the Presidency in 1800, and finally in the Burr-Hamilton duel at Weehawken in 1804.

Burr

Hamilton, if he rides you down, remember
That I was here to speak, and so to save

ON THE WAY

Your fabric from catastrophe. That's good;
For I perceive that you observe him also.
A President, a-riding of his horse,
May dust a General and be forgiven;
But why be dusted—when we're all alike,
All equal, and all happy? Here he comes—
And there he goes. And we, by your new patent,
Would seem to be two kings here by the wayside,
With our two hats off to his Excellency.
Why not his Majesty, and done with it?
Forgive me if I shook your meditation,
But you that weld our credit should have eyes
To see what's coming. Bury me first if *I* do.

Hamilton

There's always in some pocket of your brain
A care for me; wherefore my gratitude
For your attention is commensurate
With your concern. Yes, Burr, we are two kings;
We are as royal as two ditch-diggers;
But owe me not your sceptre. These are the days
When first a few seem all; but if we live
We may again be seen to be the few
That we have always been. These are the days
When men forget the stars, and are forgotten.

Burr

But why forget them? They're the same that winked
Upon the world when Alcibiades
Cut off his dog's tail to induce distinction.
There are dogs yet, and Alcibiades
Is not forgotten.

COLLECTED POEMS

Hamilton

      Yes, there are dogs enough,
God knows; and I can hear them in my dreams.

Burr

Never a doubt. But what you hear the most
Is your new music, something out of tune
With your intention. How in the name of Cain,
I seem to hear you ask, are men to dance,
When all men are musicians. Tell me that,
I hear you saying, and I'll tell you the name
Of Samson's mother. But why shroud yourself
Before the coffin comes? For all you know,
The tree that is to fall for your last house
Is now a sapling. You may have to wait
So long as to be sorry; though I doubt it,
For you are not at home in your new Eden
Where chilly whispers of a likely frost
Accumulate already in the air.
I think a touch of ermine, Hamilton,
Would be for you in your autumnal mood
A pleasant sort of warmth along the shoulders.

Hamilton

If so it is you think, you may as well
Give over thinking. We are done with ermine.
What I fear most is not the multitude,
But those who are to loop it with a string
That has one end in France and one end here.
I'm not so fortified with observation
That I could swear that more than half a score
Among us who see lightning see that ruin
Is not the work of thunder. Since the world

ON THE WAY

Was ordered, there was never a long pause
For caution between doing and undoing.

BURR

Go on, sir; my attention is a trap
Set for the catching of all compliments
To Monticello, and all else abroad
That has a name or an identity.

HAMILTON

I leave to you the names—there are too many;
Yet one there is to sift and hold apart,
As now I see. There comes at last a glimmer
That is not always clouded, or too late.
But I was near and young, and had the reins
To play with while he manned a team so raw
That only God knows where the end had been
Of all that riding without Washington.
There was a nation in the man who passed us,
If there was not a world. I may have driven
Since then some restive horses, and alone,
And through a splashing of abundant mud;
But he who made the dust that sets you on
To coughing, made the road. Now it seems dry,
And in a measure safe.

BURR

    Here's a new tune
From Hamilton. Has your caution all at once,
And over night, grown till it wrecks the cradle?
I have forgotten what my father said
When I was born, but there's a rustling of it
Among my memories, and it makes a noise

About as loud as all that I have held
And fondled heretofore of your same caution.
But that's affairs, not feelings. If our friends
Guessed half we say of them, our enemies
Would itch in our friends' jackets. Howsoever,
The world is of a sudden on its head,
And all are spilled—unless you cling alone
With Washington. Ask Adams about that.

Hamilton

We'll not ask Adams about anything.
We fish for lizards when we choose to ask
For what we know already is not coming,
And we must eat the answer. Where's the use
Of asking when this man says everything,
With all his tongues of silence?

Burr

I dare say.
I dare say, but I won't. One of those tongues
I'll borrow for the nonce. He'll never miss it.
We mean his Western Majesty, King George.

Hamilton

I mean the man who rode by on his horse.
I'll beg of you the meed of your indulgence
If I should say this planet may have done
A deal of weary whirling when at last,
If ever, Time shall aggregate again
A majesty like his that has no name.

Burr

Then you concede his Majesty? That's good,
And what of yours? Here are two majesties.

ON THE WAY

Favor the Left a little, Hamilton,
Or you'll be floundering in the ditch that waits
For riders who forget where they are riding.
If we and France, as you anticipate,
Must eat each other, what Cæsar, if not yourself,
Do you see for the master of the feast?
There may be a place waiting on your head
For laurel thick as Nero's. You don't know.
I have not crossed your glory, though I might
If I saw thrones at auction.

Hamilton

Yes, you might.
If war is on the way, I shall be—here;
And I've no vision of your distant heels.

Burr

I see that I shall take an inference
To bed with me to-night to keep me warm.
I thank you, Hamilton, and I approve
Your fealty to the aggregated greatness
Of him you lean on while he leans on you.

Hamilton

This easy phrasing is a game of yours
That you may win to lose. I beg your pardon,
But you that have the sight will not employ
The will to see with it. If you did so,
There might be fewer ditches dug for others
In your perspective; and there might be fewer
Contemporary motes of prejudice
Between you and the man who made the dust.
Call him a genius or a gentleman,

COLLECTED POEMS

A prophet or a builder, or what not,
But hold your disposition off the balance,
And weigh him in the light. Once (I believe
I tell you nothing new to your surmise,
Or to the tongues of towns and villages)
I nourished with an adolescent fancy—
Surely forgivable to you, my friend—
An innocent and amiable conviction
That I was, by the grace of honest fortune,
A savior at his elbow through the war,
Where I might have observed, more than I did,
Patience and wholesome passion. I was there,
And for such honor I gave nothing worse
Than some advice at which he may have smiled.
I must have given a modicum besides,
Or the rough interval between those days
And these would never have made for me my friends,
Or enemies. I should be something somewhere—
I say not what—but I should not be here
If he had not been there. Possibly, too,
You might not—or that Quaker with his cane.

Burr

Possibly, too, I should. When the Almighty
Rides a white horse, I fancy we shall know it.

Hamilton

It was a man, Burr, that was in my mind;
No god, or ghost, or demon—only a man:
A man whose occupation is the need
Of those who would not feel it if it bit them;
And one who shapes an age while he endures
The pin pricks of inferiorities;
A cautious man, because he is but one;

ON THE WAY

A lonely man, because he is a thousand.
No marvel you are slow to find in him
The genius that is one spark or is nothing:
His genius is a flame that he must hold
So far above the common heads of men
That they may view him only through the mist
Of their defect, and wonder what he is.
It seems to me the mystery that is in him
That makes him only more to me a man
Than any other I have ever known.

BURR

I grant you that his worship is a man.
I'm not so much at home with mysteries,
May be, as you—so leave him with his fire:
God knows that I shall never put it out.
He has not made a cripple of himself
In his pursuit of me, though I have heard
His condescension honors me with parts.
Parts make a whole, if we've enough of them;
And once I figured a sufficiency
To be at least an atom in the annals
Of your republic. But I must have erred.

HAMILTON

You smile as if your spirit lived at ease
With error. I should not have named it so,
Failing assent from you; nor, if I did,
Should I be so complacent in my skill
To comb the tangled language of the people
As to be sure of anything in these days.
Put that much in account with modesty.

BURR

What in the name of Ahab, Hamilton,
Have you, in the last region of your dreaming,
To do with "people"? You may be the devil
In your dead-reckoning of what reefs and shoals
Are waiting on the progress of our ship
Unless you steer it, but you'll find it irksome
Alone there in the stern; and some warm day
There'll be an inland music in the rigging,
And afterwards on deck. I'm not affined
Or favored overmuch at Monticello,
But there's a mighty swarming of new bees
About the premises, and all have wings.
If you hear something buzzing before long,
Be thoughtful how you strike, remembering also
There was a fellow Naboth had a vineyard,
And Ahab cut his hair off and went softly.

HAMILTON

I don't remember that he cut his hair off.

BURR

Somehow I rather fancy that he did.
If so, it's in the Book; and if not so,
He did the rest, and did it handsomely.

HAMILTON

Commend yourself to Ahab and his ways
If they inveigle you to emulation;
But where, if I may ask it, are you tending
With your invidious wielding of the Scriptures?
You call to mind an eminent archangel
Who fell to make him famous. Would you fall
So far as he, to be so far remembered?

ON THE WAY

BURR

Before I fall or rise, or am an angel,
I shall acquaint myself a little further
With our new land's new language, which is not—
Peace to your dreams—an idiom to your liking.
I'm wondering if a man may always know
How old a man may be at thirty-seven;
I wonder likewise if a prettier time
Could be decreed for a good man to vanish
Than about now for you, before you fade,
And even your friends are seeing that you have had
Your cup too full for longer mortal triumph.
Well, you have had enough, and had it young;
And the old wine is nearer to the lees
Than you are to the work that you are doing.

HAMILTON

When does this philological excursion
Into new lands and languages begin?

BURR

Anon—that is, already. Only Fortune
Gave me this afternoon the benefaction
Of your blue back, which I for love pursued,
And in pursuing may have saved your life—
Also the world a pounding piece of news:
Hamilton bites the dust of Washington,
Or rather of his horse. For you alone,
Or for your fame, I'd wish it might have been so.

HAMILTON

Not every man among us has a friend
So jealous for the other's fame. How long

Are you to diagnose the doubtful case
Of Demos—and what for? Have you a sword
For some new Damocles? If it's for me,
I have lost all official appetite,
And shall have faded, after January,
Into the law. I'm going to New York.

Burr

No matter where you are, one of these days
I shall come back to you and tell you something.
This Demos, I have heard, has in his wrist
A pulse that no two doctors have as yet
Counted and found the same, and in his mouth
A tongue that has the like alacrity
For saying or not for saying what most it is
That pullulates in his ignoble mind.
One of these days I shall appear again,
To tell you more of him and his opinions;
I shall not be so long out of your sight,
Or take myself so far, that I may not,
Like Alcibiades, come back again.
He went away to Phrygia, and fared ill.

Hamilton

There's an example in Themistocles:
He went away to Persia, and fared well.

Burr

So? Must I go so far? And if so, why so?
I had not planned it so. Is this the road
I take? If so, farewell.

Hamilton

Quite so. Farewell.

JOHN BROWN

Though for your sake I would not have you now
So near to me tonight as now you are,
God knows how much a stranger to my heart
Was any cold word that I may have written;
And you, poor woman that I made my wife,
You have had more of loneliness, I fear,
Than I—though I have been the most alone,
Even when the most attended. So it was
God set the mark of his inscrutable
Necessity on one that was to grope,
And serve, and suffer, and withal be glad
For what was his, and is, and is to be,
When his old bones, that are a burden now,
Are saying what the man who carried them
Had not the power to say. Bones in a grave,
Cover them as they will with choking earth,
May shout the truth to men who put them there,
More than all orators. And so, my dear,
Since you have cheated wisdom for the sake
Of sorrow, let your sorrow be for you,
This last of nights before the last of days,
The lying ghost of what there is of me
That is the most alive. There is no death
For me in what they do. Their death it is
They should heed most when the sun comes again
To make them solemn. There are some I know
Whose eyes will hardly see their occupation,
For tears in them—and all for one old man;
For some of them will pity this old man,
Who took upon himself the work of God
Because he pitied millions. That will be
For them, I fancy, their compassionate

Best way of saying what is best in them
To say; for they can say no more than that,
And they can do no more than what the dawn
Of one more day shall give them light enough
To do. But there are many days to be,
And there are many men to give their blood,
As I gave mine for them. May they come soon!

May they come soon, I say. And when they come,
May all that I have said unheard be heard,
Proving at last, or maybe not—no matter—
What sort of madness was the part of me
That made me strike, whether I found the mark
Or missed it. Meanwhile, I've a strange content,
A patience, and a vast indifference
To what men say of me and what men fear
To say. There was a work to be begun,
And when the Voice, that I have heard so long,
Announced as in a thousand silences
An end of preparation, I began
The coming work of death which is to be,
That life may be. There is no other way
Than the old way of war for a new land
That will not know itself and is tonight
A stranger to itself, and to the world
A more prodigious upstart among states
Than I was among men, and so shall be
Till they are told and told, and told again;
For men are children, waiting to be told,
And most of them are children all their lives.
The good God in his wisdom had them so,
That now and then a madman or a seer
May shake them out of their complacency
And shame them into deeds. The major file
See only what their fathers may have seen,

JOHN BROWN

Or may have said they saw when they saw nothing.
I do not say it matters what they saw.
Now and again to some lone soul or other
God speaks, and there is hanging to be done,—
As once there was a burning of our bodies
Alive, albeit our souls were sorry fuel.
But now the fires are few, and we are poised
Accordingly, for the state's benefit,
A few still minutes between heaven and earth.
The purpose is, when they have seen enough
Of what it is that they are not to see,
To pluck me as an unripe fruit of treason,
And then to fling me back to the same earth
Of which they are, as I suppose, the flower—
Not given to know the riper fruit that waits
For a more comprehensive harvesting.

Yes, may they come, and soon. Again I say,
May they come soon!—before too many of them
Shall be the bloody cost of our defection.
When hell waits on the dawn of a new state,
Better it were that hell should not wait long,—
Or so it is I see it who should see
As far or farther into time tonight
Than they who talk and tremble for me now,
Or wish me to those everlasting fires
That are for me no fear. Too many fires
Have sought me out and seared me to the bone—
Thereby, for all I know, to temper me
For what was mine to do. If I did ill
What I did well, let men say I was mad;
Or let my name for ever be a question
That will not sleep in history. What men say
I was will cool no cannon, dull no sword,
Invalidate no truth. Meanwhile, I was;

And the long train is lighted that shall burn,
Though floods of wrath may drench it, and hot feet
May stamp it for a slight time into smoke
That shall blaze up again with growing speed,
Until at last a fiery crash will come
To cleanse and shake a wounded hemisphere,
And heal it of a long malignity
That angry time discredits and disowns.

Tonight there are men saying many things;
And some who see life in the last of me
Will answer first the coming call to death;
For death is what is coming, and then life.
I do not say again for the dull sake
Of speech what you have heard me say before,
But rather for the sake of all I am,
And all God made of me. A man to die
As I do must have done some other work
Than man's alone. I was not after glory,
But there was glory with me, like a friend,
Throughout those crippling years when friends were few,
And fearful to be known by their own names
When mine was vilified for their approval.
Yet friends they are, and they did what was given
Their will to do; they could have done no more.
I was the one man mad enough, it seems,
To do my work; and now my work is over.
And you, my dear, are not to mourn for me,
Or for your sons, more than a soul should mourn
In Paradise, done with evil and with earth.
There is not much of earth in what remains
For you; and what there may be left of it
For your endurance you shall have at last
In peace, without the twinge of any fear
For my condition; for I shall be done

JOHN BROWN

With plans and actions that have heretofore
Made your days long and your nights ominous
With darkness and the many distances
That were between us. When the silence comes,
I shall in faith be nearer to you then
Than I am now in fact. What you see now
Is only the outside of an old man,
Older than years have made him. Let him die,
And let him be a thing for little grief.
There was a time for service and he served;
And there is no more time for anything
But a short gratefulness to those who gave
Their scared allegiance to an enterprise
That has the name of treason—which will serve
As well as any other for the present.
There are some deeds of men that have no names,
And mine may like as not be one of them.
I am not looking far for names tonight.
The King of Glory was without a name
Until men gave Him one; yet there He was,
Before we found Him and affronted Him
With numerous ingenuities of evil,
Of which one, with His aid, is to be swept
And washed out of the world with fire and blood.

Once I believed it might have come to pass
With a small cost of blood; but I was dreaming—
Dreaming that I believed. The Voice I heard
When I left you behind me in the north,—
To wait there and to wonder and grow old
Of loneliness,—told only what was best,
And with a saving vagueness, I should know
Till I knew more. And had I known even then—
After grim years of search and suffering,
So many of them to end as they began—

After my sickening doubts and estimations
Of plans abandoned and of new plans vain—
After a weary delving everywhere
For men with every virtue but the Vision—
Could I have known, I say, before I left you
That summer morning, all there was to know—
Even unto the last consuming word
That would have blasted every mortal answer
As lightning would annihilate a leaf,
I might have trembled on that summer morning;
I might have wavered; and I might have failed.

And there are many among men today
To say of me that I had best have wavered.
So has it been, so shall it always be,
For those of us who give ourselves to die
Before we are so parcelled and approved
As to be slaughtered by authority.
We do not make so much of what they say
As they of what our folly says of us;
They give us hardly time enough for that,
And thereby we gain much by losing little.
Few are alive to-day with less to lose
Than I who tell you this, or more to gain;
And whether I speak as one to be destroyed
For no good end outside his own destruction,
Time shall have more to say than men shall hear
Between now and the coming of that harvest
Which is to come. Before it comes, I go—
By the short road that mystery makes long
For man's endurance of accomplishment.
I shall have more to say when I am dead.

THE FALSE GODS

"We are false and evanescent, and aware of our deceit,
From the straw that is our vitals to the clay that is our feet.
You may serve us if you must, and you shall have your wage
    of ashes,—
Though arrears due thereafter may be hard for you to meet.

"You may swear that we are solid, you may say that we are
    strong,
But we know that we are neither and we say that you are
    wrong;
You may find an easy worship in acclaiming our indulgence,
But your large admiration of us now is not for long.

"If your doom is to adore us with a doubt that's never still,
And you pray to see our faces—pray in earnest, and you will.
You may gaze at us and live, and live assured of our confusion:
For the False Gods are mortal, and are made for you to kill.

"And you may as well observe, while apprehensively at ease
With an Art that's inorganic and is anything you please,
That anon your newest ruin may lie crumbling unregarded,
Like an old shrine forgotten in a forest of new trees.

"Howsoever like no other be the mode you may employ,
There's an order in the ages for the ages to enjoy;
Though the temples you are shaping and the passions you are
    singing
Are a long way from Athens and a longer way from Troy.

"When we promise more than ever of what never shall arrive,
And you seem a little more than ordinarily alive,
Make a note that you are sure you understand our obligations—
For there's grief always auditing where two and two are five.

"There was this for us to say and there was this for you to know,
Though it humbles and it hurts us when we have to tell you so.
If you doubt the only truth in all our perjured composition,
May the True Gods attend you and forget us when we go."

ARCHIBALD'S EXAMPLE

OLD ARCHIBALD, in his eternal chair,
Where trespassers, whatever their degree,
Were soon frowned out again, was looking off
Across the clover when he said to me:

"My green hill yonder, where the sun goes down
Without a scratch, was once inhabited
By trees that injured him—an evil trash
That made a cage, and held him while he bled.

"Gone fifty years, I see them as they were
Before they fell. They were a crooked lot
To spoil my sunset, and I saw no time
In fifty years for crooked things to rot.

"Trees, yes; but not a service or a joy
To God or man, for they were thieves of light.
So down they came. Nature and I looked on,
And we were glad when they were out of sight.

"Trees are like men, sometimes; and that being so,
So much for that." He twinkled in his chair,
And looked across the clover to the place
That he remembered when the trees were there.

LONDON BRIDGE

"Do I hear them? Yes, I hear the children singing—and what
 of it?
Have you come with eyes afire to find me now and ask me that?
If I were not their father and if you were not their mother,
We might believe they made a noise. . . . What are you—
 driving at!"

"Well, be glad that you can hear them, and be glad they are so
 near us,—
For I have heard the stars of heaven, and they were nearer still.
All within an hour it is that I have heard them calling,
And though I pray for them to cease, I know they never will;
For their music on my heart, though you may freeze it, will
 fall always,
Like summer snow that never melts upon a mountain-top.
Do you hear them? Do you hear them overhead—the children
 —singing?
Do you hear the children singing? . . . God, will you make
 them stop!"

"And what now in His holy name have you to do with moun-
 tains?
We're back to town again, my dear, and we've a dance tonight.
Frozen hearts and falling music? Snow and stars, and—what
 the devil!
Say it over to me slowly, and be sure you have it right."

"God knows if I be right or wrong in saying what I tell you,
Or if I know the meaning any more of what I say.
All I know is, it will kill me if I try to keep it hidden—
Well, I met him. . . . Yes, I met him, and I talked with him—
 today."

"You met him? Did you meet the ghost of someone you had
    poisoned,
Long ago, before I knew you for the woman that you are?
Take a chair; and don't begin your stories always in the
    middle.
Was he man, or was he demon? Anyhow, you've gone too far
To go back, and I'm your servant. I'm the lord, but you're
    the master.
Now go on with what you know, for I'm excited."

                                      "Do you mean—
Do you mean to make me try to think that you know less than
    I do?"

"I know that you foreshadow the beginning of a scene.
Pray be careful, and as accurate as if the doors of heaven
Were to swing or to stay bolted from now on for evermore."

"Do you conceive, with all your smooth contempt of every
    feeling,
Of hiding what you know and what you must have known
    before?
Is it worth a woman's torture to stand here and have you
    smiling,
With only your poor fetish of possession on your side?
No thing but one is wholly sure, and that's not one to scare
    me;
When I meet it I may say to God at last that I have tried.
And yet, for all I know, or all I dare believe, my trials
Henceforward will be more for you to bear than are your own;
And you must give me keys of yours to rooms I have not
    entered.
Do you see me on your threshold all my life, and there alone?
Will you tell me where you see me in your fancy—when it
    leads you
Far enough beyond the moment for a glance at the abyss?"

LONDON BRIDGE

"Will you tell me what intrinsic and amazing sort of nonsense
You are crowding on the patience of the man who gives you—
   this?
Look around you and be sorry you're not living in an attic,
With a civet and a fish-net, and with you to pay the rent.
I say words that you can spell without the use of all your
   letters;
And I grant, if you insist, that I've a guess at what you
   meant."

"Have I told you, then, for nothing, that I met him? Are you
   trying
To be merry while you try to make me hate you?"

                                                        "Think again,
My dear, before you tell me, in a language unbecoming
To a lady, what you plan to tell me next. If I complain,
If I seem an atom peevish at the preference you mention—
Or imply, to be precise—you may believe, or you may not,
That I'm a trifle more aware of what he wants than you are.
But I shouldn't throw that at you. Make believe that I forgot.
Make believe that he's a genius, if you like,—but in the
   meantime
Don't go back to rocking-horses. There, there, there, now."

                                                        "Make believe!
When you see me standing helpless on a plank above a whirl-
   pool,
Do I drown, or do I hear you when you say it? Make believe?
How much more am I to say or do for you before I tell you
That I met him! What's to follow now may be for you to
   choose.
Do you hear me? Won't you listen? It's an easy thing to
   listen. . . ."

"And it's easy to be crazy when there's everything to lose."

"If at last you have a notion that I mean what I am saying,
Do I seem to tell you nothing when I tell you I shall try?
If you save me, and I lose him—I don't know—it won't much matter.
I dare say that I've lied enough, but now I do not lie."

"Do you fancy me the one man who has waited and said nothing
While a wife has dragged an old infatuation from a tomb?
Give the thing a little air and it will vanish into ashes.
There you are—piff! presto!"

"When I came into this room,
It seemed as if I saw the place, and you there at your table,
As you are now at this moment, for the last time in my life;
And I told myself before I came to find you, 'I shall tell him,
If I can, what I have learned of him since I became his wife.'
And if you say, as I've no doubt you will before I finish,
That you have tried unceasingly, with all your might and main,
To teach me, knowing more than I of what it was I needed,
Don't think, with all you may have thought, that you have tried in vain;
For you have taught me more than hides in all the shelves of knowledge
Of how little you found that's in me and was in me all along.
I believed, if I intruded nothing on you that I cared for,
I'd be half as much as horses,—and it seems that I was wrong;
I believed there was enough of earth in me, with all my nonsense
Over things that made you sleepy, to keep something still awake;
But you taught me soon to read my book, and God knows I have read it—
Ages longer than an angel would have read it for your sake.
I have said that you must open other doors than I have entered,

LONDON BRIDGE

But I wondered while I said it if I might not be obscure.
Is there anything in all your pedigrees and inventories
With a value more elusive than a dollar's? Are you sure
That if I starve another year for you I shall be stronger
To endure another like it—and another—till I'm dead?"

"Has your tame cat sold a picture?—or more likely had a
 windfall?
Or for God's sake, what's broke loose? Have you a bee-hive
 in your head?
A little more of this from you will not be easy hearing
Do you know that? Understand it, if you do; for if you
 won't. . . .
What the devil are you saying! Make believe you never said it,
And I'll say I never heard it. . . . Oh, you. . . . If you. . . ."

"If I don't?"

"There are men who say there's reason hidden somewhere in a
 woman,
But I doubt if God himself remembers where the key was
 hung."

"He may not; for they say that even God himself is growing.
I wonder if He makes believe that He is growing young;
I wonder if He makes believe that women who are giving
All they have in holy loathing to a stranger all their lives
Are the wise ones who build houses in the Bible. . . ."

"Stop—you devil!"

". . . Or that souls are any whiter when their bodies are called
 wives.
If a dollar's worth of gold will hoop the walls of hell together,
Why need heaven be such a ruin of a place that never was?

And if at last I lied my starving soul away to nothing,
Are you sure you might not miss it? Have you come to such a pass
That you would have me longer in your arms if you discovered
That I made you into someone else. . . . Oh! . . . Well, there are worse ways.
But why aim it at my feet—unless you fear you may be sorry. . . .
There are many days ahead of you."

"I do not see those days."

"I can see them. Granted even I am wrong, there are the children.
And are they to praise their father for his insight if we die?
Do you hear them? Do you hear them overhead—the children —singing?
Do you hear them? Do you hear the children?"

"Damn the children!"

"Why?
What have *they* done? . . . Well, then,—do it. . . . Do it now, and have it over."

"Oh, you devil! . . . Oh, you. . . ."

"No, I'm not a devil, I'm a prophet—
One who sees the end already of so much that one end more
Would have now the small importance of one other small illusion,
Which in turn would have a welcome where the rest have gone before.
But if I were you, my fancy would look on a little farther
For the glimpse of a release that may be somewhere still in sight.

TASKER NORCROSS

Furthermore, you must remember those two hundred invitations
For the dancing after dinner. We shall have to shine tonight.
We shall dance, and be as happy as a pair of merry spectres,
On the grave of all the lies that we shall never have to tell;
We shall dance among the ruins of the tomb of our endurance;
And I have not a doubt that we shall do it very well.
There!—I'm glad you've put it back; for I don't like it. Shut
    the drawer now.
No—no—don't cancel anything. I'll dance until I drop.
I can't walk yet, but I'm going to. . . . Go away somewhere,
    and leave me. . . .
Oh, you children! Oh, you children! . . . God, will they never
    stop!"

TASKER NORCROSS

"WHETHER all towns and all who live in them—
So long as they be somewhere in this world
That we in our complacency call ours—
Are more or less the same, I leave to you.
I should say less. Whether or not, meanwhile,
We've all two legs—and as for that, we haven't—
There were three kinds of men where I was born:
The good, the not so good, and Tasker Norcross.
Now there are two kinds."

                      "Meaning, as I divine,
Your friend is dead," I ventured.

                              Ferguson,
Who talked himself at last out of the world
He censured, and is therefore silent now,
Agreed indifferently: "My friends are dead—
Or most of them."

                        "Remember one that isn't,"
I said, protesting. "Honor him for his ears;
Treasure him also for his understanding."
Ferguson sighed, and then talked on again:
"You have an overgrown alacrity
For saying nothing much and hearing less;
And I've a thankless wonder, at the start,
How much it is to you that I shall tell
What I have now to say of Tasker Norcross,
And how much to the air that is around you.
But given a patience that is not averse
To the slow tragedies of haunted men—
Horrors, in fact, if you've a skilful eye
To know them at their firesides, or out walking,—"

"Horrors," I said, "are my necessity;
And I would have them, for their best effect,
Always out walking."

                        Ferguson frowned at me:
"The wisest of us are not those who laugh
Before they know. Most of us never know—
Or the long toil of our mortality
Would not be done. Most of us never know—
And there you have a reason to believe
In God, if you may have no other. Norcross,
Or so I gather of his infirmity,
Was given to know more than he should have known,
And only God knows why. See for yourself
An old house full of ghosts of ancestors,
Who did their best, or worst, and having done it,
Died honorably; and each with a distinction
That hardly would have been for him that had it,
Had honor failed him wholly as a friend.
Honor that is a friend begets a friend.

TASKER NORCROSS

Whether or not we love him, still we have him;
And we must live somehow by what we have,
Or then we die. If you say chemistry,
Then you must have your molecules in motion,
And in their right abundance. Failing either,
You have not long to dance. Failing a friend,
A genius, or a madness, or a faith
Larger than desperation, you are here
For as much longer than you like as may be.
Imagining now, by way of an example,
Myself a more or less remembered phantom—
Again, I should say less—how many times
A day should I come back to you? No answer.
Forgive me when I seem a little careless,
But we must have examples, or be lucid
Without them; and I question your adherence
To such an undramatic narrative
As this of mine, without the personal hook."

"A time is given in Ecclesiastes
For divers works," I told him. "Is there one
For saying nothing in return for nothing?
If not, there should be." I could feel his eyes,
And they were like two cold inquiring points
Of a sharp metal. When I looked again,
To see them shine, the cold that I had felt
Was gone to make way for a smouldering
Of lonely fire that I, as I knew then,
Could never quench with kindness or with lies.
I should have done whatever there was to do
For Ferguson, yet I could not have mourned
In honesty for once around the clock
The loss of him, for my sake or for his,
Try as I might; nor would his ghost approve,
Had I the power and the unthinking will

To make him tread again without an aim
The road that was behind him—and without
The faith, or friend, or genius, or the madness
That he contended was imperative.

After a silence that had been too long,
"It may be quite as well we don't," he said;
"As well, I mean, that we don't always say it.
You know best what I mean, and I suppose
You might have said it better. What was that?
Incorrigible? Am I incorrigible?
Well, it's a word; and a word has its use,
Or, like a man, it will soon have a grave.
It's a good word enough. Incorrigible,
May be, for all I know, the word for Norcross.
See for yourself that house of his again
That he called home: An old house, painted white,
Square as a box, and chillier than a tomb
To look at or to live in. There were trees—
Too many of them, if such a thing may be—
Before it and around it. Down in front
There was a road, a railroad, and a river;
Then there were hills behind it, and more trees.
The thing would fairly stare at you through trees,
Like a pale inmate out of a barred window
With a green shade half down; and I dare say
People who passed have said: 'There's where he lives.
We know him, but we do not seem to know
That we remember any good of him,
Or any evil that is interesting.
There you have all we know and all we care.'
They might have said it in all sorts of ways;
And then, if they perceived a cat, they might
Or might not have remembered what they said.
The cat might have a personality—

TASKER NORCROSS

And maybe the same one the Lord left out
Of Tasker Norcross, who, for lack of it,
Saw the same sun go down year after year;
All which at last was my discovery.
And only mine, so far as evidence
Enlightens one more darkness. You have known
All round you, all your days, men who are nothing—
Nothing, I mean, so far as time tells yet
Of any other need it has of them
Than to make sextons hardy—but no less
Are to themselves incalculably something,
And therefore to be cherished. God, you see,
Being sorry for them in their fashioning,
Indemnified them with a quaint esteem
Of self, and with illusions long as life.
You know them well, and you have smiled at them;
And they, in their serenity, may have had
Their time to smile at you. Blessed are they
That see themselves for what they never were
Or were to be, and are, for their defect,
At ease with mirrors and the dim remarks
That pass their tranquil ears."

       "Come, come," said I;
"There may be names in your compendium
That we are not yet all on fire for shouting.
Skin most of us of our mediocrity,
We should have nothing then that we could scratch.
The picture smarts. Cover it, if you please,
And do so rather gently. Now for Norcross."

Ferguson closed his eyes in resignation,
While a dead sigh came out of him. "Good God!"
He said, and said it only half aloud,
As if he knew no longer now, nor cared,

If one were there to listen: "Have I said nothing—
Nothing at all—of Norcross? Do you mean
To patronize him till his name becomes
A toy made out of letters? If a name
Is all you need, arrange an honest column
Of all the people you have ever known
That you have never liked. You'll have enough;
And you'll have mine, moreover. No, not yet.
If I assume too many privileges,
I pay, and I alone, for their assumption;
By which, if I assume a darker knowledge
Of Norcross than another, let the weight
Of my injustice aggravate the load
That is not on your shoulders. When I came
To know this fellow Norcross in his house,
I found him as I found him in the street—
No more, no less; indifferent, but no better.
'Worse' were not quite the word: he was not bad;
He was not . . . well, he was not anything.
Has your invention ever entertained
The picture of a dusty worm so dry
That even the early bird would shake his head
And fly on farther for another breakfast?"

"But why forget the fortune of the worm,"
I said, "if in the dryness you deplore
Salvation centred and endured? Your Norcross
May have been one for many to have envied."

"Salvation? Fortune? Would the worm say that?
He might; and therefore I dismiss the worm
With all dry things but one. Figures away,
Do you begin to see this man a little?
Do you begin to see him in the air,
With all the vacant horrors of his outline

TASKER NORCROSS

For you to fill with more than it will hold?
If so, you needn't crown yourself at once
With epic laurel if you seem to fill it.
Horrors, I say, for in the fires and forks
Of a new hell—if one were not enough—
I doubt if a new horror would have held him
With a malignant ingenuity
More to be feared than his before he died.
You smile, as if in doubt. Well, smile again.
Now come into his house, along with me:
The four square sombre things that you see first
Around you are four walls that go as high
As to the ceiling. Norcross knew them well,
And he knew others like them. Fasten to that
With all the claws of your intelligence;
And hold the man before you in his house
As if he were a white rat in a box,
And one that knew himself to be no other.
I tell you twice that he knew all about it,
That you may not forget the worst of all
Our tragedies begin with what we know.
Could Norcross only not have known, I wonder
How many would have blessed and envied him!
Could he have had the usual eye for spots
On others, and for none upon himself,
I smile to ponder on the carriages
That might as well as not have clogged the town
In honor of his end. For there was gold,
You see, though all he needed was a little,
And what he gave said nothing of who gave it.
He would have given it all if in return
There might have been a more sufficient face
To greet him when he shaved. Though you insist
It is the dower, and always, of our degree
Not to be cursed with such invidious insight,

Remember that you stand, you and your fancy,
Now in his house; and since we are together,
See for yourself and tell me what you see.
Tell me the best you see. Make a slight noise
Of recognition when you find a book
That you would not as lief read upside down
As otherwise, for example. If there you fail,
Observe the walls and lead me to the place,
Where you are led. If there you meet a picture
That holds you near it for a longer time
Than you are sorry, you may call it yours,
And hang it in the dark of your remembrance,
Where Norcross never sees. How can he see
That has no eyes to see? And as for music,
He paid with empty wonder for the pangs
Of his infrequent forced endurance of it;
And having had no pleasure, paid no more
For needless immolation, or for the sight
Of those who heard what he was never to hear.
To see them listening was itself enough
To make him suffer; and to watch worn eyes,
On other days, of strangers who forgot
Their sorrows and their failures and themselves
Before a few mysterious odds and ends
Of marble carted from the Parthenon—
And all for seeing what he was never to see,
Because it was alive and he was dead—
Here was a wonder that was more profound
Than any that was in fiddles and brass horns.

"He knew, and in his knowledge there was death.
He knew there was a region all around him
That lay outside man's havoc and affairs,
And yet was not all hostile to their tumult,

TASKER NORCROSS

Where poets would have served and honored him,
And saved him, had there been anything to save.
But there was nothing, and his tethered range
Was only a small desert. Kings of song
Are not for thrones in deserts. Towers of sound
And flowers of sense are but a waste of heaven
Where there is none to know them from the rocks
And sand-grass of his own monotony
That makes earth less than earth. He could see that,
And he could see no more. The captured light
That may have been or not, for all he cared,
The song that is in sculpture was not his,
But only, to his God-forgotten eyes,
One more immortal nonsense in a world
Where all was mortal, or had best be so,
And so be done with. 'Art,' he would have said,
'Is not life, and must therefore be a lie;'
And with a few profundities like that
He would have controverted and dismissed
The benefit of the Greeks. He had heard of them,
As he had heard of his aspiring soul—
Never to the perceptible advantage,
In his esteem, of either. 'Faith,' he said,
Or would have said if he had thought of it,
'Lives in the same house with Philosophy,
Where the two feed on scraps and are forlorn
As orphans after war. He could see stars,
On a clear night, but he had not an eye
To see beyond them. He could hear spoken words,
But had no ear for silence when alone.
He could eat food of which he knew the savor,
But had no palate for the Bread of Life,
That human desperation, to his thinking,
Made famous long ago, having no other.
Now do you see? Do you begin to see?"

I told him that I did begin to see;
And I was nearer than I should have been
To laughing at his malign inclusiveness,
When I considered that, with all our speed,
We are not laughing yet at funerals.
I see him now as I could see him then,
And I see now that it was good for me,
As it was good for him, that I was quiet;
For Time's eye was on Ferguson, and the shaft
Of its inquiring hesitancy had touched him,
Or so I chose to fancy more than once
Before he told of Norcross. When the word
Of his release (he would have called it so)
Made half an inch of news, there were no tears
That are recorded. Women there may have been
To wish him back, though I should say, not knowing,
The few there were to mourn were not for love,
And were not lovely. Nothing of them, at least,
Was in the meagre legend that I gathered
Years after, when a chance of travel took me
So near the region of his nativity
That a few miles of leisure brought me there;
For there I found a friendly citizen
Who led me to his house among the trees
That were above a railroad and a river.
Square as a box and chillier than a tomb
It was indeed, to look at or to live in—
All which had I been told. "Ferguson died,"
The stranger said, "and then there was an auction.
I live here, but I've never yet been warm.
Remember him? Yes, I remember him.
I knew him—as a man may know a tree—
For twenty years. He may have held himself
A little high when he was here, but now . . .
Yes, I remember Ferguson. Oh, yes."

SOUVENIR

Others, I found, remembered Ferguson,
But none of them had heard of Tasker Norcross.

A SONG AT SHANNON'S

Two men came out of Shannon's, having known
The faces of each other for as long
As they had listened there to an old song,
Sung thinly in a wastrel monotone
By some unhappy night-bird, who had flown
Too many times and with a wing too strong
To save himself, and so done heavy wrong
To more frail elements than his alone.

Slowly away they went, leaving behind
More light than was before them. Neither met
The other's eyes again or said a word.
Each to his loneliness or to his kind,
Went his own way, and with his own regret,
Not knowing what the other may have heard.

SOUVENIR

A VANISHED house that for an hour I knew
By some forgotten chance when I was young
Had once a glimmering window overhung
With honeysuckle wet with evening dew.
Along the path tall dusky dahlias grew,
And shadowy hydrangeas reached and swung
Ferociously; and over me, among
The moths and mysteries, a blurred bat flew.

Somewhere within there were dim presences
Of days that hovered and of years gone by.
I waited, and between their silences
There was an evanescent faded noise;
And though a child, I knew it was the voice
Of one whose occupation was to die.

DISCOVERY

WE told of him as one who should have soared
And seen for us the devastating light
Whereof there is not either day or night,
And shared with us the glamour of the Word
That fell once upon Amos to record
For men at ease in Zion, when the sight
Of ills obscured aggrieved him and the might
Of Hamath was a warning of the Lord.

Assured somehow that he would make us wise,
Our pleasure was to wait; and our surprise
Was hard when we confessed the dry return
Of his regret. For we were still to learn
That earth has not a school where we may go
For wisdom, or for more than we may know.

FIRELIGHT

TEN years together without yet a cloud,
They seek each other's eyes at intervals
Of gratefulness to firelight and four walls
For love's obliteration of the crowd.
Serenely and perennially endowed
And bowered as few may be, their joy recalls

INFERENTIAL

No snake, no sword; and over them there falls
The blessing of what neither says aloud.

Wiser for silence, they were not so glad
Were she to read the graven tale of lines
On the wan face of one somewhere alone;
Nor were they more content could he have had
Her thoughts a moment since of one who shines
Apart, and would be hers if he had known.

THE NEW TENANTS

The day was here when it was his to know
How fared the barriers he had built between
His triumph and his enemies unseen,
For them to undermine and overthrow;
And it was his no longer to forego
The sight of them, insidious and serene,
Where they were delving always and had been
Left always to be vicious and to grow.

And there were the new tenants who had come,
By doors that were left open unawares,
Into his house, and were so much at home
There now that he would hardly have to guess,
By the slow guile of their vindictiveness,
What ultimate insolence would soon be theirs.

INFERENTIAL

Although I saw before me there the face
Of one whom I had honored among men
The least, and on regarding him again.

Would not have had him in another place,
He fitted with an unfamiliar grace
The coffin where I could not see him then
As I had seen him and appraised him when
I deemed him unessential to the race.

For there was more of him than what I saw.
And there was on me more than the old awe
That is the common genius of the dead.
I might as well have heard him: "Never mind;
If some of us were not so far behind,
The rest of us were not so far ahead."

THE RAT

As often as he let himself be seen
We pitied him, or scorned him, or deplored
The inscrutable profusion of the Lord
Who shaped as one of us a thing so mean—
Who made him human when he might have been
A rat, and so been wholly in accord
With any other creature we abhorred
As always useless and not always clean.

Now he is hiding all alone somewhere,
And in a final hole not ready then;
For now he is among those over there
Who are not coming back to us again.
And we who do the fiction of our share
Say less of rats and rather more of men.

RAHEL TO VARNHAGEN

RAHEL TO VARNHAGEN

NOTE.—Rahel Robert and Varnhagen von Ense were married, after many protestations on her part, in 1814. The marriage—so far as he was concerned at any rate—appears to have been satisfactory.

> Now you have read them all; or if not all,
> As many as in all conscience I should fancy
> To be enough. There are no more of them—
> Or none to burn your sleep, or to bring dreams
> Of devils. If these are not sufficient, surely
> You are a strange young man. I might live on
> Alone, and for another forty years,
> Or not quite forty,—are you happier now?—
> Always to ask if there prevailed elsewhere
> Another like yourself that would have held
> These aged hands as long as you have held them,
> Not once observing, for all I can see,
> How they are like your mother's. Well, you have read
> His letters now, and you have heard me say
> That in them are the cinders of a passion
> That was my life; and you have not yet broken
> Your way out of my house, out of my sight,—
> Into the street. You are a strange young man.
> I know as much as that of you, for certain;
> And I'm already praying, for your sake,
> That you be not too strange. Too much of that
> May lead you bye and bye through gloomy lanes
> To a sad wilderness, where one may grope
> Alone, and always, or until he feels
> Ferocious and invisible animals
> That wait for men and eat them in the dark.
> Why do you sit there on the floor so long,
> Smiling at me while I try to be solemn?

Do you not hear it said for your salvation,
When I say truth? Are you, at four and twenty,
So little deceived in us that you interpret
The humor of a woman to be noticed
As her choice between you and Acheron?
Are you so unscathed yet as to infer
That if a woman worries when a man,
Or a man-child, has wet shoes on his feet
She may as well commemorate with ashes
The last eclipse of her tranquillity?
If you look up at me and blink again,
I shall not have to make you tell me lies
To know the letters you have not been reading
I see now that I may have had for nothing
A most unpleasant shivering in my conscience
When I laid open for your contemplation
The wealth of my worn casket. If I did,
The fault was not yours wholly. Search again
This wreckage we may call for sport a face,
And you may chance upon the price of havoc
That I have paid for a few sorry stones
That shine and have no light—yet once were stars,
And sparkled on a crown. Little and weak
They seem; and they are cold, I fear, for you.
But they that once were fire for me may not
Be cold again for me until I die;
And only God knows if they may be then.
There is a love that ceases to be love
In being ourselves. How, then, are we to lose it?
You that are sure that you know everything
There is to know of love, answer me that.
Well? . . . You are not even interested.

Once on a far off time when I was young,
I felt with your assurance, and all through me,

RAHEL TO VARNHAGEN

That I had undergone the last and worst
Of love's inventions. There was a boy who brought
The sun with him and woke me up with it,
And that was every morning; every night
I tried to dream of him, but never could,
More than I might have seen in Adam's eyes
Their fond uncertainty when Eve began
The play that all her tireless progeny
Are not yet weary of. One scene of it
Was brief, but was eternal while it lasted;
And that was while I was the happiest
Of an imaginary six or seven,
Somewhere in history but not on earth,
For whom the sky had shaken and let stars
Rain down like diamonds. Then there were clouds,
And a sad end of diamonds; whereupon
Despair came, like a blast that would have brought
Tears to the eyes of all the bears in Finland,
And love was done. That was how much I knew.
Poor little wretch! I wonder where he is
This afternoon. Out of this rain, I hope.

At last, when I had seen so many days
Dressed all alike, and in their marching order,
Go by me that I would not always count them,
One stopped—shattering the whole file of Time,
Or so it seemed; and when I looked again,
There was a man. He struck once with his eyes,
And then there was a woman. I, who had come
To wisdom, or to vision, or what you like,
By the old hidden road that has no name,—
I, who was used to seeing without flying
So much that others fly from without seeing,
Still looked, and was afraid, and looked again.
And after that, when I had read the story

Told in his eyes, and felt within my heart
The bleeding wound of their necessity,
I knew the fear was his. If I had failed him
And flown away from him, I should have lost
Ingloriously my wings in scrambling back,
And found them arms again. If he had struck me
Not only with his eyes but with his hands,
I might have pitied him and hated love,
And then gone mad. I, who have been so strong—
Why don't you laugh?—might even have done all that.
I, who have learned so much, and said so much,
And had the commendations of the great
For one who rules herself—why don't you cry?—
And own a certain small authority
Among the blind, who see no more than ever,
But like my voice,—I would have tossed it all
To Tophet for one man; and he was jealous.
I would have wound a snake around my neck
And then have let it bite me till I died,
If my so doing would have made me sure
That one man might have lived; and he was jealous.
I would have driven these hands into a cage
That held a thousand scorpions, and crushed them,
If only by so poisonous a trial
I could have crushed his doubt. I would have wrung
My living blood with mediaeval engines
Out of my screaming flesh, if only that
Would have made one man sure. I would have paid
For him the tiresome price of body and soul,
And let the lash of a tongue-weary town
Fall as it might upon my blistered name;
And while it fell I could have laughed at it,
Knowing that he had found out finally
Where the wrong was. But there was evil in him
That would have made no more of his possession

RAHEL TO VARNHAGEN

Than confirmation of another fault;
And there was honor—if you call it honor
That hoods itself with doubt and wears a crown
Of lead that might as well be gold and fire.
Give it as heavy or as light a name
As any there is that fits. I see myself
Without the power to swear to this or that
That I might be if he had been without it.
Whatever I might have been that I was not,
It only happened that it wasn't so.
Meanwhile, you might seem to be listening:
If you forget yourself and go to sleep,
My treasure, I shall not say this again.
Look up once more into my poor old face,
Where you see beauty, or the Lord knows what,
And say to me aloud what else there is
Than ruins in it that you most admire.

No, there was never anything like that;
Nature has never fastened such a mask
Of radiant and impenetrable merit
On any woman as you say there is
On this one. Not a mask? I thank you, sir,
But you see more with your determination,
I fear, than with your prudence or your conscience;
And you have never met me with my eyes
In all the mirrors I've made faces at.
No, I shall never call you strange again:
You are the young and inconvincible
Epitome of all blind men since Adam.
May the blind lead the blind, if that be so?
And we shall need no mirrors? You are saying
What most I feared you might. But if the blind,
Or one of them, be not so fortunate
As to put out the eyes of recollection,

She might at last, without her meaning it,
Lead on the other, without his knowing it,
Until the two of them should lose themselves
Among dead craters in a lava-field
As empty as a desert on the moon.
I am not speaking in a theatre,
But in a room so real and so familiar
That sometimes I would wreck it. Then I pause,
Remembering there is a King in Weimar—
A monarch, and a poet, and a shepherd
Of all who are astray and are outside
The realm where they should rule. I think of him,
And save the furniture; I think of you,
And am forlorn, finding in you the one
To lavish aspirations and illusions
Upon a faded and forsaken house
Where love, being locked alone, was nigh to burning
House and himself together. Yes, you are strange,
To see in such an injured architecture
Room for new love to live in. Are you laughing?
No? Well, you are not crying, as you should be.
Tears, even if they told only gratitude
For your escape, and had no other story,
Were surely more becoming than a smile
For my unwomanly straightforwardness
In seeing for you, through my close gate of years
Your forty ways to freedom. Why do you smile?
And while I'm trembling at my faith in you
In giving you to read this book of danger
That only one man living might have written—
These letters, which have been a part of me
So long that you may read them all again
As often as you look into my face,
And hear them when I speak to you, and feel them
Whenever you have to touch me with your hand,—

RAHEL TO VARNHAGEN

Why are you so unwilling to be spared?
Why do you still believe in me? But no,
I'll find another way to ask you that.
I wonder if there is another way
That says it better, and means anything.
There is no other way that could be worse?
I was not asking you; it was myself
Alone that I was asking. Why do I dip
For lies, when there is nothing in my well
But shining truth, you say? How do you know?
Truth has a lonely life down where she lives;
And many a time, when she comes up to breathe,
She sinks before we seize her, and makes ripples.
Possibly you may know no more of me
Than a few ripples; and they may soon be gone,
Leaving you then with all my shining truth
Drowned in a shining water; and when you look
You may not see me there, but something else
That never was a woman—being yourself.
You say to me my truth is past all drowning,
And safe with you for ever? You know all that?
How do you know all that, and who has told you?
You know so much that I'm an atom frightened
Because you know so little. And what is this?
You know the luxury there is in haunting
The blasted thoroughfares of disillusion—
If that's your name for them—with only ghosts
For company? You know that when a woman
Is blessed, or cursed, with a divine impatience
(Another name of yours for a bad temper)
She must have one at hand on whom to wreak it
(That's what you mean, whatever the turn you give it),
Sure of a kindred sympathy, and thereby
Effect a mutual calm? You know that wisdom,
Given in vain to make a food for those

Who are without it, will be seen at last,
And even at last only by those who gave it,
As one or more of the forgotten crumbs
That others leave? You know that men's applause
And women's envy savor so much of dust
That I go hungry, having at home no fare
But the same changeless bread that I may swallow
Only with tears and prayers? Who told you that?
You know that if I read, and read alone,
Too many books that no men yet have written,
I may go blind, or worse? You know yourself,
Of all insistent and insidious creatures,
To be the one to save me, and to guard
For me their flaming language? And you know
That if I give much headway to the whim
That's in me never to be quite sure that even
Through all those years of storm and fire I waited
For this one rainy day, I may go on,
And on, and on alone, through smoke and ashes,
To a cold end? You know so dismal much
As that about me? . . . Well, I believe you do.

NIMMO

Since you remember Nimmo, and arrive
At such a false and florid and far drawn
Confusion of odd nonsense, I connive
No longer, though I may have led you on.

So much is told and heard and told again,
So many with his legend are engrossed,
That I, more sorry now than I was then,
May live on to be sorry for his ghost.

NIMMO

You knew him, and you must have known his eyes,—
How deep they were, and what a velvet light
Came out of them when anger or surprise,
Or laughter, or Francesca, made them bright.

No, you will not forget such eyes, I think,—
And you say nothing of them. Very well.
I wonder if all history's worth a wink,
Sometimes, or if my tale be one to tell.

For they began to lose their velvet light;
Their fire grew dead without and small within;
And many of you deplored the needless fight
That somewhere in the dark there must have been.

All fights are needless, when they're not our own,
But Nimmo and Francesca never fought.
Remember that; and when you are alone,
Remember me—and think what I have thought.

Now, mind you, I say nothing of what was,
Or never was, or could or could not be:
Bring not suspicion's candle to the glass
That mirrors a friend's face to memory.

Of what you see, see all,—but see no more;
For what I show you here will not be there.
The devil has had his way with paint before,
And he's an artist,—and you needn't stare.

There was a painter and he painted well:
He'd paint you Daniel in the lion's den,
Beelzebub, Elaine, or William Tell.
I'm coming back to Nimmo's eyes again.

The painter put the devil in those eyes,
Unless the devil did, and there he stayed;
And then the lady fled from paradise,
And there's your fact. The lady was afraid.

She must have been afraid, or may have been,
Of evil in their velvet all the while;
But sure as I'm a sinner with a skin,
I'll trust the man as long as he can smile.

I trust him who can smile and then may live
In my heart's house, where Nimmo is today.
God knows if I have more than men forgive
To tell him; but I played, and I shall pay.

I knew him then, and if I know him yet,
I know in him, defeated and estranged,
The calm of men forbidden to forget
The calm of women who have loved and changed.

But there are ways that are beyond our ways,
Or he would not be calm and she be mute,
As one by one their lost and empty days
Pass without even the warmth of a dispute.

God help us all when women think they see;
God save us when they do. I'm fair; but though
I know him only as he looks to me,
I know him,—and I tell Francesca so.

And what of Nimmo? Little would you ask
Of him, could you but see him as I can,
At his bewildered and unfruitful task
Of being what he was born to be—a man.

PEACE ON EARTH

Better forget that I said anything
Of what your tortured memory may disclose;
I know him, and your worst remembering
Would count as much as nothing, I suppose.

Meanwhile, I trust him; and I know his way
Of trusting me, and always in his youth.
I'm painting here a better man, you say,
Than I, the painter; and you say the truth.

PEACE ON EARTH

He took a frayed hat from his head,
And "Peace on Earth" was what he said.
"A morsel out of what you're worth,
And there we have it: Peace on Earth.
Not much, although a little more
Than what there was on earth before
I'm as you see, I'm Ichabod,—
But never mind the ways I've trod;
I'm sober now, so help me God."

I could not pass the fellow by.
"Do you believe in God?" said I;
"And is there to be Peace on Earth?"

"Tonight we celebrate the birth,"
He said, "of One who died for men;
The Son of God, we say. What then?
Your God, or mine? I'd make you laugh
Were I to tell you even half
That I have learned of mine today
Where yours would hardly seem to stay.

Could He but follow in and out
Some anthropoids I know about,
The god to whom you may have prayed
Might see a world He never made."

"Your words are flowing full," said I;
"But yet they give me no reply;
Your fountain might as well be dry."

"A wiser One than you, my friend,
Would wait and hear me to the end;
And for his eyes a light would shine
Through this unpleasant shell of mine
That in your fancy makes of me
A Christmas curiosity.
All right, I might be worse than that;
And you might now be lying flat;
I might have done it from behind,
And taken what there was to find.
Don't worry, for I'm not that kind.
'Do I believe in God?' Is that
The price tonight of a new hat?
Has he commanded that his name
Be written everywhere the same?
Have all who live in every place
Identified his hidden face?
Who knows but he may like as well
My story as one you may tell?
And if he show me there be Peace
On Earth, as there be fields and trees
Outside a jail-yard, am I wrong
If now I sing him a new song?
Your world is in yourself, my friend,
For your endurance to the end;
And all the Peace there is on Earth

LATE SUMMER

Is faith in what your world is worth,
And saying, without any lies,
Your world could not be otherwise."

"One might say that and then be shot,"
I told him; and he said: "Why not?"
I ceased, and gave him rather more
Than he was counting of my store.
"And since I have it, thanks to you,
Don't ask me what I mean to do,"
Said he. "Believe that even I
Would rather tell the truth than lie—
On Christmas Eve. No matter why."

His unshaved, educated face,
His inextinguishable grace.
And his hard smile, are with me still,
Deplore the vision as I will;
For whatsoever he be at,
So droll a derelict as that
Should have at least another hat.

LATE SUMMER

(ALCAICS)

CONFUSED, he found her lavishing feminine
Gold upon clay, and found her inscrutable;
    And yet she smiled. Why, then, should horrors
Be as they were, without end, her playthings?

And why were dead years hungrily telling her
Lies of the dead, who told them again to her?
    If now she knew, there might be kindness
Clamoring yet where a faith lay stifled.

A little faith in him, and the ruinous
Past would be for time to annihilate,
   And wash out, like a tide that washes
Out of the sand what a child has drawn there.

God, what a shining handful of happiness,
Made out of days and out of eternities,
   Were now the pulsing end of patience—
Could he but have what a ghost had stolen!

What was a man before him, or ten of them,
While he was here alive who could answer them,
   And in their teeth fling confirmations
Harder than agates against an egg-shell?

But now the man was dead, and would come again
Never, though she might honor ineffably
   The flimsy wraith of him she conjured
Out of a dream with his wand of absence.

And if the truth were now but a mummery,
Meriting pride's implacable irony,
   So much the worse for pride. Moreover,
Save her or fail, there was conscience always.

Meanwhile, a few misgivings of innocence,
Imploring to be sheltered and credited,
   Were not amiss when she revealed them.
Whether she struggled or not, he saw them.

Also, he saw that while she was hearing him
Her eyes had more and more of the past in them;
   And while he told what cautious honor
Told him was all he had best be sure of,

LATE SUMMER

He wondered once or twice, inadvertently,
Where shifting winds were driving his argosies,
    Long anchored and as long unladen,
Over the foam for the golden chances.

"If men were not for killing so carelessly,
And women were for wiser endurances,"
    He said, "we might have yet a world here
Fitter for Truth to be seen abroad in;

"If Truth were not so strange in her nakedness,
And we were less forbidden to look at it,
    We might not have to look." He stared then
Down at the sand where the tide threw forward

Its cold, unconquered lines, that unceasingly
Foamed against hope, and fell. He was calm enough,
    Although he knew he might be silenced
Out of all calm; and the night was coming.

"I climb for you the peak of his infamy
That you may choose your fall if you cling to it.
    No more for me unless you say more.
All you have left of a dream defends you:

"The truth may be as evil an augury
As it was needful now for the two of us.
    We cannot have the dead between us.
Tell me to go, and I go."—She pondered:

"What you believe is right for the two of us
Makes it as right that you are not one of us.
    If this be needful truth you tell me,
Spare me, and let me have lies hereafter."

She gazed away where shadows were covering
The whole cold ocean's healing indifference.
  No ship was coming. When the darkness
Fell, she was there, and alone, still gazing.

AN EVANGELIST'S WIFE

"Why am I not myself these many days,
You ask? And have you nothing more to ask?
I do you wrong? I do not hear your praise
To God for giving you me to share your task?

"Jealous—of Her? Because her cheeks are pink,
And she has eyes? No, not if she had seven.
If you should only steal an hour to think,
Sometime, there might be less to be forgiven.

"No, you are never cruel. If once or twice
I found you so, I could applaud and sing.
Jealous of—What? You are not very wise.
Does not the good Book tell you anything?

"In David's time poor Michal had to go.
Jealous of God? Well, if you like it so."

THE OLD KING'S NEW JESTER

You that in vain would front the coming order
With eyes that meet forlornly what they must,
And only with a furtive recognition
See dust where there is dust,—
Be sure you like it always in your faces,

THE OLD KING'S NEW JESTER

Obscuring your best graces,
Blinding your speech and sight,
Before you seek again your dusty places
Where the old wrong seems right.

Longer ago than cave-men had their changes
Our fathers may have slain a son or two,
Discouraging a further dialectic
Regarding what was new;
And after their unstudied admonition
Occasional contrition
For their old-fashioned ways
May have reduced their doubts, and in addition
Softened their final days.

Farther away than feet shall ever travel
Are the vague towers of our unbuilded State;
But there are mightier things than we to lead us,
That will not let us wait.
And we go on with none to tell us whether
Or not we've each a tether
Determining how fast or how far we go;
And it is well, since we must go together,
That we are not to know.

If the old wrong and all its injured glamour
Haunts you by day and gives your night no peace,
You may as well, agreeably and serenely,
Give the new wrong its lease;
For should you nourish a too fervid yearning
For what is not returning,
The vicious and unfused ingredient
May give you qualms—and one or two concerning
The last of your content.

LAZARUS

"No, Mary, there was nothing—not a word.
Nothing, and always nothing. Go again
Yourself, and he may listen—or at least
Look up at you, and let you see his eyes.
I might as well have been the sound of rain,
A wind among the cedars, or a bird;
Or nothing. Mary, make him look at you;
And even if he should say that we are nothing,
To know that you have heard him will be something.
And yet he loved us, and it was for love
The Master gave him back. Why did he wait
So long before he came? Why did he weep?
I thought he would be glad—and Lazarus—
To see us all again as he had left us—
All as it was, all as it was before."

Mary, who felt her sister's frightened arms
Like those of someone drowning who had seized her,
Fearing at last they were to fail and sink
Together in this fog-stricken sea of strangeness,
Fought sadly, with bereaved indignant eyes,
To find again the fading shores of home
That she had seen but now could see no longer
Now she could only gaze into the twilight,
And in the dimness know that he was there,
Like someone that was not. He who had been
Their brother, and was dead, now seemed alive
Only in death again—or worse than death;
For tombs at least, always until today,
Though sad were certain. There was nothing certain
For man or God in such a day as this;
For there they were alone, and there was he—

LAZARUS

Alone; and somewhere out of Bethany,
The Master—who had come to them so late,
Only for love of them and then so slowly,
And was for their sake hunted now by men
Who feared Him as they feared no other prey—
For the world's sake was hidden. "Better the tomb
For Lazarus than life, if this be life,"
She thought; and then to Martha, "No, my dear,"
She said aloud; "not as it was before.
Nothing is ever as it was before,
Where Time has been. Here there is more than Time;
And we that are so lonely and so far
From home, since he is with us here again,
Are farther now from him and from ourselves
Than we are from the stars. He will not speak
Until the spirit that is in him speaks;
And we must wait for all we are to know,
Or even to learn that we are not to know.
Martha, we are too near to this for knowledge,
And that is why it is that we must wait.
Our friends are coming if we call for them,
And there are covers we'll put over him
To make him warmer. We are too young, perhaps,
To say that we know better what is best
Than he. We do not know how old he is.
If you remember what the Master said,
Try to believe that we need have no fear.
Let me, the selfish and the careless one,
Be housewife and a mother for tonight;
For I am not so fearful as you are,
And I was not so eager."

       Martha sank
Down at her sister's feet and there sat watching
A flower that had a small familiar name

That was as old as memory, but was not
The name of what she saw now in its brief
And infinite mystery that so frightened her
That life became a terror. Tears again
Flooded her eyes and overflowed. "No, Mary,"
She murmured slowly, hating her own words
Before she heard them, "you are not so eager
To see our brother as we see him now;
Neither is he who gave him back to us.
I was to be the simple one, as always,
And this was all for me." She stared again
Over among the trees where Lazarus,
Who seemed to be a man who was not there,
Might have been one more shadow among shadows,
If she had not remembered. Then she felt
The cool calm hands of Mary on her face,
And shivered, wondering if such hands were real.

"The Master loved you as he loved us all,
Martha; and you are saying only things
That children say when they have had no sleep.
Try somehow now to rest a little while;
You know that I am here, and that our friends
Are coming if I call."

      Martha at last
Arose, and went with Mary to the door,
Where they stood looking off at the same place,
And at the same shape that was always there
As if it would not ever move or speak,
And always would be there. "Mary, go now,
Before the dark that will be coming hides him.
I am afraid of him out there alone,
Unless I see him; and I have forgotten
What sleep is. Go now—make him look at you—

LAZARUS

And I shall hear him if he stirs or whispers.
Go!—or I'll scream and bring all Bethany
To come and make him speak. Make him say once
That he is glad, and God may say the rest.
Though He say I shall sleep, and sleep for ever,
I shall not care for that . . . Go!"

                                                      Mary, moving
Almost as if an angry child had pushed her,
Went forward a few steps; and having waited
As long as Martha's eyes would look at hers,
Went forward a few more, and a few more;
And so, until she came to Lazarus,
Who crouched with his face hidden in his hands,
Like one that had no face. Before she spoke,
Feeling her sister's eyes that were behind her
As if the door where Martha stood were now
As far from her as Egypt, Mary turned
Once more to see that she was there. Then, softly,
Fearing him not so much as wondering
What his first word might be, said, "Lazarus,
Forgive us if we seemed afraid of you;"
And having spoken, pitied her poor speech
That had so little seeming gladness in it,
So little comfort, and so little love.

There was no sign from him that he had heard,
Or that he knew that she was there, or cared
Whether she spoke to him again or died
There at his feet. "We love you, Lazarus,
And we are not afraid. The Master said
We need not be afraid. Will you not say
To me that you are glad? Look, Lazarus!
Look at my face, and see me. This is Mary."

She found his hands and held them. They were cool,
Like hers, but they were not so calm as hers.
Through the white robes in which his friends had wrapped him
When he had groped out of that awful sleep,
She felt him trembling and she was afraid.
At last he sighed; and she prayed hungrily
To God that she might hear again the voice
Of Lazarus, whose hands were giving her now
The recognition of a living pressure
That was almost a language. When he spoke,
Only one word that she had waited for
Came from his lips, and that word was her name.

"I heard them saying, Mary, that he wept
Before I woke." The words were low and shaken,
Yet Mary knew that he who uttered them
Was Lazarus; and that would be enough
Until there should be more . . . "Who made him come,
That he should weep for me? . . . Was it you, Mary?"
The questions held in his incredulous eyes
Were more than she would see. She looked away;
But she had felt them and should feel for ever,
She thought, their cold and lonely desperation
That had the bitterness of all cold things
That were not cruel. "I should have wept," he said,
"If I had been the Master. . . ."

         Now she could feel
His hands above her hair—the same black hair
That once he made a jest of, praising it,
While Martha's busy eyes had left their work
To flash with laughing envy. Nothing of that
Was to be theirs again; and such a thought
Was like the flying by of a quick bird
Seen through a shadowy doorway in the twilight.

LAZARUS

For now she felt his hands upon her head,
Like weights of kindness: "I forgive you, Mary. . . .
You did not know—Martha could not have known—
Only the Master knew. . . . Where is he now?
Yes, I remember. They came after him.
May the good God forgive him. . . . I forgive him.
I must; and I may know only from him
The burden of all this. . . Martha was here—
But I was not yet here. She was afraid. . . .
Why did he do it, Mary? Was it—you?
Was it for you? . . . Where are the friends I saw?
Yes, I remember. They all went away.
I made them go away. . . . Where is he now? . . .
What do I see down there? Do I see Martha—
Down by the door? . . . I must have time for this."

Lazarus looked about him fearfully,
And then again at Mary, who discovered
Awakening apprehension in his eyes,
And shivered at his feet. All she had feared
Was here; and only in the slow reproach
Of his forgiveness lived his gratitude.
Why had he asked if it was all for her
That he was here? And what had Martha meant?
Why had the Master waited? What was coming
To Lazarus, and to them, that had not come?
What had the Master seen before he came,
That he had come so late?

      "Where is he, Mary?"
Lazarus asked again. "Where did he go?"
Once more he gazed about him, and once more
At Mary for an answer. "Have they found him?
Or did he go away because he wished

535

Never to look into my eyes again? . . .
That, I could understand. . . . Where is he, Mary?"

"I do not know," she said. "Yet in my heart
I know that he is living, as you are living—
Living, and here. He is not far from us.
He will come back to us and find us all—
Lazarus, Martha, Mary—everything—
All as it was before. Martha said that.
And he said we were not to be afraid."
Lazarus closed his eyes while on his face
A tortured adumbration of a smile
Flickered an instant. "All as it was before,"
He murmured wearily. "Martha said that;
And he said you were not to be afraid . . .
Not you . . . Not you . . . Why should you be afraid?
Give all your little fears, and Martha's with them,
To me; and I will add them unto mine,
Like a few rain-drops to Gennesaret."

"If you had frightened me in other ways,
Not willing it," Mary said, "I should have known
You still for Lazarus. But who is this?
Tell me again that you are Lazarus;
And tell me if the Master gave to you
No sign of a new joy that shall be coming
To this house that he loved. Are you afraid?
Are you afraid, who have felt everything—
And seen . . . ?"

But Lazarus only shook his head,
Staring with his bewildered shining eyes
Hard into Mary's face. "I do not know,
Mary," he said, after a long time.
"When I came back, I knew the Master's eyes

LAZARUS

Were looking into mine. I looked at his,
And there was more in them than I could see.
At first I could see nothing but his eyes;
Nothing else anywhere was to be seen—
Only his eyes. And they looked into mine—
Long into mine, Mary, as if he knew."

Mary began to be afraid of words
As she had never been afraid before
Of loneliness or darkness, or of death,
But now she must have more of them or die:
"He cannot know that there is worse than death,"
She said. "And you . . ."

"Yes, there is worse than death."
Said Lazarus; "and that was what he knew;
And that is what it was that I could see
This morning in his eyes. I was afraid,
But not as you are. There is worse than death,
Mary; and there is nothing that is good
For you in dying while you are still here.
Mary, never go back to that again.
You would not hear me if I told you more,
For I should say it only in a language
That you are not to learn by going back.
To be a child again is to go forward—
And that is much to know. Many grow old,
And fade, and go away, not knowing how much
That is to know. Mary, the night is coming,
And there will soon be darkness all around you.
Let us go down where Martha waits for us,
And let there be light shining in this house."

He rose, but Mary would not let him go:
"Martha, when she came back from here, said only

That she heard nothing. And have you no more
For Mary now than you had then for Martha?
Is Nothing, Lazarus, all you have for me?
Was Nothing all you found where you have been?
If that be so, what is there worse than that—
Or better—if that be so? And why should you,
With even our love, go the same dark road over?"

"I could not answer that, if that were so,"
Said Lazarus,—"not even if I were God.
Why should He care whether I came or stayed,
If that were so? Why should the Master weep—
For me, or for the world,—or save himself
Longer for nothing? And if that were so,
Why should a few years' more mortality
Make him a fugitive where flight were needless,
Had he but held his peace and given his nod
To an old Law that would be new as any?
I cannot say the answer to all that;
Though I may say that he is not afraid,
And that it is not for the joy there is
In serving an eternal Ignorance
Of our futility that he is here.
Is that what you and Martha mean by Nothing?
Is that what you are fearing? If that be so,
There are more weeds than lentils in your garden.
And one whose weeds are laughing at his harvest
May as well have no garden; for not there
Shall he be gleaning the few bits and orts
Of life that are to save him. For my part,
I am again with you, here among shadows
That will not always be so dark as this;
Though now I see there's yet an evil in me
That made me let you be afraid of me.
No, I was not afraid—not even of life.

LAZARUS

I thought I was . . . I must have time for this;
And all the time there is will not be long.
I cannot tell you what the Master saw
This morning in my eyes. I do not know.
I cannot yet say how far I have gone,
Or why it is that I am here again,
Or where the old road leads. I do not know.
I know that when I did come back, I saw
His eyes again among the trees and faces—
Only his eyes; and they looked into mine—
Long into mine—long, long, as if he knew."

AVON'S HARVEST, ETC.

(1921)

To Seth Ellis Pope

AVON'S HARVEST

Fear, like a living fire that only death
Might one day cool, had now in Avon's eyes
Been witness for so long of an invasion
That made of a gay friend whom we had known
Almost a memory, wore no other name
As yet for us than fear. Another man
Than Avon might have given to us at least
A futile opportunity for words
We might regret. But Avon, since it happened,
Fed with his unrevealing reticence
The fire of death we saw that horribly
Consumed him while he crumbled and said nothing.

So many a time had I been on the edge,
And off again, of a foremeasured fall
Into the darkness and discomfiture
Of his oblique rebuff, that finally
My silence honored his, holding itself
Away from a gratuitous intrusion
That likely would have widened a new distance
Already wide enough, if not so new.
But there are seeming parallels in space
That may converge in time; and so it was
I walked with Avon, fought and pondered with him,
While he made out a case for So-and-so,
Or slaughtered What's-his-name in his old way,
With a new difference. Nothing in Avon lately

Was, or was ever again to be for us,
Like him that we remembered; and all the while
We saw that fire at work within his eyes
And had no glimpse of what was burning there.

So for a year it went; and so it went
For half another year—when, all at once,
At someone's tinkling afternoon at home
I saw that in the eyes of Avon's wife
The fire that I had met the day before
In his had found another living fuel.
To look at her and then to think of him,
And thereupon to contemplate the fall
Of a dim curtain over the dark end
Of a dark play, required of me no more
Clairvoyance than a man who cannot swim
Will exercise in seeing that his friend
Off shore will drown except he save himself.
To her I could say nothing, and to him
No more than tallied with a long belief
That I should only have it back again
For my chagrin to ruminate upon,
Ingloriously, for the still time it starved;
And that would be for me as long a time
As I remembered Avon—who is yet
Not quite forgotten. On the other hand,
For saying nothing I might have with me always
An injured and recriminating ghost
Of a dead friend. The more I pondered it
The more I knew there was not much to lose,
Albeit for one whose delving hitherto
Had been a forage of his own affairs,
The quest, however golden the reward,
Was irksome—and as Avon suddenly
And soon was driven to let me see, was needless.

AVON'S HARVEST

It seemed an age ago that we were there
One evening in the room that in the days
When they could laugh he called the Library.
"He calls it that, you understand," she said,
"Because the dictionary always lives here.
He's not a man of books, yet he can read,
And write. He learned it all at school."—He smiled,
And answered with a fervor that rang then
Superfluous: "Had I learned a little more
At school, it might have been as well for me."
And I remember now that he paused then,
Leaving a silence that one had to break.
But this was long ago, and there was now
No laughing in that house. We were alone
This time, and it was Avon's time to talk.

I waited, and anon became aware
That I was looking less at Avon's eyes
Than at the dictionary, like one asking
Already why we make so much of words
That have so little weight in the true balance.
"Your name is Resignation for an hour,"
He said; "and I'm a little sorry for you.
So be resigned. I shall not praise your work,
Or strive in any way to make you happy.
My purpose only is to make you know
How clearly I have known that you have known
There was a reason waited on your coming,
And, if it's in me to see clear enough,
To fish the reason out of a black well
Where you see only a dim sort of glimmer
That has for you no light."

"I see the well,"
I said, "but there's a doubt about the glimmer—

Say nothing of the light. I'm at your service;
And though you say that I shall not be happy,
I shall be if in some way I may serve.
To tell you fairly now that I know nothing
Is nothing more than fair."—"You know as much
As any man alive—save only one man,
If he's alive. Whether he lives or not
Is rather for time to answer than for me;
And that's a reason, or a part of one,
For your appearance here. You do not know him,
And even if you should pass him in the street
He might go by without your feeling him
Between you and the world. I cannot say
Whether he would, but I suppose he might."

"And I suppose you might, if urged," I said,
"Say in what water it is that we are fishing.
You that have reasons hidden in a well,
Not mentioning all your nameless friends that walk
The streets and are not either dead or living
For company, are surely, one would say
To be forgiven if you may seem distraught—
I mean distrait. I don't know what I mean.
I only know that I am at your service,
Always, yet with a special reservation
That you may deem eccentric. All the same
Unless your living dead man comes to life,
Or is less indiscriminately dead,
I shall go home."

       "No, you will not go home,"
Said Avon; "or I beg that you will not."
So saying, he went slowly to the door
And turned the key. "Forgive me and my manners,
But I would be alone with you this evening.

AVON'S HARVEST

The key, as you observe, is in the lock;
And you may sit between me and the door,
Or where you will. You have my word of honor
That I would spare you the least injury
That might attend your presence here this evening."

"I thank you for your soothing introduction,
Avon," I said. "Go on. The Lord giveth,
The Lord taketh away. I trust myself
Always to you and to your courtesy.
Only remember that I cling somewhat
Affectionately to the old tradition."—
"I understand you and your part," said Avon;
"And I dare say it's well enough, tonight,
We play around the circumstance a little.
I've read of men that half way to the stake
Would have their little joke. It's well enough;
Rather a waste of time, but well enough."

I listened as I waited, and heard steps
Outside of one who paused and then went on;
And, having heard, I might as well have seen
The fear in his wife's eyes. He gazed away,
As I could see, in helpless thought of her,
And said to me: "Well, then, it was like this.
Some tales will have a deal of going back
In them before they are begun. But this one
Begins in the beginning—when he came.
I was a boy at school, sixteen years old,
And on my way, in all appearances,
To mark an even-tempered average
Among the major mediocrities
Who serve and earn with no especial noise
Or vast reward. I saw myself, even then,
A light for no high shining; and I feared

No boy or man—having, in truth, no cause.
I was enough a leader to be free,
And not enough a hero to be jealous.
Having eyes and ears, I knew that I was envied,
And as a proper sort of compensation
Had envy of my own for two or three—
But never felt, and surely never gave,
The wound of any more malevolence
Than decent youth, defeated for a day,
May take to bed with him and kill with sleep.
So, and so far, my days were going well,
And would have gone so, but for the black tiger
That many of us fancy is in waiting,
But waits for most of us in fancy only.
For me there was no fancy in his coming,
Though God knows I had never summoned him,
Or thought of him. To this day I'm adrift
And in the dark, out of all reckoning,
To find a reason why he ever was,
Or what was ailing Fate when he was born
On this alleged God-ordered earth of ours.
Now and again there comes one of his kind—
By chance, we say. I leave all that to you.
Whether it was an evil chance alone,
Or some invidious juggling of the stars,
Or some accrued arrears of ancestors
Who throve on debts that I was here to pay,
Or sins within me that I knew not of,
Or just a foretaste of what waits in hell
For those of us who cannot love a worm,—
Whatever it was, or whence or why it was,
One day there came a stranger to the school.
And having had one mordacious glimpse of him
That filled my eyes and was to fill my life,
I have known Peace only as one more word

AVON'S HARVEST

Among the many others we say over
That have an airy credit of no meaning.
One of these days, if I were seeing many
To live, I might erect a cenotaph
To Job's wife. I assume that you remember;
If you forget, she's extant in your Bible."

Now this was not the language of a man
Whom I had known as Avon, and I winced
Hearing it—though I knew that in my heart
There was no visitation of surprise.
Unwelcome as it was, and off the key
Calamitously, it overlived a silence
That was itself a story and affirmed
A savage emphasis of honesty
That I would only gladly have attuned
If possible, to vinous innovation.
But his indifferent wassailing was always
Too far within the measure of excess
For that; and then there were those eyes of his.
Avon indeed had kept his word with me,
And there was not much yet to make me happy.

"So there we were," he said, "we two together,
Breathing one air. And how shall I go on
To say by what machinery the slow net
Of my fantastic and increasing hate
Was ever woven as it was around us?
I cannot answer; and you need not ask
What undulating reptile he was like,
For such a worm as I discerned in him
Was never yet on earth or in the ocean,
Or anywhere else than in my sense of him.
Had all I made of him been tangible,
The Lord must have invented long ago

Some private and unspeakable new monster
Equipped for such a thing's extermination;
Whereon the monster, seeing no other monster
Worth biting, would have died with his work done.
There's a humiliation in it now,
As there was then, and worse than there was then;
For then there was the boy to shoulder it
Without the sickening weight of added years
Galling him to the grave. Beware of hate
That has no other boundary than the grave
Made for it, or for ourselves. Beware, I say;
And I'm a sorry one, I fear, to say it,
Though for the moment we may let that go
And while I'm interrupting my own story
I'll ask of you the favor of a look
Into the street. I like it when it's empty.
There's only one man walking? Let him walk.
I wish to God that all men might walk always,
And so, being busy, love one another more."

"Avon," I said, now in my chair again,
"Although I may not be here to be happy,
If you are careless, I may have to laugh.
I have disliked a few men in my life,
But never to the scope of wishing them
To this particular pedestrian hell
Of your affection. I should not like that.
Forgive me, for this time it was your fault."

He drummed with all his fingers on his chair,
And, after a made smile of acquiescence,
Took up again the theme of his aversion,
Which now had flown along with him alone
For twenty years, like Io's evil insect,
To sting him when it would. The decencies

AVON'S HARVEST

Forbade that I should look at him for ever,
Yet many a time I found myself ashamed
Of a long staring at him, and as often
Essayed the dictionary on the table,
Wondering if in its interior
There was an uncompanionable word
To say just what was creeping in my hair,
At which my scalp would shrink,—at which, again,
I would arouse myself with a vain scorn,
Remembering that all this was in New York—
As if that were somehow the banishing
For ever of all unseemly presences—
And listen to the story of my friend,
Who, as I feared, was not for me to save,
And, as I knew, knew also that I feared it.

"Humiliation," he began again,
"May be or not the best of all bad names
I might employ; and if you scent remorse,
There may be growing such a flower as that
In the unsightly garden where I planted,
Not knowing the seed or what was coming of it.
I've done much wondering if I planted it;
But our poor wonder, when it comes too late,
Fights with a lath, and one that solid fact
Breaks while it yawns and looks another way
For a less negligible adversary.
Away with wonder, then; though I'm at odds
With conscience, even tonight, for good assurance
That it was I, or chance and I together,
Did all that sowing. If I seem to you
To be a little bitten by the question,
Without a miracle it might be true;
The miracle is to me that I'm not eaten
Long since to death of it, and that you sit

With nothing more agreeable than a ghost.
If you had thought a while of that, you might,
Unhappily, not have come; and your not coming
Would have been desolation—not for you,
God save the mark!—for I would have you here.
I shall not be alone with you to listen;
And I should be far less alone tonight
With you away, make what you will of that.

"I said that we were going back to school,
And we may say that we are there—with him.
This fellow had no friend, and, as for that,
No sign of an apparent need of one,
Save always and alone—myself. He fixed
His heart and eyes on me, insufferably,—
And in a sort of Nemesis-like way,
Invincibly. Others who might have given
A welcome even to him, or I'll suppose so—
Adorning an unfortified assumption
With gold that might come off with afterthought—
Got never, if anything, more out of him
Than a word flung like refuse in their faces,
And rarely that. For God knows what good reason,
He lavished his whole altered arrogance
On me; and with an overweening skill,
Which had sometimes almost a cringing in it,
Found a few flaws in my tight mail of hate
And slowly pricked a poison into me
In which at first I failed at recognizing
An unfamiliar subtle sort of pity.
But so it was, and I believe he knew it;
Though even to dream it would have been absurd—
Until I knew it, and there was no need
Of dreaming. For the fellow's indolence,
And his malignant oily swarthiness

AVON'S HARVEST

Housing a reptile blood that I could see
Beneath it, like hereditary venom
Out of old human swamps, hardly revealed
Itself the proper spawning-ground of pity.
But so it was. Pity, or something like it,
Was in the poison of his proximity;
For nothing else that I have any name for
Could have invaded and so mastered me
With a slow tolerance that eventually
Assumed a blind ascendency of custom
That saw not even itself. When I came in,
Often I'd find him strewn along my couch
Like an amorphous lizard with its clothes on,
Reading a book and waiting for its dinner.
His clothes were always odiously in order,
Yet I should not have thought of him as clean—
Not even if he had washed himself to death
Proving it. There was nothing right about him.
Then he would search, never quite satisfied,
Though always in a measure confident,
My eyes to find a welcome waiting in them,
Unwilling, as I see him now, to know
That it would never be there. Looking back,
I am not sure that he would not have died
For me, if I were drowning or on fire,
Or that I would not rather have let myself
Die twice than owe the debt of my survival
To him, though he had lost not even his clothes.
No, there was nothing right about that fellow;
And after twenty years to think of him
I should be quite as helpless now to serve him
As I was then. I mean—without my story.
Be patient, and you'll see just what I mean—
Which is to say, you won't. But you can listen,
And that's itself a large accomplishment

Uncrowned; and may be, at a time like this,
A mighty charity. It was in January
This evil genius came into our school,
And it was June when he went out of it—
If I may say that he was wholly out
Of any place that I was in thereafter.
But he was not yet gone. When we are told
By Fate to bear what we may never bear,
Fate waits a little while to see what happens;
And this time it was only for the season
Between the swift midwinter holidays
And the long progress into weeks and months
Of all the days that followed—with him there
To make them longer. I would have given an eye,
Before the summer came, to know for certain
That I should never be condemned again
To see him with the other; and all the while
There was a battle going on within me
Of hate that fought remorse—if you must have it—
Never to win, . . . never to win but once,
And having won, to lose disastrously,
And as it was to prove, interminably—
Or till an end of living may annul,
If so it be, the nameless obligation
That I have not the Christian revenue
In me to pay. A man who has no gold,
Or an equivalent, shall pay no gold
Until by chance or labor or contrivance
He makes it his to pay; and he that has
No kindlier commodity than hate,
Glossed with a pity that belies itself
In its negation and lacks alchemy
To fuse itself to—love, would you have me say?
I don't believe it. No, there is no such word.
If I say tolerance, there's no more to say.

AVON'S HARVEST

And he who sickens even in saying that—
What coin of God has he to pay the toll
To peace on earth? Good will to men—oh, yes!
That's easy; and it means no more than sap,
Until we boil the water out of it
Over the fire of sacrifice. I'll do it;
And in a measurable way I've done it—
But not for him. What are you smiling at?
Well, so it went until a day in June.
We were together under an old elm,
Which now, I hope, is gone—though it's a crime
In me that I should have to wish the death
Of such a tree as that. There were no trees
Like those that grew at school—until he came.
We stood together under it that day,
When he, by some ungovernable chance,
All foreign to the former crafty care
That he had used never to cross my favor,
Told of a lie that stained a friend of mine
With a false blot that a few days washed off.
A trifle now, but a boy's honor then—
Which then was everything. There were some words
Between us, but I don't remember them.
All I remember is a bursting flood
Of half a year's accumulated hate,
And his incredulous eyes before I struck him.
He had gone once too far; and when he knew it,
He knew it was all over; and I struck him.
Pound for pound, he was the better brute;
But bulking in the way then of my fist
And all there was alive in me to drive it,
Three of him misbegotten into one
Would have gone down like him—and being larger,
Might have bled more, if that were necessary.
He came up soon; and if I live for ever,

The vengeance in his eyes, and a weird gleam
Of desolation—if I make you see it—
Will be before me as it is tonight.
I shall not ever know how long it was
I waited his attack that never came;
It might have been an instant or an hour
That I stood ready there, watching his eyes,
And the tears running out of them. They made
Me sick, those tears; for I knew, miserably,
They were not there for any pain he felt.
I do not think he felt the pain at all.
He felt the blow. . . . Oh, the whole thing was bad—
So bad that even the bleaching suns and rains
Of years that wash away to faded lines,
Or blot out wholly, the sharp wrongs and ills
Of youth, have had no cleansing agent in them
To dim the picture. I still see him going
Away from where I stood; and I shall see him
Longer, sometime, than I shall see the face
Of whosoever watches by the bed
On which I die—given I die that way.
I doubt if he could reason his advantage
In living any longer after that
Among the rest of us. The lad he slandered,
Or gave a negative immunity
No better than a stone he might have thrown
Behind him at his head, was of the few
I might have envied; and for that being known,
My fury became sudden history,
And I a sudden hero. But the crown
I wore was hot; and I would happily
Have hurled it, if I could, so far away
That over my last hissing glimpse of it
There might have closed an ocean. He went home
The next day, and the same unhappy chance

AVON'S HARVEST

That first had fettered me and my aversion
To his unprofitable need of me
Brought us abruptly face to face again
Beside the carriage that had come for him.
We met, and for a moment we were still—
Together. But I was reading in his eyes
More than I read at college or at law
In years that followed. There was blankly nothing
For me to say, if not that I was sorry;
And that was more than hate would let me say—
Whatever the truth might be. At last he spoke,
And I could see the vengeance in his eyes,
And a cold sorrow—which, if I had seen
Much more of it, might yet have mastered me.
But I would see no more of it. 'Well, then,'
He said, 'have you thought yet of anything
Worth saying? If so, there's time. If you are silent,
I shall know where you are until you die.'
I can still hear him saying those words to me
Again, without a loss or an addition;
I know, for I have heard them ever since.
And there was in me not an answer for them
Save a new roiling silence. Once again
I met his look, and on his face I saw
There was a twisting in the swarthiness
That I had often sworn to be the cast
Of his ophidian mind. He had no soul.
There was to be no more of him—not then.
The carriage rolled away with him inside,
Leaving the two of us alive together
In the same hemisphere to hate each other.
I don't know now whether he's here alive,
Or whether he's here dead. But that, of course,
As you would say, is only a tired man's fancy.
You know that I have driven the wheels too fast

Of late, and all for gold I do not need.
When are we mortals to be sensible,
Paying no more for life than life is worth?
Better for us, no doubt, we do not know
How much we pay or what it is we buy."
He waited, gazing at me as if asking
The worth of what the universe had for sale
For one confessed remorse. Avon, I knew,
Had driven the wheels too fast, and not for gold.

"If you had given him then your hand," I said,
"And spoken, though it strangled you, the truth,
I should not have the melancholy honor
Of sitting here alone with you this evening.
If only you had shaken hands with him,
And said the truth, he would have gone his way,
And you your way. He might have wished you dead,
But he would not have made you miserable.
At least," I added, indefensibly,
"That's what I hope is true."

                              He pitied me,
But had the magnanimity not to say so.
"If only we had shaken hands," he said,
"And I had said the truth, we might have been
In half a moment rolling on the gravel.
If I had said the truth, I should have said
That never at any moment on the clock
Above us in the tower since his arrival
Had I been in a more proficient mood
To throttle him. If you had seen his eyes
As I did, and if you had seen his face
At work as I did, you might understand.
I was ashamed of it, as I am now,
But that's the prelude to another theme;

AVON'S HARVEST

For now I'm saying only what had happened
If I had taken his hand and said the truth.
The wise have cautioned us that where there's hate
There's also fear. The wise are right sometimes.
There may be now, but there was no fear then.
There was just hatred, hauled up out of hell
For me to writhe in; and I writhed in it."

I saw that he was writhing in it still;
But having a magnanimity myself,
I waited. There was nothing else to do
But wait, and to remember that his tale,
Though well along, as I divined it was,
Yet hovered among shadows and regrets
Of twenty years ago. When he began
Again to speak, I felt them coming nearer.

"Whenever your poet or your philosopher
Has nothing richer for us," he resumed,
"He burrows among remnants, like a mouse
In a waste-basket, and with much dry noise
Comes up again, having found Time at the bottom
And filled himself with its futility.
'Time is at once,' he says, to startle us,
'A poison for us, if we make it so,
And, if we make it so, an antidote
For the same poison that afflicted us.'
I'm witness to the poison, but the cure
Of my complaint is not, for me, in Time.
There may be doctors in eternity
To deal with it, but they are not here now.
There's no specific for my three diseases
That I could swallow, even if I should find it,
And I shall never find it here on earth."

"Mightn't it be as well, my friend," I said,
"For you to contemplate the uncompleted
With not such an infernal certainty?"

"And mightn't it be as well for you, my friend,"
Said Avon, "to be quiet while I go on?
When I am done, then you may talk all night—
Like a physician who can do no good,
But knows how soon another would have his fee
Were he to tell the truth. Your fee for this
Is in my gratitude and my affection;
And I'm not eager to be calling in
Another to take yours away from you,
Whatever it's worth. I like to think I know.
Well then, again. The carriage rolled away
With him inside; and so it might have gone
For ten years rolling on, with him still in it,
For all it was I saw of him. Sometimes
I heard of him, but only as one hears
Of leprosy in Boston or New York
And wishes it were somewhere else. He faded
Out of my scene—yet never quite out of it:
'I shall know where you are until you die,'
Were his last words; and they are the same words
That I received thereafter once a year,
Infallibly on my birthday, with no name;
Only a card, and the words printed on it.
No, I was never rid of him—not quite;
Although on shipboard, on my way from here
To Hamburg, I believe that I forgot him.
But once ashore, I should have been half ready
To meet him there, risen up out of the ground,
With hoofs and horns and tail and everything.
Believe me, there was nothing right about him,

AVON'S HARVEST

Though it was not in Hamburg that I found him.
Later, in Rome, it was we found each other,
For the first time since we had been at school.
There was the same slow vengeance in his eyes
When he saw mine, and there was a vicious twist
On his amphibious face that might have been
On anything else a smile—rather like one
We look for on the stage than in the street.
I must have been a yard away from him
Yet as we passed I felt the touch of him
Like that of something soft in a dark room.
There's hardly need of saying that we said nothing,
Or that we gave each other an occasion
For more than our eyes uttered. He was gone
Before I knew it, like a solid phantom;
And his reality was for me some time
In its achievement—given that one's to be
Convinced that such an incubus at large
Was ever quite real. The season was upon us
When there are fitter regions in the world—
Though God knows he would have been safe enough—
Than Rome for strayed Americans to live in,
And when the whips of their itineraries
Hurry them north again. I took my time,
Since I was paying for it, and leisurely
Went where I would—though never again to move
Without him at my elbow or behind me.
My shadow of him, wherever I found myself,
Might horribly as well have been the man—
Although I should have been afraid of him
No more than of a large worm in a salad.
I should omit the salad, certainly,
And wish the worm elsewhere. And so he was,
In fact; yet as I go on to grow older,
I question if there's anywhere a fact

That isn't the malevolent existence
Of one man who is dead, or is not dead,
Or what the devil it is that he may be.
There must be, I suppose, a fact somewhere,
But I don't know it. I can only tell you
That later, when to all appearances
I stood outside a music-hall in London,
I felt him and then saw that he was there.
Yes, he was there, and had with him a woman
Who looked as if she didn't know. I'm sorry
To this day for that woman—who, no doubt,
Is doing well. Yes, there he was again;
There were his eyes and the same vengeance in them
That I had seen in Rome and twice before—
Not mentioning all the time, or most of it,
Between the day I struck him and that evening.
That was the worst show that I ever saw,
But you had better see it for yourself
Before you say so too. I went away,
Though not for any fear that I could feel
Of him or of his worst manipulations,
But only to be out of the same air
That made him stay alive in the same world
With all the gentlemen that were in irons
For uncommendable extravagances
That I should reckon slight compared with his
Offence of being. Distance would have made him
A moving fly-speck on the map of life,—
But he would not be distant, though his flesh
And bone might have been climbing Fujiyama
Or Chimborazo—with me there in London,
Or sitting here. My doom it was to see him,
Be where I might. That was ten years ago;
And having waited season after season
His always imminent evil recrudescence,

AVON'S HARVEST

And all for nothing, I was waiting still,
When the *Titanic* touched a piece of ice
And we were for a moment where we are,
With nature laughing at us. When the noise
Had spent itself to names, his was among them;
And I will not insult you or myself
With a vain perjury. I was far from cold.
It seemed as for the first time in my life
I knew the blessedness of being warm;
And I remember that I had a drink,
Having assuredly no need of it.
Pity a fool for his credulity,
If so you must. But when I found his name
Among the dead, I trusted once the news;
And after that there were no messages
In ambush waiting for me on my birthday.
There was no vestige yet of any fear,
You understand—if that's why you are smiling."

I said that I had not so much as whispered
The name aloud of any fear soever,
And that I smiled at his unwonted plunge
Into the perilous pool of Dionysus.
"Well, if you are so easily diverted
As that," he said, drumming his chair again,
"You will be pleased, I think, with what is coming;
And though there be divisions and departures,
Imminent from now on, for your diversion
I'll do the best I can. More to the point,
I know a man who if his friends were like him
Would live in the woods all summer and all winter,
Leaving the town and its iniquities
To die of their own dust. But having his wits,
Henceforth he may conceivably avoid

The adventure unattended. Last October
He took me with him into the Maine woods,
Where, by the shore of a primeval lake,
With woods all round it, and a voyage away
From anything wearing clothes, he had reared somehow
A lodge, or camp, with a stone chimney in it,
And a wide fireplace to make men forget
Their sins who sat before it in the evening,
Hearing the wind outside among the trees
And the black water washing on the shore.
I never knew the meaning of October
Until I went with Asher to that place,
Which I shall not investigate again
Till I be taken there by other forces
Than are innate in my economy.
'You may not like it,' Asher said, 'but Asher
Knows what is good. So put your faith in Asher,
And come along with him.' He's an odd bird,
Yet I could wish for the world's decency
There might be more of him. And so it was
I found myself, at first incredulous,
Down there with Asher in the wilderness,
Alive at last with a new liberty
And with no sore to fester. He perceived
In me an altered favor of God's works,
And promptly took upon himself the credit,
Which, in a fashion, was as accurate
As one's interpretation of another
Is like to be. So for a frosty fortnight
We had the sunlight with us on the lake,
And the moon with us when the sun was down.
'God gave his adjutants a holiday,'
Asher assured me, 'when He made this place';
And I agreed with him that it was heaven,—
Till it was hell for me for then and after.

AVON'S HARVEST

"There was a village miles away from us
Where now and then we paddled for the mail
And incidental small commodities
That perfect exile might require, and stayed
The night after the voyage with an antique
Survival of a broader world than ours
Whom Asher called The Admiral. This time,
A little out of sorts and out of tune
With paddling, I let Asher go alone,
Sure that his heart was happy. Then it was
That hell came. I sat gazing over there
Across the water, watching the sun's last fire
Above those gloomy and indifferent trees
That might have been a wall around the world,
When suddenly, like faces over the lake,
Out of the silence of that other shore
I was aware of hidden presences
That soon, no matter how many of them there were,
Would all be one. I could not look behind me,
Where I could hear that one of them was breathing,
For, if I did, those others over there
Might all see that at last I was afraid;
And I might hear them without seeing them,
Seeing that other one. You were not there;
And it is well for you that you don't know
What they are like when they should not be there.
And there were chilly doubts of whether or not
I should be seeing the rest that I should see
With eyes, or otherwise. I could not be sure;
And as for going over to find out,
All I may tell you now is that my fear
Was not the fear of dying, though I knew soon
That all the gold in all the sunken ships
That have gone down since Tyre would not have paid
For me the ferriage of myself alone

To that infernal shore. I was in hell,
Remember; and if you have never been there
You may as well not say how easy it is
To find the best way out. There may not be one.
Well, I was there; and I was there alone—
Alone for the first time since I was born;
And I was not alone. That's what it is
To be in hell. I hope you will not go there.
All through that slow, long, desolating twilight
Of incoherent certainties, I waited;
Never alone—never to be alone;
And while the night grew down upon me there,
I thought of old Prometheus in the story
That I had read at school, and saw mankind
All huddled into clusters in the dark,
Calling to God for light. There was a light
Coming for them, but there was none for me
Until a shapeless remnant of a moon
Rose after midnight over the black trees
Behind me. I should hardly have confessed
The heritage then of my identity
To my own shadow; for I was powerless there,
As I am here. Say what you like to say
To silence, but say none of it to me
Tonight. To say it now would do no good,
And you are here to listen. Beware of hate,
And listen. Beware of hate, remorse, and fear,
And listen. You are staring at the damned,
But yet you are no more the one than he
To say that it was he alone who planted
The flower of death now growing in his garden.
Was it enough, I wonder, that I struck him?
I shall say nothing. I shall have to wait
Until I see what's coming, if it comes,
When I'm a delver in another garden—

AVON'S HARVEST

If such an one there be. If there be none,
All's well—and over. Rather a vain expense,
One might affirm—yet there is nothing lost.
Science be praised that there is nothing lost."

I'm glad the venom that was on his tongue
May not go down on paper; and I'm glad
No friend of mine alive, far as I know,
Has a tale waiting for me with an end
Like Avon's. There was here an interruption,
Though not a long one—only while we heard,
As we had heard before, the ghost of steps
Faintly outside. We knew that she was there
Again; and though it was a kindly folly,
I wished that Avon's wife would go to sleep.

"I was afraid, this time, but not of man—
Or man as you may figure him," he said.
"It was not anything my eyes had seen
That I could feel around me in the night,
There by that lake. If I had been alone,
There would have been the joy of being free,
Which in imagination I had won
With unimaginable expiation—
But I was not alone. If you had seen me,
Waiting there for the dark and looking off
Over the gloom of that relentless water,
Which had the stillness of the end of things
That evening on it, I might well have made
For you the picture of the last man left
Where God, in his extinction of the rest,
Had overlooked him and forgotten him.
Yet I was not alone. Interminably
The minutes crawled along and over me,
Slow, cold, intangible, and invisible,

As if they had come up out of that water.
How long I sat there I shall never know,
For time was hidden out there in the black lake,
Which now I could see only as a glimpse
Of black light by the shore. There were no stars
To mention, and the moon was hours away
Behind me. There was nothing but myself,
And what was coming. On my breast I felt
The touch of death, and I should have died then.
I ruined good Asher's autumn as it was,
For he will never again go there alone,
If ever he goes at all. Nature did ill
To darken such a faith in her as his,
Though he will have it that I had the worst
Of her defection, and will hear no more
Apologies. If it had to be for someone,
I think it well for me it was for Asher.
I dwell on him, meaning that you may know him
Before your last horn blows. He has a name
That's like a tree, and therefore like himself—
By which I mean you find him where you leave him.
I saw him and The Admiral together
While I was in the dark, but they were far—
Far as around the world from where I was;
And they knew nothing of what I saw not
While I knew only I was not alone.
I made a fire to make the place alive,
And locked the door. But even the fire was dead,
And all the life there was was in the shadow
It made of me. My shadow was all of me;
The rest had had its day, and there was night
Remaining—only night, that's made for shadows,
Shadows and sleep and dreams, or dreams without it.
The fire went slowly down, and now the moon,
Or that late wreck of it, was coming up;

AVON'S HARVEST

And though it was a martyr's work to move,
I must obey my shadow, and I did.
There were two beds built low against the wall,
And down on one of them, with all my clothes on,
Like a man getting into his own grave,
I lay—and waited. As the firelight sank,
The moonlight, which had partly been consumed
By the black trees, framed on the other wall
A glimmering window not far from the ground.
The coals were going, and only a few sparks
Were there to tell of them; and as they died
The window lightened, and I saw the trees.
They moved a little, but I could not move,
More than to turn my face the other way;
And then, if you must have it so, I slept.
We'll call it so—if sleep is your best name
For a sort of conscious, frozen catalepsy
Wherein a man sees all there is around him
As if it were not real, and he were not
Alive. You may call it anything you please
That made me powerless to move hand or foot,
Or to make any other living motion
Than after a long horror, without hope,
To turn my face again the other way.
Some force that was not mine opened my eyes,
And, as I knew it must be,—it was there."

Avon covered his eyes—whether to shut
The memory and the sight of it away,
Or to be sure that mine were for the moment
Not searching his with pity, is now no matter.
My glance at him was brief, turning itself
To the familiar pattern of his rug,
Wherein I may have sought a consolation—
As one may gaze in sorrow on a shell,

Or a small apple. So it had come, I thought;
And heard, no longer with a wonderment,
The faint recurring footsteps of his wife,
Who, knowing less than I knew, yet knew more.
Now I could read, I fancied, through the fear
That latterly was living in her eyes,
To the sure source of its authority.
But he went on, and I was there to listen:

"And though I saw it only as a blot
Between me and my life, it was enough
To make me know that he was watching there—
Waiting for me to move, or not to move,
Before he moved. Sick as I was with hate
Reborn, and chained with fear that was more than fear,
I would have gambled all there was to gain
Or lose in rising there from where I lay
And going out after it. 'Before the dawn,'
I reasoned, 'there will be a difference here.
Therefore it may as well be done outside.'
And then I found I was immovable,
As I had been before; and a dead sweat
Rolled out of me as I remembered him
When I had seen him leaving me at school.
'I shall know where you are until you die,'
Were the last words that I had heard him say;
And there he was. Now I could see his face,
And all the sad, malignant desperation
That was drawn on it after I had struck him,
And on my memory since that afternoon.
But all there was left now for me to do
Was to lie there and see him while he squeezed
His unclean outlines into the dim room,
And half erect inside, like a still beast
With a face partly man's, came slowly on

AVON'S HARVEST

Along the floor to the bed where I lay,
And waited. There had been so much of waiting,
Through all those evil years before my respite—
Which now I knew and recognized at last
As only his more venomous preparation
For the vile end of a deceiving peace—
That I began to fancy there was on me
The stupor that explorers have alleged
As evidence of nature's final mercy
When tigers have them down upon the earth
And wild hot breath is heavy on their faces.
I could not feel his breath, but I could hear it;
Though fear had made an anvil of my heart
Where demons, for the joy of doing it,
Were sledging death down on it. And I saw
His eyes now, as they were, for the first time—
Aflame as they had never been before
With all their gathered vengeance gleaming in them,
And always that unconscionable sorrow
That would not die behind it. Then I caught
The shadowy glimpse of an uplifted arm,
And a moon-flash of metal. That was all. . . .

"When I believed I was alive again
I was with Asher and The Admiral,
Whom Asher had brought with him for a day
With nature. They had found me when they came;
And there was not much left of me to find.
I had not moved or known that I was there
Since I had seen his eyes and felt his breath;
And it was not for some uncertain hours
After they came that either would say how long
That might have been. It should have been much longer.
All you may add will be your own invention,
For I have told you all there is to tell.

Tomorrow I shall have another birthday,
And with it there may come another message—
Although I cannot see the need of it,
Or much more need of drowning, if that's all
Men drown for—when they drown. You know as much
As I know about that, though I've a right,
If not a reason, to be on my guard;
And only God knows what good that will do.
Now you may get some air. Good night!—and thank
 you."
He smiled, but I would rather he had not.

I wished that Avon's wife would go to sleep,
But whether she found sleep that night or not
I do not know. I was awake for hours,
Toiling in vain to let myself believe
That Avon's apparition was a dream,
And that he might have added, for romance,
The part that I had taken home with me
For reasons not in Avon's dictionary.
But each recurrent memory of his eyes,
And of the man himself that I had known
So long and well, made soon of all my toil
An evanescent and a vain evasion;
And it was half as in expectancy
That I obeyed the summons of his wife
A little before dawn, and was again
With Avon in the room where I had left him,
But not with the same Avon I had left.
The doctor, an august authority,
With eminence abroad as well as here,
Looked hard at me as if I were the doctor
And he the friend. "I have had eyes on Avon
For more than half a year," he said to me,
"And I have wondered often what it was

MR. FLOOD'S PARTY

That I could see that I was not to see.
Though he was in the chair where you are looking,
I told his wife—I had to tell her something—
It was a nightmare and an aneurism;
And so, or partly so, I'll say it was.
The last without the first will be enough
For the newspapers and the undertaker;
Yet if we doctors were not all immune
From death, disease, and curiosity,
My diagnosis would be sorry for me.
He died, you know, because he was afraid—
And he had been afraid for a long time;
And we who knew him well would all agree
To fancy there was rather more than fear.
The door was locked inside—they broke it in
To find him—but she heard him when it came.
There are no signs of any visitors,
Or need of them. If I were not a child
Of science, I should say it was the devil.
I don't believe it was another woman,
And surely it was not another man."

MR. FLOOD'S PARTY

OLD Eben Flood, climbing alone one night
Over the hill between the town below
And the forsaken upland hermitage
That held as much as he should ever know
On earth again of home, paused warily.
The road was his with not a native near;
And Eben, having leisure, said aloud,
For no man else in Tilbury Town to hear:

"Well, Mr. Flood, we have the harvest moon
Again, and we may not have many more;
The bird is on the wing, the poet says,
And you and I have said it here before.
Drink to the bird." He raised up to the light
The jug that he had gone so far to fill,
And answered huskily: "Well, Mr. Flood,
Since you propose it, I believe I will."

Alone, as if enduring to the end
A valiant armor of scarred hopes outworn,
He stood there in the middle of the road
Like Roland's ghost winding a silent horn.
Below him, in the town among the trees,
Where friends of other days had honored him,
A phantom salutation of the dead
Rang thinly till old Eben's eyes were dim.

Then, as a mother lays her sleeping child
Down tenderly, fearing it may awake,
He set the jug down slowly at his feet
With trembling care, knowing that most things break;
And only when assured that on firm earth
It stood, as the uncertain lives of men
Assuredly did not, he paced away,
And with his hand extended paused again:

"Well, Mr. Flood, we have not met like this
In a long time; and many a change has come
To both of us, I fear, since last it was
We had a drop together. Welcome home!"
Convivially returning with himself,
Again he raised the jug up to the light;
And with an acquiescent quaver said:
"Well, Mr. Flood, if you insist, I might.

BEN TROVATO

"Only a very little, Mr. Flood—
For auld lang syne. No more, sir; that will do."
So, for the time, apparently it did,
And Eben evidently thought so too;
For soon amid the silver loneliness
Of night he lifted up his voice and sang,
Secure, with only two moons listening,
Until the whole harmonious landscape rang—

"For auld lang syne." The weary throat gave out,
The last word wavered; and the song being done,
He raised again the jug regretfully
And shook his head, and was again alone.
There was not much that was ahead of him,
And there was nothing in the town below—
Where strangers would have shut the many doors
That many friends had opened long ago.

BEN TROVATO

THE deacon thought. "I know them," he began,
"And they are all you ever heard of them—
Allurable to no sure theorem,
The scorn or the humility of man.
You say 'Can I believe it?'—and I can;
And I'm unwilling even to condemn
The benefaction of a stratagem
Like hers—and I'm a Presbyterian.

"Though blind, with but a wandering hour to live,
He felt the other woman in the fur
That now the wife had on. Could she forgive
All that? Apparently. Her rings were gone,

Of course; and when he found that she had none,
He smiled—as he had never smiled at her."

THE TREE IN PAMELA'S GARDEN

PAMELA was too gentle to deceive
Her roses. "Let the men stay where they are,"
She said, "and if Apollo's avatar
Be one of them, I shall not have to grieve."
And so she made all Tilbury Town believe
She sighed a little more for the North Star
Than over men, and only in so far
As she was in a garden was like Eve.

Her neighbors—doing all that neighbors can
To make romance of reticence meanwhile—
Seeing that she had never loved a man,
Wished Pamela had a cat, or a small bird,
And only would have wondered at her smile
Could they have seen that she had overheard.

VAIN GRATUITIES

NEVER was there a man much uglier
In eyes of other women, or more grim:
"The Lord has filled her chalice to the brim,
So let us pray she's a philosopher,"
They said; and there was more they said of her—
Deeming it, after twenty years with him,
No wonder that she kept her figure slim
And always made you think of lavender.

LOST ANCHORS

But she, demure as ever, and as fair,
Almost, as they remembered her before
She found him, would have laughed had she been there;
And all they said would have been heard no more
Than foam that washes on an island shore
Where there are none to listen or to care.

JOB THE REJECTED

They met, and overwhelming her distrust
With penitence, he praised away her fear;
They married, and Job gave him half a year
To wreck the temple, as we knew he must.
He fumbled hungrily to readjust
A fallen altar, but the road was clear
By which it was her will to disappear
That evening when Job found him in the dust.

Job would have deprecated such a way
Of heaving fuel on a sacred fire,
Yet even the while we saw it going out,
Hardly was Job to find his hour to shout;
And Job was not, so far as we could say,
The confirmation of her soul's desire.

LOST ANCHORS

Like a dry fish flung inland far from shore,
There lived a sailor, warped and ocean-browned,
Who told of an old vessel, harbor-drowned
And out of mind a century before,

Where divers, on descending to explore
A legend that had lived its way around
The world of ships, in the dark hulk had found
Anchors, which had been seized and seen no more.

Improving a dry leisure to invest
Their misadventure with a manifest
Analogy that he may read who runs,
The sailor made it old as ocean grass—
Telling of much that once had come to pass
With him, whose mother should have had no sons.

RECALLED

LONG after there were none of them alive
About the place—where there is now no place
But a walled hole where fruitless vines embrace
Their parent skeletons that yet survive
In evil thorns—none of us could arrive
At a more cogent answer to their ways
Than one old Isaac in his latter days
Had humor or compassion to contrive.

I mentioned them, and Isaac shook his head:
"The Power that you call yours and I call mine
Extinguished in the last of them a line
That Satan would have disinherited.
When we are done with all but the Divine,
We die." And there was no more to be said.

MODERNITIES

SMALL knowledge have we that by knowledge met
May not some day be quaint as any told
In almagest or chronicle of old,

AFTERTHOUGHTS

Whereat we smile because we are as yet
The last—though not the last who may forget
What cleavings and abrasions manifold
Have marked an armor that was never scrolled
Before for human glory and regret.

With infinite unseen enemies in the way
We have encountered the intangible,
To vanquish where our fathers, who fought well,
Scarce had assumed endurance for a day;
Yet we shall have our darkness, even as they,
And there shall be another tale to tell.

AFTERTHOUGHTS

We parted where the old gas-lamp still burned
Under the wayside maple and walked on,
Into the dark, as we had always done;
And I, no doubt, if he had not returned,
Might yet be unaware that he had earned
More than earth gives to many who have won—
More than it has to give when they are gone—
As duly and indelibly I learned.

The sum of all that he came back to say
Was little then, and would be less today:
With him there were no Delphic heights to climb,
Yet his were somehow nearer the sublime.
He spoke, and went again by the old way—
Not knowing it would be for the last time.

CAPUT MORTUUM

Not even if with a wizard force I might
Have summoned whomsoever I would name,
Should anyone else have come than he who came,
Uncalled, to share with me my fire that night;
For though I should have said that all was right,
Or right enough, nothing had been the same
As when I found him there before the flame,
Always a welcome and a useful sight.

Unfailing and exuberant all the time,
Having no gold he paid with golden rhyme,
Of older coinage than his old defeat,
A debt that like himself was obsolete
In Art's long hazard, where no man may choose
Whether he play to win or toil to lose.

MONADNOCK THROUGH THE TREES

Before there was in Egypt any sound
Of those who reared a more prodigious means
For the self-heavy sleep of kings and queens
Than hitherto had mocked the most renowned,—
Unvisioned here and waiting to be found,
Alone, amid remote and older scenes,
You loomed above ancestral evergreens
Before there were the first of us around.

And when the last of us, if we know how,
See farther from ourselves than we do now,
Assured with other sight than heretofore

MANY ARE CALLED

That we have done our mortal best and worst,—
Your calm will be the same as when the first
Assyrians went howling south to war.

THE LONG RACE

Up the old hill to the old house again
Where fifty years ago the friend was young
Who should be waiting somewhere there among
Old things that least remembered most remain,
He toiled on with a pleasure that was pain
To think how soon asunder would be flung
The curtain half a century had hung
Between the two ambitions they had slain.

They dredged an hour for words, and then were done.
"Good-bye! . . . You have the same old weather-vane—
Your little horse that's always on the run."
And all the way down back to the next train,
Down the old hill to the old road again,
It seemed as if the little horse had won.

MANY ARE CALLED

The Lord Apollo, who has never died,
Still holds alone his immemorial reign,
Supreme in an impregnable domain
That with his magic he has fortified;
And though melodious multitudes have tried
In ecstasy, in anguish, and in vain,

With invocation sacred and profane
To lure him, even the loudest are outside.

Only at unconjectured intervals,
By will of him on whom no man may gaze,
By word of him whose law no man has read,
A questing light may rift the sullen walls,
To cling where mostly its infrequent rays
Fall golden on the patience of the dead.

REMBRANDT TO REMBRANDT

(AMSTERDAM, 1645)

AND there you are again, now as you are.
Observe yourself as you discern yourself
In your discredited ascendency;
Without your velvet or your feathers now,
Commend your new condition to your fate,
And your conviction to the sieves of time.
Meanwhile appraise yourself, Rembrandt van Ryn,
Now as you are—formerly more or less
Distinguished in the civil scenery,
And once a painter. There you are again,
Where you may see that you have on your shoulders
No lovelier burden for an ornament
Than one man's head that's yours. Praise be to God
That you have that; for you are like enough
To need it now, my friend, and from now on;
For there are shadows and obscurities
Immediate or impending on your view,
That may be worse than you have ever painted
For the bewildered and unhappy scorn

REMBRANDT TO REMBRANDT

Of injured Hollanders in Amsterdam
Who cannot find their fifty florins' worth
Of Holland face where you have hidden it
In your new golden shadow that excites them,
Or see that when the Lord made color and light
He made not one thing only, or believe
That shadows are not nothing. Saskia said,
Before she died, how they would swear at you,
And in commiseration at themselves.
She laughed a little, too, to think of them—
And then at me. . . . That was before she died.

And I could wonder, as I look at you,
There as I have you now, there as you are,
Or nearly so as any skill of mine
Has ever caught you in a bilious mirror,—
Yes, I could wonder long, and with a reason,
If all but everything achievable
In me were not achieved and lost already,
Like a fool's gold. But you there in the glass,
And you there on the canvas, have a sort
Of solemn doubt about it; and that's well
For Rembrandt and for Titus. All that's left
Of all that was is here; and all that's here
Is one man who remembers, and one child
Beginning to forget. One, two, and three,
The others died, and then—then Saskia died;
And then, so men believe, the painter died.
So men believe. So it all comes at once.
And here's a fellow painting in the dark,—
A loon who cannot see that he is dead
Before God lets him die. He paints away
At the impossible, so Holland has it,
For venom or for spite, or for defection,
Or else for God knows what. Well, if God knows,

And Rembrandt knows, it matters not so much
What Holland knows or cares. If Holland wants
Its heads all in a row, and all alike,
There's Franz to do them and to do them well—
Rat-catchers, archers, or apothecaries,
And one as like a rabbit as another.
Value received, and every Dutchman happy.
All's one to Franz, and to the rest of them,—
Their ways being theirs, are theirs.—But you, my friend,
If I have made you something as you are,
Will need those jaws and eyes and all the fight
And fire that's in them, and a little more,
To take you on and the world after you;
For now you fare alone, without the fashion
To sing you back and fling a flower or two
At your accusing feet. Poor Saskia saw
This coming that has come, and with a guile
Of kindliness that covered half her doubts
Would give me gold, and laugh . . . before she died.

And if I see the road that you are going,
You that are not so jaunty as aforetime,
God knows if she were not appointed well
To die. She might have wearied of it all
Before the worst was over, or begun.
A woman waiting on a man's avouch
Of the invisible, may not wait always
Without a word betweenwhiles, or a dash
Of poison on his faith. Yes, even she.
She might have come to see at last with others,
And then to say with others, who say more,
That you are groping on a phantom trail
Determining a dusky way to nowhere;
That errors unconfessed and obstinate
Have teemed and cankered in you for so long

REMBRANDT TO REMBRANDT

That even your eyes are sick, and you see light
Only because you dare not see the dark
That is around you and ahead of you.
She might have come, by ruinous estimation
Of old applause and outworn vanities,
To clothe you over in a shroud of dreams,
And so be nearer to the counterfeit
Of her invention than aware of yours.
She might, as well as any, by this time,
Unwillingly and eagerly have bitten
Another devil's-apple of unrest,
And so, by some attendant artifice
Or other, might anon have had you sharing
A taste that would have tainted everything,
And so had been for two, instead of one,
The taste of death in life—which is the food
Of art that has betrayed itself alive
And is a food of hell. She might have heard
Unhappily the temporary noise
Of louder names than yours, and on frail urns
That hardly will ensure a dwelling-place
For even the dust that may be left of them,
She might, and angrily, as like as not,
Look soon to find your name, not finding it.
She might, like many another born for joy
And for sufficient fulness of the hour,
Go famishing by now, and in the eyes
Of pitying friends and dwindling satellites
Be told of no uncertain dereliction
Touching the cold offence of my decline.
And even if this were so, and she were here
Again to make a fact of all my fancy,
How should I ask of her to see with me
Through night where many a time I seem in vain
To seek for new assurance of a gleam

That comes at last, and then, so it appears,
Only for you and me—and a few more,
Perchance, albeit their faces are not many
Among the ruins that are now around us.
That was a fall, my friend, we had together—
Or rather it was my house, mine alone,
That fell, leaving you safe. Be glad for that.
There's life in you that shall outlive my clay
That's for a time alive and will in time
Be nothing—but not yet. You that are there
Where I have painted you are safe enough,
Though I see dragons. Verily, that was a fall—
A dislocating fall, a blinding fall,
A fall indeed. But there are no bones broken;
And even the teeth and eyes that I make out
Among the shadows, intermittently,
Show not so firm in their accoutrement
Of terror-laden unreality
As you in your neglect of their performance,—
Though for their season we must humor them
For what they are: devils undoubtedly,
But not so parlous and implacable
In their undoing of poor human triumph
As easy fashion—or brief novelty
That ails even while it grows, and like sick fruit
Falls down anon to an indifferent earth
To break with inward rot. I say all this,
And I concede, in honor of your silence,
A waste of innocent facility
In tints of other colors than are mine.
I cannot paint with words, but there's a time
For most of us when words are all we have
To serve our stricken souls. And here you say,
"Be careful, or you may commit your soul
Soon to the very devil of your denial."

REMBRANDT TO REMBRANDT

I might have wagered on you to say that,
Knowing that I believe in you too surely
To spoil you with a kick or paint you over.

No, my good friend, Mynheer Rembrandt van Ryn—
Sometime a personage in Amsterdam,
But now not much—I shall not give myself
To be the sport of any dragon-spawn
Of Holland, or elsewhere. Holland was hell
Not long ago, and there were dragons then
More to be fought than any of these we see
That we may foster now. They are not real,
But not for that the less to be regarded;
For there are slimy tyrants born of nothing
That harden slowly into seeming life
And have the strength of madness. I confess,
Accordingly, the wisdom of your care
That I look out for them. Whether I would
Or not, I must; and here we are as one
With our necessity. For though you loom
A little harsh in your respect of time
And circumstance, and of ordained eclipse,
We know together of a golden flood
That with its overflow shall drown away
The dikes that held it; and we know thereby
That in its rising light there lives a fire
No devils that are lodging here in Holland
Shall put out wholly, or much agitate,
Except in unofficial preparation
They put out first the sun. It's well enough
To think of them; wherefore I thank you, sir,
Alike for your remembrance and attention.

But there are demons that are longer-lived
Than doubts that have a brief and evil term

To congregate among the futile shards
And architraves of eminent collapse.
They are a many-favored family,
All told, with not a misbegotten dwarf
Among the rest that I can love so little
As one occult abortion in especial
Who perches on a picture (when it's done)
And says, "What of it, Rembrandt, if you do?"
This incubus would seem to be a sort
Of chorus, indicating, for our good,
The silence of the few friends that are left:
"What of it, Rembrandt, even if you know?"
It says again; "and you don't know for certain.
What if in fifty or a hundred years
They find you out? You may have gone meanwhile
So greatly to the dogs that you'll not care
Much what they find. If this be all you are—
This unaccountable aspiring insect—
You'll sleep as easy in oblivion
As any sacred monk or parricide;
And if, as you conceive, you are eternal,
Your soul may laugh, remembering (if a soul
Remembers) your befrenzied aspiration
To smear with certain ochres and some oil
A few more perishable ells of cloth,
And once or twice, to square your vanity,
Prove it was you alone that should achieve
A mortal eye—that may, no less, tomorrow
Show an immortal reason why today
Men see no more. And what's a mortal eye
More than a mortal herring, who has eyes
As well as you? Why not paint herrings, Rembrandt?
Or if not herrings, why not a split beef?
Perceive it only in its unalloyed
Integrity, and you may find in it

REMBRANDT TO REMBRANDT

A beautified accomplishment no less
Indigenous than one that appertains
To gentlemen and ladies eating it.
The same God planned and made you, beef and human;
And one, but for His whim, might be the other."

That's how he says it, Rembrandt, if you listen;
He says it, and he goes. And then, sometimes,
There comes another spirit in his place—
One with a more engaging argument,
And with a softer note for saying truth
Not soft. Whether it be the truth or not,
I name it so; for there's a string in me
Somewhere that answers—which is natural,
Since I am but a living instrument
Played on by powers that are invisible.
"You might go faster, if not quite so far,"
He says, "if in your vexed economy
There lived a faculty for saying yes
And meaning no, and then for doing neither;
But since Apollo sees it otherwise,
Your Dutchmen, who are swearing at you still
For your pernicious filching of their florins,
May likely curse you down their generation,
Not having understood there was no malice
Or grinning evil in a golden shadow
That shall outshine their slight identities
And hold their faces when their names are nothing.
But this, as you discern, or should by now
Surmise, for you is neither here nor there:
You made your picture as your demon willed it;
That's about all of that. Now make as many
As may be to be made,—for so you will,
Whatever the toll may be, and hold your light
So that you see, without so much to blind you

As even the cobweb-flash of a misgiving,
Assured and certain that if you see right
Others will have to see—albeit their seeing
Shall irk them out of their serenity
For such a time as umbrage may require.
But there are many reptiles in the night
That now is coming on, and they are hungry;
And there's a Rembrandt to be satisfied
Who never will be, howsoever much
He be assured of an ascendency
That has not yet a shadow's worth of sound
Where Holland has its ears. And what of that?
Have you the weary leisure or sick wit
That breeds of its indifference a false envy
That is the vermin on accomplishment?
Are you inaugurating your new service
With fasting for a food you would not eat?
You are the servant, Rembrandt, not the master,—
But you are not assigned with other slaves
That in their freedom are the most in fear.
One of the few that are so fortunate
As to be told their task and to be given
A skill to do it with a tool too keen
For timid safety, bow your elected head
Under the stars tonight, and whip your devils
Each to his nest in hell. Forget your days,
And so forgive the years that may not be
So many as to be more than you may need
For your particular consistency
In your peculiar folly. You are counting
Some fewer years than forty at your heels;
And they have not pursued your gait so fast
As your oblivion—which has beaten them,
And rides now on your neck like an old man
With iron shins and fingers. Let him ride

REMBRANDT TO REMBRANDT

(You haven't so much to say now about that),
And in a proper season let him run.
You may be dead then, even as you may now
Anticipate some other mortal strokes
Attending your felicity; and for that,
Oblivion heretofore has done some running
Away from graves, and will do more of it."

That's how it is your wiser spirit speaks,
Rembrandt. If you believe him, why complain?
If not, why paint? And why, in any event,
Look back for the old joy and the old roses,
Or the old fame? They are all gone together,
And Saskia with them; and with her left out,
They would avail no more now than one strand
Of Samson's hair wound round his little finger
Before the temple fell. Nor more are you
In any sudden danger to forget
That in Apollo's house there are no clocks
Or calendars to say for you in time
How far you are away from Amsterdam,
Or that the one same law that bids you see
Where now you see alone forbids in turn
Your light from Holland eyes till Holland ears
Are told of it; for that way, my good fellow,
Is one way more to death. If at the first
Of your long turning, which may still be longer
Than even your faith has measured it, you sigh
For distant welcome that may not be seen,
Or wayside shouting that will not be heard,
You may as well accommodate your greatness
To the convenience of an easy ditch,
And, anchored there with all your widowed gold,
Forget your darkness in the dark, and hear
No longer the cold wash of Holland scorn.